HISTORY OF THE FLOWER BULB INDUSTRY
IN WASHINGTON STATE

Charles J. Gould
Plant Pathologist, Emeritus
Washington State University

Northwest Bulb Growers Association
Mount Vernon
Washington

1993

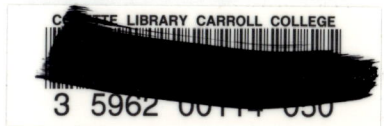

Published by Northwest Bulb Growers Association, P.O. Box 303, Mount Vernon, WA 98273

Library of Congress Catalog Card Number 92-63379
ISBN 0-9635438-0-6

Printed in the United States of America

Distributed by Western Watershed Publishing Co., 9792 Edmonds Way, Suite 178, Edmonds, WA 98020

Cover Photography:
Front: Narcissus field in Puyallup Valley with Mt. Rainier, by author.
Back: Tulip field near Mount Vernon with Mt. Baker, © by Dave Curran, Bainbridge Island, WA.

To Dorothy Ebersole Gould

without whose encouragement, assistance and culinary ability
this book would never have been completed

ACKNOWLEDGMENTS

No book represents the unaided work of a single individual and many people have helped me with this one. Although it's impossible to list them all, I especially want to thank:

The Northwest Bulb Growers Association (NWBGA) for sponsoring the book.

Dr. Arlen Davison, Assistant Dean and Superintendent of the Washington State University Research and Extension Center at Puyallup, for his encouragement and assistance including the use of facilities at the Center.

Phototypesetter Joyce Weber who adapted tables, made maps and typeset the final manuscript which is a tribute to her ability and expertise with both word processing and computers.

Sherrill Carlson of Western Watershed Publishing for her valuable editorial comments, for managing the publication of the color insert and other photographs and the marketing of the book.

Former Secretary Rosie Hueneka for her patience in transcribing my handwriting when she typed many chapters of the early drafts of the book before retiring in May 1992.

Pat Patterson, Betty Barstow, Melna Forrester and Earl Otis for their helpful assistance at many times during the years of book preparation.

Richard Nowadnick for much data, for handling financial details of publication and for his encouraging support during the entire project.

All who prepared bar and line charts and maps: my son, James F. Gould (Figures 3-2, 7-1, 10-1, 10-2 and 12-1); Dr. Peter Bristow (3-3 and 8-2); Vernene Scheurer (4-1 and 8-1); Joyce Weber (2-3, 3-1 and 4-2).

My son, Carl David Gould, for assistance with examples and advice on using the computerized index program.

Dr. Gary Chastagner and Dr. Ralph Byther for sharing the bulb history files at WSU and for general assistance and advice.

Ted Sabelis for information and comments on many aspects of bulb production and marketing, including the estimates used in Tables 8-4 and 8-5.

Neil Van Lierop for his willing assistance at all times and for providing pre-sale book storage space.

Leo Roozen for his continued encouragement during the project and for help in obtaining many of the photographs.

Those who reviewed all or parts of the book and provided additional information: Dr. Wilbur Anderson, Dr. Ralph Byther, Dr. Gary Chastagner, Francis Chervenka, Robin Clausen, Dorothy Gould, Roger Knutson, Tom Knutson, Edward McRae, Dr. James Menzies, Richard Nowadnick, Earl Otis, Leo Roozen, William A. (Bill) Roozen, Ted Sabelis, Wallace Staatz and Neil Van Lierop.

William M. Roozen, past president of the NWBGA, for his overall support and for obtaining the photograph of the 1990 flood damage in Skagit County.

Roger Knutson for historical data on the founding of the Puget Sound Bulb Exchange and the Puyallup Valley Flower Cooperative.

Dr. Marc Cathey for Dr. Griffith's photograph and for an article unobtainable through usual sources.

Ir. Henk van Os, Director of the Bloembollenkeuringsdienst at Lisse, for data on bulb acreages in Holland.

Mrs. Marilyn Bell and Mr. Bill Merrill who discovered and shared with me many previously unknown facts about George Gibbs.

Dorothy Peterkin of the Sumner Historical Museum for making the newspaper files and the photographic collection of the Puyallup Valley Daffodil Festival available.

Hertitage Quest for permission to use their newspaper files.

The librarians of the Pierce County Reference Library, the Bellingham Herald, the Washington State Historical Society, the Tacoma Public Library and the Holland Library at WSU in Pullman for help in finding references and photographs.

George Clark and Chauncey Wight for their personal reminiscences about Edwin Wines.

Dorothy Neil of Oak Harbor for information about bulb activities on Whidbey Island.

Tom Dabalos of the Washington State Department of Agriculture for data on bulb inspections and inspectors.

All those who generously loaned photographs. I regret that space limitations prevented the use of so many of them.

From the Author

This history originally was to have been a Washington State University bulletin and I expected to finish it in six weeks, but the weeks grew into months, the months became years and the bulletin became a book.

It is not a picture book of bulb flowers nor a manual on how to grow them. Primarily, it is intended as a reference source for writers, bulb growers, bulb hobbyists, historians, genealogists, horticulturists and other scientists. The general public should find the less technical parts of interest, particularly the chapters on flower festivals, on individual bulb growers, on George Gibbs, the first commercial bulb grower, and on Dr. David Griffiths whose research put bulb growing in Washington on a sound basis.

Washington State is the major producer of bulbous Iris, Narcissus and Tulips in the United States. Most of the book deals with these three crops although Gladiolus and Lilies are discussed also. Lilies *(Lilium)* include the Easter Lily as well as the Asiatic, Oriental and trumpet types. All major species of the genus *Narcissus* (Daffodils) are included except the polyanthus group which is not grown commercially in Washington State. All members of the genus *Tulipa* are included, but only the bulbous type of *Iris*.

Technical names of genera including *Gladiolus*, *Iris* and *Narcissus* are capitalized. Common names such as Tulips *(Tulipa)* and Lilies *(Lilium)* are used instead of their technical names and they, too, have been capitalized.

Tables, figures and photographs are numbered in sequence in each chapter. A reference to Table 3-2 refers to the second table in Chapter 3.

I have always been interested in history and began to collect items about the bulb industry when I arrived in 1941 at the Washington State University Research and Extension Center at Puyallup where I was assigned to study the cause and control of diseases of bulbs and other ornamental crops. During the course of my work I met many of the "old timers" in the bulb industry as well as later growers and my goal in writing this book is to preserve the memory of the growers and to record available data about the industry before more of it is lost.

The project became very interesting but also very frustrating because most of the older growers discarded their records when they retired and most of them are now dead. Consequently, much of the information obtained was so fragmentary that I felt as if I were assembling a jig-saw puzzle.

During the research, we, fortunately, were able to find several growers, spouses, neighbors and friends who added enough detail to the published material to make it possible for us to prepare 128 brief biographies of past and present growers and a few others closely connected with the industry. I should emphasize that the estimates and some conclusions are "educated guesses." In view of this and the volume of data presented, there are undoubtedly errors which might be corrected with further research and I would appreciate receiving additional comments and records for that purpose.

Articles written by Rachel Wyman (154), R. L. Nowadnick (95) and Terri Horstman (68) provided many useful leads to other sources of information. Some data were found in newspapers, magazines, festival brochures, research publications and especially in reports of the Northwest Bulb Growers Association, the Washington State Bulb Commission and the Washington State Department of Agriculture.

In some instances, we found more information than we could use but all of the collected material is available for study in the bulb history files at Washington State University Puyallup.

In addition to the biographies of people who worked with bulbs, I have described a number of the major changes in the industry such as the planting and digging of bulbs by machine instead of by hand; the growing of bulbs in rows rather than "Dutch beds"; the use of tractors instead of horses; the disappearahce of many small farms and the rise of a few large ones; the sale of flowers instead of bulbs as a major source of income; the shift of the centers of bulb growing from Whatcom County south to Pierce County and back north to Skagit County and many changes in marketing, exporting and importing.

I've also included an overview of the university and federal research work on the problems of commercial bulb growing. I regret that lack of time and space prevented an expanded discussion of mechanization, of biographical sketches of the scientists and of their research. These topics could easily fill another book.

The Northwest Bulb Growers Association has published this book and any profits from sales will be used to support additional bulb research by Washington State University scientists.

Undoubtedly, more information is available. Researching local news-papers and magazines is time-consuming work but could make excellent projects for senior citizens or high school or college term papers and would be useful contributions to the history of the bulb industry, the counties and the state. Each subject and every person listed in this book is worthy of a more comprehensive report.

Charles J. Gould

Puyallup, Washington
February 28, 1993

CONTENTS

CHAPTER 1

The Washington Bulb Industry in Perspective

Flower bulbs, especially Iris, Narcissus (Daffodils) and Tulips, flourish in Washington's mild climate and rich soils. Since the first commercial bulbs were planted on Orcas Island in 1892, bulb crops have contributed much to the state's agricultural income and have brightened the landscape for its non-agricultural citizens.

Before discussing the flower bulb industry in Washington State in detail, it may be of interest to compare its size with that in other countries which also produce Iris, Narcissus and Tulip bulbs. Although commercial production of these bulbs has been tried at various times in many regions of the world, major production is now centered in temperate countries with comparatively mild climates. Generally, these countries are in the north temperate zone between 30° and 55° latitude, where the extremes of winter and summer are moderated by winds from nearby oceans or other large bodies of water.

The major producing countries and their bulb acreages are listed in Table 1-1. The data in this table are not strictly comparable from country to country because they were reported in different years and because some are only estimates, such as those for the United States, but they do provide a general overview of the world's flower bulb industry.

Holland (The Netherlands) had the largest total bulb acreage in 1991, followed in sequence by the United States, England, Japan, France, Poland, Israel and Canada. The United States leads in Gladiolus. England has been the major producer of Narcissus for many years with the center of production in Lincolnshire. Bulb production in France is found in Brittany and the southwest area of the country. In Israel, most of the Iris are raised in Galilee and most of the Lilies in the Golan Heights. Holland is the major supplier for all types of bulbs except for Narcissus and had increased its acreage of Iris, Narcissus and Tulips from 11,263 acres in 1956 to 23,899 acres by 1992.

Commercial bulb production of bulbous Iris, Narcissus and Tulips has been tried in many regions of the United States. The major producing areas were listed by Hill in 1929/30 (67), by Gould in 1956 (50) and again in 1967 in the World Production of Bulbs, *Florists Review*, V. 140, July 13. Some scattered pockets of production still exist outside of Washington State but most of these are maintained by small growers or hobbyists who can provide their bulbs with a great deal of care.

Because of favorable climates and other factors, major commercial bulb production has gradually become localized in certain areas in the United States. Florida is the center for the field-cut flower production of Gladiolus. Michigan leads in the production of Gladiolus corms. Most Easter Lilies are grown in the coastal area of northwestern California and southwestern Oregon while Washington State produces the majority of bulbous Iris, Narcissus and Tulip bulbs. Iris and Narcissus bulbs are also planted in large numbers for field-cut flower production in both Washington and in coastal California from San Diego to San Francisco. Washington's neighbors, Oregon and British Columbia, formerly produced many more Iris, Narcissus and Tulip bulbs than they do today.

Table 1-1. Number of acres of bulbs in major producing countries.*

Country	Year	Gladiolus	Hyacinth	Iris-Bulbous	Lilies	Narcissus	Tulip	Total-INT**	Total-All
Canada (BC)	1991	40	0	4	12	367	28	399	451
England	1989	267	0	79	0	9,788	314	10,181	10,448
France	1991	717	74	259	99	49	457	765	1,655
Israel	1991	15	0	110	65	400	0	510	590
Japan	1990	353	52	264	941	101	1,532	1,897	3,243
Netherlands	1992	4,872	2,195	1,782	6,135	3,786	18,331	23,899	37,101
Poland	1990	395	0	0	351	178	432	610	1,356
USA	1991	5,967	0	475	1,950	1,400	650	2,525	10,442
TOTAL		12,626	2,321	2,973	9,553	16,069	21,744	40,786	65,286
USA-WA State	1991	100	0	368	44	959	493	1,820	1,964

* SOURCES: Personal communications or reports from: **Canada** (BC), Ben Warmerdam, Aldergrove, BC (10/25/91) and Ian Van Treight, Victoria, BC (9/15/91). **England and Wales**, J.B. Briggs, Bulbs Technical Notes #30, ADAS, Boston, U.K. (2/11/91). **France**, Marcel Le Nard, INRA, Ploudaniel (6/12/91). **Israel**, A.H. Halevy, Hebrew University of Jerusalem, Rehovot (5/28/91). **Japan**, Masayuki Yamashita, Embassy of Japan, Washington, DC (8/2/91). **Netherlands**, Flowerbulb Inspection Service (BKD), Lisse (7/9/92). **Poland**, Maciej Mynett, Institute Pomology and Floriculture, Skierniewice (8/1/91). **United States of America**, Gladiolus estimate by R.O. Magie, Bradenton, FL (3/23/92). Lilies by A. De Hertogh (3/23/92) and others by the author. **United States-WA**. Gladiolus estimate by the author. Other data from 1991 report by Washington State Department of Agriculture.

**Total of Iris, Narcissus and Tulips.

3

CHAPTER 2

George Gibbs
Commercial Father of the Washington Bulb Industry

One hundred and one years ago in 1892, George William Gibbs planted a handful of bulbs which were destined to become the first recorded commercial bulb farm in Washington State.

Homeowners and nurserymen, such as John Bennett at Bellingham, had grown and used Tulips and other bulbs in their landscaping before 1892. There were also commercial bulb farms in Virginia and other eastern states in the 1800s but it was Gibbs who first saw and seriously acted upon the commercial opportunity for growing bulbs in Washington State (Figure 2-1).

Figure 2-1. Mr. and Mrs. George Gibbs. (Courtesy Marilyn Bell)

Gibbs led an eventful life. He was born May 2, 1830 to William and Mary (Walker) Gibbs in Tewkesbury, England. Emigrating to the United States in 1847, he worked on farms near Buffalo, NY. About 1849, he bought his first farm near Ann Arbor, MI. George attended the University of Michigan for a time, married Miss Lucina West (126) and then joined in the Gold Rush to California with very successful results. In 1853, he returned to Michigan, sold his original farm and bought another. He must have prospered because he spent much of 1862 traveling in England. By 1863, he was back in Michigan, sold his second farm and became manager of a packing plant owned by Englishmen (78).

The following year he was in Iowa where he was "engaged in the grain and lumber business" for the next four years. Gibbs truly must have had the wanderlust. In 1870 he moved again, this time to Holden, MO where he became a very successful wheat farmer. He was still there in 1880/81 (78). Up to this point he had had an obviously profitable financial career. What prompted him to leave Missouri and settle on Orcas Island is unknown but his many moves show that he thoroughly enjoyed new areas and new challenges.

A report by A. W. Thornton, a friend of Gibbs, implies that he arrived on Orcas Island about 1883; other reports indicate 1886 or 1887. Thornton, himself, had settled in Ferndale on the mainland in 1883 and met Gibbs because of their mutual love for horticulture. He writes that "at that time Captain Gibbs had settled on a fruit farm [on Orcas] and had taken up an investigation of hazelnuts" (140).

By the time he arrived on Orcas Island, Gibbs had published many articles on agriculture, some of which had been reprinted in England. According to Thornton, Gibbs "was a fluent and very interesting speaker with a vast range of general information to draw upon" (140).

The exact area on the island where Gibbs first grew apples and nuts is unknown but, in 1890, he leased 121.45 acres of land near the town of Orcas from the County Commissioners (118) at $10 a year and began to establish a fruit and nut orchard there (Figures 2-2 and 2-3). In 1891, when bank failures all over the United States caused a panic in the financial markets, sales of fruit from the San Juan Islands dropped drastically. This may have caused Gibbs to try such a new crop as flowering bulbs. Judging from the fact that he was asked by the Orcas Island Fruit Growers Association in 1899 to help prepare a constitution for their organization, he must then still have been raising fruit (127).

5

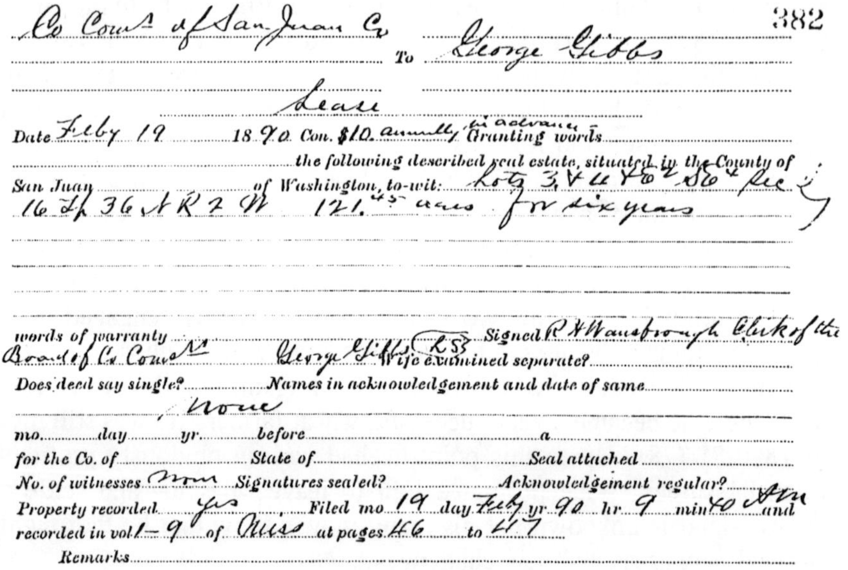

Co Court of San Juan Co To George Gibbs 382

Lease

Date Feby 19 1890 Con. $10 annually in advance Granting words

the following described real estate, situated in the County of San Juan of Washington, to-wit: Lots 3 & 4 & E½ SE¼ Sec 16 Tp 36 N R 2 W 121.45 acres for six years

words of warranty Signed R H Wansbrough Clerk of the Board of Co Court George Gibbs (LS) Wife examined separate?

Does deed say single? Names in acknowledgement and date of same

None

mo. day yr. before a

for the Co. of State of Seal attached

No. of witnesses none Signatures sealed? Acknowledgement regular?

Property recorded yes Filed mo 19 day Feby yr 90 hr 9 min 40 AM and recorded in vol 1-9 of Miss at pages 46 to 47

Remarks

Figure 2-2. Copy of lease from records of Island Title Co., Friday Harbor, Wash. Deeds, p. 382. (Courtesy Mrs. Art Grove)

According to Thornton, again, Gibbs started in bulbs by growing Hyacinths. His first bulbs were accidentally damaged during planting and, when they were harvested, he found many small bulblets growing around the injured bases. This development stimulated his interest and "he then turned his indefatigable energy into boosting [bulbs]" (140).

In 1892 he "invested $5 in flower bulbs including hyacinths, tulips, narcissi, crocuses and several lilies, leaving them in the ground for two seasons. When he dug them up in 1894, the enormous increase in bulbs amazed him and, from that time on he devoted all his energies toward the development of what he believed would become one of the richest industries of Puget Sound although he at no time had more than an acre devoted to bulbs at Orcas" (110). At one time or another, he apparently experimented with all the common genera of bulbs.

Gibbs then began to expand his bulb plantings using the Dutch-bed system and, in an effort to learn more about bulb culture, soon "put himself in touch with leading growers in Holland who guarded the details as the strictest kind of investment." Gibbs must have bragged about his results and was told by one Dutch grower "to beware that he was not

Orcas Island, Washington

Figure 2-3. Location of Gibbs lease on Orcas Island, WA.

heading for a fall . . . [as] it was impossible for a grown man to succeed in the business of bulb culture without having been familiarized with the industry from childhood." This statement "got the Captain's dander up" and he sent samples of his bulbs to a grower in Holland for examination. The Dutchman admitted that Gibbs's bulbs were good and later visited him at Orcas "to see for himself another land which could grow bulbs equal to Holland" (140).

Gibbs persisted in his bulb venture, became a member of the Society of American Florists and promoted interest in bulbs with exhibitions at several local and national shows (110). Then in May 1898, a party of expert bulb growers from Holland made a special visit to his gardens and reported, "We were astonished to see such fine plants grown in that part of the world by a man who has never been trained in bulb culture. Here we saw Lilies and other plants growing stronger than we had ever seen them before in any country" (41).

Later in 1898, with assistance from President C. X. Larrabee of the Fairhaven Land Co., Gibbs sent four large boxes of 300 bulbs to be exhibited at the Trans-Mississippi and International Exposition in Omaha, NE (14,110). He entered three varieties of Narcissus, two of Iris, one of Hyacinth, two of Crocus, four of Tulips and one of *Lilium candidum*

7

Figure 2-4. Silver medal awarded to
George Gibbs by SAF, 1898. (Courtesy Marilyn Bell)

(Madonna Lily). The judging committee awarded him a silver medal (Figure 2-4) and commented on the bulbs' fine quality, especially that of *L. candidum* ["the largest and finest ever seen by the committee"] and stated that "the whole exhibit is extremely interesting and valuable as an indication of the possibilities of bulb culture in some sections of our own country" (92).

Gibbs imported 50,000 more bulbs from Holland in the fall of 1898 and planted these as well as his own in beds which were up to 10-15 feet wide (41), much wider than the usual Dutch bed of about three feet. At this time, Gibbs still probably had no more than one to one and a half acres of bulbs but that would be equal to three to four acres in the row system now used. All of his bulbs were dug and planted by hand.

In 1899, Gibbs moved his bulb stocks to the brickyard site of old Fort Bellingham on Marietta Road near the town of Bellingham. He did this while "working in connection with C. T. Canfield" who presumably helped to finance this move. They planted two acres that year and this planting may have been the "Marietta Bulb Farm." Also in 1899, Canfield sent samples of some of their bulbs to florists in Philadelphia who pronounced them "as fine as Holland can produce" (113).

Gibbs's next move was to the Clearbrook area near Lynden in 1902 where his son-in-law, S. A. Weide, provided ample land for his bulb enterprises (109). Gibbs's home was on Swanson Road, also near Lynden (150). It is presumed that Gibbs and Canfield dissolved their partnership about the time of this move.

By 1904, Gibbs had over two acres (110) of various bulbs but had begun to specialize in Freesias and *L. candidum*. He was still using the bed system rather than the row method that Canfield was using (41).

Gibbs continued to carry on an extensive correspondence in an effort to learn as much as possible about bulb culture. He was one of the first to bring the possibility of raising bulbs commercially in Washington State to the attention of the United States Department of Agriculture (USDA). In this effort he was joined by others in Whatcom County including John Macrae Smith who sent samples of his own bulbs to the USDA in 1902 (30). The USDA sent Gibbs 15,000 imported Dutch bulbs in November 1905 to be planted and grown for two years under contract for experimental purposes (119). The efforts of Gibbs and others were so successful that in 1908 the USDA established a "Bulb Garden" near Bellingham (30), at a location which may have been at Gibbs's old 1899 site.

Five years later, in 1913, a USDA bulletin included an interesting statement that "Mr. George Gibbs, of Clearbrook, WA, more than fourscore years of age, is enthusiastic over the results of his experiments in bulb growing, as outlined in his early correspondence with the Department of Agriculture and is firmly convinced that Dutch bulbs equal to, and possibly in some respects superior to, those grown in other countries can be grown in that region. Under date of April 19, 1903, he wrote that he wished 'to see the industry started correctly and early put upon a paying basis, with the very best varieties money can buy.' Mr. Gibbs has lived to see the Department of Agriculture take up the work, and he may yet realize his hopes as to the commercial production of bulbs in the Puget Sound region" (30).

Meanwhile, Gibbs continued to grow and exhibit his bulbs. He presented "a fine display of Tulip and Hyacinth bulbs" at a meeting of the Pacific Coast Association of Nurserymen in Tacoma on July 11 and 12, 1906 (93). He had also been experimenting with a wide assortment of other bulbs furnished by the USDA. His major income for several years, however, apparently came from the sale of *L. candidum* bulbs to the Vaughn Seed Store in Chicago (92).

About 1905-1907, Gibbs seems to have been struggling financially. One report in 1907 stated that "although seriously handicapped for want of sufficient capital to take advantage of the natural expansion of the business, he has about five acres of bulbs under cultivation" (139). This would be the equivalent of twelve acres in the row system used today.

9

Before that, we find evidence of his problems when C. X. Larrabee sent Gibbs's bulbs to the Omaha Exposition in 1898 for him; when he moved to Bellingham in 1899 with the assistance of Canfield who also financed the shipment of bulb samples to the Philadelphia florists; and when Gibbs moved to his son-in-law's farm near Lynden in 1902. The sale of bulbs was not, so far, a money maker for anyone. John Macrae Smith of Bellingham wrote the USDA on December 8, 1902 that "Bulb growing so far has been very discouraging financially" (30).

Although by today's standards, the extent of George Gibbs's acreage is not very impressive, it must be remembered that most of the work was done by hand and that the cultivation of two, not to mention five, acres of bulbs represented a lot of backbreaking work to plant and to harvest. Also, when he moved to the Bellingham area from Orcas, he was 69 years old and was still growing bulbs at the age of 77 in 1907. Little is known of Gibbs's bulb activities after 1907. He monitored the Clearbrook weather station from March 2, 1903 until July 31, 1915 (150). In 1917 he moved to the County Farm near Bellingham where he died, in 1919, of "apoplexy" at the age of 89 (Figure 2-5) (147).

In 1921, A. W. Thornton wrote in his article that "Captain Gibbs was the first introducer of the Dutch bulb industry in Whatcom County. The old pioneers of Whatcom County twenty-five years ago. . .stocked their gardens with Captain Gibbs's home-grown Puget Sound bulbs" (140).

Dr. Fletcher of Cornell University wrote in 1904 that: "The honor of being the pioneer bulb grower of Washington belongs to Mr. George Gibbs of Bellingham" (41).

Because George Gibbs was a man of such energy, knowledge and enterprise and because of his great willingness to speak freely on his favorite subject, flowering bulbs, he undoubtedly stimulated others to undertake bulb growing in Whatcom County about 1900. His results, exhibits at shows, and his speeches must have contributed to the interest in bulb growing in other counties, too, between 1900 and 1910, especially Skagit County [Mary Stewart] and Pierce County [Edwin Wines]. Perhaps George Gibbs should be compared with other innovators who helped develop an industry from which those who came later profited far more than they ever did.

For the many reasons mentioned in the preceding pages, the title of The Commercial Father of the Bulb Industry in Washington State surely belongs to George William Gibbs.

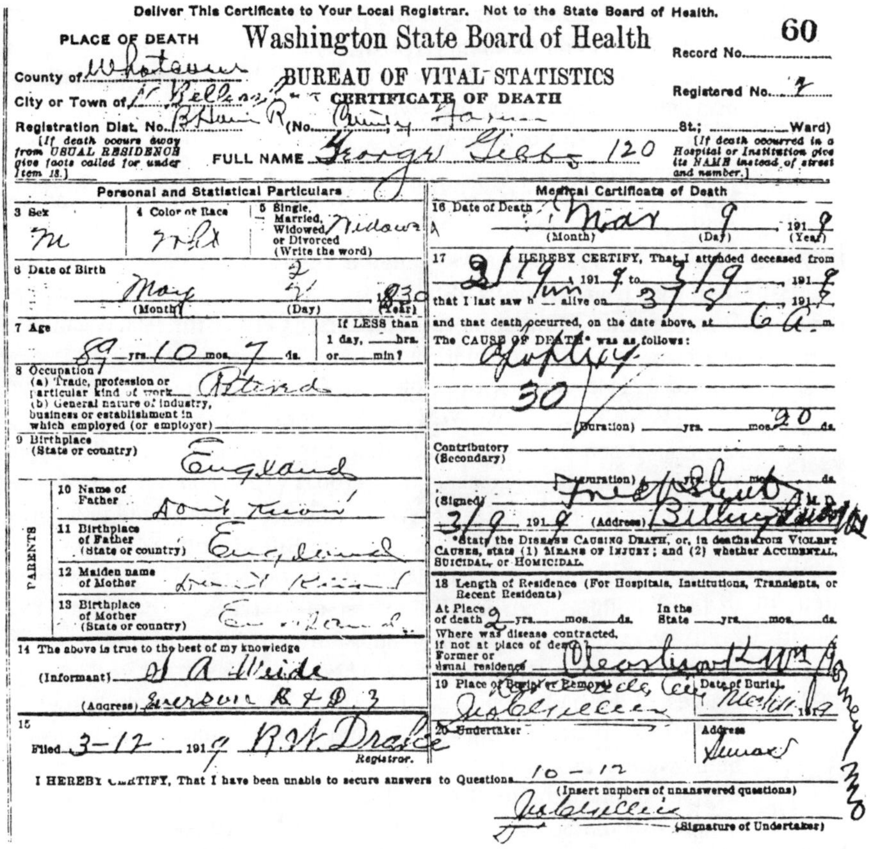
Deliver This Certificate to Your Local Registrar. Not to the State Board of Health.

PLACE OF DEATH Washington State Board of Health 60

Record No.

County of Whatcom BUREAU OF VITAL STATISTICS

City or Town of CERTIFICATE OF DEATH Registered No. 7

Registration Dist. No. (No. St.; Ward)

[If death occurs away from USUAL RESIDENCE give facts called for under Item 18.]

FULL NAME George Gibbs 120

[If death occurred in a Hospital or Institution give its NAME instead of street and number.]

Personal and Statistical Particulars

3 Sex M

4 Color or Race White

5 Single, Married, Widowed or Divorced (Write the word) Widower

6 Date of Birth May 2 1830 (Month) (Day) (Year)

7 Age 89 yrs. 10 mos. 7 ds. If LESS than 1 day, —hrs. or —min?

8 Occupation (a) Trade, profession or particular kind of work Retired (b) General nature of industry, business or establishment in which employed (or employer)

9 Birthplace (State or country) England

PARENTS

10 Name of Father Dont know

11 Birthplace of Father (State or country) England

12 Maiden name of Mother Dont know

13 Birthplace of Mother (State or country) England

14 The above is true to the best of my knowledge

(Informant)

(Address) Everson R F D 3

15 Filed 3-12 1919 Registrar.

Medical Certificate of Death

16 Date of Death Mar 9 1919 (Month) (Day) (Year)

17 I HEREBY CERTIFY, That I attended deceased from 2/19 1919 to 3/9 1919 that I last saw h alive on 3/8 1919 and that death occurred, on the date above, at 6 a.m.

The CAUSE OF DEATH* was as follows: Apoplexy

(Duration) yrs. mos. 20 ds.

Contributory (Secondary)

(Duration) yrs. mos. ds.

(Signed) M.D.

3/9 1919 (Address) Bellingham

*State the DISEASE CAUSING DEATH, or, in deaths from VIOLENT CAUSES, state (1) MEANS OF INJURY; and (2) whether ACCIDENTAL, SUICIDAL, or HOMICIDAL.

18 Length of Residence (For Hospitals, Institutions, Transients, or Recent Residents)

At Place of death 2 yrs. mos. ds. In the State yrs. mos. ds.

Where was disease contracted, if not at place of death? Former or usual residence

19 Place of Burial or Removal Date of Burial 1919

20 Undertaker Address

I HEREBY CERTIFY, That I have been unable to secure answers to Questions 10 – 12

(Insert numbers of unanswered questions)

(Signature of Undertaker)

Figure 2-5. Death certificate of George Gibbs. (Courtesy Marilyn Bell)

Table 2-1. Events in George Gibbs's life.

1830	Born in Tewkesbury, Gloucestershire, England on May 2. Parents were William Gibbs and Mary (Walker) Gibbs (10).
1847	Emigrated to the United States and began working on a farm near Buffalo, NY (78).
1848(?)	Worked for another farmer in the Buffalo area for one year (78).
1849(?)	Moved to Michigan, bought land, began farming (78) and entered the University of Michigan (126).
1850	Married Lucina West [spelled as Lucinda in some reports] of Ann Arbor, Michigan on December 1 (10).
1851(?)	Joined in the California gold rush and was very successful (78).
1853	Returned to Michigan, sold his original farm and bought another (78).

1862	Traveled in England. Wrote many articles on agriculture which were copied in all parts of Great Britain (78).
1863	Returned to the United States, sold his Michigan farm and became manager of a packing house owned by Englishmen (78).
1864	Went to Iowa and became involved in the grain and lumber business for four years (78).
1870	Moved to Holden, MO and became a very successful wheat farmer (78).
1882(?)	Moved to Orcas Island, Washington Territory, in Puget Sound and went into fruit farming (140).
1889	Was listed as a farmer in the Territorial Census for Island County, Washington Territory (148).
1890	Leased 121.45 acres (Gov. Lots 3 & 4 in the SE quarter of Section 16, TWN 36N, R2W WM WA) from the San Juan County Commissioners for six years at $10 a year in advance (118). This area included Assessor's parcels #2616-41001, 41002 and 44001 to 44008 and is near the present Orcas ferry landing on Orcas Island in an area known as "Warm Valley," according to Bill Merrill (84).
1891(?)	Planted some injured Hyacinths just for flowers. Had an excellent yield of bulblets and decided to test other types of bulbs in 1892 (140). Was still raising apples and other crops at that time.
1892	Planted $5 worth of various bulbs (110).
1894	Harvested the bulb crop planted in 1892. The yield was so good that he decided to expand bulb production (110). Some of his Hyacinth bulbs were 9 inches in circumference (94).
189?	Began exhibiting bulbs at many local and national shows. Became a member of the Society of American Florists (110).
1898	March 10. Was elected president of the "Orcas Entertainers" (73). April 14. Sold wild currants in Eastern markets (74). October 27. Planted 50,000 bulbs imported from Holland (75). May. Was visited by a group of Dutch bulb growers who were very impressed with his results (41). Sent 300 bulbs of different varieties of Hyacinths, Narcissus, Tulips, Iris, Crocus and Lilies for exhibition at the Trans-Mississippi and International Exposition in Omaha. Awarded silver medal and a commendation by the Society of American Florists for his display (92).
1899	Gibbs and two other fruit growers developed a constitution and by-laws for the Orcas Island Fruit Growers Association (127). Moved his bulb stocks to the brickyard area of old Fort Bellingham in cooperation with C. T. Canfield. Planted two acres. Area may have been called the Marietta Bulb Farm. Canfield sent samples of bulbs to Philadelphia florists who pronounced them "as fine as Holland can produce" (113).

1900	Was listed in the Federal Census as living on Marietta Road in Bellingham (141).
1902	Apparently separated from Canfield. Moved to Clearbrook area near Lynden, WA where S. A. Weide, a son-in-law, provided him with 65 acres to use (109). His residence there was on Swanson Road (150).
1903	April 19. Wrote to the USDA commending the western Washington area for its potential for raising bulbs (30). March 2. Became an observer for the U.S. Clearbrook Weather Station (150).
1904	Was listed as the pioneer bulb grower of Washington State and pictures of his bulb fields were printed in the *Seattle Post-Intelligencer* on February 7 (41). Had two acres in bulbs of various types. Began specializing in Freesias and *L. candidum* (110).
1906	Was reported in the *Northwest Horticulturist* to have been supplying *L. candidum* bulbs to Vaughn's Seed Store in Chicago for several years. He had also been experimenting with many different genera of bulbs furnished by the USDA (92). On July 11 and 12 displayed a collection of Tulip and Hyacinth bulbs at a meeting of the Pacific Coast Association of Nurserymen in Tacoma (93). Gibbs's Hyacinths were pictured in *The Northwest Horticulturist* (94) in October.
1907	Was reported to have five acres of bulbs under cultivation at Clearbrook but "was seriously handicapped for want of sufficient capital to take advantage of the natural expansion of the business" (139).
1910	Was listed in U.S. Census of 1910 as a florist with eight children (four living), residing at the home of S. A. Weide, his son-in-law, at Clearbrook, WA (142).
1913	Lucina West Gibbs died of pneumonia on December 9 (150).
1915	July 31. Retired as an observer for U.S. Weather Service (150).
1917	Entered Whatcom County Farm Home near Bellingham (147).
1919	March 9. Died of apoplexy at the County Farm in North Bellingham at age 89 (147). He and Lucina are buried at Lakeside Cemetery (formerly Clearbrook Cemetery) on Pangborn Road in the Clearbrook area near Sumas (150).

Addenda

The Gibbs had eight children of whom four daughters were still alive in 1919 as well as thirteen grandchildren and twelve great grandchildren (126).

One daughter, Lillie E., married S. A. Weide in 1880. Their son, Jack Weide, Sr., of Custer, WA, was the last surviving grandchild of the Gibbs and died in 1989 at the age of 98. His daughter, Mrs. Marilyn Bell, of Woodinville, WA is researching the Gibbs family lines and reported that Otto Reise, Sr., a pioneer bulb grower in the 1920s in the Puyallup Valley, was a cousin of Jack Weide, Sr.'s first wife, Emma (10).

There seem to have been three "George Gibbs" in Washington State in the past 150 years. One was the bulb-grower whose biography appears in this chapter, a second was a geologist in the mid-1800s and a third was listed as a marine insurance underwriter in a 1928 glass negative in the Washington State Historical Society files in Tacoma. The third Gibbs may have been the "Captain" referred to by Thornton in his article for the *Bellingham Herald* in 1921. He probably knew the underwriter also and may have confused him with his friend, the bulb grower, who died in 1919. The George Gibbs of this chapter is never referred to as Captain in any other reference.

CHAPTER 3

Washington State's Bulb Acreage

The commercial production of Iris, Narcissus and Tulips (INT) in Washington is confined to the west side of the state where the winter weather is moist and usually cool, but not so cold that bulb roots cannot continue to grow. The dry and warm, but not hot, summers of this region also provide a very favorable climate for the maturing, digging and curing of the bulbs. These conditions help to produce bulbs of superior quality. Weather records at the Seattle-Tacoma International Airport are representative of the region and show an average temperature in January of 39.1°F with 6.04 inches of precipitation and in July of 64.8°F with 0.74 inches of precipitation.

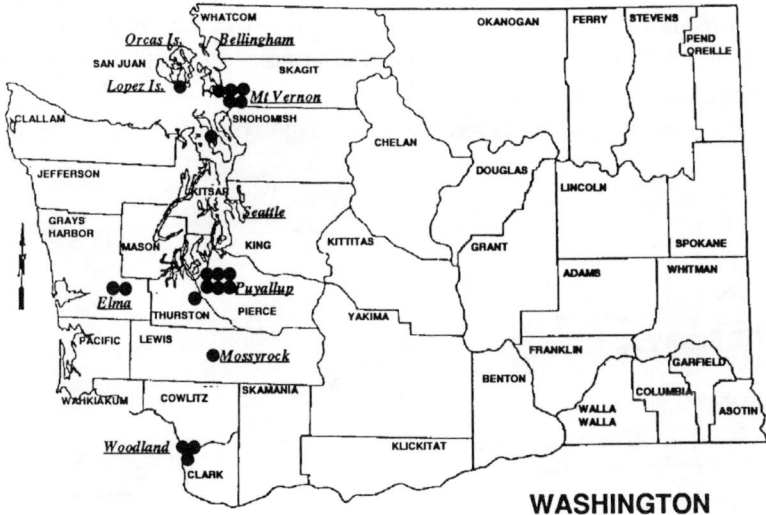

Figure 3-1. Location of Iris, Narcissus and Tulip bulb farms in 1990.

15

The major bulb growing area in western Washington in 1992 extended from Woodland in the south to Mount Vernon in the north, a distance of approximately 180 miles, located at about 46° to 48° 30" latitude (Figure 3-1). During the early 1900s, the center of bulb production was located further north in Whatcom County but, because of repeated severe freezes, most growers either quit or moved south to the Skagit Valley where nearby hills offered better protection from the winter storms which periodically came down the Fraser River Canyon .

The only information about bulb acreage before 1920 in Washington has been gleaned from a few scattered stories in newspapers and magazines. Probably not more than five acres of INT bulbs were grown in the state in 1900 and George Gibbs, himself, planted two of those near Bellingham. Total INT acreage in Washington rose to perhaps 30 acres in 1910 and to 100 by 1920 and continued to increase to 1,880 acres in 1949. Acreage then dropped to a low of 1,285 in 1959, rose again to a peak of 2,015 in 1988 and declined to 1,708 acres in 1992.

Based upon fragmentary information, again, it is believed that the most popular bulb types grown before 1900 were Hyacinths and Tulips, along with smaller numbers of Lilies and other bulbs. Narcissus became increasingly popular after 1900. Since 1920, Narcissus has been the most common bulb type grown, except for a period of six years in the late 1960s and 1970s. Tulips, which were so popular in 1900, lost ground to Narcissus in the 1920s and to Iris in the 1930s. Since 1980, however, they have frequently exceeded Iris in acreage (Figure 3-2).

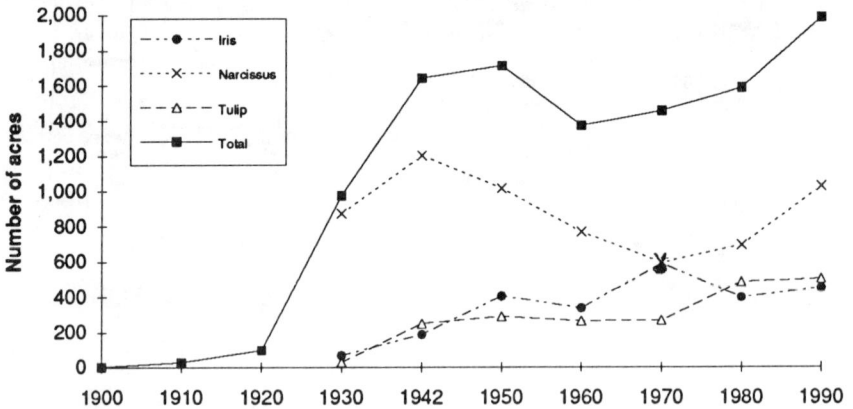

Figure 3-2. Number of acres of Iris, Narcissus and Tulips.

16

Sources of Data

The best data available on bulb acreages are found in the annual reports of the Washington State Department of Agriculture Nursery Inspection Service, starting in 1928 and continuing to the present. Unfortunately, records are missing for the years 1936-1941 and for 1946. Because of lack of storage space, the Department now keeps such records for only 3-7 years and then discards them. Fortunately, data for the other years have been retained in the historical bulb files at WSU Puyallup. Inspection reports for 1928-1935 listed only the number of bulbs planted. For purposes of comparison, the number of Narcissus bulbs was converted to acres by dividing it by 75,000, the estimated planting rate at that time.

Inspection in recent years has been done upon request by growers. The inspectors accept growers' estimates of the acreages involved, which may or may not include all bulbs planted. Since the formation of the Bulb Commission in 1956, it has not been necessary for growers to report the acreage of bulbs used for flower production only, although many growers have continued to provide the total. Recently, the increasing shortage of good land and other related factors has forced growers to plant more densely. Because of these variables, the available data can best be used to show general trends in the shifting areas of production and in the changing proportions of types of bulbs grown, rather than exact comparisons of figures for any two specific years.

Acreage data for minor bulb crops was collected only intermittently by inspectors. The Gladiolus and Lily industries were both flourishing on a small scale at one time, but Gladiolus and Lily growers did not usually raise Iris, Narcissus or Tulips. For this reason, the limited information about Gladiolus and Lilies is reported in separate chapters. Hyacinths, Crocus, Colchicum and other minor bulb crops have been, and still are, grown in small quantities, but there is even less information about them and their total acreage has probably never exceeded 50 to 100 acres annually.

Additional information was obtained from newspapers, magazines and other sources. All the data collected is listed in Table 3-3. Brief summaries of some of this information are given in the following discussions.

17

Iris

Bulbous Iris were less popular in the early 1900s than they are today and only twelve acres of them were grown in 1928. Since then, the acreages have fluctuated greatly in response to supply and demand and weather conditions. The twelve acres in 1928 had increased to 475 acres by 1945. Most of the bulbs were sold for forcing in greenhouses and the demand remained relatively stable until after World War II when increasing imports gradually created serious surpluses both in the United States and in Holland. Iris growers in Washington plowed under about 25% of their acreage in 1953 and Iris acreage dropped from 414 acres in 1953 to 339 in 1954. Dutch bulb growers also reduced their Iris plantings in 1953. A very severe freeze in Holland the next winter killed many Iris bulbs and Dutch exporters purchased bulbs from Washington growers in order to fill their orders, as described in Chapter 8. Demand persisted for Washington bulbs because of their high quality and Iris acreage began to increase, reaching a peak of 742 acres in 1979. A very severe freeze in the winter of 1978/79 injured many Washington bulbs and Iris acreage dropped to 400 acres the next year. By 1983, it had reached a low level of 262 acres and was only 312 acres in 1992.

The major market for Iris bulbs has always been for greenhouse forcing, primarily in the United States at first, but in Europe as well from 1955 until 1981. Although the U.S. greenhouse market remains an important one, an even larger outlet has developed for sales to growers of field-cut flowers in coastal California from San Diego to San Francisco. Some Iris are also forced by local growers and a few go into the dry sale trade.

Narcissus

Narcissus acreage has fluctuated many times. Narcissus were the first bulbs to be grown commercially in large numbers in Washington and they have continued to be the most popular type except for a few years in the late 1960s and early 1970s when Iris became more important. Narcissus represented 79% to 90% of all bulb acreage from 1928 to 1935, when the demand for Iris and Tulips began to increase. Narcissus acreage declined slightly in the Depression years of 1933 and 1934, then increased to a record 1,200 acres in 1942. After that, acreage remained relatively stable until 1953 when surpluses developed and these caused a decline to a low point of 597 acres in 1970. By 1991, the acreage was back up to 892 acres which represented 52% of the INT acreage in the state.

As described in Chapter 8, greenhouse forcers in other states created the most important market for Washington Narcissus bulbs in the 1930s and 1940s. As that market declined, more bulbs were sold to the dry sale trade and an increasing number began to be used for cut flower sales by growers themselves. At present, most Narcissus bulbs are used by growers for their own greenhouse forcing and for field-cut flowers, or are sold to the dry sale trade with only a few being sold to greenhouses elsewhere.

Tulips

Tulip acreage as a percentage of total bulb acreage in Washington State was usually less than that of Iris and Narcissus between 1929 and 1980. During the last 50 years, Tulip acreage has ranged from a low of 201 acres in 1962 and 1963 to a high of 505 in 1990 and has surpassed Iris acreage in seven of the years since 1980.

During the 1930s and 1940s most Washington Tulip bulbs were sold for forcing in greenhouses elsewhere. The dry sale trade gradually became more important but now most growers retain their large bulbs for their own forcing and for the production of field-cut flowers. About 30% are sold to the dry sale trade.

Number of Bulb Growers

The total number of commercial bulb growers in Washington State is surprising. There were at least 520 persons who grew Iris, Narcissus and Tulips or various combinations of them between 1892 and 1992; 357 who primarily raised Lilies; and another 134 who concentrated on Gladiolus. Some of these growers raised more than one type of bulb, but after duplication of names was eliminated, there still were more than 900 individual growers who raised bulbs in Washington State during the past 100 years. During the late 1940s and early 1950s, there were probably 250 to 300 growers raising Iris, Narcissus, Tulips, Gladiolus and Croft Lilies, or a combination of these at any one time. Those who grew the major INT crops are listed in Appendix Table A; the names of Gladiolus growers are shown in Appendix Table B; the names of Lily growers are found in Appendix Table C.

It has been difficult to find accurate figures for the number of growers of specific bulb types before 1956. Most of the information was found in occasional reports of the Washington State Department of Agriculture, the Northwest Bulb Growers Association and in newspaper articles.

Most reports dealt with the number of growers of Narcissus and relatively few listed those of other bulb crops. To add to the confusion, in some years, the number of rhizomatous Iris farmers was apparently included in the total with those growing bulbous Iris. For these reasons, the data listed in Table 3-1 are limited to the four years when the number of growers was specified for each of several bulb crops.

Table 3-1. Numbers of growers of various bulb types. *

Year	Gladiolus	Hyacinth	Iris	Lilies	Narcissus	Tulips	TOTAL INT
1942	?	?	52	?	103	?	141 (IN)
1947	29	?	34	178	64	42	80 (INT)
1956	?	6	32	4	57	28	71 (INT)
1989	4	?	8	3	15	9	20 (INT)

* Sources: Reports by the Washington State Department of Agriculture, Northwest Bulb Growers Association and miscellaneous articles. The 1989 data included three INT growers who produced only flowers.

The announcement in 1922 by the USDA that a quarantine would be imposed against the importation of Narcissus bulbs after 1926, stimulated a large number of farmers to begin raising this and other bulb crops, beginning in the mid-1920s. By 1929, there were 162 Narcissus growers. A few growers dropped out during the Depression years and more stopped growing bulbs during the 1940s. Only 15 Narcissus growers were left in 1989.

By 1990, only five farms of the 152 which began raising Narcissus before 1933 were still in business. They were started by Marinus Lefeber (now the Lefeber Bulb farms); Si Van Lierop (now Van Lierop Bulb Farms); E. C. Orton (now Knutson Farms); Neal Noorlag (now Skagit Valley Bulb Farms, owned by Tom De Goede); and Mrs. Lubbe Lee (now run by the Lubbe family).

The first year for which data are available concerning the number of persons raising all three major crops is 1947, when there were 80 growers. This number gradually declined until the 1970s when it seemed to stabilize between 16 and 21 individuals in any given year. In 1989, there were 17 INT bulb farmers plus another 3 who sold only flowers.

The Gladiolus industry also had its ups and downs. The peak years were 1945 through 1955, after which the number of growers declined. Twenty-nine growers raised Glads in 1946, 81 in 1950, but only four in 1989.

The Croft Easter Lily industry peaked at about the same time as did the Gladiolus industry. There were 178 Lily growers in 1947 but the number declined rapidly after 1955. Recently, there has been an expansion in the growing of Asiatic and Oriental Lilies for forcing and dry sales, but only three growers were involved with them in 1989.

Lily and Gladiolus production are discussed in separate chapters. It should be pointed out that most growers of these crops were specialists in them and few of them raised INT crops, nor did many INT growers raise either Gladiolus or Lilies, except on a trial basis.

Size of Farms

The first bulb farms were small as would be expected with a new industry, especially when most of the work had to be done by hand. In 1929, Narcissus farms averaged only three acres each. The average size increased to 16 acres in 1947 and to 64 in 1990. The increased size of the acreage was accompanied by a decrease in the number of Narcissus growers, which dropped from 162 in 1929 to 64 in 1947 and to 16 in 1990. During the same period, from 1929 to 1990, the percentage of the total INT acreage planted to Narcissus decreased from 86% in 1929 to 56% in 1947 and to 52% in 1990 as Iris and Tulips became more popular.

The first year for which data are available on the number of INT growers and the extent of their acreage in different crops is 1947. At that time, the average INT farm contained 22 acres of bulbs, a number which increased to 27 acres in 1960, to 69 in 1970, to 75 in 1980 and to 117 acres in 1990. As farm size increased, the number of growers decreased from 80 in 1947, to 51 in 1960, to 21 in 1970, and to 17 in 1990 (Figure 3-3 and Table 3-3). The data on growers in Figure 3-3 for 1929 is only for Narcissus, and for 1942 it is only for Iris plus Narcissus, but these crops represented 86% and 85% respectively of the total INT acreage in those years. All other data include all three major crops.

21

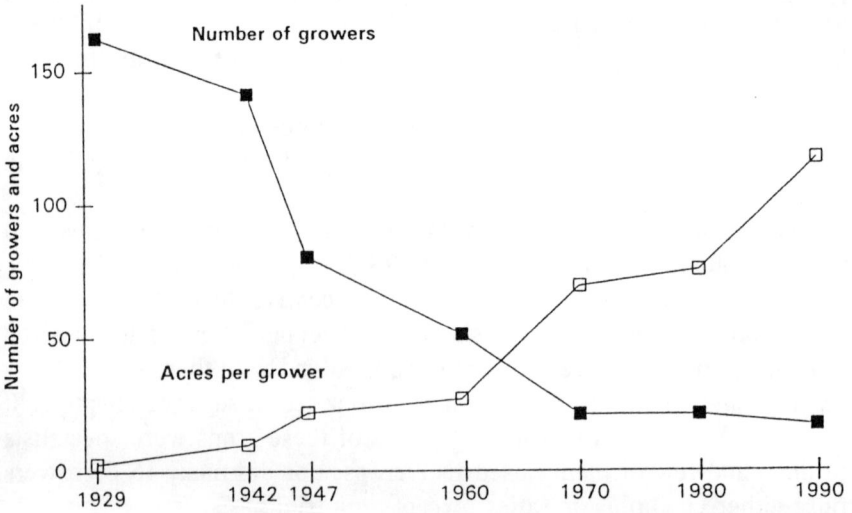

**Figure 3-3. Number of bulb growers and average size of farm.
See Table 3-3 for details.**

The data listed above show the strong trend toward larger bulb farms. This trend would not have been possible without the increased mechanization of all operations as discussed in Chapter 6.

Only 15 farms in the state have raised more than 100 acres of INT bulbs during the last 100 years. Eight of these were still active in 1992 and are so marked in Table 3-2. One of these, the Washington Bulb Company, with 1,260 acres of INT bulbs in 1989, is the largest farm for these bulb types in the United States.

Table 3-2. Approximate peak year and acreage of INT bulb farms of 100 or more acres.[*]

County	Bulb farm	Peak year	Number of acres of INT
Clark + Cowlitz	United Bulb Company	1948	250-400
Lewis	*DeGoede Bulb Farms	1970	250
Pierce	*Knutson Farms	1989	269
	Orton, C. W.	1963	200
	Orton, E. C.	1957	200
	*Staatz Bulb Farms	1964	140
	*Van Lierop Bulb Farms	1965	120
	Van Zonneveld of Washington	1939	165
Skagit + Island	*Darst Bulb Farms	1967	137
	*Lefeber Bulb Company	1978	110
	Tulip Grange	1956	153
	*Washington Bulb Company	1989	1,260
	*West Shore Acres	1987	120
Thurston	Lawlers Bulbs	1941	200
Whatcom	Van Zanten Bulb Farms	1932	120

[*] Still growing bulbs in 1992.

Table 3-3. Number of acres, bulb sales, Iris exports, number of growers and average acreage from 1900 to 1992 in Washington state.*

Year	Iris	Narcissus	Tulips	Total INT	Gladi-olus	Lilies	Misc	Grand total	Iris	Narcissus	Tulips	Total	No. Iris exported in millions	Number of INT growers**	Average acres per grower of INT
										No. bulbs sold in millions					
1900	Estimated							5							
1910	"							30							
1920	"							100							
1928	12	565	60	637											
1929	48	561	45	654											
y1930	70	875	30	975					2.6	11.1	.4	14.1		162(N)	3(N)
1931	116	785	20	921						7.7		7.7		157(N)	6(N)
1932	100	890	30	1,020						10.8		10.8		136(N)	6(N)
1933	100	687	40	827										152(N)	6(N)
1934	133	650	40	823										132(N)	5(N)
1935	60	720	30	810						9.0		9.0		44(I)	1(I)
1936-1941 Data not available															
1942	190	1,200	250	1,640	60	18	78	1,796						141(IN)	10(IN)
1943	225	950	300	1,475	70	26		1,571							
1944	350	896	335	1,581	80	65		1,726							
1945	475	900	365	1,740	80	90		1,910							
1946 Data not available														Below—All INT	
1947	400	1,000	380	1,780	125	100		2,005		11.5		11.5	11.5	80	22
1948	300	1,030	395	1,725	115	110	50	2,000						51	34
1949	410	1,120	350	1,880	120	105	50	2,155							

* Sources of data: Mostly from annual reports of the Washington State Department of Agriculture, and the Washington State Bulb Commission, supplemented, when necessary in a few cases by newspaper reports, etc. Acreages estimated for 1900, 1910 and 1920. 1930 bulb sales data from Riemann (105) and Eade (37). Numbers of growers after 1955 from Bulb Commission records.

** (I) Iris, (N) Narcissus, (T) Tulips.

*** Data include 1989 figures and additional acreage used for field-cut flower production, obtained from growers in a survey by the author.

Table 3-3. Number of acres, bulb sales, Iris exports, number of growers and average acreage from 1900 to 1992 in Washington state.* Continued.

Year	Number of acres — Iris	Narcissus	Tulips	Total INT	Gladiolus	Lilies	Misc	Grand total	No. bulbs sold in millions — Iris	Narcissus	Tulips	Total	No. Iris exported in millions	Number of INT growers**	Average acres per grower of INT
1950	405	1,015	290	1,710	118	110	55	1,993							
1951	424	904	226	1,554	120	112	50	1,836							
1952	428	960	226	1,614	100	102	51	1,867							
1953	414	809	294	1,517	100	95	51	1,763							
1954	339	864	283	1,486	85	90	55	1,716	22.3	12.8	7.3	42.4	2.0	68	21
1955	322	875	250	1,447	65	85	58	1,655	21.3	12.3	6.2	39.8		71	20
1956	336	830	270	1,436		36	16	1,488						72(?)	19
1957	324	799	239	1,362			8	1,370	23.3	11.9	6.5	41.7	1.8	56	24
1958	367	730	245	1,342			12	1,354	25.6	12.4	7.1	45.1	1.6	53	24
1959	341	693	251	1,285	50	50	15	1,400	22.8	11.7	8.3	42.7	1.7	51	27
1960	338	770	264	1,372				1,372	22.2	12.1	6.2	40.4		46	29
1961	364	733	236	1,333			158	1,491	30.3	11.3	7.0	48.6	11.2	42	31
1962	362	743	201	1,306			155	1,461	30.4	11.2	5.9	47.5	10.2	36	38
1963	409	745	201	1,355			155	1,510	35.8	10.4	6.1	52.3	14.7	36	40
1964	474	720	230	1,424			209	1,633	51.1	10.0	5.6	66.6	25.1	32	47
1965	622	657	236	1,515				1,515						32	49
1966	640	693	245	1,578			260	1,838					34.9	25	66
1967	707	681	260	1,648			265	1,913					33.9	25	63
1968	670	630	278	1,578			190	1,768					25.4	21	77
1969	720	614	281	1,615			223	1,838					19.5	21	69
1970	590	597	269	1,456			170	1,626	60.6	9.4	9.9	79.8	34.9	21	76
1971	686	599	321	1,606			173	1,779					28.2	19	80
1972	716	632	327	1,675			52	1,727					21.9	19	80
1973	617	645	250	1,512			32	1,544					16.6		87
1974	580	720	358	1,658			13	1,671					11.6		

Table 3-3. Number of acres, bulb sales, Iris exports, number of growers and average acreage from 1900 to 1992 in Washington state.* Continued.

Year	Iris	Narcissus	Tulips	Total INT	Gladi-olus	Lilies	Misc	Grand total	Iris	Narcissus	Tulips	Total	No. Iris exported in millions	Number of INT growers**	Average acres per grower of INT
		Number of acres							No. bulbs sold in millions						
1975	462	589	348	1,399			8	1,407					18.1	19	74
1976	527	717	368	1,612			67	1,679					16.7	19	85
1977	614	663	413	1,690				1,690					18.2	21	80
1978	727	701	389	1,817			1	1,818	52.5	9.6	14.4	76.5	12.5	20	91
1979	742	772	352	1,866				1,866	16.0	7.4	11.7	35.1	15.6	18	104
1980	400	696	488	1,584			35	1,619	25.1	10.4	16.8	52.2	14.9	21	75
1981	392	659	420	1,471			81	1,552					13.3	20	74
1982	482	711	373	1,566			41	1,607					1.5	16	98
1983	262	746	313	1,321			16	1,337					1.5	21	63
1984	387	947	338	1,672			38	1,710					.4	19	88
1985	390	746	381	1,517			33	1,550					.04	16	95
1986	363	880	361	1,604			37	1,641					.8	16	100
1987	360	964	375	1,699		56	4	1,759						16	106
1988	519	1,041	455	2,015		59		2,074	33.4	24.6	22.5	80.5		16	126
1989	400	817	442	1,659		34		1,693	26.4	24.8	19.5	70.6		17	98
1989***	517	1,097	608	2,222	50	77	6	2,355						20	111
1990	454	1,027	505	1,986		24		2,010	27.0	19.9	21.6	68.5		17	117
1991	368	959	493	1,820	100	44		1,964						17	107
1992	312	892	504	1,708		53		1,761						17	100

26

CHAPTER 4

Counties and Their Bulb Histories

Commercial bulb growing began in Washington State when George Gibbs planted $5 worth of Hyacinths and other bulbs on Orcas Island in 1892. When he moved his bulbs to Bellingham in 1899, others in Whatcom County became interested and this area remained the main bulb producing county for many years. After 1900, the interest in bulb growing slowly spread to other counties including Skagit (Mrs. Mary Stewart on Samish Island) and Pierce (Edwin Wines on Fox Island).

The first large-scale bulb grower was George Lawler of Fife in Pierce County who began raising bulbs in 1910 and rapidly increased his acreage. Information is sketchy about other growers between 1910 and 1920, but general reports indicate that there were many persons who were growing bulbs in small acreages by the early 1920s, primarily in King, Pierce and Whatcom Counties.

With the scheduled approach of the "Daffodil Quarantine" in 1926, more people decided to try their hands at raising bulbs, especially Narcissus. They probably assumed that, because of the restricted imports of Narcissus bulbs, shortages would develop and profits would be high. Narcissus were soon being grown in 14 of the 16 western Washington counties, excepting only Skamania and Wahkiakum. Bulb growing was even tried in eastern Washington but the climate there proved to be unsuitable for Narcissus, although good for Gladiolus and Lilies.

The earliest comprehensive county data we have about bulb growing were collected in 1929 by the Washington State Department of Agriculture which inspected Narcissus fields for nematodes and bulb flies. The inspectors recorded the number of Narcissus planted and the number of growers. In all, there were 162 growers, with 58 in King County, 38 in Pierce, 16 in Snohomish, 14 in Whatcom, 9 in Thurston, 5 each in Skagit and Clark, 4 each in Kitsap and Mason, 3 in Pacific, 2 each in Cowlitz and Spokane, and 1 each in Clallam and Jefferson.

Of the total 42 million bulbs planted in Washington State in 1929, 58% were grown in Pierce County, 15% in Whatcom and 12% in King.

Other counties with less than 5% were, in order: Thurston, Snohomish, Clark + Cowlitz, Pacific, Skagit, Clallam and Mason. Unfortunately, comparable data on Iris and Tulip acreages in different counties are not available for 1929, but 86% of all INT bulb acreage that year was planted with Narcissus.

In 1930, two new growers started in Grays Harbor County, while seven former growers dropped out elsewhere. By 1931 the number of Narcissus growers was down to 136. There were 45 in Pierce County, 32 in King County, 14 in Whatcom County, 10 in Thurston County, 9 in Snohomish County and 6 or fewer in all other counties. Every grower in Spokane, Clallam and Jefferson counties quit in 1931. One started in Asotin County in 1932 but soon quit the business, too. Another grower repeated the same experience in Yakima County a little later.

The next available county data from the Washington State Department of Agriculture show the number of acres in each county which were planted with each bulb type in 1955/56. Of all the counties, Pierce County had the largest total bulb acreage and the greatest number of acres planted in Narcissus. Skagit + Island Counties had the largest acreage in Tulips and Iris. The bulb acreages in other counties were 12% or less of the total that year.

By 1989, Skagit County was far ahead of all other counties in the state with 71% of Washington State's total INT bulb acreage. Pierce County ranked second in total acreage with 18% and other counties had less than 5% (Figure 4-1 and Table 4-1).

The Washington State Bulb Commission has collected data on the number of INT bulbs sold by growers since 1956 and their data for representative years are shown in Table 8-1. Pierce County continued to lead in total sales of INT bulbs until 1960 and also in sales of Narcissus until 1970. After those years, Skagit County became the leader and produced 60% of all bulbs sold in Washington in 1989. Counties which produced fewer bulbs are listed in descending order: Lewis, Pierce, Clark + Cowlitz, Grays Harbor and Thurston. The acreage of individual INT bulb and flower producers in 1989 is shown by counties in Table 4-2.

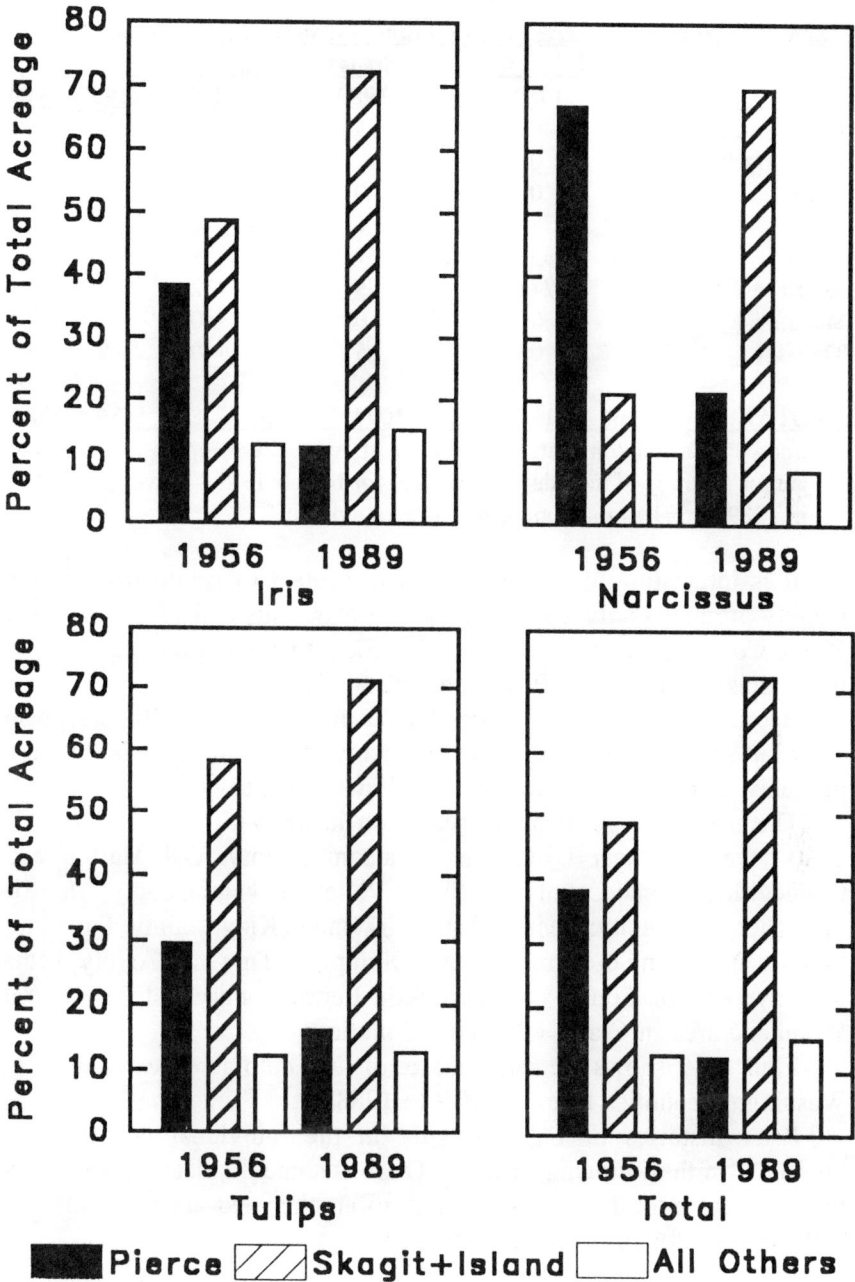

Figure 4-1. Percent of bulb acreage in Pierce, Skagit + Island
and all other counties in 1956 and 1989.

Table 4-1. Number of acres of INT bulbs in counties in 1956 and 1989.*

	Iris		Narcissus		Tulips		Total	
	1956	1989	1956	1989	1956	1989	1956	1989
Clark + Cowlitz	41	40	90	33	30	35	161	108
Grays Harbor	0	0	0	37	0	2	0	39
King	1	0	Tr	0	2	0	3	0
Lewis	0	38	0	0	0	40	0	78
Pierce	130	65	558	237	80	99	768	401
Skagit + Island	164	374	175	765	157	432	495	1571
Snohomish	0	0	1	0	0	0	1	0
Thurston	Tr	0	6	25	1	0	8	25
TOTAL	336	517	829	1097	270	608	1436	2222

* Source: Washington State Department of Agriculture report for 1956 and author's survey to include acreage used for both bulb and flower production in 1989. Tr=less than one acre. Data rounded off.

It is interesting to note the shifts in centers of production. Skagit County produced only 1% of the salable Narcissus bulbs in 1932 while Pierce County produced 65%. In 1989, Skagit County produced 70% of the Narcissus bulbs, and Pierce only 22%.

Because Skagit County planted 71% of the state's bulb acreage in 1989 but sold only 60% of the bulbs, many of the bulbs produced were probably used only for flower production by the growers.

The main centers of bulb production in the various counties since 1920 have been near Lynden in Whatcom County; Oak Harbor and Coupeville in Island County; the Skagit Valley in Skagit County; Monroe in Snohomish County; Redmond and Kirkland in King County; Puyallup, Sumner and Orting in Pierce County; Olympia in Thurston County; Elma in Grays Harbor County; Mossyrock in Lewis County and the general Woodland area in Clark + Cowlitz Counties.

Figure 4-2 shows the relative size of INT bulb acreages in western Washington counties from 1918/19 to 1988/89.

Brief histories of bulb growing in the individual counties are presented in the following section. There is some duplication because a few growers moved from one county to another and are mentioned in both counties for the sake of continuity.

1918/19

WHATCOM
SKAGIT
SAN JUAN
ISLAND
CLALLAM
SNOHOMISH
JEFFERSON
KITSAP
KING
GRAYS'
HARBOR
MASON
THURSTON
PIERCE
LEWIS
PACIFIC
WAHKIAKUM
CLARK
SKAMANIA

INT (Est.)
COWLITZ

1929/30

WHATCOM
SKAGIT
SAN JUAN
ISLAND
SNOHOMISH
CLALLAM
JEFFERSON
KITSAP
KING
GRAYS'
HARBOR
MASON
THURSTON
PIERCE
LEWIS
PACIFIC
WAHKIAKUM
CLARK
SKAMANIA

Narcissus
COWLITZ

1955/56

WHATCOM
SKAGIT
SAN JUAN
ISLAND
CLALLAM
SNOHOMISH
JEFFERSON
KITSAP
KING
GRAYS'
HARBOR
MASON
THURSTON
PIERCE
LEWIS
PACIFIC
WAHKIAKUM
CLARK
SKAMANIA

INT
COWLITZ

1988/90

WHATCOM
SKAGIT
SAN JUAN
ISLAND
CLALLAM
SNOHOMISH
JEFFERSON
KITSAP
KING
GRAYS'
HARBOR
MASON
THURSTON
PIERCE
LEWIS
PACIFIC
WAHKIAKUM
CLARK
SKAMANIA

INT
COWLITZ

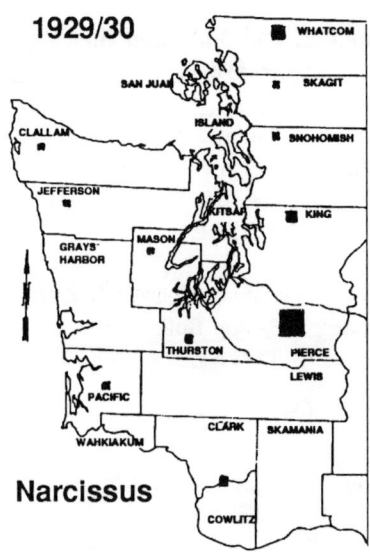

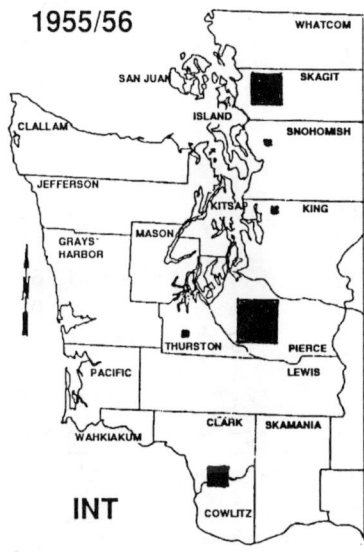

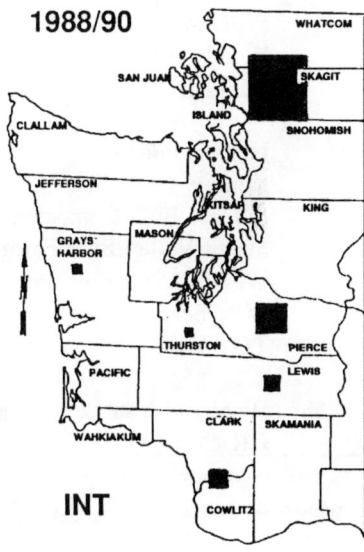

Figure 4-2. Relative size of INT (Iris, Narcissus and Tulip) bulb
acreages in different counties from 1918/19 to 1988/89 (100 acres = ■).

31

Table 4-2. INT bulb and flower producers and their acreages by counties in 1989[*].

County	Name	Iris	Narcissus	Tulips	Total
Clark +	Holland America Bulb Farms	20	0	25	45
Cowlitz	Northwest Rose Growers	20	33	0	53
	Van der Salm Bulbfarm, Inc.	0	0	10	10
	TOTAL	**40**	**33**	**35**	**108**
Grays	Lubbe, Charles & Kurt	0	27	0	27
Harbor	Satsop Bulb Farm	0	10	2	12
	TOTAL	**0**	**37**	**2**	**39**
Island	Darst, Earle	5	0	0	5
Lewis	DeGoede Bulb Farms	38	0	40	78
Pierce	Bowen Bulb Farm	0	10	0	10
	Knutson Farms	60	135	74	269
	Staatz, Wallace	0	Tr	0	Tr
	Van Lierop Bulb Farms, Inc.	5	60	25	90
	Williams, E. G., Jr.	0	30	0	30
	Woodward Bulb Farms	0	2	0	2
	TOTAL	**65**	**237**	**99**	**401**
Skagit	Hulbert Farms	0	65	0	65
	Koning, Cornelius	Tr	Tr	Tr	Tr
	Lefeber Bulb Company, Inc.	14	80	0	94
	Skagit Valley Bulb Farm	25	0	27	52
	Washington Bulb Company	330	530	400	1,260
	Westshore Acres	0	90	5	95
	TOTAL	**369**	**765**	**432**	**1,566**
Thurston	Ward and Van Lierop Farms	0	25	0	25
	GRAND TOTAL	**517**	**1,097**	**608**	**2,222**

[*] Source: Author's survey to include acreage used for both bulb and flower production in 1989. Tr=Less than 1 acre.

These two counties are combined since most bulb production has been in the general area around Woodland and plantings often cross county lines. Some bulbs also were grown near Battleground and La Center in the 1940s.

Bulb growing started early in Clark County. An encouraging report in the *Seattle Post Intelligencer* for February 7, 1904 stated that G. Kloniger at Washougal had "built up a fine trade in Oregon and California for Lilies of the Valley." The next record jumps to 1929 when the United Bulb Company, then owned by Ted De Groot, Sr., moved some of its bulbs from Michigan to seven acres of leased land near Woodland. United subsequently bought land there and became one of the largest bulb growers in Washington. Unfortunately, they lost most of their stock during the Columbia and Lewis River floods in 1948. Undaunted, they purchased bulbs from several sources and rapidly recovered, so that, by the 1960s, they were again growing 200 or more acres.

Ladd and Holden were reported to have had 16 acres of Narcissus near Battleground in 1933 and Ladd and Marble grew 70 acres in 1942. Ralph Marble, a retired horticultural inspector, then raised bulbs independently in the same area from 1943 to 1948, at least, according to available records.

In 1947, Dr. Clyde Homan (Tulips Inc.) planted 65 acres of bulbs in the Woodland area in beds. This is the equivalent of over 160 acres planted in rows. Unfortunately, the Columbia River flood destroyed all his bulbs in 1948.

In 1978 the United Bulb Company sold its holdings to the Woodland Bulb Farms Company owned by Ted De Groot, Jr., and Ed Maggi. Woodland Farms suffered a disastrous fire in 1980 and most of its remaining assets were purchased by the Northwest Rose Growers at Woodland. By 1989, the Northwest Rose Growers had 53 acres of Iris and Narcissus but lost some of the Narcissus and 80% of the Iris from freeze damage that spring.

Two other firms also began growing in the Woodland area in 1980. One was Holland America Bulb Farms, Inc. which had 55 acres of Iris, Tulips and Lilies in 1989. The other was the Van der Salm Bulbfarm, Inc. which is now concentrating on Lilies. Earlier they had grown some Tulips.

33

The total area devoted to bulbs in the Woodland area in 1989 was approximately 150 acres, which were about equally divided between Iris, Lilies, Narcissus and Tulips. By 1992 Lilies were becoming more important.

Grays Harbor County

Commercial bulb growing began in Grays Harbor County when Aaron Kanouse started raising Gladiolus in 1922 and Narcissus about 1926 at Cedarville. There were undoubtedly other growers for whom there are no records because on May 12, 1929 the *Seattle Times* reported that "Grays Harbor Plans Second Tulip Show," and Tulip shows need more than one grower. J. R. McLean started at Raymond with Narcissus in 1933, moving to Elma in 1936. At one time, he was reported to have had 40 acres in all types of bulbs. He shifted his plantings to Orting in 1953 and is discussed in more detail under Pierce County.

A boom in Croft Easter Lilies developed in the 1940s and 1950s when it appeared that almost everyone with a backyard wanted to get into the Lily business. Grays Harbor even had a Lily Festival at one time. Eventually, the interest in Easter Lilies diminished in Washington and the industry became concentrated in the coastal areas of southwest Oregon and northwest California. Refer to Chapter 15 for more details.

There was a period of a few years when no bulbs were raised commercially in Grays Harbor, but, in 1971, the Lubbes moved their Narcissus plantings from Sumner to Elma. Mrs. Lucille Lubbe Lee started growing Narcissus in 1931 at Puyallup and her son Charles (Chuck) Lubbe began in 1949. Chuck grew 27 acres and his son, Kurt, 9 acres, in 1989 at Elma. Chuck's two daughters, Mrs. Kristen Edem and Mrs. Karel Smith, raised 12 acres of Narcissus and Tulips in 1989 on their Satsop Bulb Farms, forced bulbs in their greenhouse and ran a retail flower and bulb shop.

Island County

Island County is combined with Skagit County in the statistical reports because the largest growers moved most of their bulbs to the Skagit Valley in the 1930s, but still maintained their warehouses on Whidbey Island. Their operations on the Island, however, are discussed in this section.

Neal Noorlag (1906-1989, Noorlag Bulb Farms, Oak Harbor) pioneered bulb growing on Whidbey Island with his first plantings of Narcissus and Iris in 1931. Glenn and Earle Darst bought Iris planting stock from him in 1932. In 1934 the Engle family (Carl, Will and Robert) got their first Iris bulbs from C. W. Orton who raised Iris on Whidbey Island from about 1933 to 1935. The Roodzant Brothers got into bulb production in the mid-1930s. Noorlag and the Darsts, Engles and Roodzants were the four largest growers and they continued to expand not only in Iris, the main crop, but into other bulb types as well, growing them mostly in the Coupeville and Oak Harbor areas.

Neal Noorlag later added Hyacinths to his bulb farm and may have been the leading producer of this crop in the state at one time. Meanwhile, Earle Darst had begun growing Gladiolus in eastern Washington and, at one time, had about 95 acres there.

At least two growers on Whidbey Island did some hybridizing of Iris. Burch Lemon had several promising types which were lost when he died suddenly. Earle Darst began hybridizing in 1955 and developed several varieties, some of which, such as Moonlight Mist, are still being grown commercially.

Several other growers are believed to have been farming fewer than 10 acres each. Those for whom we have names, but few details, are: George Cooke, Ralph Engle, Luke Hollguts, Jim Houslin, Tom Howell, Burch Lemon, Andrew Otterson, G. A. Palmer, George and Knight Smith, the Segers Brothers, H. T. Wanamaker and Adrian Youngsman. They are listed in Appendix Table A-1.

The chief advantage of Whidbey Island as a bulb growing location was its climate. It was warmer and drier than the mainland, making it possible for Iris and other bulbs to mature 10-14 days earlier. These could be forced in greenhouses that much earlier, and the resulting flowers commanded a premium price. However, when the benefit of artificial heat curing was discovered by USDA and WSU scientists in 1948, the Island Iris bulbs lost most of their advantage. Island growers also had the disadvantage of drier soil and their Iris bulbs were smaller than those produced on the mainland. In addition, many slabs (daughter bulbs) were lost during mechanical digging and Tulip skins often cracked and were thinner. Consequently, where at one time there were 16 or more growers on Whidbey Island, only Earle Darst was left in 1992, growing a few acres each of Gladiolus and Iris, as a hobby and for cut-flower sales.

The growers who kept their homes and warehouses on Whidbey Island and were the last to stop growing bulbs were Neal Noorlag, who moved his bulbs to the Skagit Valley in 1937, and Glenn and Earle Darst, who moved most of their plantings to the Valley in 1948. Earle sold his bulbs to Sun Valley Bulb Farms in 1982 and Neal sold his bulbs to Tom De Goede in 1983.

Many Whidbey Island pioneers came from Holland so it was logical to expect an appropriate festival to develop. It is called "Holland Happenings," is held at Oak Harbor, and is discussed in Chapter 16.

King County

Fragmentary records indicate many small growers were more or less experimenting with bulbs as early as 1904. These included J. Hopkins, a florist, F. Anton and Charles Malmo. The latter reportedly had been testing bulbs for ten years.

The earliest grower for whom there is much information was E. Albertson of Seattle who began growing Tulips and Narcissus sometime before 1920 and added King Alfred Narcissus to his collection that year. The King Alfreds did so well that he soon stopped growing the others.

John Van Aalst also started raising Tulips some time during the 1920s near Redmond and, at one time, was reported to be one of the largest Tulip growers in the state. He also grew Iris and Narcissus and was manager for Segers Bros. Bulb Farm before they moved to Lynden.

In 1924 Case Van Lierop (Vans Bulb Farm) began growing Tulips at Bothell and later added greenhouses for forcing his surplus bulbs. He sold the flowers at his roadside stand for several years and eventually developed a cut flower trade supplying the entire West Coast. In 1940 he bought a farm in Conway and raised bulbs there to force in his greenhouse at Bothell. After Case's death in 1962, his son Cornelius (Cornie) ran the company until his death in 1973 when Cornie's widow sold the business.

Fred Winters was another pioneer who started with Narcissus in 1924 near Bellevue, added Iris later, and farmed until he retired in 1943 and moved to Vashon Island.

There must have been many others who started bulb growing in the early 1920s because Joe Smith reported in 1925 that he was buying bulbs (at 6-10¢/lb.) from many discouraged growers who had tried to raise them on soils around Lake Washington that were either too heavy or too wet. In 1929, however, King County still had more Narcissus growers (58) than any other county in the state.

Other King County growers about whom there is little information include Mrs. Frank Curtis, Ira Edwards, Paul Failor, Olaf Monrad, Segers Bros. (who moved later to Lynden) and Steuber and Richardson. These and the others are listed in Appendix Table A.

Lilies also were produced in King County at various times. F. S. Flickinger was reported to have had 500,000 Regal and Easter Lily bulbs in 1925 at Richmond Beach and George Sheffield began with Regal Lilies in 1928 on Vashon Island. By 1931 there were about 35 others growing 3 million bulbs and all were members of the Vashon Island Lily Growers Association.

Gladiolus used to be more popular than they are today. One of the leading hybridists in the United States was Ralph Pommert of Pacific, who started growing Gladiolus in 1925, developed the first All America Glad (Royal Stewart) and several other hybrids. He turned the business over to his son Robert (1923-1985) about 1950 but continued to hybridize and test new varieties as a hobby for many years.

Orville Roe (1900-1952) started at Auburn in 1935 and was probably the largest Gladiolus grower in western Washington at one time with 43 acres. His son-in-law, Clyde Painter, joined him in 1951 and carried on the business with Mrs. Roe after Orville died in 1952. In 1954 they sold the business to Ira Gregg.

There were, also, several retail and wholesale dealers handling bulbs and flowers. Joe Berger and Co., Harry Sharp and Son, and Multiflora, Inc. (Joe Frantzen) are discussed in Chapter 5. Others for whom only names are available include David L. Jones, Monrad Bulb Company, Monrad-Peeter Bulb Co., Peter McFarlane, Cameron and Co., Rosaia Brothers, Thomas Floral and Mt. Rainier Bulb Co. owned by Joe Feroe.

Lewis County

The first commercial bulb farm in Lewis County was that of the Van Zonneveld Brothers who planted Narcissus in 1925 at Onalaska and Toledo. When they needed more land in 1926, they moved to Chehalis, but the soil proved to be too heavy so they moved again in 1927, this time to Orting in Pierce County and are discussed under that county. There were some other growers, including Erle Moran who raised several acres of Gladiolus at Chehalis, but there is little information about them.

In 1977, Henry DeGoede moved his bulbs from Mount Vernon to a 725 acre farm near Mossyrock where, with his sons Jack, Bob and Dennis, he raised about 78 acres of Iris and Tulips in 1989 in addition to 50 acres of miscellaneous bulbs and perennials. They also operate several greenhouses, a display garden and a retail shop. The DeGoedes cooperate with the Mossyrock Chamber of Commerce in putting on a Tulip Festival which is described in Chapter 16.

Pierce County

The Pierce County story begins in 1907 with an article by A. Lingham, a nurseryman, on "The Adaptability of Our Valley Soil for Bulb Growing." He had raised some parrot Tulips and reported that others had grown large Gladiolus (83).

Edwin Wines may have been the first commercial grower of Narcissus in this county. He built and ran the Sylvan Lodge on Fox Island and, reportedly (133), started to grow bulbs about 1905 but, since Lingham did not mention his name in 1907, Wines was probably just getting started. By 1910, Wines had a large planting and was selling flowers in Tacoma, taking them there by steamboat. He continued for several years but abandoned his plantings and left the Island in 1920 after his wife died, later returning to Tacoma where he died about 1934.

In the late 1920s, W. C. and A. E. Wight collected the remaining volunteer bulbs on Fox Island and established their own bulb farm, selling both bulbs and flowers. After they left the island in 1942, Bill and Frances Ward collected and sold flowers from the fields for several years.

Wines's sales of Narcissus flowers in Tacoma may have been the stimulus which interested George Lawler in planting bulbs in 1910 at Fife (Gardenville). Lawler soon became the largest bulb grower in the county, dealing first in cut flowers and then, as his plantings multiplied, in bulbs. Lawler started at Fife and enlarged his acreage at North Puyallup with help from his son, George Ward. Later they moved to Roy and, finally, to Monroe in Snohomish County.

While Lawler was expanding his business, two others began raising bulbs. Joe Smith, a seed and bulb catalog dealer and nurseryman, was growing bulbs at least as early as 1919 at Longbranch. In 1925 he decided to enlarge and moved his operations to the Olympia area and is discussed under Thurston County.

Clifford Van Slyke, a Puyallup High School sophomore, started with a few Tulip bulbs in 1921, imported more from Holland and, by 1923, had over 200 varieties of Narcissus, Tulips and Gladiolus. He was one of the 12 charter members of the Puget Sound Bulb Exchange in 1926.

In April 1923, Senator W. H. Paulhamus was visited by a South Dakota boyhood friend, Dr. David Griffiths, who was then in charge of the USDA Bulb Station at Bellingham. Griffiths was impressed with the possibilities of the Puyallup Valley area and recommended that a few farmers make some test plantings of bulbs. Paulhamus subsequently wrote a pertinent "letter to the editor" to the local newspapers on April 21, 1923 (99). The only growers who responded to this suggestion apparently were Frank Chervenka and H. F. Gronen who planted some bulbs that fall (27, 90).

Paulhamus continued his investigations into bulb growing and called a meeting on March 22, 1924 at Puyallup. As one reporter commented, "The meeting was suggested by Senator Paulhamus whose fertile mind is looking about for some culture of a practical nature that will help to break the one crop [berries] aspect of our horticulture." (103) A. G. Pruyser, grower and salesman from Michigan, who already had an experimental bulb planting at Marysville, was asked to speak. The 100 persons who attended came from Kent, Elma and many places in between. Joe Smith brought flower samples to exhibit and George Lawler made a few comments. Pruyser recommended trying one or two varieties of Narcissus first, because imports of these bulbs were to be restricted after January 1, 1926. The meeting ended with the formation of a temporary organization which was called the Northwest Bulb Growers Association. George Ward Lawler was elected president and Joe Smith, the secretary. The goal of the Association was to collect and distribute information on bulb growing to interested parties. Following this meeting, the Western Washington Experiment Station (WSU Puyallup) listed several pertinent USDA bulletins on bulb growing in the *Puyallup Valley Tribune* on March 29, 1924.

The meeting was followed by other talks, editorials and articles in the local newspapers, including a reference to the Tulip Festival at Bellingham which had attracted 50,000 visitors in 1924. On June 6, 1924, Paulhamus wrote an article for the newspapers in which he included suggestions regarding trial plantings and stating that he expected to order 4,000 King Alfred bulbs at $125/1,000 for fall planting. He invited others to join him for a "pooled purchase." The number of responses to this is not known but Charles Orton may have been among them since he planted 4,000 bulbs that fall (97). Frank Chervenka and Ed Orton also bought a carload of bulbs from Pruyser in 1924.

Meanwhile, certain importers and others were trying to overturn the anticipated quarantine against Narcissus bulbs, a situation which may have made local farmers reluctant to plunge heavily into such a new enterprise as bulb growing. Favorable speeches, articles and editorials by Lawler, Smith, Chervenka and others continued, however, and several local farmers including Reise, Orton, Hatch, Gronen and Locklin later ordered 55 tons of Narcissus bulbs from Holland in the fall of 1925.

Interest in bulbs began growing rapidly and the Western Washington Experiment Station (WSU Puyallup) held a special Bulb Short Course on January 15, 1926, to give growers the latest information about bulb culture. The third annual meeting of the Northwest Bulb Growers Association was held later the same day.

In 1926, about 95 tons of foreign bulbs were imported into Pierce County under special permits. Most of these were Narcissus but 400,000 bulbous Iris also were brought in. The growers' interest in bulbs may have been sharpened by the heavy loss of their raspberry crops from a severe freeze in the winter of 1924/25 in the Puyallup Valley.

By 1928, about 150 acres of bulbs were being grown in the Puyallup Valley, of which 90% were Narcissus. The acreage rapidly expanded. By 1930, the 120-acre Van Zonneveld Farm at Orting was reported to be the largest in the state and sold 190 tons of Narcissus bulbs that year.

Twelve growers banded together in 1926 to form a marketing organization called the Puget Sound Bulb Exchange which is discussed in Chapter 17. These 12 were joined by 15 other local growers before the end of 1926, leaving only Lawler Farms at Fife and Van Zonneveld of Washington at Orting as independents. Eventually the total number climbed to 47 and included several from Mount Vernon. In 1992 there were only five members left. The Exchange was a major stabilizing influence on the industry at several crucial times and helped to pioneer the sale of Iris to Europe.

Interest in bulb growing slowed during the Depression years and many small growers quit, but others began, such as the Van Lierops, Staatzes and Karl Koehler, whose farm became a famous showplace. By 1948, bulb production was so large that 111 railroad cars were needed to transport the 23,754,840 bulbs shipped from Pierce County. Meanwhile, in order to speed up operations and reduce labor costs, the larger growers had started mechanizing their operations. By 1955/56 Pierce County was producing over one half of all the Tulips, Iris and Narcissus in Washington State. Unfortunately, industrial and residential development began to reduce the amount of suitable land available for proper rotation of bulb crops. In 1969, Frank C. Jackson, County Agent, predicted the approaching end for bulb production in the Puyallup Valley because of foreign competition, rising costs and the increasing shortage of good land (115). This warning was repeated by Roger Knutson and Neil Van Lierop in 1992 (82).

By 1989 there were only five growers and fewer than 400 acres of bulbs left in Pierce County, representing about 13% of Washington State's total acreage of Iris, Narcissus and Tulips. Of the pioneering bulb farms before 1940, only the Van Lierop, Williams, Staatz and Ed Orton (now Knutson) farms remain in the business. Even so, 400 acres of flowering bulbs are still a beautiful sight and they attract many visitors during the blooming season.

Pierce County growers were primarily responsible for the organization of the Northwest Bulb Growers Association, the Puget Sound Bulb Exchange, the Puyallup Valley Flower Coop and the Puyallup Valley Daffodil Festival, all of which are discussed in separate chapters.

Several of the growers, including Frank and Francis Chervenka, Howard Mansfield, Otto Reise, Harold Knutson and John Colyn were pioneers in the mechanization of the digging, treating and planting of bulbs which enabled the industry to compete with lower-priced Dutch imports.

Finally, in the bulb history of Pierce County, the Puyallup Valley Daffodil Festival should be mentioned. This festival did not develop overnight but evolved gradually with the increasing use of Narcissus flowers for decorations at banquets in Sumner, the organization of bulb shows in Sumner and Tacoma and similar events. A Daffodil Parade was organized and a Queen selected in 1934. The complete festival has been held annually since then with the exception of the years during World War II. More details are given in Chapter 16 on festivals.

San Juan County

Orcas Island has the distinction of being the birthplace of commercial bulb production in Washington State according to available records. George Gibbs, an Englishman, rented 121 acres of school land near Orcas and began raising hazel nuts and apples in 1890. In 1892 he planted $5 worth of Hyacinths and other bulbs. He later moved to Whatcom County and at one time had five acres of bulbs planted in beds. Gibbs died in 1919. For more details see his biography in Chapter 2. He is certainly entitled to be called the Commercial Father of Bulb Growing in Washington.

The only other pioneer bulb grower in San Juan County for whom a record was found was Samuel Shorey who was getting excellent results with his bulbs at Deer Harbor on Orcas Island in 1904. At present, Gary and Alberta Franco (Madrona Farms) on Lopez Island are the only commercial bulb growers in San Juan County, raising bulbs on four acres for cut flowers.

Skagit County

Although bulb growing started early in Skagit County, it increased more slowly there than in many other counties. It was not until the 1930s that the acreage began to expand. It increased more rapidly after 1940 and now (1992) Skagit is the leading bulb producing area in the state.

Mrs. Mary Stewart planted her first bulbs about 1908 and, by 1910, was selling bulbs and flowers to visitors and, later, by retail catalog, to others. She imported bulbs from Holland for resale in addition to raising some on her small farm on Samish Island. Her son, Sam, returned home to assist her in 1925. They expanded in 1931 by planting 5 acres on leased land on McLean Road in the Skagit Valley, purchased 15 acres in 1937, and later bought another farm on Bradshaw Road. The latter became their home place. In 1947, Mary's husband died. She retired and Sam became the sole owner of the business. By 1954, he had 145 acres in bulbs. Sam died in 1971 and most of his bulbs were sold to the United Bulb Company. Bert Hart, a brother-in-law, was his office manager and salesman from 1946 to 1970.

Meanwhile, H. L. Willis, a dairyman, had begun growing Narcissus soon after Mary Stewart started. He proved that the Skagit Valley could produce excellent bulbs and flowers which, at first, he gave to friends and to the Camp Fire Girls. Later, he enlarged his operations and was a commercial grower until 1956 at least.

Neal Noorlag began growing Iris, Narcissus and Tulips near Oak Harbor in Island County in 1931, and, in 1937, moved to a farm on the McLean Road in the Skagit Valley where he added Hyacinths. At one time he was the largest grower of these bulbs in the state. His farm was bought by Tom DeGoede in 1983.

Harold Kenealy, a chemist, began growing bulbs part-time in 1929 and full-time in 1941 near Mount Vernon. By 1961 he had 50 acres.

Glenn Darst started in 1932 at Coupeville and grew mostly Iris although he dabbled in Tulips and Narcissus. He, with his son Earle, moved most of their plantings to the Skagit Valley in 1948. Glenn died in 1971 and Earle continued growing bulbs until 1982, when he sold them to Sun Valley Bulb Farms in Oregon. Recently, he resumed growing Iris and Gladiolus for cut flower purposes.

Marinus Lefeber moved his bulb planting from Lynden to the Skagit Valley in 1936 because of the frequent severe winters in Whatcom County. His son, Bill, took over in 1972 and Bill's son, Dan, is now (1992) operating the farm.

John Onderwater came to Washington from Holland in 1941 and grew bulbs from about 1946 until he died in 1961. He sponsored both Henry DeGoede and Bill Roozen when they decided to emigrate from Holland.

Gerrit Van Zanten also started growing bulbs in Whatcom County but got tired of the losses from periodic freezing and moved his Iris operations to Skagit County in 1945.

Joe Berger and Cornelius (Cor) Roozekrans organized the Washington Bulb Company in 1949 and raised all major bulb types plus Lilies. In 1956 Joe sold his share of the business to Bill Roozen and Cor and then organized his own wholesale firm, Joe Berger and Co., with a head office in Seattle and a branch office in Portland.

Bill Roozen came to work for Onderwater in 1946 and started on his own in 1950 with five acres of bulbs. He bought Joe Berger's share of the Washington Bulb Company in 1956 and Cor Roozenkrans's share in 1963. He and his wife, Helen, raised five sons and five daughters. All of the sons (John, Leo, William M., Richard and Michael) and one daughter (Bernadette) are actively engaged in the family business (the Washington Bulb Company) at Mount Vernon. They farmed 1,310 acres of bulbs and several hundred acres of vegetables and seed crops in 1989.

Their farm produces more Iris, Narcissus and Tulips than any bulb farm in the United States. They also operate 7½ acres of greenhouses for cut flower production as well as a display garden and retail shop.

Henry (Hank) DeGoede (DeGoede Bulb Farms) is another Hollander who came in 1947 to work for Onderwater and started on his own in 1951. He also developed a large farm at Mount Vernon with his sons Jack, Bob and Dennis and was assisted by two brothers, John and Tom. In 1978, Hank and his sons moved their bulbs to Mossyrock in Lewis County where more land was available for proper rotation of their crops.

Tom DeGoede (Skagit Valley Bulb Company) came to Washington in 1953, worked first with his brother, Hank, then with Neal Noorlag and, in 1983, bought Neal's bulb business. John DeGoede also worked with Hank from 1955 until he moved to Pierce County in 1966 to start a greenhouse business in forcing bulbs, raising other plants and operating an adjacent retail shop.

John Gardner (West Shore Acres) started in the bulb business near Mount Vernon in 1964 and grew 96 acres of Narcissus and Tulips in 1989. He and his wife, Marilyn, also manage a display garden and a retail shop. They suffered a disastrous fire in 1982 which destroyed much of their bulb stock, shed and equipment.

Bob and Jim Hulbert (Hulbert Farms, Inc.) grow over 1,000 acres of vegetables, berries, bulbs, seed and other crops. They began to raise Narcissus in 1974 and, by 1989, had 65 acres of them.

Case and Cornelius Van Lierop raised bulbs at Conway but their office and greenhouse were in Bothell so they are listed under King County. Several other growers for whom little detailed information is available include Eerkes Bros., Eddie Gordon, George Hubbard, Jim Leckenby and A. Clizbe.

All the Skagit County growers who were in business before 1935 give much credit to Dr. David Griffiths of the USDA Bulb Station at Bellingham for his encouragement and assistance. Several of them, including the Stewarts, Lefeber and Willis, actively assisted Griffiths by running cooperative experiments with him on their farms. Dr. Griffiths's work is described in detail in Chapter 18.

Skagit County has suffered major problems such as fires, floods by the Skagit River (especially November and December 1990) and severe freezes (November 1955, the winter of 1978/79 and February of both 1989 and 1990).

In general, however, Skagit County has been blessed with an excellent climate, a good work force, progressive growers and a fair amount of excellent well-drained land. The Skagit Valley is now the center for Iris, Narcissus and Tulip production in the United States. Unfortunately, the amount of suitable land for bulbs is limited and is in danger of being lost to development, a misfortune which has already happened to much of the Pierce County bulb land.

During the 1940s and 1950s, most of the Skagit growers sold their bulbs directly to jobbers or sometimes went out on selling trips themselves. Several growers organized the Skagit Valley Flower Cooperative in the late 1950s to sell their flowers. After it ceased operations in 1962, some growers sold their flowers through the Puyallup Valley Flower Cooperative. A few of them also joined the Puget Sound Bulb Exchange as a bulb sales outlet in the 1960s.

Many Skagit growers were blessed with mechanical skills and were able to develop their own diggers, planters and other equipment. Among these were Sam Stewart, Bill Lefeber, Earle Darst and John Roozen.

Bulb flowers naturally seem to give rise to shows and festivals. The first in Skagit County was a Tulip Show sponsored by the LaConner Civic Garden Club which ran from about 1946 to 1971. In 1984, the Mount Vernon Chamber of Commerce organized a Skagit Valley Tulip Festival. Later, other communities added their support and it has become an outstanding 16-day success during April, with all types of festivities except a parade. Of course, the best event of all is the annual pilgrimage to visit the spectacular fields and display gardens with Narcissus and Tulips in full bloom. Eastman Kodak even builds a viewing platform for picture taking near one of the fields.

Snohomish County

Snohomish County had many small growers of bulbs at one time. They raised primarily Gladiolus, Hyacinths and Tulips according to Case Van Lierop, who helped them organize the Snohomish County Bulb Growers Association. The Association president was H. H. Palmer, who grew Narcissus between 1933 and 1948. The largest grower in Snohomish County was George Ward Lawler (known as Ward), who moved from Roy to Monroe in 1941 and, by 1943, was growing 100 acres of bulbs. He sold all his Narcissus bulbs in the field to the United Bulb Company after they lost their bulbs in the Columbia River flood in

1948. However, United missed some Narcissus while digging, so Ward collected these and, by 1954, had five acres of King Alfred and Fortune varieties under cultivation. He finally sold the farm and the bulbs and retired in 1962.

Thurston County

The early beginnings of bulb growing in Thurston County were associated with three men, two of whom started in other counties.

Joe Smith was growing Iris, at least, as early as 1919 at Longbranch in Pierce County. His business flourished and, in 1924, he contracted with W. R. Taylor to raise an acre of Pheasants Eye Narcissus at Olympia. In that same year he helped to organize the Northwest Bulb Growers Association, was elected secretary and was re-elected in 1925. Also, in 1925, Smith expanded again, by contracting with Taylor to grow Lilies, Gladiolus, Tulips and more Narcissus. Smith moved all of his bulbs to Olympia in 1926.

He contracted with A. N. Kanouse in 1927 to grow Gladiolus for him and, in 1928 asked him to become superintendent of his Olympia Bulb Company located on 40 acres south of Tumwater. According to Kanouse, the 1929-1931 years were good ones, but the Depression forced the company into bankruptcy in 1932 or 1933.

Aaron Kanouse (Floravista, Olympia) had been growing Gladiolus and some other bulbs primarily as a hobby at Cedarville in Grays Harbor County since at least 1922. In 1927, he grew Gladiolus for Joe Smith and in 1928 took charge of Smith's company. When the company went bankrupt in 1932 or 1933, Aaron was asked by the receiver to continue running it until the bulb harvest the next year. Meanwhile, he had been gradually building up his own stock and, in 1929, had established his own farm, Floravista. Aaron specialized in newer varieties and in novelty Narcissus and gradually built up a strong retail catalog trade in bulbs and retail sales of cut flowers. He and his wife hybridized Narcissus, specializing in pink colors. They introduced several hybrids.

After Walter R. Taylor grew bulbs for Smith from 1924 to 1928, he apparently went into business for himself, raising and selling both bulbs and flowers locally. In 1930 or 1931 he issued his first retail catalog, presumably of Narcissus. During the 1930s Taylor also raised over 70 varieties of Lilies, but, in 1942, reported that "unfriendly weather accomplished our defeat" (136).

46

Jac Lefeber, one of the Lefeber brothers from Holland, began growing bulbs first at Olympia in 1948, and then at Nisqually, but neither location proved acceptable so he moved to Mount Vernon in 1956. He raised Tulips, Hyacinths and, particularly, Narcissus, of which about 50 were his own hybrids. His most famous variety was the popular Flower Record.

Pete Van Lierop and Mervin Lee Ward (Ward-Van Lierop Farms) are the only remaining bulb growers in Thurston County. They began to raise Narcissus in 1981 and, by 1989, had 25 acres from which they sold both bulbs and flowers.

Several other bulb growers were active in the Olympia area about 1928 including H. R. Watson, T. E. and S. G. Chambers, J. D. Koren, Mrs. Frank McCandless and E. B. Stookey.

Whatcom County

George Gibbs, who had begun growing bulbs on Orcas Island in 1892, moved his operation to the old Fort Bellingham site in 1899 in cooperation with C. T. Canfield. In 1902, he moved to the Lynden area and began concentrating on Freesias and Madonna Lilies. His interesting career with bulbs is described in Chapter 2.

Canfield continued to grow bulbs, but used the row system in preference to the Dutch bed system favored by Gibbs. About the same time, C. X. Larrabee also imported bulbs for field planting, but no other records are available on his bulb activities. Nor is it known when John Macrae Smith began growing bulbs. He did send samples of Tulips and other bulbs to the USDA in 1902. Smith apparently began cooperating with the USDA in experiments in 1903, according to a newspaper article (139), and his cooperation must have helped influence the decision to locate a Test Garden (Bulb Station) in Bellingham in 1908 on 10 acres of the old Fort Bellingham site.

In 1918 the Bulb Station was expanded by the donation of a 60-acre field by Cyrus Gates, William McKay and Mrs. Frances Larrabee. Dr. David Griffiths was placed in charge about 1917 and did a great deal to publicize the possibilities of the Pacific Northwest for bulb growing. He also encouraged and helped growers who were starting to raise bulbs. After his death in 1935, the USDA bulb tests were discontinued at the Station.

47

The USDA Station was the largest bulb producer in the county, and perhaps in the state, for many years. It probably served as the major source of the Tulips used at the Bellingham Tulip Festival which began in 1920 and lasted until 1930, when it was discontinued because of the Depression. This Festival had a Queen, a parade of decorated floats and many other activities including a baseball team which was called the "Tulips." Spectators came by boat from Victoria, by trains from Seattle and Vancouver, BC and by car caravans from all over the Northwest. It is described in more detail in Chapter 16.

Rutgert Vallentgoed resigned from the USDA in 1922 to help organize the Holland-American Bulb Company. In 1923 he was manager of the Bellingham Bulb Company and, in 1926, was listed in the firm of Vallentgoed & Murray.

Henry Juenemann also worked at the USDA Station but resigned in 1924 to organize the Juenemann Bulb Company. He was still active in 1926.

About 1925, the Segers Brothers from Holland planted bulbs at Redmond, but moved to the Lynden area in 1926 or 1927 and soon became one of the largest growers in Washington State. Frank Van Aalst was their first company manager at Lynden and was followed by Harry Van Waveren. The Segers apparently stopped growing bulbs during the late 1930s but Harry continued on his own at least until 1949.

The Van Zanten Brothers from Holland bought 100 acres of land near Lynden and planted Narcissus there in 1926. They added Iris later, issued their own catalog and enlarged the farm to 110 acres by 1929. Unfortunately, they lost many bulbs in the severe winter of 1929/30 when the temperature dropped to 7° below zero and the frigid weather continued for 21 days according to Marinus Lefeber (81). The Van Zantens replanted and, by 1932, were back up to 115 acres of Narcissus and 5 of Iris, making their bulb farm one of the largest in the state. Repeated losses from freezes, however, eventually forced them, and other growers, to either go out of business or to move to Skagit County. The Van Zantens moved their Iris to Mount Vernon and gradually sold off their Narcissus. Gerrit Van Zanten was the first manager of the firm, and was joined in 1931 by his cousin, Maurice, who cooperated on the bulb growing but also began raising greenhouse azaleas. About 1949 Gerrit and Maurice purchased the farm from the parent company in Holland and divided it. Gerrit took the bulbs and Maurice, the azaleas. Maurice's son still carries on the azalea business in Lynden.

48

Marinus Lefeber was another Hollander who began growing bulbs near Lynden in 1928 and had enlarged his plantings to 15 acres of Narcissus by 1936. The severe winters finally forced him, too, to move to Skagit County in 1936 and he is discussed there.

Many new varieties were hybridized or selected by Whatcom growers. Dr. Griffiths developed several hybrids of Pacific Coast Lilies which were eventually combined and sold as the "Bellingham Hybrids" by the Oregon Bulb Farms. LeVern Freimann, county agent for many years, had a life-long hobby of hybridizing Lilies. One of these, Scarlet Delight, a brilliant red, is his most popular Lily. Frank and Lucie Wilson, from Everson, discovered an unusual *Lilium speciosum rubrum* in a chicken yard near Deming. They bought the bulbs in 1943, propagated and distributed them under the name "Lucie Wilson" and the variety became very popular.

Other Whatcom County growers, for whom we have only names are C. R. S. Egbert, O. L. Giese, W. E. Longley, Floral Exchange, Lynden Bulb Company and Tulip Town Bulb Gardens.

Why did so many Dutch immigrants settle in the Lynden area? A major factor, in addition to the abundance of good soil, was the presence of a well-established Dutch community. Their Dutch heritage is remembered even today in their annual festival, called "Holland Days," which is held in early May.

Whatcom County has much to be proud of. It nurtured the early bulb industry and, for many years, was the major producing area in the state, losing out to weather but not to man.

CHAPTER 5

Washington Bulb Growers

The effort to obtain information about growers of bulbs has been both fascinating and frustrating. Fascinating, because I was fortunate in knowing so many of them during my career, but frustrating because the available information about most of them is so very fragmentary. Unfortunately, most of the old timers just discarded their records when they retired.

Information was compiled from reports from the Washington State Department of Agriculture, Northwest Bulb Growers Association and Washington State Bulb Commission; from articles in newspapers and magazines; and, in some cases, from estimates by persons, usually spouses or neighbors, familiar with a certain grower's bulb growing activities. Consequently, both the years and the acreages are often educated guesses but are still the best information available.

Too often the information about a grower was just a name and a year on a list. With assistance from many persons and reports, however, it was possible to accumulate enough details to prepare brief biographies of 117 growers of Iris, Tulips and Narcissus and a few other individuals who were associated with and contributed much to the industry. The 8 Gladiolus and Lily growers for whom information was available are discussed in their respective chapters. The names of all known growers, together with certain pertinent data about them, are shown in tables in the Appendix. The list of more than 900 names includes 520 Iris, Narcissus and/or Tulip growers (Appendix Table A); 134 Gladiolus growers (Appendix Table B); and 357 Lily growers (Appendix Table C). Detailed biographies of George Gibbs (Commercial Father of the Bulb Industry) and Dr. David Griffiths (Scientific Father of the Washington Bulb Industry) are given in Chapters 2 and 18.

In general, most bulb growers before 1922 were Washingtonians; many of the later ones came from Holland. By 1930, the latter included the Van Lierops and Van Zonnevelds in Pierce County and John Van

Aalst in King County. Most Hollanders headed for Whatcom County in the 1920s. These included the Van Zantens, Segers Bros. and Marinus Lefeber. Among those coming from other countries were Frank Chervenka from Czechoslovakia, Karl Koehler from Germany, George Gibbs from England and John Macrae Smith from Scotland.

It is logical to assume that bulb growers started out as general farmers but such was not always the case. Mrs. Mary Stewart had been a school teacher in Ohio, Edwin Wines was an "advance" man for a vaudeville company, George Lawler was a realtor, Sam Stewart had been a quartermaster on a ship, Harold Kenealy and Miles Hatch were both chemists, Stan Staatz studied to be a lawyer, J. R. McLean started out as a logger and the Williams Brothers originally were produce merchants in Tacoma. They all quickly learned how to grow bulbs and contributed much to the industry.

Sooner or later most of the pioneers experimented with several types of bulbs and most grew more than one type commercially. A few growers and companies specialized in one or two types. For example, the Darsts concentrated on Iris and Gladiolus while the Hulberts, West Shore Acres, Williams Brothers, Ward and Van Lierop have grown mostly Narcissus. None of the larger growers seemed to raise Tulips only. Most Lily and Gladiolus growers raised only those crops. Sometimes the choice was a personal one but, at other times, it was necessitated by location, weather, markets or other factors. The Chervenkas, for example, had to stop growing Tulips because of repeated losses from hailstorms in their particular location in the Puyallup Valley.

The length of the following individual biographies does not necessarily reflect the size or importance of a grower's business. Very little information was available about many of them—especially the pioneers. Additional research in local newspapers might yield more information and this could be an excellent project for senior citizens and for high school and college students writing term papers.

Albertson, E.

E. Albertson (1856----, Seattle) was an accountant who, because of problems from eye strain, went into bulb growing. He began with Tulips and Gladiolus sometime before 1920 and later added Narcissus, raising them on his lots near Green Lake, Seattle. In 1920 he planted 6,000 King Alfreds. They grew so well and their flowers brought such a premium price (12-14¢ each versus 5-6¢ for the common Golden Spur) that by 1924 he decided to discard his other bulbs and concentrate on the King Alfreds. He may have been the largest grower of this variety in the state at that time (100).

Berger, Joe

Joe Berger (1913-1985, Joe Berger & Company, Seattle) first began raising Lilies with his brother in the Brookings, OR area. He moved to Mount Vernon about 1946 and, in 1949, joined Cornelius (Cor) Roozekrans to form the Washington Bulb Company to raise Iris, Lilies, Narcissus and Tulips. Joe did the growing and Cor did the selling.

By 1955/56 they had 32 acres of Iris, Lilies, Narcissus and Tulips but the severe freeze in November of 1955 caused so much damage that Joe decided to sell his share of the company and its name to Bill Roozen and Cor in 1956. He joined the Mount Rainier Bulb Company for about one year and next organized his own wholesale company, the Joe Berger & Company, with the head office in Seattle. Later, he and Dave Wolfkill opened a branch in Portland selling both bulbs and florists' supplies.

Joe sold his company in 1973 so that he could spend his winters playing golf in Arizona! Later, he reopened the old Portland Wholesale Company but hired a manager to run it for him until 1980 when he finally retired.

The old Washington Bulb Company was probably the first to sell Washington-grown Iris to Holland importers in 1952 and/or 1953 before the big 1953/54 freeze in Holland which fueled the subsequent rapid increase in Iris exports from many Washington growers to Europe. Dorothy Berger recalled that they sold mostly to Rotteveel (jobber) and to Leo Berbee and Sons (forcers) in Holland.

Bergman, Henry

Henry (Hank) Bergman (1909-1962, Mount Vernon) came from Holland under the sponsorship of Cornelius Koning about 1947. By 1949 he was reported growing 25 acres of bulbs. He passed away on May 11, 1962.

Bowen Bulb Farms

Clarence Bowen (1926-1983, Bowen Bulb Farms, Puyallup) came to Washington in 1935 and worked first for Ed Orton and later for Harold Knutson. He began buying bulbs for his own use in 1959. In 1963 Clarence bought a farm near McMillin and started full-time farming. By 1977 he had 35 acres planted to Iris, Narcissus and Tulips. Clarence died in 1983 but his sons, Bernie and Robin, and his widow, Mable, continued to grow bulbs. In 1985 Mable married Sam Nearhood and they continued the bulb business. By 1989, however, they had put part of their farm into Christmas trees and had only 10 acres of Narcissus left.

Canfield, Chauncey T.

Chauncey Canfield (1851----, Bellingham) was raised on a farm in Connecticut, arrived in Bellingham in 1889, later became an auditor and, by 1926, was the manager of the Bellingham Abstract Company. In 1899 he helped George Gibbs move to Bellingham and cooperated with him in the bulb business until Gibbs moved to the Lynden area in 1902. In the same year Canfield sent bulb samples (presumably from Gibbs) to Philadelphia florists who pronounced them "as fine as Holland can produce. (113)" Canfield continued farming in the Bellingham area and raised bulbs until at least 1904, planting in 18" rows, unlike Gibbs's bed system.

Chervenka, Frank A.

Frank Chervenka (1880-1966, Chervenka Farms, Sumner) was born in Czechoslovakia, came to the United States in 1888, went to Amherst Agricultural College, MA, worked in nurseries and greenhouses in several states and arrived in Sumner in 1919. He and two partners bought Woodland Park Floral in 1920 but Frank sold his share in 1926 in order to concentrate on growing bulbs and roses. He was one of the first to grow bulbs commercially in the Puyallup-Sumner area, beginning in 1923. He and Ed Orton reportedly bought a surplus carload of Narcissus bulbs from A. Pruyser of the General Bulb Company in Michigan in 1924 and were the two largest local Narcissus growers at that time with over 1 million bulbs each (27,28,97).

Narcissus were Chervenka's major crop at first but he later added

Iris, Tulips and Lilies. He eventually gave up Tulips because his location was subject to hail damage. In 1926 Frank bought a 60-acre farm near Sumner and, in 1927, a 20-acre farm near Fife. The latter was sold in 1933 because the soil was too wet for bulbs. In 1934 he and Stanley Staatz began raising 40 acres of Narcissus near the junction of the Puyallup and Stuck Rivers. In 1937, he and Stan bought a 100-acre farm near Orting, which is now the location of the Hi Cedars Golf Course. Staatz bought out Frank's share in 1940. Frank also owned a bulb and berry farm at Watsonville, CA and grew Narcissus there from 1938 to about 1946. In general, he raised mostly Narcissus, Iris and roses. He also produced rose root stock and even developed several new rose varieties. Frank sold out to his son, Francis, in 1944.

Chervenka was one of the founders and later president of the Northwest Bulb Growers Association. He also helped found the Puget Sound Bulb Exchange of which he was both president and sales manager from 1926 to 1928.

Frank was very active in local and national florist associations and spent much time promoting the bulb industry locally as well as representing it before congressional committees, the Tariff Commission, etc., in Washington, DC. He was the person mainly instrumental in obtaining funds from both the United States Department of Agriculture and the Pierce County Commissioners to develop and staff the USDA Bulb Insect Laboratory at Sumner in 1928. He also strongly supported Washington State University when he was a state representative from 1938 to 1945 and was chairman of the House Agricultural Committee. His daughter, Olive, was a princess during the 1935 Daffodil Festival and Frank was a chaperon.

Chervenka, Francis A.

Francis Chervenka (Chervenka Farms, Inc., Sumner) helped plant Narcissus for his father in 1923 and later worked for him full-time after graduation from college. He bought the farm from Frank in 1944 and continued growing Narcissus and Iris until an arson fire in 1971 destroyed the barn, most of his equipment and all of his Iris planting stock. In 1951 he had purchased 14 acres of land at Santa Barbara, CA and raised Iris for field-cut flowers until his wife died in 1956. He then sold the California acreage and returned to the home farm at Puyallup.

Francis was one of the first to begin mechanizing bulb operations and was the first to develop a self-propelled digger and a planter. In 1956 he won the Conservation Award of the year for his excellent and diversified year-round operation in raising Narcissus, Iris, rose rootstock and dwarf apple rootstock.

Francis was president of and very active in the Northwest Bulb Growers Association; he also helped to organize the Puyallup Valley Flower Cooperative and managed it from 1956 to 1961. He served on the bulb research and other committees and actively supported the research program and the WSU Bulb Growers Short Courses. Since 1971 he has concentrated his efforts on the production of dwarf apple rootstock which he began growing in 1946 and of which he was once the largest producer not only in Washington but in the United States.

Darst, Glenn and Earle

Glenn Darst (1893-1971, Darst Bulb Farms, Coupeville) bought Wedgwood Iris planting stock from Neal Noorlag in 1932 and gave 5% of it to each of his two sons, Earle and Gerald. They grew cooperatively, purchasing additional stock locally and from Holland until 1941 when Earle left for the Army and his father and Gerald concentrated on vegetables. When Earle returned home, he and Glenn formed a partnership, discarded all the old Iris stock and bought new bulbs, including some from Captain C. R. Wilson in British Columbia. Then, in 1948, they moved their plantings to the Skagit Valley, intermittently planting part of the stock on Whidbey Island where bulbs matured earlier but did not achieve the size of mainland bulbs. According to Earle, the Darst Farms reached its peak in acreage about 1967/68 with their 137 acres producing 16 million salable Iris bulbs. Unfortunately, they suffered a heavy bulb loss the next year from flooding.

They experimented with Tulips, Lilies and Narcissus but grew them for only a short time. Earle had begun growing Gladiolus in 1964 at George in eastern Washington and continued until about 1969, reaching a peak of 95 acres in 1967. He also raised Glads on Whidbey Island and in the Skagit Valley until he sold his stock in 1976. Glenn died in 1971 and Earle gradually began to specialize in Iris. In 1978/79 he had another catastrophe when the severe freeze that winter destroyed 80% of his salable bulbs as well as a third of his planting stock. In 1982 he sold all of his Iris to Sun Valley Bulb Farms.

Earle began to hybridize Iris about 1955 and later introduced several new varieties, including Moonlight Mist, Enchantress and Blue Pacific. The DeGoede Bulb Farms is now growing Moonlight Mist and some of Earle's other hybrids, primarily for the dry sale trade.

About 1985, Earle repurchased some of his Iris hybrids from Sun Valley Farms and again began growing them and Gladiolus on Whidbey Island as a hobby and for commercial field-cut flower production. In 1992 he had about eight acres of Iris and ten of Gladiolus.

Deeds, George H.

George Deeds (1874-1969, Puyallup) bought a 10-acre farm in Puyallup in 1919 and grew a variety of crops including raspberries, rhubarb, vegetables and various bulbs. Of the latter he sold both flowers and bulbs. He was raising Narcissus in 1933 and continued until about 1965. At the peak of his production, George probably had about 10 acres of Narcissus, Iris and Tulips. He was also secretary-treasurer for a Puyallup Valley insurance firm and at one time was a horticultural inspector. A relative, D. A. Balch, was a manager for Deeds during his last years in the bulb business.

DeGoede, Henry

Henry (Hank) DeGoede (DeGoede Bulb Farms, Mossyrock) learned bulb growing on his father's farm in Holland and came to the United States in 1947, $200 in debt, to work for John Onderwater at Mount Vernon. He began growing bulbs independently in 1951 and bought all of Onderwater's stock in 1952. By 1956 he had 12 acres in Iris and 12 in Tulips at Mount Vernon. In 1957 he grew about 35 acres of Gladiolus in eastern Washington and continued growing Glads there until 1966 as well as some at Mount Vernon. Hank continued enlarging his plantings with all bulb types and by about 1964 was farming 250 acres of bulbs and seed crops on his own land plus about 150 acres of leased land. By 1970 he had about 250 acres in all types of bulbs.

The shortage of good land in Skagit Valley and the expense associated with farming 15-20 scattered leased parcels prompted Hank and his family to buy and begin moving to a 725-acre farm in Mossyrock in 1977 where the company raised about 110 acres of Iris and Tulips, and 65 more of miscellaneous bulbs and perennial crops in 1991. They also have several greenhouses for forcing bulbs and other crops as well as a large retail flower and gift shop. Hank's three sons, Jack, Bob and Dennis, went to WSU and are now in the family business, each with his own specialty.

Hank and his wife, Hildegarde, originally developed the beautiful Chuckanut Display Gardens at Mount Vernon, managed by John Conijn (1928-1992), a brother-in-law. The DeGoedes now have another display garden at their Mossyrock farm and also cooperate with the local Chamber of Commerce in putting on a Tulip Festival each spring.

Hank was president and sales manager of the Skagit Valley Flower Cooperative from about 1959 until 1962 when it was disbanded.

DeGoede, John P.

John DeGoede (Windmill Greenhouse and Nursery, Sumner) first stepped on United States soil in 1955 when he came from Holland. In Mount Vernon, he worked with his brother, Henry, on Henry's bulb farm which became one of the largest in the Skagit Valley.

John met Ansje Jungerhans and, after they were married, three sons soon followed. John moved to Sumner in 1966 and worked at the Puget Sound Bulb Exchange until he purchased Henry Koch's old greenhouse business in 1968. John first forced Tulips for flowers in the winter and spring months, and later included Iris and Narcissus.

In 1980, John's sons, Ben, Phil and Paul, joined the business full-time and they soon added a retail store. It is now a full-service florist, nursery and garden center open the year around.

The DeGoede family business still sells to the wholesale market also. They force over two million Tulip and Narcissus bulbs annually and also raise winter primroses and fuchsias. They employ over eighty people to do this at peak season.

John is still very active in the business. Ben, his oldest son, runs the retail store while Phil is wholesale sales manager and Paul is production manager.

DeGoede, Anthony, Sr.

Anthony (Tom) DeGoede (Skagit Valley Bulb Farm, Mount Vernon) emigrated from Holland to Canada in 1952 and to Washington in 1953. He worked with his brother, Henry, from 1955 to 1976 in Mount Vernon and then became manager for Neal Noorlag. After Neal had a stroke in 1983, Tom bought his bulbs and rented his farm and equipment. At that time Neal had 25 acres of Iris, Narcissus and Tulips. By 1989 Tom had eliminated the Narcissus and was growing 25 acres of Iris and 27 of Tulips. He and his wife, Jeanette, run a retail shop at the farm but most of their bulbs are sold wholesale.

De Groot, Theodore, Sr.

Theodore (Ted) De Groot, Sr. (1893-1982, United Bulb Company, Woodland) was apparently the major pioneer grower of Narcissus in the Clark + Cowlitz area. He began raising Narcissus in Michigan in 1925 but saw some Washington bulbs in 1927, admired their quality, and decided to investigate the area. Two years later he planted Narcissus and Tulip bulbs on 7 acres of rented Washington land and in 1930 bought an 80-acre farm which he subsequently enlarged. Later he also grew Lilies.

By 1948 the United Bulb Company was one of the largest bulb farms in Washington. Unfortunately, all their bulbs were destroyed by the Columbia and Lewis River floods that spring. Some growers estimated that between 200 and 300 acres were lost but, in 1991, Arie Guldemond, a part owner, recalled that it might have been closer to 402 acres, with 200 in Narcissus, 125 in Iris, 75 in Tulips and 2 in Lilies. The company immediately contracted with Lawler and others to buy planting stock which they planted on surrounding hills for the next two or three years. In 1954 they planted 170 acres of Iris, Tulips and Narcissus. During the 1960s some estimates indicate that they may have had as many as 250-300 acres in bulbs.

The United Bulb Company was incorporated in 1929 by De Groot who owned 70% of the stock. Co-owners were Leo and Gerald Aalbersberg. Ted De Groot, Jr. also was a partner at one time. Arie Guldemond joined the firm in 1944 and eventually became the sole owner.

The first manager of the United Bulb Company was Gerald Aalbersberg and the next, starting in 1941 and continuing for another 33 years, was Dirk Kroon. Dirk was another "import" from Holland who worked first for United Bulb Company in Michigan and then moved to the Woodland farm in 1939.

58

De Groot, Theodore, Jr.

Theodore (Ted) De Groot, Jr. (1926-1984, Woodland Bulb Farms, Woodland) worked for his father for many years at the United Bulb Company farm at Woodland. In 1978 he and Ed Maggi bought the farm and renamed it the "Woodland Bulb Farms." They continued to grow all types of bulbs and may have had about 80 acres at their peak. In 1980 they suffered a disastrous fire and later were forced to sell the farm. Most of the assets were acquired by the Northwest Rose Growers Company of Woodland, WA. Ted next organized the Hilltop Farms and sold a few Iris in 1980 but that was his last year as a bulb grower. He was a co-owner of the United Bulb Company at one time. He also was a past president of the Northwest Bulb Growers Association. His hobby was painting.

Delkin, Fred

Fred Delkin (Delkin Bulb Farm, Bellevue) grew bulbs at least from 1933 to 1950. He raised Iris, Narcissus and Lilies and, in 1942, had 20 acres in Narcissus. He was both a grower and a wholesaler, issued a catalog and, reportedly, was one of the first dealers to sell Northwest Iris to eastern greenhouses for forcing. Unfortunately, we have no more information about him.

Dobbe, Benno

Benno Dobbe (Holland America Bulb Farms, Inc., Woodland) began raising bulbs in Holland in 1965 when he was 15 years old. He emigrated in 1980 with his wife, Klazina, and their three children to Woodland where they have continued to grow bulbs on 125 acres of land with the assistance of 7 full-time and 60-80 part-time employees. In 1989 they had 20 acres of Iris, 10 of Asiatic Lilies and 25 of Tulips. In that same year they handled about 36 million salable bulbs of their own and imported stocks. Their 20,000 square foot warehouse contains 14 storage rooms for heating or cooling bulbs and this makes it possible for them to ship bulbs to flower producers on a weekly basis throughout the year.

Edem, Mrs. Kristen Lubbe

Kristen (Kris) Edem (Satsop Bulb Farms, Elma) and her sister, Mrs. Karel Smith, daughters of Chuck Lubbe, planted the bulbs their grandmother (Mrs. Lubbe Lee) gave Kris in 1976 which included 125 varieties of Narcissus and 20 of Tulips. By 1989 they had enlarged their plantings to 10 acres of Narcissus and 1½ acres of Tulips. In addition to selling bulbs, they also force them in a greenhouse for sale in their retail bulb and flower shop where Kris said "her heart is."

Edmondson, Henry D.

Henry (Hank) Edmondson (1901-1979, of Mansfield and Edmondson, Sumner) worked in a shipyard and sawmill before going to work for C. W. Orton in 1931, first as foreman and later as warehouse manager. He and Howard Mansfield began growing Tulips in 1946 and later added Narcissus. Their peak year was about 1951 when they had a total of 20 acres. They continued growing bulbs until about 1962 when Hank retired. He was president of the Northwest Bulb Growers Association in 1952/53.

Engles

The Engle family (Carl T., Will C. and Robert E., Coupeville) bought their first Iris planting stock from C. W. Orton about 1935, paying $1 a pound for the bulbs. In 1937 Carl (father) and Will (brother) decided to sell their shares to Robert who continued growing bulbs until the 1960s, reaching a peak of about 25 acres of Iris, 2 of Tulips and 2 of Narcissus. Also in 1937, Robert was one of the first to adopt the method of planting by just scattering bulbs in an open furrow and covering, instead of carefully spacing and setting them upright by hand as had been customary. Other growers soon adopted this technique. Engle usually plowed out the bulbs with an old horse plow since his soil type was not conducive to mechanical digging. In the fall of 1955, a sudden freeze destroyed most of the bulbs in his warehouse and his Iris acreage dropped from 15 acres in 1955/56 to 2 the next year. Robert's uncle, Ralph, also raised 1 to 2 acres of Iris for a few years.

Franco, Gary

Gary and Alberta Franco (Madrona Farms, Lopez Island) began growing berries several years ago and, in 1985, added bulbs. They are now raising Gladiolus, Iris, Lilies, Narcissus and Tulips, primarily for cut-flower production.

Frantzen, Johannes H.

Johannes (Joe) Frantzen (Multiflora, Inc., Redmond) was born in Holland, worked on a bulb farm in Sweden and then became a bulb salesman in Sweden. He came to the United States in 1957 and worked for an eastern firm until he became the assistant manager of the Puget Sound Bulb Exchange in 1961 and manager in 1970 when Ted Sabelis left to become a salesman for Gloeckner & Company. Joe was also manager of the Puyallup Valley Flower Cooperative from 1961 until 1972 when he retired from both jobs, built some greenhouses and later organized his own flower wholesaling business called Multiflora, Inc.

Fryar, Richard G.

Richard (Dick) Fryar (1892-1981, Sumner) was a pharmacist who sold his drug store in 1927 and in 1929 became assistant manager of the Puget Sound Bulb Exchange and then manager from 1946 to 1956. Dick never raised bulbs but he had a knack for merchandizing them. He was very active in the Northwest Bulb Growers Association and during his tenure was the main representative for the Northwest Bulb Growers in their fights to retain the quarantine, keep or increase tariffs and reduce freight rates. It was his suggestion to include a Narcissus flower show in the 1931 Daffodil Festival and he ran it until 1936. He also started a newsletter for bulb growers and published it for the Association from 1948 until 1951.

Gardner, John

John Gardner (West Shore Acres, Mount Vernon) has had varied experiences. He started out with a dairy herd and general farming after which he became an Alaskan fisherman but continued to farm on the side and leased out part of his land. One year Sam Stewart grew some bulbs on part of John's land and John became so interested in them that about 1964 he began growing five acres of Flower Carpet Narcissus. By 1987, he had expanded his plantings to 120 acres of three varieties of Narcissus. This was one of the largest Narcissus plantings in Washington at that time. In 1989 John joined the general trend toward thicker plantings per acre and, by 1990, was planting the same number of bulbs on only 96 acres. He also had another six acres in Tulips.

John has had two major catastrophes: a 50% loss of bulbs during the severe freezing winter of 1978/79 and a fire in 1982 in which he lost his barn, greenhouses, some machinery, 250,000 salable Iris bulbs, all the Tulip planting stock and a considerable portion of his Narcissus stock. Fortunately, during the crisis, Bob Hulbert, a nearby grower, arrived in time to help save much movable equipment. Two years later, a sharp February freeze resulted in a loss of profit from about 2 million Narcissus flowers. They were too short-stemmed to sell!

In 1982 John and his wife, Marilyn, began developing a beautiful two-acre display garden of over 60,000 bulbs with more than 100 different varieties of Narcissus and Tulips. The bulbs are planted in scattered designs in a wooded area surrounding their 1886 Victorian house. The Gardners have a retail catalog business and also operate a retail shop in conjunction with the display garden where they sell both flowers and bulbs.

Gibbs, George

George Gibbs was the Commercial Father of Washington State's Bulb Industry and his story can be found in Chapter 2.

Goelzer, Lester

Lester (Les) Goelzer (1901-1975, G. R. Kirk and Company, Puyallup) began as a radio operator on a ship, later worked for Hofert and Co. on Christmas trees and other crops and, in 1929, went to work for G. R. Kirk and Company. He and Otto Reise later recommended to Kirk that the company should get into the bulb business and it did, some time before 1942. This cooperative relationship between Kirk and Goelzer lasted until about 1958. They grew a few Tulips but mostly Narcissus, reaching a peak of about 60 acres in 1945. Their main business was in cut flowers but they also sold bulbs to the dry sale trade.

Les later raised strawberries and Christmas trees, retailing the latter in California.

Gronen, Hamilton F.

H. F. Gronen (1874-1968, Puyallup) was a veteran of the Spanish-American War and an engineer who helped build Alder Dam near Eatonville and other projects. Because of impaired health, he left engineering, bought a farm in Puyallup in 1919 and began raising raspberries and vegetables. Gronen may have started growing a few bulbs in 1923 (90) but it was in 1925 when he expanded his planting with 9 tons of Narcissus and Iris planted on 2 acres. He actively continued growing until 1947 when his son, Robert, joined him as a partner. Hamilton sold his share of the business about 1950 and Robert sold the remaining bulbs to Si Van Lierop around 1952. The Gronen peak acreage was about 13 acres, mostly in Narcissus.

Gronen helped organize the Puget Sound Bulb Exchange and was its secretary-treasurer from 1926 to 1932 and its sales manager from 1933 to 1946. He also organized and was president of the American Narcissus Growers Association, an organization of about 150 growers in 11 states organized to fight for the continuance of Quarantine 37 and to retain the tariffs on bulbs. Gronen retired from the Bulb Exchange in 1946. He was very active in the bulb associations and carried on a life-long battle to protect their interests. He even tried some hybridizing of bulbs in his spare time. Gronen moved to Santa Cruz, CA in 1947 and died there in 1968.

Guldemond, Arie

Arie Guldemond (United Bulb Co., Mount Clemens, MI) was born in Lisse, Holland and went into bulb growing there in 1935. He later came to the United States and became a partner with Ted De Groot in the United Bulb Company in 1944. Arie estimated that their peak acreage at Woodland was 1947/48, the year they lost about 400 acres of bulbs when the Columbia River backed up the Lewis River and flooded their fields. Arie said they owned about 450 acres of land and leased another 200-300 acres at this time.

Eventually, Arie became the sole owner of the business in Michigan and subsequently, passed the company along to his son. Their business

63

is now about two-thirds in cut flowers and one-third in bulbs. Refer to Ted De Groot for more details about Arie and the United Bulb Company.

Harm, William C.

William (Bill) Harm (Puyallup) began growing Narcissus about 1939 and continued until 1968. His peak acreage was about 13 acres in 1956. In 1968 he sold his bulbs, trays and some of his land to Clarence Bowen and retired.

Hatch, L. M. and Miles B.

Lewis Miles Hatch (1880-1964, Hatch Bulb Ranch, Puyallup) was a civil engineer who graduated from WSU in 1902 and returned to the farm in Alderton to help his father in 1911. His main interest was berries but, in 1925, he bought some Narcissus and continued growing bulbs until he turned the operation over to his son, Miles, in 1948. Lewis was a charter member of the Puget Sound Bulb Exchange and was active in the Northwest Bulb Growers Association as well as in the Fruit Growers Association, the Farm Loan Association and in other groups. At his peak he grew about 17 acres of Iris, Narcissus and Tulips although bulbs were a sideline as most of his acreage was still in berries.

His son, Miles B. Hatch, was a Professor of Chemistry at Oregon State University until he resigned in 1948 to return and help his father with the farm at Puyallup. Miles continued growing bulbs and developed a display garden of them adjacent to the Sumner-Orting highway with Mount Rainier in the background. It was a favorite spot for years for photographers. In 1972 Miles sold all of his bulbs to the Puget Sound Bulb Exchange and retired from active farming. His peak year was about 1960 when he grew 20 acres of Narcissus and Iris.

Homan, Dr. Clyde

Dr. Clyde Homan (1903-1984, Tulips Inc., Terre Haute, IN) may have known more about the growing and forcing of Tulips than anyone else in the United States and perhaps as much as anyone else in the world when he was still active. He raised Tulips and other bulbs at different times in Washington, Oregon, Tennessee and even Chile (one year) and forced them in his greenhouses, first near Chicago and later at Terre Haute, IN. Homan was raising bulbs, mostly Tulips, at least as early as 1938 in the Portland area and, by 1940, he had about 100 acres there in bulbs. During World War II, the Dutch even sent stocks of many new Tulip varieties to Homan in an effort to save them. Unfortunately, they were lost when the ship was sunk.

Tulips Inc. was a subsidiary of Vaughan's Seed Company from 1934 until 1960 when it was purchased by Homan. After his death, his wife Viola, who had assisted Clyde in the business, sold it to Jim and Dru Adams who renamed it "The Tulip Company." A generous gift by Homan in 1983 enabled the University of Chicago to develop a state-of-the-art "Dr. Clyde Homan Plant Environmental Genetics Laboratory."

Homan had a reputation for producing high quality flowers and, because of it, he was able to convince flower wholesalers that he needed a premium price for his flowers which he usually got. He was the only large grower in Washington who still planted bulbs in beds in 1947. In 1940, Homan, with the help of Ray Thomas and some others, developed and patented a special machine for harvesting bulbs in beds. In 1947 he planted 20 acres of Narcissus, 5 of Iris and 40 of Tulips at Woodland but lost all the bulbs and a new home in the disastrous Columbia and Lewis River floods in early 1948. Homan subsequently raised his bulbs in Oregon and Tennessee for a few years and then began importing all he needed for forcing at Terre Haute.

Hulbert, Robert and James

Robert (Bob) and James (Jim) Hulbert (with his sons Tom and Jack, Hulbert Farms, Inc., Mount Vernon) operate one of the most diversified and progressive farms in Washington. On their 1,000-plus acres they raised strawberries, seed crops, vegetables and 65 acres of Narcissus in 1989. The Hulberts started growing Narcissus in 1974 and began forcing them in greenhouses in 1983. Both Jim and Bob are WSU graduates. Bob has been a very active leader in state support for agriculture and in 1977 was named WSU Dad of the Year.

Johnson, Arthur O.

Arthur (Art) Johnson (Sumner) worked at Si Van Lierop's farm for one or two years and then started his own bulb farm about 1950. He

65

began with Narcissus and later added Tulips and Iris. Our first recorded date for him is 1950 and the last was 1975. At his peak, about 1965, he probably had 15 acres, mostly in Iris and Tulips. His sister was Mrs. Si Van Lierop. According to Neil Van Lierop, Art had a natural green thumb.

Jonkheer, Anthony William

Anthony (Tony) Jonkheer (Mount Vernon Bulb Company, Mount Vernon) was born in Holland in 1905,came to the United States in 1939, and moved with his family to Washington State in 1949. He worked for Harold Kenealy for about three years and then organized the Mount Vernon Bulb Company. Tony raised a few bulbs but he was primarily a salesman and jobber from 1952 until he retired in 1969 and moved to Woodburn, OR. His son, Theodore Anthony (Ted) of Jonkheer Greenhouses, Mount Vernon, worked on bulbs with his father until 1969. Since then he has been forcing various bulb crops, primarily Tulips.

Juenemann, Henry E.

Henry Juenemann (Juenemann Bulb Company, Bellingham) was a propagator and supervisor at the USDA Bulb Gardens in Bellingham from 1908 until April of 1924 when he retired to go into commercial bulb production. He organized the Juenemann Bulb Company which was still active in 1926 and had a salesman named Halsey Watson, but that is all that is known of him or his company.

Kanouse, Aaron N.

Aaron Kanouse (1902-1980, Floravista, Olympia) began raising Gladiolus in 1922 on his father's farm at Cedarville in eastern Grays Harbor County. In 1926 he salvaged enough Narcissus bulbs from a deserted homestead to begin growing them commercially. In 1927 he raised 1½ acres of Gladiolus under contract for Joe Smith who, in 1928, asked Aaron to manage the Olympia Bulb Company for him. The company eventually expanded to about 40 acres of various bulbs with about half the land planted with Narcissus. The years from 1929 to 1931 were good years but the Depression hit and the company went bankrupt in 1932. Kanouse continued as manager for the receivership until 1933.

Meanwhile, Aaron had been building up his own stock of bulbs "whenever extra cash was available." After his marriage in 1929, he and his wife established "Floravista Gardens" in Olympia. They sold bulbs through the Puget Sound Bulb Exchange at first but later developed a flourishing catalog business of their own. They also sold cut flowers to local florists. He and his wife developed about 60 new hybrid varieties of Narcissus and were noted for their collection of new and novelty Narcissus in addition to Lilies, Tulips and other bulb types. Aaron retired about 1973 but retained a few of his seedlings in order to observe their performance. He was also an avid rockhounder.

Kapteyn, John

John Kapteyn (Holland Bulb Co., Portland, OR) came from a long line of bulb growers and exporters in Holland. He was born in Holland in 1920, raised a few Tulips there and emigrated to the United States in late 1945. During 1946 he worked for Sam Stewart who permitted John to plant about an acre of his imported Tulips on Sam's field. John sold these Tulips to E. P. Gordon in 1947 in order to concentrate on his new firm, the Holland Bulb Growers (later called the Holland Bulb Co.) which was incorporated on January 1, 1947. He hired his first full-time salesman in 1951 and moved into a warehouse in Mount Vernon. In 1954 Pete Walker became warehouse manager for him but resigned in late 1962 when John moved the company to Portland. John retired in 1984 and turned the business over to his son, Bruce. The company now has a 65,000 square foot warehouse, 35 full-time employees and 11 full-time outside salesmen.

Kaylor, Floyd C.

Floyd Kaylor (1876-1960, Kaylor Nurseries, Arlington) planted his first bulbs at Blaine in 1910 when his congressman sent him several Narcissus and Hyacinth bulbs. Floyd continued raising bulbs there until he sold the farm about 1915. In 1926 he had to repossess the farm and, subsequently, went back into bulb growing, adding Tulips first and Gladiolus later. He stayed there until 1940 when he moved to Arlington. In a letter written to the author in 1954, Floyd stated that he was still growing Narcissus, Tulips, Hyacinths and Gladiolus on a small scale but, because of low prices, planned to dispose of them as soon as possible and concentrate on his nursery stock. Floyd was another grower who actively cooperated with Dr. Griffiths, and described him as a very reserved gentleman and that it took 2-3 years of personal association for him to "open up."

Kenealy, Harold R.

Harold Kenealy (1900-1975, Mount Vernon) was a chemist who first worked for Darigold Creamery in Mount Vernon. As a sideline in 1929 he started growing some Hyacinths, Narcissus and Tulips. He proceeded to add more bulbs, including Wedgwood Iris in 1930. In 1941 he retired from Darigold, purchased a farm, put up a warehouse and began full time bulb farming. By 1956 he had 54 acres in all types of bulbs. He decided to retire in 1965 and sold his bulbs to Bill Roozen. Harold died in 1975. He was rather shy and retiring but very knowledgeable. A shopping mall now occupies the site of his former bulb farm just north of Mount Vernon beside the I-5 freeway.

Kenly, David

David (Dave) Kenly (Northwest Rose Growers, Woodland) is a large rose grower who lives near Phoenix, AZ. He and the United Bulb Company organized the Northwest Rose Growers at Woodland in 1966 with assistance from Monty McGuire. Kenly bought United Bulb Company's share in 1976. They concentrated on roses until they added Narcissus in 1978 and Iris in 1979. Then, when Woodland Bulb Farms went bankrupt, Kenly acquired most of its remaining assets and began enlarging their bulb operations. By 1989 they had 20 acres in Iris and 33 in Narcissus. They lost some Narcissus and about 80% of the Iris from freezing damage in the spring of 1989 so their acreage in 1990 was down to 3-4 acres of Iris and 30 acres of Narcissus.

The manager and salesman for the company is Monty McGuire who has been with the company from the beginning and helped organize the original operation. He reported that they sell about one million Narcissus flowers a year. Their major emphasis, however, is on "jobbing" bulbs, buying them from other growers and then reselling them. They also purchase and resell large numbers of roses and other nursery stock.

68

Kern, Raymond F.

Raymond (Ray) Kern (Sumner) began growing Narcissus in cooperation with the Williams Brothers on 10 acres of leased land near McMillin in 1940 or 1941. They later added Tulips and Iris, raising them on a farm near Orting purchased for that purpose by the Williams. Kern and Williams split up in 1949 with each taking half the stock. Ray continued growing all three types of bulbs on five or more acres until at least 1951 or 1952. He was also a Horticultural Inspector with the Washington State Department of Agriculture at Sumner from 1946 until about 1955 when he became an assistant supervisor of the Horticulture Division in the Department of Agriculture in charge of inspection in eastern Washington. Ray was subsequently appointed a supervisor and retired in 1965.

Kirk, George and Paul, Sr.

George and Paul Kirk (G. R. Kirk and Company, Tacoma) were in the "greens" and Christmas tree business when Les Goelzer went to work for them in 1929. Les and Otto Reise recommended that the company also get into the cut-flower bulb business, which Kirk and Goelzer did in partnership some time before 1942. They raised a few Tulips but most of the acreage was in Narcissus. Their peak year was about 1945 when they grew approximately 60 acres of bulbs. They stopped growing bulbs in Washington about 1958. Kirk and Company independently also owned Narcissus farms in Eureka, CA and Siletz, OR. This provided a continuous supply of cut flowers over a 6-8 week period in the spring. Although their main interest was in cut flowers, they did sell bulbs to the dry sale trade through their contacts in the floral and greenhouse trades.

Knoblauch, Theodore A.

Theodore (Ted) Knoblauch (1908-1990, Everett) was raised in the Sumner area, attended WSU and grew Narcissus about 1930 on land rented from Alfred Scholz's father. Ted later became an inspector with the Washington State Department of Agriculture at Sumner. Later, he was transferred to Everett but remained active in bulb inspection in both areas.

Knutson, Harold

Harold Knutson (1913-1977, Knutson Farms, Sumner) is another bulb grower who began at the bottom and worked his way to the top. He arrived in Sumner in 1939 from the dust bowl of South Dakota with holes in the bottom of his shoes and just $5 in his pocket. Harold went to work for Ed Orton and soon became his foreman. In 1957, Harold bought the farm from Ed, as well as his equipment and 200 acres of land, most of it in bulbs. By that time, he and Marion, his wife, knew the business from the ground up. Through diligence and hard work, Knutsons became one of the largest bulb farms in the United States.

Harold made numerous innovations which included the use of a helicopter to spray bulbs when the soil was waterlogged. He also developed one of the first successful bulb diggers. Harold continued to enlarge the farm and, in 1965, incorporated it, with his wife and sons all becoming shareholders. He was elected president of the Puget Sound Bulb Exchange in 1958 and continued in that position until he died in 1977. Harold helped to found the Puyallup Valley Flower Cooperative in 1956 and was its president until his death. At various times, he was chairman of the Washington State Bulb Commission, president of the Northwest Bulb Growers Association, a director and secretary of the Western Washington Fair, a director and first president of the Puyallup Valley Bank and a director of the Puyallup Valley Daffodil Festival Board. He was also a past president of the Sumner Rhubarb Association and, in 1967, designed and built the first practical rhubarb digger.

His widow, Marion, and sons have continued to run and to expand the business since Harold's death. Tom and Roger both grew up working on the farm. Roger is now president and manager of Knutson Farms, Inc., the Puyallup Valley Flower Co-op and the Puget Sound Bulb Exchange. Roger is also chairman of the Washington State Bulb Commission, is a director of the Puyallup Valley Bank and was Time Magazine-Pierce County Newsmaker of Tomorrow in 1983.

Colleen Knutson, Roger's oldest daughter, was crowned Sumner's Daffodil Princess in 1988 and was one of 5 of 22 Daffodil Valley Festival princesses chosen to be in the Royal Court. In 1991, Amy Knutson, Roger's middle daughter, was also crowned as Sumner's Daffodil Princess. She, too, was chosen to be one of 5 of 21 Festival princesses in the Court.

Tom Knutson graduated from high school in 1955, attended Central Washington University and then joined the Army in 1957. While in the service, he served at the National Security Agency. In 1960, he returned home to work on the farm. Tom is primarily concerned with field operations and equipment. He has served on the Board of Directors of the Puyallup Valley Daffodil Festival and is now on the Board of Directors of the Washington Rhubarb Growers Association. Tom is also currently president of the Sumner School District Board, having served on the Board since 1982.

Erik, Tom's oldest son, was the national winner of the Proficiency Award in Floriculture at the National FFA convention at Kansas City in 1989.

Knutson Farms is the largest bulb farm in Pierce County and, in 1989, raised 135 acres of 60 varieties of Narcissus, 60 acres of 15 Iris varieties and 74 acres of 20 varieties of Tulips. Unfortunately, most of their salable Iris and many Tulip bulbs were lost from waterlogging and freezing in the winter of 1990/91.

Roger and Tom have automated their Iris and Tulip digging and processing equipment and have added field and hothouse rhubarb and peonies to their farming operations. Recently, they built five greenhouses in which they force some of their bulbs.

Koehler, Karl

Karl Koehler (1874-1942, Orting) was a Master Gardener in Germany, came to Orting in 1892 and, in 1902, bought a 53-acre farm in cooperation with his brother, Paul, who died in 1905. Karl raised hops, apples and also had a dairy herd. In 1920, he had a prize-winning yield of over 2 tons of hops per acre. However, after Arie Van Zonneveld began growing bulbs nearby in 1927, Karl gradually quit the other crops and began to raise bulbs. By 1930, he had enough Narcissus to exhibit several varieties at a Tacoma Flower Show and, by 1942, was growing about 15 acres of Crocus, Hyacinths, Narcissus and Tulips. He leased the remainder of his land (104 acres) to Van Zonneveld for whom he also worked part time. Although Narcissus was his first bulb crop, Tulips became Karl's greatest love. By 1942, he had over 800 varieties of Tulips and had introduced three new hybrids of his own. He died of a heart attack in October 1942, the same month in which a beautifully illustrated and highly complimentary article about him was published in

71

the *National Geographic*. Other magazines such as *Colliers*, *Saturday Evening Post* and *Holiday* also ran pictures and stories showing the Koehlers' old gray-weathered hop barn surrounded by brilliant bulb flowers with Mount Rainier in the background. His farm was a mecca for photographers.

Karl's widow, Elsie, continued growing bulbs to fill their mail order and roadside stand business, but the drop in bulb prices after World War II and her poor health forced her to gradually reduce the acreage. She quit the bulb business in 1960.

Their daughters, Louise Marie and Helene, and a son, Karl, sold cut flowers when they were children to help the family and to raise spending money. Helene (Williamson) later moved to Tacoma but Louise (Anderson) again started raising bulbs in 1958 and forced some in her greenhouse, selling both bulbs and flowers in a roadside stand until about 1966. She was head gardener at the Hi Cedars Golf Course near Orting from 1977 to 1987. Louise is now retired and enjoys her hobbies of collecting local historical information, growing flowers and picking mushrooms.

Koning, Cornelius

Cornelius Koning (Mount Vernon) arrived in the United States in 1934 from Holland and came to Washington in 1948. He raised bulbs, sometimes under contract, from about 1950 to 1988. Koning reached a peak during the 1960s with 20 acres of Iris, Narcissus and Tulips but discontinued selling bulbs in 1988. Subsequently, he continued to grow an acre or so of bulbs as a hobby and for cut-flower sales. Koning sponsored Henry Bergman when he emigrated to the United States about 1947.

Korsten, Ben

Ben Korsten (Sumner) began growing bulbs in Holland in 1925 while still a teenager. He later attended the Government Bulb College in Lisse and worked summers for various bulb growers. Ben began to sell bulbs in the United States in 1937. At the onset of World War II in 1939 in Europe, he decided to stay in Washington State. He started raising Tulips on 12 acres near Sumner in 1942, added Narcissus in 1943 and Iris in

1946. In 1948, he bought 28 acres of land from C. W. Orton and built a modern bulb shed which included temperature-controlled rooms.

From 1954 until 1968 Ben forced bulbs, especially Narcissus, under artificial light. He displayed Tulip flowers for 13 years at the Frederick and Nelson department store in Seattle and sold bulbs for fall delivery.

Ben's father sold bulbs for the Dutch firm of Van Waveren & Sons. After his death in 1952, Ben became their West Coast representative. He also sold his own bulbs until he joined the Puget Sound Bulb Exchange in 1964 and sold his own flowers until 1956 when he and others organized the Puyallup Valley Flower Co-op of which he was their first secretary.

At Ben's peak in 1956, he owned 61 acres in bulbs, mostly Narcissus, and another 49 acres in cover crop. When he sold most of his planting stock to Henry DeGoede in 1968 he had 55 acres in bulbs. Ben retained 500 bulbs of certain new varieties of Narcissus to grow as a hobby and from which he sold flowers. In 1978 he sold all the remaining bulbs to Dusty Backeberg. Wiebrand (Wieb) Van Zonneveld was his warehouse manager from 1952 until 1968.

Ben had three disasters during his bulb career: the flooding of the Stuck River on December 15, 1955 which caused severe waterlogging and the loss of many bulbs, and two serious fires in his warehouse. One occurred on March 4, 1956 and another on November 17, 1965, and both caused heavy damage.

With three other associates, Ben began raising turfgrass sod on part of his land in 1961. They formed the Emerald Turfgrass Company and, eventually, were producing 400 acres of sod annually. Ben sold his interest in the farm in 1986.

Larrabee, Charles X.

Charles Larrabee (1843-1914, Bellingham) arrived in Bellingham in 1890, soon after finding and selling a valuable ore claim in Montana. He was an active and versatile businessman and helped promote the bulb and other industries. In 1898 he "induced a party of expert bulb growers from Holland to pass judgment upon the possibilities [of bulb production] and their verdict was highly favorable" (110). This was probably the same group that visited Gibbs on Orcas Island that year. We know little about Larrabee's own bulb business except that one year he ordered 15,000 bulbs from a Chicago florist and several thousand from Holland.

In 1917, his widow, Frances, together with Cyrus Gates and William McKay, donated 60 acres of logged-off land along the Guide Meridian Highway to the United States Department of Agriculture so that the latter could enlarge its experimental plots. Dr. Griffiths subsequently named one of his hybrid Lilies after Frances, in appreciation.

Lawler, George

George Lawler (1861-1948, Lawler's Bulbs, Fife) arrived in Tacoma in 1888. He was first an accountant, next a lumberman, and then got into real estate. George was very active in developing the Tacoma tideflats which earned him the nicknames "King of the Tideflats" or "Tideflats Lawler." In 1910, he purchased 15 acres of land near Fife (Gardenville) of which he sold 10 acres (106). He built a house on the remaining 5 acres and planted 2,200 Narcissus and Tulip bulbs worth $50. The bulbs grew well and the flowers sold easily in Tacoma, so he planted another 9,000 bulbs in 1911. By 1918, Lawler was producing more bulb flowers than the Tacoma florists needed so he started selling them directly to the public through street sales. He also featured weekend specials at the Rhodes Department Store in Tacoma. By 1923, he needed more land and leased 15 acres in North Puyallup. Lawler planted in Dutch-type beds at both Fife and Puyallup. Some of his bulbs were infested with nematodes, so he imported a hot water treating tank from England in 1924, perhaps the first in the state.

By 1926, Lawler again needed more land so he bought 383 acres near Roy. Eventually, he and his son, George Ward Lawler, were growing about 100 acres of Narcissus and another 100 acres of other bulb types. In 1928 George made his first selling trip to greenhouses in the eastern United States. Subsequently, Ward did the selling. They also had their own retail catalogs and were doing very well at Roy until 1941 when the United States government took their farm in order to enlarge the military base at Fort Lewis, paying them $52,500 for the 383 acres. Apparently, Ward ran the business after that and moved it to Monroe. In 1948 their Narcissus and Iris stocks were sold to the United Bulb Company which had lost theirs in the Columbia River flood. The remaining Lawler Tulips and other bulbs went to other growers.

George Lawler was an industrious person and, even at age 85, was still farming, having planted 50,000 Lily of the Valley bulbs the year before, which he planned to harvest in three years! He and Dr. Griffiths were good friends. Lawler promoted the bulb industry vigorously in the 1920s, giving many talks and writing many articles. He helped to organize the Northwest Bulb Growers Association in 1924. He is credited with suggesting that "Bulb Sundays" be held in the Puyallup Valley in 1932, after getting the idea from a Dutch newspaper. He was also, reportedly, the first person in Washington to purchase the excellent Fortune variety of Narcissus bulbs, for $75 each.

Lawler, George Ward

George Ward Lawler (1886-1974, Lawler's Bulbs, Monroe) was a lawyer, but joined his father in the real estate and bulb business some time before 1910. George, Sr. is supposed to have told his son, "Now, my boy, I want you to remember one thing: You've got to get along with Me; I'm not going to try to get along with You" (134). Apparently, the combination worked well although Ward was somewhat overshadowed by his father.

Ward ran most of the business after they moved the bulbs to Monroe in 1941. When the Lawler bulb stocks were sold to the United Bulb Company in 1948, the diggers missed a sizable number of King Alfred and Fortune Narcissus bulbs so Ward collected these and, by 1954, was growing five acres of them. He sold the farm and bulbs in 1962 and retired to Wesley Gardens near Seattle. Ward also helped organize the Northwest Bulb Growers Association in 1924 and was elected its first president.

Lee, Mrs. Lucille Lubbe

Ralph (1904-1987) and Lucille Lubbe (1904-1989) began raising Narcissus in 1931 at Puyallup. They were divorced in 1940. Lucille then married Robert E. Lee (1904-1949). After Lee's death, she moved to Sumner and then to Elma in 1971. At her peak, Lucille probably had about 15 acres, selling bulbs through the Puget Sound Bulb Exchange and also retailing flowers. From 1972 until her death, she managed the retail flower and bulb shop at the Satsop Bulb Farms near Elma. In 1976, Lucille gave all her bulbs and equipment to a granddaughter, Kris Edem. Meanwhile, Lucille had also passed along her love of flowers to her son, Chuck, as well as to her other grandchildren, Kurt Lubbe and Karel Smith. All are bulb growers.

Lefeber, Dan

Dan Lefeber (Lefeber Bulb Company, Mount Vernon) worked with his father, Bill, for many years and in 1989 bought his bulbs. In 1990 Dan grew 80 acres of eight varieties of Narcissus, 19 acres of Iris and a few Tulips. Over half of the company's business is in flower sales. They have also diversified into the sod business. Dan is the third generation of bulb-growing Lefebers in the United States, following father, William, and grandfather, Marinus.

Lefeber, Jac

Jac Lefeber (Mount Vernon) arrived in the United States in 1948 and first settled in Olympia but moved to Nisqually in 1950 to raise his bulbs. By 1956, he had about 5 acres of Narcissus plus 3-5 more in Iris, Hyacinths and Tulips. At that time, he was reported to have had about 1,000 varieties of Narcissus but many of his bulbs were lost due to frost and flooding so he moved to Mount Vernon where he grew them until he retired about 1967, selling his stock to Henry DeGoede.

Jac was one of eight bulb-growing brothers raised in Holland. One lived in South Carolina, Marinus was in Mount Vernon while the others remained in Holland. Jac's main love was hybridizing Narcissus and, by 1956, he had more than 50 new hybrids to his credit. One, Flower Record, which he developed in 1943 in Holland, became an excellent commercial type.

Lefeber, Marinus

Marinus Lefeber (1893-1982, Lefeber Bulb Company, Mount Vernon) came from a bulb-growing family in Holland. He moved to the United States in 1913, worked in the oil fields of Texas and other areas and arrived in Lynden in 1928. He planted imported stocks of Narcissus (at $1,000/ton) and Iris (at $160/1,000) but lost many in the severe winters of 1929 and later despite his efforts with mulching and building windbreaks. He then experimented with growing bulbs at Point Roberts, Lawrence and on Whidbey Island. The Whidbey planting was done on three acres in cooperation with Gerrit Van Zanten and the Segers Brothers under the supervision of Neal Noorlag. They had a good crop the first year but Marinus chose to relocate in the Skagit Valley in 1936.

At the time he left Lynden, he was growing 15 acres of Narcissus. He was already acquainted with Dr. Griffiths at the Bellingham Bulb Station who became a good friend and helped Marinus in many ways. Marinus continued to enlarge his land and bulb holdings and, by 1967, had 58 acres in Iris, Narcissus and Tulips. In 1970, he sold the business to his son, William. Bill Jansen, another Hollander, worked for the Lefeber Bulb Company as warehouse manager and salesman from 1941 until his death in 1970.

About 1938, Marinus, together with Neal Noorlag and Sam Stewart, purchased a horse-drawn sprayer for $65 to help control leaf diseases on their Iris. Before that, they had used hand sprayers and it must have been quite a challenge to keep ahead of the fungi on 15 or more acres of bulbs.

Lefeber, William

William (Bill) Lefeber (Lefeber Bulb Company, Mount Vernon) worked as a young man on the bulb farm with his father, Marinus. He began growing bulbs independently in the late 1940s and, in 1970, purchased the home farm from Marinus. Bill continued expanding until, by 1978, he had 34 acres of Iris and 76 of Narcissus. He was especially interested in machinery and built most of the digging and planting equipment now used on the farm. Bill moved to Anacortes in 1984 and, in 1989, sold the bulbs to his son Dan.

Lemon, Burch

Burch Lemon (Coupeville) has been described as an eccentric old hermit who was fun to visit! According to Earle Darst, Burch developed some promising Iris hybrids but died suddenly and they were all lost. He grew 2 to 3 acres of Iris plus a few Tulips and Narcissus from about 1944 to 1950.

Locklin, Harrison D.

Harrison (Harry) D. Locklin (1891-1979, Puyallup) came to Puyallup in 1923 as a horticulturist at the Western Washington Experiment Station (WSU Puyallup). He bought his first bulbs in 1924 and sold out in 1935 or 1936. Bulbs were a sideline with him and he probably never planted more than one acre. Harry helped to organize the Northwest Bulb Growers Association and was its first treasurer in 1924 or 1925. He was also a charter member of the Puget Sound Bulb Exchange in 1926.

Loeb, C. E.

C. E. Loeb (Puyallup) bought a berry farm in 1937 but gradually replaced berries with King Alfred Narcissus and, by 1957, was growing 14 acres of them. He also raised rhododendrons.

Lubbe, Charles and Kurt

Charles (Chuck) Lubbe (Sumner/Elma) got his start in bulb growing when he bought Leroy Merritt's Narcissus in 1949. Chuck raised them at Sumner until 1971 when he moved to Elma with his mother and his children in order to have more land for expansion and rotation. By 1989, he had 27 acres of Narcissus under cultivation.

His children are also in the business. Kurt Lubbe has been growing bulbs since his father gave him a case of Narcissus bulbs when he was 8 years old. Kurt is still growing bulbs in cooperation with his father and now has 9 acres of his own. Chuck's daughters, Kris Edem and Karel Smith, also grow, force and retail bulbs nearby at Satsop.

McColley, Everett and Eugene

This father and son combination (Sumner) began growing bulbs in 1942 when Eugene (Gene) bought Tulip planting stock from Si Van Lierop for a Future Farmers of America project. The next year Everett (1897-1975) purchased a ton of King Alfred bulbs from Charles Orton. The McColleys gradually expanded, primarily in Narcissus, reaching a peak about 1976 with 15 acres. Meanwhile, Gene continued with Tulips and also added Wedgwood Iris in 1962. Everett quit in 1965. Gene continued until the severe freeze of 1979 caused so much damage that he sold his remaining bulbs and retired in 1980.

McLean, J. R.

J. R. McLean (1897-1977, McLean Bulb Farms, Puyallup) started in the lumber business in the Willapa area. He began growing Scillas and

Narcissus at Raymond in 1933 and then moved to Elma in 1936. At his peak in Elma he had 32 acres in Narcissus, 4 in Tulips and 4 in Iris. He also developed a retail business, issued catalogs and sold his own bulbs "on the road." About 1946 he built a warehouse in Puyallup and, in 1953, moved his bulbs from Elma to Orting where he bought about 100 acres of the old Van Zonneveld farm. By 1954, he was growing an estimated 46 acres of Narcissus, Iris, Tulips and miscellaneous bulbs. He quit farming about 1962 and concentrated on his wholesale bulb and nursery supply business which he had started some time before. After World War II, he made several trips to Japan to buy Lilies and other bulbs. McLean was a pioneer in the promotion of plastic pots for use in greenhouses and nurseries. He sold his bulb and nursery supply business to J. M. McConkey and retired in 1965.

Wayne Grubb was associated with the firm from about 1944 to 1958, primarily as a salesman. Wayne was also an inspector for the Washington Department of Agriculture from 1960 to 1964 and later ran a greenhouse for a number of years.

Mansfield, Howard

Howard Mansfield (1907-1992, Mansfield & Edmondson, Sumner) went to work for C. W. Orton in 1929. He became, essentially, the equipment manager for Orton and was one of the pioneers in building new bulb machinery. Most of the diggers, planters and graders used on the Orton farm were built by him. He and Hank Edmondson began to grow bulbs as a sideline in 1946, expanding to a peak of about 12 acres of Narcissus and 8 of Tulips about 1951. They discontinued growing bulbs in 1962 when Hank retired from the Orton farm and Howard was made manager. Mr. Orton died in 1963 and the estate was sold the next year. At that time, Howard and his wife, Margaret, went to work for Wally Staatz until they decided to retire in 1972. Howard was general manager while Margaret was in charge of the warehouse at the Staatz Farm.

Marble, Ralph

Ralph Marble (1898-1983, Battleground) was one of the first nursery inspectors in the Washington State Department of Agriculture. He started this work about 1927 and continued until 1930 or longer at Sumner with

Henry Reynolds as his assistant. Alfred Scholz (Puyallup) helped Ralph get into the bulb business in the early 1930s by leasing him land and planting Narcissus bulbs for him. They planted the bulbs by hand and used mules for cultivating. Ralph also grew a few Tulips given to him by Dr. David Griffiths.

After retiring from the Department of Agriculture, Ralph moved to the Battleground area to become manager of Ladd and Holden, Narcissus growers. This company started at Canby, OR but moved to Battleground in the mid-1930s. Ralph later became a partner with Ladd and, by 1942, they had 70 acres of Narcissus under cultivation. In 1943, Marble became independent and apparently continued raising Narcissus until at least 1948. He specialized in King Alfred and Golden Harvest varieties. At one time he also raised Gladiolus near Yakima.

Noorlag, Neal

Neal Noorlag (1906-1989, Noorlag Bulb Farms, Oak Harbor) pioneered bulb growing in Island County, thanks to Harry Van Waveren's whetting his interest in them when Neal worked for him one summer at Lynden. Neal purchased $800 worth of King Alfred and other Narcissus varieties from Harry in December 1930. The bulbs had already been planted at Lynden so Neal took delivery in 1931 and moved them to Whidbey Island. He paid for them partly in cash and partly in labor during the summers of 1930 and 1931. Neal also planted Iris in 1931 and later added Tulips. By 1933 he apparently had one acre in bulbs according to a Bulb Association assessment report. In 1935 he grew 1½ acres of King Alfreds and one acre of Iris plus another 4 acres of Iris for Gerrit Van Zanten Bulb Farms. About this time, Neal also managed a test planting of 3 acres of Iris on Whidbey Island for Van Zanten, Lefeber and Segers Brothers.

Neal continued growing bulbs in different locations on the Island but the yields were often poor because of dry weather although the bulbs matured earlier than on the mainland and commanded premium prices. In 1937 he and Sam Stewart purchased a 30-acre farm near Mount Vernon for $179 an acre and divided it between them. Neal and his wife, Elsie, also became full-time residents in Oak Harbor that year. Before 1937, they had spent their winters working in California.

Neal began to expand his Iris plantings in 1935 and also branched out into Hyacinths, at one time having one of the largest acreages in

Washington. However, so much hand labor was required with Hyacinths at the peak of the bulb season that eventually he had to give them up. He also reduced his Narcissus planting at that time. At his peak, Neal had about 46 acres of all four types of bulbs. He also tried forcing Wedgwood Iris in California in the winter of 1938/39 with the assistance of Mr. and Mrs. Tony Van Waveren, but the results were not sufficiently promising to justify continuing.

Neal sold his bulbs locally and to jobbers at first but, in 1939, he made the first of his selling trips to the eastern United States and later to California. In 1983, he had a stroke which partially disabled him and he sold his bulbs to Tom DeGoede who had been working for him since 1976. Neal retained samples of a few of his favorite varieties which Tom raised for him. Neal often visited the fields to observe them. The last time he enjoyed them was just four days before his death from a heart attack in 1989.

Neal had many hobbies including the raising and showing of Shetland and Hackney ponies, growing orchids and singing. He also had a dairy herd during World War II and raised beef cattle for a few years afterward. Tony Van Waveren was his farm manager from about 1946 until 1967. Since Tony also raised some bulbs on his own, he is discussed separately.

Nowadnick, Richard L.

Richard (Dick) Nowadnick (Mount Vernon) was born in Chehalis and raised on a farm. He attended Washington State University, majored in dairy science, received his B.S. degree in 1948, and worked on his parents' farm in Chehalis from 1948 to 1950. Dick returned to WSU in the fall of 1950, receiving a bachelor's degree in education in 1951. Later he earned a master's degree in higher education at WSU in 1968.

Dick was an instructor at Sedro-Woolley High School in 1951/52 and then became an instructor at Skagit Valley College in Mount Vernon in 1952. He was appointed dean of instruction in 1977. Dick retired in 1982 to spend more time playing golf and coaching high school golf teams.

Dick and his wife, Jean, had three children. They travelled extensively and have conducted groups on tours to United States and overseas locations. He also led an archaeological group to Guatemala in 1974.

Dick was appointed secretary/treasurer of the Northwest Bulb Growers Association in March 1954 and of the Washington State Bulb Commission in February of 1961 and has continued in those offices to the present. He edited the Northwest Bulb Growers Newsletter from 1953 until 1964. Dick has been of great assistance to the author in providing details and data concerning the Bulb Association, the Bulb Commission, and many other aspects of the Washington State bulb industry.

Oliver, Orno

Orno Oliver (1901-1990, Puyallup) was born in Tacoma and went to the University of Washington but spent most of his life in Puyallup. He grew bulbs in rotation with berries and other crops on a 50-acre farm at Alderton from about 1934 to 1975. In 1975, his peak year, he had about 20 acres of Narcissus plus 5 acres of Tulips. When he retired, he sold his planting stock to Wilmer Reise.

Onderwater, John O.

John Onderwater (1890-1962, Mount Vernon) was on a selling trip from Holland to the United States when World War II broke out and he settled in the Mount Vernon area. He worked summers for Marinus Lefeber on his farm and then sold bulbs for him during the winter on the road. John began growing his own bulbs about 1947. He tried Lilies and Narcissus but finally gave them up in order to concentrate on Iris, Tulips and Hyacinths. By 1956 he had 18 acres of these. John was one of the first in Skagit County to develop a hopper-type planter. He sponsored both Henry DeGoede and Bill Roozen when they decided to emigrate to the United States. John died in 1962 and his bulbs were sold to Henry DeGoede.

Orton, Charles W.

C. (Charley) Orton (1879-1963, Sumner) arrived in Tacoma in 1900, worked for a year or two on Senator Paulhamus's farm and then with his brother, William (Will), bought an 80-acre farm in 1903. He later added 40 more acres. Will sold his share to Charley in 1911 and moved to Renton. Charley developed one of the finest dairy herds in the state and also grew berries and rhubarb before starting in bulbs in 1924 when he planted 4,000 Narcissus, apparently on a trial basis. They must have performed well because he expanded heavily in 1925.

Charley Orton is often given credit for being the first bulb grower in the Puyallup Valley, but he was not. The *Sumner American Standard* (Sept. 18, 1925) made the interesting comment: "Ordinarily Charley Orton is a leader and a good one but he is now a follower and will no doubt be a better follower than the run of the trailers of the valley . . . He is planting bulbs on his show farm for the first time this fall" (3). This comment apparently refers to a large ($2,200 worth) planting, since he told the author in 1954 that he had made a trial planting of 4,000 Narcissus bulbs in the fall of 1924 (97,104).

The locally famous Daffodil Tea, sponsored by the Sumner Home and Country Club, Parent Teachers Association and Sumner Civic Club was held on April 6, 1926 at the Orton residence when about 300-500 growers, garden club members and dignitaries from several cities and Fort Lewis gathered to see a display of many Narcissus varieties and to hear Orton discuss the promising new bulb industry. This tea was an important event, but only one of many leading to the development of the present Puyallup Valley Daffodil Festival which is discussed in Chapter 16.

Orton did not remain a "follower" for very long. He was an early member of the Northwest Bulb Growers Association and a charter member of the Puget Sound Bulb Exchange, promoted bulb growing in speeches, added Iris to his farm in 1928 and Tulips in 1932 or 1933. By 1931, he was entirely out of other crops and on his way to becoming one of the top bulb producers in Washington.

Orton was willing to experiment. He even tried growing Narcissus at Tillamook, OR for 2-3 years in order to obtain earlier blooming bulbs. In the early 1930s Orton began hybridizing Iris, trying to develop superior yellow and bicolor varieties. One called Blue Princess is still being grown commercially on a small scale. He grew Wedgwood Iris from about 1932 to 1935 on Whidbey Island because they matured earlier there. The volunteer bulbs which escaped his digging served as a nucleus for some other Whidbey farmers who wanted to get into Iris growing. The yield on the island was lower than that on the mainland because of the drier climate, so about 1936 Orton moved all of his bulbs back to the home farm at Sumner.

83

By 1954, he was growing 140 acres of bulbs and subsequently reached a peak about 1963 with 200 acres, composed of 70 in Iris, 100 in Narcissus and 30 in Tulips. Orton was partially disabled by a stroke about 1960 but continued farming until his death in 1963.

Orton began mechanizing early with the excellent assistance of Howard Mansfield, one of his managers, who was a natural inventor. His first warehouse manager was Maynard Smit, followed by Henry Edmondson and Mansfield. He was also assisted at times by two relatives, John Twohy and Henry Orton.

C.W. Orton was very active in public affairs, at different times serving as president of the Northwest Bulb Growers Association, the Puget Sound Bulb Exchange, the Western Washington Horticultural Association and the Fruit Growers Association. He was also a Tacoma Port Commissioner and president of the Board of Regents of WSU. Unfortunately, he left no children to carry on the business, and all his bulbs and equipment were sold in 1964, the year after his death.

Orton, Edward C.

Edward (Ed) Orton (1881-1975, Sumner) was one of four brothers who came to western Washington from Iowa. Charles and Will arrived in 1900 and Ed came in 1904. He worked for his brothers until 1906 when he bought his own farm, developed a dairy herd and began raising raspberries and blackberries. He was the largest grower of blackberries in the state at one time with 90 acres.

Ed got into bulb growing in 1924 when August Pruyser sold him and Frank Chervenka a "rejected" carload of Narcissus. This date is based, in part, on an article Ed wrote for the *Sumner News Index* on May 22, 1925 stating "since my experience is limited to less than one year's operations." He gave many speeches and wrote articles for the newspapers extolling the benefits of growing bulbs. He emphasized the poor returns that berry growers had received since 1922 and encouraged those interested in growing bulbs to contact George Lawler or Frank Chervenka "who had had more experience."

In 1927 or 1928 he bought his first Iris and Tulips and rapidly expanded his plantings of all three bulb types. He even paid as much as $200 per bulb for a new variety which was a lot of money in those days. Unfortunately, the Depression soon forced Ed and most of the other growers to reduce operations. At one time he even paid his workers, such as Si Van Lierop, in flowers and bulbs which they sold in Tacoma. Ed also lost about 20 acres of bulbs during the Puyallup River flood, about 1930. By the end of 1956, he was one of Washington's largest bulb growers with 170 acres in Iris, Narcissus and Tulips. He was also an early member of the Northwest Bulb Growers Association, a charter member of the Puget Sound Bulb Exchange and president of the Washington Berry Growers Association for 13 years. At one time he was also the largest producer of roses and hothouse rhubarb in Washington State. At his peak, he grew about 200 acres of bulbs. At the age of 76, he decided to retire and play pinochle, selling out to Harold Knutson, his foreman.

Orton, Stanley

Stanley (Stan) Orton (Sumner) sold flowers at a roadside stand as a kid and later worked for his father, Ed, before entering the Air Force in 1943. After discharge in 1946, Stan bought Iris and Narcissus bulbs and farmed on rented land. At his peak he had about 8 acres in King Alfreds and 4 in Wedgwood Iris but he decided to sell out about 1952. Stan was an experimental aide at WSU Puyallup from 1960 to 1985 and, after retirement, organized a successful mole trapping company. His daughter, Corinne, was a Daffodil Princess from Sumner in 1970.

Paulhamus, W. H.

State Senator and berry farmer W. H. Paulhamus (1864-1925, Puyallup) should be recognized for his active promotion of the bulb industry in the Puyallup Valley at a time when the hop industry had been decimated by insects, disease and prohibition, and the berry industry had reached a surplus situation. After a visit in 1923 by Dr. David Griffiths, a boyhood chum, Paulhamus wrote letters to the local newspapers, urging farmers to run some tests with Narcissus on their farms. In this connection, one reporter described him as one "whose fertile mind is looking about for some culture of a practical nature that will help to break the one crop aspect of our horticulture" (103).

However, his advice was generally not acted upon in 1923 except by Frank Chervenka and, perhaps by H. F. Gronen. So, in the spring of 1924 he arranged for two bulb growers, George Lawler and Joe Smith, and a bulb jobber, August Pruyser from Michigan, to talk to members of the Puyallup Chamber of Commerce and farmers who might be interested. Paulhamus followed this up in June with a statement that he was going to buy 4,000 King Alfred bulbs at $125/1,000 (a high price in those days) to plant in the fall. He invited others to pool their orders with him and apparently several did so, probably including C. W. Orton. Unfortunately, Paulhamus did not live to harvest his bulbs or even to see the result of his efforts for the industry, as he died on April 14, 1925.

Paulhamus was very energetic and civic minded. He helped organize the Western Washington Fair, the local fruit and poultry associations and others. He was also a legislator and, among his other contributions, helped to reactivate the Western Washington Experiment Station (WSU Puyallup) in the early 1900s.

Picha, Lloyd and Warren

Warren and Lloyd Picha (Puyallup) grew bulbs together. Warren started first, about 1942, with Narcissus. Lloyd began a few years later. They raised a few acres of Iris and Tulips but concentrated mainly on Narcissus. Their peak acreage was in 1957 when they had a total of about 30 acres in bulbs. They began selling off in the late 1950s and, in 1961, disposed of their remaining Narcissus to Ben Korsten.

Pruyser, August G.

A. G. Pruyser (General Bulb Company, Michigan and later Puyallup) started growing bulbs in Michigan but moved to Washington where he planted bulbs, first at Marysville in 1923 and later at Puyallup and on Fox Island. He was still raising them in 1933. However, he was primarily a salesman by nature and was sales manager for the Puget Sound Bulb Exchange from 1929 to 1931. He was one of the experts invited by Senator Paulhamus to promote the bulb industry at the meeting in Sumner in 1924.

Reise, Otto Carl

Otto Reise (1896-1981, Puyallup) began farming on his own in 1917 with hops and dairy cattle. He quit these in 1921 and went into caneberries. In 1925 Ed Orton talked him into growing bulbs so he bought 2½ tons of King Alfred and other varieties of Narcissus. As his bulb acreage increased, the berries came out and, by 1935, were gone. About 1927, he bought part of the home farm near McMillan from his father, Ludvig. In 1959, he sold the farm and the bulbs to his son, Wilmer.

Otto was as much interested in mechanization as he was in the bulbs themselves and developed or improved much equipment including self-propelled diggers and planters. One of his most important innovations was a hot water treatment tank he developed in 1950. Previously, treating bulbs involved hand dumping them from trays into crates which were then covered and lowered into the treating tank by hand with the temperature of the tank controlled manually. Otto, with help from Glen Cushing, an engineer with Puget Sound Power and Light, devised a tank with a platform so trays could be trucked on, the stacks quickly covered, the platform lowered by means of an electrical hoist and the temperature regulated by a thermostat with a warning alarm and a recorder. The operation was so effective and precise that many growers had Otto do all the treating of their bulbs. Before this, there had been many failures in the industry by growers who treated their own bulbs. One grower reportedly lost over 200 tons of Narcissus one year because of a faulty thermostat.

Among his other innovations, Otto was one of the first to: add 1½ inch cleats to the top and bottom of trays so they could be stacked more easily; use the disk plow to more effectively turn under the cover crop; use a portable irrigation system to irrigate the cover crop and hasten its decomposition as well as soften the bulb soil in dry years to facilitate digging. In the late 1930s he made one of the very first mechanical diggers by putting a Ford Model-T engine on a potato digger to run the conveyer belt. He and his son Wilmer did custom digging for many local growers for the next 3-4 years.

Otto liked variety and new projects. He was warehouse manager for the Puget Sound Bulb Exchange in the summer of 1928, and at one time was hired by the Oregon Bulb Farms at Gresham, OR to organize, renovate and update their bulb equipment.

He was a charter member of the Bulb Exchange and an active member of the Northwest Bulb Growers Association. He served in both World War I and in World War II with the Seabees. He owned and ran the McMillan/Alderton water system, and in 1959 developed the Sunrise Terrace residential project on the hill above his farm. Otto was also an active Grange member all his life. He moved to Lummi Island in 1967 and died in 1981.

Mrs. Otto (Florence) Reise also worked on their farm in the 1930s. Flossie specialized in selling cut flowers of Narcissus and Tulips at a roadside stand and to wholesalers, including the Williams Brothers Produce Co. in Tacoma.

Reise, Otto, Jr.

The only data available on Otto, Jr. (Puyallup) is that he was apparently an active grower from about 1947 to 1956 and had about 10 acres of Narcissus in 1956.

Reise, Wilmer

Wilmer Reise (Puyallup) bought his first bulbs, four tons of Narcissus, from Harry Locklin in 1936. He eventually raised Iris, Narcissus, and Tulips and reached a peak of 35 acres about 1957. Wilmer helped his father, Otto, do custom digging for other growers for a few years in the late 1930s. He sold his bulbs and equipment to Pete Van Lierop in 1982, leased his land for Christmas tree production and retired so that he and his wife could travel.

Reynolds, Henry J.

Henry (Hank) Reynolds (1899-1972, Sumner) began his bulb career as an assistant nursery inspector in the Washington State Department of Agriculture under Ralph Marble. About 1936 he became manager of the Puyallup Valley Daffodil Flower Show. Hank continued as a horticultural inspector until about 1942. He became a bulb grower in 1941 in cooperation with the Vaughn Seed Co. of Chicago, planting Tulips near Auburn in the fall that year. A few months later, after the onset of World War II, the government condemned the site in order to build a huge supply warehouse for military use. The contractor moved fast, covering the tulips with concrete before the bulbs could be dug, and that ended Hank's venture in bulb growing.

Hank was very creative. He was the first grower to develop a workable Tulip planter. He organized Visco Inc. in 1938 for the manufacture of pesticides, first for use on ornamentals and later for use on tree fruits. He developed Fishtox, a rotenone product to kill scrap fish so that lakes could be restocked with trout. He is especially remembered for his friendliness, his photographic memory, his inventiveness and his love for fishing.

Roberson, Leonard N.

Leonard Roberson (1904-1967, L. N. Roberson Co., Seattle) and his wife, Frances, operated an electrical supply company and also a nursery in Seattle. They planted their first Lilies, *L. longiflorum* and *L. regale*, in 1927 and, subsequently, expanded their operation with several other types of bulbs. Sometime in the early 1930s, however, they decided that their location was much better suited to alpine plants and they later reduced their bulb plantings.

Leonard was an electrical engineer and assisted other bulb growers by designing equipment for hot water treatment, for control of temperature and air circulation in storage rooms and for supplementary lighting for bulb forcing.

Roodzant Brothers

Bert Roodzant (1897-1989, Oak Harbor) and his three brothers John, Hank and Pete, all from Holland, were poultry farmers who probably bought their first Iris planting stock from Neal Noorlag about 1940. John dropped out of bulb growing after a short time, and Hank did too. Subsequently, Pete and Bert became partners and continued growing bulbs until about 1956. Their home farm was on Whidbey Island but, about 1947, they began growing most of their bulbs near Mount Vernon. They reached their peak about 1947 when they had approximately 10 acres of Narcissus, 20 of Iris and 4 of Tulips.

Roozen, William A.

William (Bill) Roozen (Washington Bulb Company, Mount Vernon). There have been many success stories in the bulb business but perhaps one of the most outstanding is that of the Roozen family. Beginning in 1950, their farm has become the largest in the United States and perhaps in the world, in the production of bulbous Iris, Narcissus, and Tulips.

The Roozen family in Holland had been growing bulbs since the 1700s and Bill's father was a famous bulb grower and consultant there. Bill went to work in the Dutch bulb fields as soon as he graduated from high school. When he emigrated to the United States in 1946, he got his start by working for three Mount Vernon growers: John Onderwater, Joe Berger and Harold Kenealy. From 1946 to 1950 he saved his money and, in 1950, leased five acres of land on which he planted 150 varieties of Tulips. About 1951 or 1952 he bought Jim Leckenby's bulbs and trays and, in 1956, he purchased, with Cornelius (Cor) Roozekrans, the Washington Bulb Company (WBC) name and a 60-acre farm with bulbs, and equipment from Joe Berger. At this time WBC had 26 acres in Iris, Narcissus, Tulips, Lilies and Hyacinths. Bill and Cor soon sold the Hyacinths. They shipped Iris bulbs to Europe in 1956 and were one of the first Washington growers to sell Iris on the island of Guernsey, starting in 1959. In 1962, Bill purchased all of Ward Lawler's Narcissus bulbs. About 1963, Cor sold his interest in the company to Bill and in 1965 Bill purchased all of Kenealy's bulbs when Harold decided to retire. Meanwhile Bill's wife, Helen, did all the bookkeeping while raising their five sons and five daughters.

By 1977, WBC had grown to 809 acres of bulbs with 157 varieties of Iris, Narcissus and Tulips. And, by 1989, the company had expanded to 1,310 acres of bulbs, which consisted of 330 acres in Iris, 530 in Narcissus, 400 in Tulips and 50 in Asiatic Lilies. This represented 58% of the INT bulb acreage in Washington that year. These were raised on 350 acres they owned and on several hundred acres rented from 44 other farmers. In addition to bulbs, they grew vegetables, seed crops and cover crops on another 1,000 acres. That year they hired over 500 persons during the summer and about 100 on a year-round basis with an annual payroll of over $3 million plus executive salaries. Their inventory included 30,000 square feet of computer-controlled storage rooms, over 25 trucks, 25 tractors, and several units of digging and planting equipment, most of which they built themselves in their highly mechanized shop. By 1990, through mechanization, they had reduced their labor requirements for digging bulbs by about 60% as compared with those in 1985. During the bulb planting season they kept 15 to 17 trucks running continuously to supply the planters with bulbs.

In 1967 WBC built its first greenhouse for forcing Iris, Narcissus, Lilies and Tulips for the cut-flower trade. By 1990, the greenhouses covered 7.5 acres with an annual production of several million flowers.

90

Because of the increase in flower sales, almost as many flower pickers are hired now as were hired formerly to dig bulbs.

In 1984 they opened "Roozengaarde," a retail division of Washington Bulb Company. It has a display garden of over 250 varieties of bulbs with a miniature Dutch-type windmill, a retail shop and a catalog business under the direction of Bernadette Roozen Miller. It is so popular that, during the blooming season, they have two parking lots with attendants present to assist visitors and tour busses.

Bill retired as president of Washington Bulb Company in 1985, turning over its management to his five sons, John, Leo, Michael, Richard and William M., all of whom graduated from Washington State University and returned to work on the home farm. Each has his own specialty. They, plus Bernadette and their parents, jointly hold shares in the company. Leo is currently the president of WBC. Their success has not been continuous. One year they lost a 25-acre field from flooding and in the winter of 1978/79 their 20 million Iris bulb crop suffered so severely from freezing that no salable bulbs were harvested. In 1989, they lost over one million dollars in flower sales as a result of a severe February freeze. Perhaps the worst incident of all occurred in November-December of 1990 when repeated heavy rains caused the Skagit River to flood 44 acres of Tulips in the Fir Island area with extensive and prolonged waterlogging in many of their other fields. Narcissus and Iris were hurt and Tulips most of all. Leo Roozen estimated (108) that they lost about 25% of their bulbs. In addition to the Roozens many other bulb growers also suffered losses from waterlogging and freezing that winter.

Bill Roozen's first partner, Cornelius (Cor) Roozekrans (1902-1984), was a bulb salesman who came from Holland. Cor was the selling partner of the WBC while Joe Berger was raising the bulbs from 1949 to 1956. When Joe sold out to Bill Roozen, Cor continued to sell for WBC until he sold his share of the business to Bill in 1963. Cor continued selling bulbs independently until he retired to Holland.

Nic Roozekrans, a nephew of Cor's, started selling bulbs in the United States in 1946 and eventually moved to Mount Vernon in 1951. He worked for Bill on the farm in the summer and sold bulbs in the winter. Since 1961 he has been supervising various activities in both the bulb and flower sheds at WBC. John Conijn (1928-1992) was a foreman at WBC for 26 years until his death from a heart attack in 1992.

Sabelis, Theodore

Theodore (Ted) Sabelis (Buckley) was raised on a bulb farm in Holland, graduated from the RTS Horticultural College and sold bulbs until the start of World War II when he flew for the Royal Dutch Air Force in Indonesia. After his discharge in 1946, he became manager for Van Zonneveld of Washington at Orting. In 1949, he was named assistant manager of the Puget Sound Bulb Exchange and became manager in 1956. In 1968, he left the Exchange to become a national bulb salesman for the Fred C. Gloeckner Company with headquarters in New York City but kept his home in Buckley, WA. During 1961 and 1962, he was a bulb grower on the side, raising several novelty Narcissus bulbs bought from the Oregon Bulb Farms.

Ted was chairman of the Washington State Bulb Commission from 1965 to 1968 and chairman of the Society of American Florists (SAF) National Affairs Committee and its International Trade Relations Committee. As chairman of the Research Committee of the Northwest Bulb Growers Association he helped raise funds for research and also for publication of the *Handbook on Bulb Growing and Forcing* in 1957.

Ted was one of the pioneers in developing the sale of Northwest Iris to Europe, beginning in 1954. Because of his broad background, his vision and extensive travels, he has been an excellent counselor for both scientists and growers as well as an excellent public relations person for the entire bulb industry. He is a frequent toastmaster at the annual Bulb Conferences and has been an invaluable source of information to the author in preparing this history.

Sather, Harry M.

Harry Sather (1912-1991, Puyallup) bought the warehouse and 68 acres of the old Van Zonneveld Bulb Farm at Orting in 1953. Fourteen acres had already been planted with Narcissus and Wedgwood Iris. To this, he added Tulips in 1954 and Gladiolus in the early 1960s. By 1955 Harry had about 20 acres of bulbs. About 1963 he sold the Orting property but continued to grow bulbs on rented land in the Puyallup Valley as well as Gladiolus on 10 acres of rented land at Mount Vernon. Harry sold cut flowers all over Washington and had a retail booth at the Western Washington Fair in Puyallup each year. He had one major disaster in 1954 when his huge warehouse at Orting burned, along with his equipment, a large quantity of cut flowers and many of his personal belongings.

Scholz, Alfred

Alfred (Al) Scholz (Puyallup) became acquainted with bulbs as a teenager when his father, Frank, raised some Narcissus belonging to Ted Knoblauch and Ralph Marble. During this time Al acquired some left-over Tulips and gradually increased his stock, continuing to work for his father and for Otto Reise. In 1940 he bought his father's farm and, in 1945, purchased 10 tons of King Alfred Narcissus and 50,000 William Pitt Tulip bulbs from Holland. Al reached his peak in bulb production with about six acres in 1948, selling his salable bulbs to the United Bulb Company. Unfortunately, he lost all his bulb stock in 1950 when it was accidentally fumigated twice by a custom applicator. He then went out of the bulb business and rented his land to his brother. For three years he drove a school bus and then worked for the United States Soil Conservation Service and the United States General Service Administration until he retired in 1982.

Segers Brothers

Segers (also spelled Seager, Zeegers, and Segus in various articles) Brothers (Lynden), a branch of the Holland firm by that name, started at Redmond in the mid-1920s under the management of John Van Aalst. They grew mostly Narcissus and Iris in Dutch-type beds. The company moved to Lynden in 1926 with Frank Van Aalst becoming manager. He was followed by Harry Van Waveren. At one time Segers Brothers was supposed to be one of the largest bulb farms in Washington but the only figure available was an estimate by Maurice Van Zanten that indicated they may have had about 60 acres in 1930. According to Neal Noorlag's account book, they were still growing bulbs in 1935. About 1935 or 1936, they cooperated with Lefeber and Van Zanten in planting test plots on Whidbey Island under the supervision and care of Neal Noorlag. Segers and other Whatcom growers suffered severely in the freeze of 1929/30. Some time after 1936, they left Washington, presumably because of repeated losses from freezing.

Sharp, Harry

Harry Sharp (Sharp-Jones Bulb Company, Seattle) and David L. Jones organized the Sharp-Jones Bulb Company in 1942 for the purpose of selling Northwest-grown Croft Lily bulbs. Harry became sole owner of the company in 1945 and added other Northwest-grown flower bulbs to the product line. He later included other horticultural products, greenhouse structures, and equipment. Harry raised Lily bulbs at Sumner about 1951/52. His son, Donn, became a partner in 1958 and full owner in 1973, incorporating the business as Harry Sharp & Sons. The company is currently a world-wide distributor of the items listed above.

Shorey, Samuel

Samuel Shorey (Deer Harbor) was an early grower but little information is available about him. George Gibbs's success with bulbs probably stimulated Shorey into trying them. The *Seattle Post Intelligencer* reported on February 7, 1904 that Samuel Shorey "is having excellent results at Deer Harbor, Orcas Island." He sent samples in 1902 to Chicago for planting in Lincoln Park and local landscape gardeners there stated they were much better than Dutch bulbs.

Smit, L. Maynard

Maynard Smit (Puyallup), a bulb grower from Holland, first worked in a greenhouse in Bellingham and about 1927 became manager for C. W. Orton. He resigned about 1947 to devote full time to his own interests. Maynard was growing Narcissus on his own at least as early as 1933 and continued until 1956. He also built and ran his own greenhouses and opened a florist shop in Puyallup. Apparently he overexpanded, went bankrupt and returned to Bellingham to work in a greenhouse there. At his peak, he probably had about 10 acres of bulbs.

Smith, Joe

Joe Smith (Olympia Bulb Company, Olympia) had a nursery at Longbranch and was growing bulbs at least as early as 1919. He also began publishing a combination catalog and newsletter that year, called *Joemma*. He bought, sold and swapped seeds, bulbs and nursery stock.

In 1924, he contracted with W. R. Taylor to grow Narcissus for him at Olympia. By 1925, he was selling Narcissus flowers in Seattle and was also buying the remaining stocks of many small bulb growers, especially in the Lake Washington area where the soil was too heavy and/or too wet for bulbs. Joe then decided to expand his operations in 1925 and he moved to Olympia where most of his bulbs (Gladiolus, Iris, Lilies, Narcissus and Tulips) were raised under contract, first by Walter R. Taylor and later by A. N. Kanouse and perhaps others. In 1928, he hired Kanouse as his manager and by 1930, they were growing about 20 acres of Narcissus and another 20 of other bulbs. He apparently overextended, however, and went bankrupt in 1932 or 1933.

In 1925, Smith organized and sold shares in the Joesmith Bulb Company (later renamed Joesmith Narcissus Company) and the Joesmith Lily Company. But, in 1928, he was found to be operating under the name of the Olympia Bulb Company.

According to other bulb growers, Joe was a "character," but very active. He carried on a large correspondence, gave many talks encouraging bulb growing and helped to organize the Northwest Bulb Growers Association in 1924, becoming its first secretary. The last record finds him in Seattle in 1947, in poor health, but still publishing *Joe's Seed Bulletin*, and confining his activities to flower seeds. He claimed that at one time he was the second largest bulb grower in the state.

Smith, John W. Macrae (MacRea)

John Smith (Bellingham) was born in Scotland in 1866 and arrived in Bellingham in 1888. He gradually turned "his attention to floriculture, with particular reference to. . .Tulips, Narcissus and the like." In 1897, he bought 14 acres of the old Fort Bellingham site on which he grew bulbs and erected greenhouses, becoming in 1926 "the proprietor of one of the best floricultural establishments in the northwest" [but he] "never lost his early love" of bulbs (112). It is not known when he started in bulbs but it was at least by 1901 because he sent samples of the Narcissus, Tulip and Hyacinth bulbs he had grown to the USDA in November of 1902 (30). Apparently, he began cooperating with the USDA in 1903 because it was reported in 1907 that on Smith's farm "the principal government experiments have been carried on the last four years" (139). He had about one acre in Narcissus in 1933 and was still growing Iris in 1942.

Smith, Mrs. Karel Lubbe

Karel Smith (Satsop Bulb Farms, Elma), a daughter of Chuck Lubbe, has been raising and forcing bulbs with her sister, Kris Edem, since 1971. She and Kris also run a retail bulb and flower shop at the farm.

Staatz, Stanley W.

Stanley (Stan) Staatz (1894-1968, Staatz Bulb Farms, Orting) was born in Kansas, moved to Washington with his parents about 1900 and eventually ended up in Tacoma. He majored in law at the University of Washington, where he was an outstanding guard on the basketball team. His studies were interrupted by the Army during World War I and he was wounded on the last day of the war.

Stan was admitted to the Washington State Bar but never practiced law. Instead, he joined his father in the feed business and later became co-owner of an insurance business in Sumner. In 1934, he joined with Frank Chervenka in raising 40 acres of Narcissus near the junction of the Puyallup and Stuck Rivers. In 1937, they purchased a 100-acre dairy farm near Orting on which they continued to grow Narcissus, adding Tulips about 1940. In 1940, Stan bought out Chervenka's interest in the farm and also purchased an adjoining 150 acres of land. In 1944 he added an adjacent 20-acre hop farm.

Stan began marketing Narcissus flowers in 1948 through a salesman. In 1954 his son, Wally, expanded the marketing efforts and sold flowers throughout the West and Midwest. When the Puyallup Valley Flower Cooperative was formed in 1956, the Staatz farm became a charter member.

In 1962, the farm was incorporated as the Staatz Bulb Farms, Inc. with Wally as a shareholder. In addition to bulbs, the Staatzes raised beef cattle, berries, vegetables and cabbage seed at various times.

Their bulbs were sold through jobbers until 1964 when they joined the Puget Sound Bulb Exchange. In 1964, they also purchased all the Iris, most of the Narcissus stock and some machinery from the C. W. Orton estate after Orton died. At this time, they also built a new warehouse with temperature-controlled rooms.

Stan was very active in the Puyallup Valley Daffodil Festival, serving as president and director until 1954 when he resigned and was succeeded by Wally who became a director and then president in 1959. Wally is the only son to have followed his father as president of the Festival. Stan was also a director and president of the Northwest Bulb Growers Association and helped to organize the Washington State Bulb Commission. He was active in the Western Washington Fair and many other organizations. Stan died from a heart attack on February 6, 1968 while landing a steelhead trout from the Puyallup River.

Staatz, Wallace T.

Wallace (Wally) Staatz (Staatz Bulb Farms, Orting) was born in Sumner and attended Oregon State University where he received his B.S. in 1949 and M.S. in 1950, working during the summers on his father's bulb farm. He served as a horticultural inspector for the Washington State Department of Agriculture in the summers of 1950 and 1951.

In 1952 Wally returned to work full time with his father on the bulb farm, taking over control partially in 1954 and, completely, in 1968 after Stan died. The peak years for the Staatz Bulb Farm were from 1964 to 1968 when they raised about 140 acres of bulbs. Bulb yields on their soil type (Orting series), however, were not as good as those on other types. This situation, as well as a decreasing net return on bulbs, prompted Wally to begin converting part of his 270-acre farm into the Hi Cedars Golf Course in 1970. At that time, he sold all of his Iris and Tulip bulbs. By 1975, Wally had sold most of the Narcissus bulbs, retaining only enough for a one-half acre planting.

Wally was director and president of the Northwest Bulb Growers Association, chairman of the Washington Bulb Commission and is still a member of the Puget Sound Bulb Exchange. He was also manager of Tulip Flowers, Inc., a flower cooperative, from 1959 until about 1964 when it merged with the Puyallup Valley Flower Cooperative. He was also the first grower to use an apple grader for grading Narcissus bulbs.

Wally was a member of the Washington National Guard Reserve, retiring in 1970 as a Lieutenant Colonel. He helped develop and manage the Crystal Mountain Ski Resort. More recently he has concentrated on the development of home sites adjacent to his two golf courses.

Stewart, Mrs. Mary Brown

Mary Stewart (1870-1958, Tulip Grange, Bow) was Skagit County's pioneer bulb grower. Her husband, who came west from Ohio, bought 40 acres of timbered and rocky school land on Samish Island, cut the timber, had it sawed at Edison and used the lumber to build a home for his family. Mary, an ex-school teacher, joined him in 1903 with their two children. Another daughter, Frances, was born in the house in 1906. According to Frances, Mary first became interested in bulbs after reading a Park Seed Company catalog and bought a few Tulips to enjoy, planting them about 1906. She had to wait two years to see the flowers bloom, however, because one of her small daughters picked all the immature buds the first year! Frances remembered seeing large masses of Siberian Squill in 1910 so Mary probably had an assortment of different bulbs by that time. She gradually planted more bulbs, as finances permitted, in Dutch-type beds in a display garden. Many visitors came to enjoy them but, apparently, Mary did not begin selling bulbs on a large scale until about 1910, except perhaps to a few friends and visitors. Mary probably entered the commercial bulb business in 1908 since she stated in her 1933 catalog that a booklet she wrote that year on bulbs was "a condensed summary of knowledge gained in twenty-five years of work and study" (129).

In 1919 Mary coined the name Tulip Grange and, in 1921, put a display in the Tulip Show in Bellingham. This was followed by ads in the *Washington Farmer* and exhibits at various fairs. The orders began to flow in! Mary next developed a catalog and mail order business. However, she had little help except from her children so her bulb farm never exceeded two to three acres in size until her son, Sam, a quartermaster on the President Cruise Line, left his job in 1925 and came home to help.

Tulip Grange was officially incorporated on July 21, 1930. Sam Stewart became president and Mary was listed as secretary. Margaret Maupin, Mary's daughter, owned five shares of stock (at $50 each) and perhaps the other daughter did also. So far as we know, Sam and Mary owned the remaining shares. After Mary's husband died in 1947, when she was 77 years old, she sold her share of the business to Sam and retired.

Mary seems to have been an excellent businesswoman and especially wanted to help rural housewives acquire some beauty for their homes and gardens by growing her bulbs. She received much assistance from Dr. David Griffiths and cooperated with him in many experiments.

Stewart, Sam

Sam Stewart (1902-1972, Tulip Grange Bulb Farm, Mount Vernon) was born in Ohio and worked on tug boats during his high school years and then as a logger for four years. He also helped his father on the farm at Bow and then served as quartermaster on the President Cruise Line but returned home in 1925 to help his mother grow bulbs. He married Sarah Hart in 1929 and they both assisted Mary with the farm and retail catalog business. Mary's husband died in 1947 and she then sold her share of the business to Sam and retired.

The Stewarts first raised a few acres of bulbs at Bow on Samish Island and then leased 5 acres of land in the Skagit Valley in 1931 where they planted King Alfred Narcissus and Wedgwood Iris. In 1937, with Neal Noorlag they bought a 30-acre parcel on McLean Road near Mount Vernon for $5,369 and divided it in half. By 1954, Sam had 145 acres of bulbs which included Narcissus (80), Tulips (40) and Iris (25). This made him one of the largest growers in Washington at that time. After his death in 1972, most of the bulbs were sold to the United Bulb Company.

Sam began issuing wholesale catalogs from Mount Vernon about 1934. He listed top size King Alfreds (DNl) at $45/1,000 in 1940 vs. $90 in 1946. Meanwhile, Mary continued with the retail catalog business at Bow, at least until 1945. They began shipping field-cut Narcissus flowers in refrigerated railroad cars to Chicago in 1936 and, in 1947, were one of the first to ship flowers by airplane from the Bow Airport.

Mrs. Margaret Maupin, Sam's sister, and Pete Walker worked for Sam for many years. Bert Hart (1905-1985, Mount Vernon) was Sam's brother-in-law. He graduated from Oregon State University in landscape architecture, served in the Army during World War II and, in 1946, went to work for Sam as office manager and salesman, a job at which he was very successful. Bert retired from bulb growing in 1970 and raised hothouse tomatoes at John Gardner's until his death.

Taylor, Walter R.

Walter Taylor (Olympia) and his wife were probably the first bulb growers in Thurston County, starting in 1924 when they raised an acre of Pheasant's Eye Narcissus under contract for Joe Smith. They continued raising Narcissus and other types of bulbs for Smith until 1928 when they went into business for themselves, selling bulbs locally and by mail order. They issued their first catalog about 1930. In the 1930s they had over 70 varieties of Lilies and records show that they continued with these until 1946 although in a letter to the author in 1962 they stated that "unfriendly weather accomplished our defeat in 1942."

Vallentgoed, Rutgert

Rutgert Vallentgoed (Holland-American Bulb Company, Bellingham) worked on bulbs at the USDA Bulb Station in Bellingham from about 1916 to 1922 when he quit in order to grow bulbs commercially. The Holland-American Bulb Company was incorporated with $60,000 capital in 1922 with Vallentgoed as president. The company planned to buy 40 acres of land and to plant 8-10 of them that fall. However, in 1923, Vallentgoed was reported to be a manager of the Bellingham Bulb Company, growing Tulips and Hyacinths on 4-5 acres. Case Van Lierop worked for him until some time in 1924 when he lost his job because the firm was having financial problems. The last record with the Vallentgoed name was in 1926 with a firm called Vallentgoed and Murray.

Van Aalst, John

John Van Aalst (Kirkland/Redmond) must have started growing Tulips about 1920 and became one of the largest Tulip growers in the state by 1929 according to the *Seattle Times* (May 12, 1929). He had about 4 acres of Narcissus in 1933 and later added Iris. John also managed Segers Brothers Farm before they moved from Kirkland to Lynden about 1927.

Van der Salm, Jerry

Jerry Van der Salm (Van der Salm Bulbfarm, Inc., Woodland) came from Holland and has been raising bulbs near Woodland since 1980. In

1986, he discontinued growing Iris and Narcissus and, by 1989, had about 25 acres of Lilies and 10 of Tulips. In 1990, he eliminated the Tulips and, by 1991, was concentrating on Asiatic, Oriental and trumpet Lilies. His farm has extensive temperature-controlled rooms which are programmed so that bulbs can be shipped weekly to greenhouse growers for year-round production. About 60% of their bulbs are now sold for that purpose. In 1990, they set up a separate company (Van der Linden Flowers Inc.) to sell their field-cut flowers and those forced in their 2½ acres of greenhouses. Ed McRae, formerly with Oregon Bulb Farms, is in charge of Lily hybridizing for the company.

Van Lierop, Case and Cornelius

Case Van Lierop (1886-1961, Bothell) was raised on a bulb farm in Holland, left school and began working in the bulb fields when he was 12 years old. He came to the United States in 1923 and worked for the Bellingham Bulb Company until they had financial problems in 1924. Case then moved to Bothell and planted Tulips from which he began selling cut flowers the next year to the passing public. In 1928 he moved his planting to Redmond and added Narcissus and Iris. He continued growing and retailing flowers and bulbs, and built a greenhouse in which he forced his excess Tulip bulbs. In 1940 Case bought a farm at Conway which enabled him to expand his production and he began selling cut flowers all over the West Coast and Alaska. He had a mishap one year when the dikes broke at Conway and the river flooded his bulbs. Estimates of his peak acreage range from 34 to 80 acres of Iris, Narcissus and Tulip bulbs. He also grew Lilies at one time. Case died in 1962 and his son, Cornelius, took over.

Cornelius (Cornie) and his family moved to Conway in 1941 to supervise his father's bulb production there but returned to Bothell in 1959. After his father's death, Cornie continued forcing and selling flowers as well as bulbs. He died in 1973 and his widow sold the business to United Bulb Company in 1974.

Van Lierop, C. Peter

C. Peter (Pete) Van Lierop (Ward-Van Lierop Farms, Inc., Olympia), a son of Si Van Lierop, was raised on his father's bulb farm at Puyallup and later grew bulbs in cooperation with his brother, Neil, from 1962 to 1964. In 1975 Pete and Mervin Lee Ward, Jr. bought a farm of 500 acres from Mervin Ward, Sr. near Olympia. In 1981, they purchased Wilmer Reise's Narcissus bulbs and imported enough more bulbs to plant 25 acres near Olympia. These were raised primarily for cut-flower purposes. Later they began to plant more densely and in 1990 planted only 16 acres. They sell both bulbs and flowers.

Each person in this corporation has his own specialty. Mervin Lee's specialty is carrots while Pete concentrates on Narcissus and strawberries with assistance from his son, Peter, Jr. Pete's son, Jeff, operates their 150 acres of turfgrass. ·

Van Lierop, Neil

Neil Van Lierop (Van Lierop Bulb Farms, Puyallup) actually started growing bulbs when he was only 12 years old. In 1960, he bought his own farm. When his father, Si, died in 1962, Neil joined forces with his mother, Beatrice, to keep the home farm going. They continued to enlarge the acreage and, by 1965, had a peak of about 60 acres in Narcissus, 40 in Iris and 20 in Tulips for a total of 120 acres. Neil later reduced the Iris acreage to 5 in 1989 but still had 60 acres in Narcissus and 25 in Tulips.

They built a greenhouse in 1966 and began forcing their own bulbs and retailing the flowers in their own shop. Neil now forces all of the Tulips he raises and most of the Narcissus, but uses most of his Iris for field-cut flowers. The forcing and retailing business now accounts for at least 85% of the company's income. The few bulbs they sell go mostly to dry sales or through their retail store.

Neil's wife, Bonnie, and their daughters, Cynthia, Anne and April are also very active in the company, particularly in supervising flower picking, managing the retail shop and organizing the display garden which is crowded with visitors who come every day in the spring. Cynthia was also president of the Northwest Bulb Growers Association from 1985 until 1989 and has organized the annual Bulb Growers Conferences for the past seven years in consultation with WSU scientists.

Neil has been extremely helpful to the author in answering many questions about bulb growing and bulb growers, both past and present.

Van Lierop, Simon

Simon (Si) Van Lierop (1900-1962, Van Lierop Bulb Farms, Puyallup) was raised on a bulb farm in Holland, sold bulbs and flowers in England and later in the United States. In 1929 he decided to stay in Washington and became a United States citizen in 1943. Si started working for Ed Orton in 1929, digging bulbs with a horse-drawn plow. Sometimes during the Depression, he was paid in flowers or bulbs which he and his wife sold on street corners or door to door in Tacoma. In 1931, he imported a handful of bulbs and these were apparently the start of his bulb empire. Si bought the home farm of 67 acres in the late 1930s and continued to enlarge his plantings of Iris, Narcissus and Tulips. He began selling bulbs in 1934 and, by 1961, had 35 acres of bulbs. Unfortunately, he died suddenly from a heart attack at age 62.

Mrs. Beatrice (Bea) Johnson Van Lierop had always believed that bulbs had a great future so, after Si's death, she and her son, Neil, continued to operate the Van Lierop Bulb Farm. They incorporated it in 1962 and, in 1972, split it into two companies—one of land and another of bulbs. The Bulb Company then bought up the shares belonging to Neil's sister, Joanne (Peterson), and to his brother, Pete. Bea concentrated on the retailing of cut flowers and, in 1968, built a flower shop and a display garden adjacent to the bulb shed. She soon became known as the "Flower Lady of the Valley." She had great vitality and was very active in church and many community projects. In 1974 Bea received the Woman of Achievement Award from the Puyallup Business and Professional Women's Club. The home that Si and Bea built was often cited by magazines as an exceptionally well-planned farm home. Bea died in 1975 and Neil has continued to raise bulbs and flowers at the home farm in Puyallup.

Van Slyke, Clifford L.

Clifford Van Slyke (Puyallup) was a sophomore at Puyallup High School when he first started growing a few Tulip bulbs in 1921. Although physically disabled, he apparently became fascinated with bulbs, since he was reported in 1923 as having 275 varieties each of Tulips and Narcissus plus 200,000 Gladiolus planted on 2 acres of land. Van Slyke also imported more bulbs from Holland that same year. He sold flowers, especially Hyacinths, on the streets of Puyallup. In 1926 he was one of the charter members of the Puget Sound Bulb Exchange, so he was definitely a commercial grower at that time. No subsequent record of him was found, except that he moved to Arizona after his father died.

Van Waveren, Anton H.

Anton (Tony) Van Waveren (1914-1979, Tony's Bulb Gardens, Mount Vernon) came to the United States in 1934 from Holland under the sponsorship of Harry Van Waveren, his brother. In 1936 he began working for Neal Noorlag and in 1938 he and his wife, Tina, forced Iris in California for Neal. Tony then went to Lynden to raise chickens, vegetables and potatoes and to manage a potato-glucose factory with his brother during World War II. In 1946 he returned to Mount Vernon as manager of the Noorlag Bulb Farms where he raised some bulbs on the side and set up a small retail shop to sell bulbs and flowers. He and his wife also displayed flowers in the Skagit Valley Tulip Show and, in 1957, won the "most popular display" contest for the third straight year, giving them permanent possession of the trophy. In 1967 or 1968 he left Mount Vernon to manage the Lakeway Mobile Estate Park in Bellingham and died there in 1979. Tony was secretary of the Skagit County Flower Coop from 1958 until it ceased operations in 1962.

Van Waveren, Harry

Harry Van Waveren (Segers Brothers, Lynden), who was from Holland, managed the Segers Brothers Bulb Farm at Lynden from about 1930 until at least 1934. He must have grown bulbs on his own also since he sold some to Neal Noorlag in 1930 and is listed as having 5 acres of them in 1949. Harry sponsored his brother, Tony, when he decided to emigrate to the United States. During World War II he and Tony farmed and operated a potato-glucose factory in Whatcom County.

Van Zanten, Gerrit J. V.

Gerrit Van Zanten (1902-1959, Van Zanten Brothers, Lynden) and Peter Duys, both from Holland, toured the United States looking for opportunities and finally decided on the Lynden area as a good one for growing bulbs. They purchased a 100-acre farm and Gerrit planted their first Narcissus in the fall of 1926. By 1929 he had added Iris, issued a wholesale catalog, planted 100 acres and had experienced a disastrous freeze that winter (1929/30) in spite of his use of a very heavy straw mulch. His cousin Maurice joined him in 1931.

In 1932, Gerrit and Maurice were reportedly growing 115 acres of Narcissus and 5 of Iris, making them one of the largest bulb growers in Washington. About 1935 or 1936 they, with Lefeber and Segers Brothers, made a trial planting of Iris on Whidbey Island and hired Neal Noorlag to manage it. There was a very good yield the first year. The Van Zantens continued to plant on the Island for a time but subsequent yields were so poor that in 1945 they moved most of their Iris to the Skagit Valley and began to phase out the Narcissus at Lynden. After another severe freeze and some water damage in 1947, they quit growing Narcissus entirely at Lynden and switched to potatoes. Meanwhile, Maurice had begun growing azaleas in greenhouses there about 1933 and eventually he concentrated all his efforts on them. About 1948 Gerrit and Maurice purchased the Lynden farm, which had belonged to the Van Zanten Brothers Company in Holland, and split it up. Gerrit took the bulbs and Maurice the azaleas.

Gerrit continued raising Iris and a few Tulips in Skagit County into the 1950s but gradually reduced his plantings. He always processed the bulbs in the warehouse at Lynden. The last record of him as a bulb grower was in 1956.

Van Zanten, Maurice

Maurice Van Zanten (Van Zanten Brothers, Lynden) came to the United States in 1931 to join his cousin, Gerrit, in operating the Van Zanten Brothers Bulb Farm. Maurice later specialized in azaleas and formed a company called Van Zanten, Inc. He is now retired and the company is being run by his son, Paul. Refer to Gerrit Van Zanten for additional details.

Van Zonneveld, Arie

Arie Van Zonneveld (1899-1948, Van Zonneveld of Washington, Orting). The Van Zonneveld farm began life as a branch of Van Zonneveld and Phillip of Holland and later became independent. It was owned jointly by Arie, other family members and Leendert (Lane) and

John Colyn. Lane was the manager and John the secretary. They first planted Narcissus at Onalaska and Toledo in 1925 but, needing more land, moved to a 60-acre farm near Chehalis in 1926. The heavy soil there, however, made digging very difficult. Reportedly, they had to break up clumps of soil with wooden mallets in order to free the bulbs at digging time! Seeking better soil, they moved to Orting in 1927, planting on leased land which they later bought and eventually enlarged to a 300-acre farm.

By 1928, they were one of Washington's largest growers with 90 acres in Narcissus. Their acreage reached 120 acres in 1930 and, by 1939, they were growing 165 acres of Iris, Narcissus and Tulips. This dropped to about 120 acres in the early 1940s. At first, Arie Van Zonneveld visited the farm only while he was on bulb-selling trips to the United States and left the active management to the Colyn brothers. Arie moved permanently to Tacoma about 1946 and died in 1948 after a prolonged illness. Meanwhile, Lane Colyn had died and John left the company in 1946 to run a Lily farm at Arcata, CA, dying in 1963.

Ted Sabelis was manager of Van Zonneveld of Washington from 1946 to 1949, leaving to become assistant manager of the Puget Sound Bulb Exchange. He was followed at Van Zonneveld's by Bos Van Der Sys as manager. After Arie died, his heirs gradually liquidated the company so that, by 1952, there were only 20 acres of bulbs left. The farm was then divided and sold to J. R. McLean and Harry Sather in 1953.

Bulbs were Van Zonneveld's main crop but the company also sold field-cut flowers. Narcissus remained the main bulb type, and over 500 varieties were grown in 1942. Iris and Tulips were also raised, beginning at least as early as 1941.

John Colyn was quite inventive and built most of the equipment used on the farm. He developed a mechanical digger for Narcissus which required 9 men to run and covered 4 acres per day. It required 20 men to dig an acre of Tulips by hand that same year. Colyn later developed diggers for Tulips and Iris. John's hobby was hybridizing Narcissus. John was the first person to build a float for display during the Daffodil Festival. The year was 1929 and the stationary float, displayed in the lobby of Tacoma's Winthrop Hotel, was in the shape of a 3 by 8 foot Dutch wooden shoe covered with 10,000 Narcissus. He and several other growers built more floats in 1930 and displayed them near the Old City Hall in Tacoma.

Walker, Peter

Peter (Pete) Walker (Mount Vernon) worked on Sam Stewart's bulb farm until he graduated from high school and then served in the Army from 1942 to 1945. After discharge, he worked full time for Sam from 1946 until 1957. His next job was that of warehouse manager for John Kapteyn (Holland Bulb Company) with whom Sam was cooperating at the time. From 1959 until 1962 Pete was also warehouse manager for the Skagit Valley Flower Cooperative. When Kapteyn decided to move his wholesale bulb business to Portland in late 1962, Pete began working at WSU's Mount Vernon Research Unit. He retired in 1982. His wife, Margie, is the daughter of Sam Stewart's sister, Margaret Maupin, and a granddaughter of Mary Stewart.

Mrs. Maupin worked for her brother, Sam Stewart, for several years and later with the Holland Bulb Company. She and Pete Walker also raised five acres of Narcissus and Tulips themselves from about 1949 to 1979, primarily for cut-flower production.

Walters, Stanley W.

Stanley (Stan) Walters (Walters Nursery, Puyallup) began raising bulbs in 1946. At his peak he had five acres of King Alfred Narcissus and three acres of Iris. Stan retired from bulb growing in 1978.

Ward, Mervin and Mervin Lee

Mervin (Merv) Ward (1906-1989, Puyallup) was a Narcissus grower from about 1950 to 1956 and, at his peak, probably had about 8 acres of King Alfred and Rembrandt varieties planted near Alderton. He also raised various berry crops and finally decided to concentrate on them and give up on bulbs. He operated the Alderton farm from 1947 to 1968 and, in 1953, bought another farm near Olympia on which he raised strawberries, carrots and other crops.

His son, Mervin Lee Ward, and Pete Van Lierop bought the Olympia farm from Mervin in 1975. They began growing Narcissus there in 1981 and by 1989 had 25 acres planted.

Wight, W. C. and A. E.

The Wights (William C. [grandfather]; Arthur E. [father]; and Chauncey E. [son]) raised Narcissus, Tulips and Gladiolus on Fox Island from about 1927 to 1942 selling both cut-flowers and bulbs. According to Chauncey, his father and grandfather got their start by digging up volunteer Narcissus in fields abandoned by Edwin Wines and others near Sylvan and the Museum on Fox Island. The Wights also grew loganberries and raised chickens for egg production but Chauncey reported that, from 1930 until they left the island in 1942, bulbs and cut flowers were their main source of income, so they must have grown several acres. W. C. is recorded as having about 3 acres of bulbs in 1933 and A. E. had 2 in 1942. Chauncey helped them but never raised bulbs himself. W. C. died in 1934. A. E. left the island in 1942 to work in the shipyards. Afterwards, Bill and Frances Ward harvested and sold flowers from the plantings for many years. Frances had picked flowers for Ed Wines when she was a teenager (about 1915).

After serving in World War II, Chauncey went into the landscaping and retail nursery business and was still actively engaged in it at Edmonds, WA as of 1992. C. Leland Wight, a brother of A. E., had a bulb farm at Woodinville and raised about 8 acres of Narcissus around 1933. Steve, another brother of A. E., also grew about one acre of Narcissus near Fox Island in the 1930s.

Williams, Elmer G., Sr.

Elmer Williams (1894-1976, Williams Brothers Produce Co., Tacoma) and Harry Smith started a produce business sometime before World War I. About 1916, Elmer joined his brother, Howard, in establishing the Williams Brothers Produce Co. of Tacoma. They got started in the bulb business in the 1930s by buying Narcissus and Tulip flowers from Mrs. Otto Reise for wholesale distribution through their contacts in the produce business.

In 1940 or 1941, the Williams Brothers started growing Narcissus bulbs, purchased from C. W. Orton, in cooperation with Ray Kern on about 10 acres of leased land near McMillan. Elmer began buying land in the Orting area the next year for bulb production and they added Tulips and, later, Iris to their collection. The company sold some bulbs but their main interest was in the cut-flower market. The cooperative venture with Ray Kern continued until about 1949 when Elmer and Ray divided the bulb stocks and grew them separately. In 1958, the Williams split up the company with Elmer taking the farm and Howard, the produce section. Elmer then turned the operation of the business over to his son, Elmer Jr., but kept an active interest in it until his death in 1976.

Williams, Elmer G., Jr.

Elmer Jr. (Ozzie) Williams (Williams Bulb Farm, Orting) graduated from the University of Washington in 1956 and then joined his father, Elmer, Sr., in the bulb business. Ozzie assumed active operation of the farm in 1958 and continued to expand, reaching a peak acreage of about 80 acres of Iris, Tulips and Narcissus in 1977. He quit Iris and Tulips after losses from the severe freeze of 1978/79 and concentrated on growing Narcissus, vegetables and Christmas trees. Ozzie gradually enlarged the farm until he owned about 400 acres of which 30 were planted to Narcissus in 1989. He sold the land in 1990 but plans to continue farming it for a few more years. By 1991, he had only 5 acres of Narcissus left. Ozzie is vice-president of the Puget Sound Bulb Exchange. He was president of the Northwest Bulb Growers Association in 1967/68 and has been active in many civic affairs.

Willis, H. L.

H. L. Willis (1869-1956, Mount Vernon) arrived at Mount Vernon in 1905 and bought some stump land on McLean Road. Although he was primarily a dairy farmer, he told a newspaper reporter in 1905 that he planned to raise Narcissus but, apparently, he did not actually begin until after Mary Stewart had already started in 1908. Several reports state that bulb growing was a hobby with him at first and he gave away bulbs and flowers to friends and to the Campfire Girls to sell. Willis was the first one to demonstrate the excellent quality of Skagit Valley soils for bulb production and cooperated with Dr. Griffiths in several experiments. In addition to bulbs, he raised rhubarb and owned a dairy herd.

Eventually, Willis's bulb acreage became large enough for him to go commercial. Records show that he was a member of the Puget Sound Bulb Exchange from at least 1943 to 1956. He had an acre of Narcissus in 1933 and was still growing 2 acres of them in 1956. He grew 5 acres of Iris from 1947 to 1956 and also raised Lilies in 1947. Willis was a member of the Northwest Bulb Growers Association from 1947 to 1956 and was in the Bulb Commission in 1956 which means that he was still growing bulbs commercially at the age of 87. Ted Sabelis remembered him well and mentioned that he was the only member of the Exchange from Mount Vernon for many years. Bill Roozen stated that Willis was very well educated and had even written books.

Wines, Edwin Hurlbut

Edwin Wines (1862-1934, Fox Island) was a traveling "advance man" for a vaudeville company who stopped traveling when he reached Fox Island. He built the Sylvan Resort Lodge at Echo Bay on Fox Island about 1905 and operated it until 1920. Wines was apparently the first commercial bulb grower in Pierce County. He is reported to have started with Narcissus and fruit trees in 1905. By 1910 he had a sizeable planting and was selling cut flowers to florists in Tacoma. C. W. Orton said that Wines had 5 acres at one time, scattered over the island, and was shipping cut flowers as far east as Minneapolis. However, some time after his wife died in 1919, he apparently quit farming and left the area. In 1927 he returned to Tacoma and died there in 1934. His abandoned fields later provided bulbs and flowers which were collected and sold by the Wights and later by Bill and Frances Ward.

Winters, Frederick W.

Frederick (Fred) Winters (1882-1968, Bellevue) began accumulating Narcissus in 1924 and, with another grower, imported a railroad carload of them in 1926. Dr. David Griffiths also gave him some Iris bulbs that year and Fred subsequently imported additional Iris planting stock for several years. He later moved his bulb plantings to Kent where he, apparently, continued growing Iris and Narcissus until he sold the home farm in 1943 and moved to Vashon Island.

Fred also had several greenhouses, first at Bellevue, in which he raised azaleas primarily and, later on, at Vashon Island where he specialized in carnations. In addition he ran a retail and wholesale flower business where he sold the flowers he produced.

Fred and Cecilia Winters constructed a "distinctive. . .Spanish Eclectic style" house in the late 1920s which the City of Bellevue was planning in 1989 to renovate as a historic structure. This house "is significant for both its distinctive architectural character and its association with the bulb growing and floricultural industry in King County and Washington State" according to a report from the city of Bellevue (152). The house is located in Mercer Slough where the land became usable after the construction of the Lake Washington Ship Canal in 1917 substantially lowered the water level of the lake.

Woodward, Wallace

Wallace Woodward (Puyallup) was born in Sumner and began raising ornamental shrubs in 1960 near Alderton as a sideline to his regular job. He added bulbs in 1963 and reached a peak of five acres in 1977. Wallace grew about an acre of Tulips at one time but concentrated on Narcissus for both the bulb and flower markets. Since retiring in 1988, he has reduced his acreage to one acre of Dutch Master Narcissus. Wallace joined the Puget Sound Bulb Exchange about 1971 and has been its secretary/treasurer for several years. He is also secretary of the Puyallup Valley Flower Cooperative.

CHAPTER 6

Producing the Bulbs

Bulb growing is a very specialized type of farming. One of the major reasons why Washington has become the bulb capital of the United States is its progressive bulb growers' development of mechanical methods of planting, digging, grading and treating bulbs in order to reduce the high cost of labor. And they did this mechanizing without any government supported research. With such creativity, they have successfully competed with cheaper overseas labor.

Labor Supply

Bulb farming was very labor intensive in the early 1900s. Workers came primarily from surrounding neighborhoods and communities. It was a mark of prestige among teenagers to work on a bulb farm and both they and adults could be counted on to return year after year. Since the late 1970s such part-time help has become increasingly difficult to obtain and is frequently unreliable. Consequently, most large growers have come to rely heavily upon migratory farm laborers for the hand labor involved in picking flowers and in harvesting, cleaning, grading and planting bulbs.

Early wages were very low and were low, also, during the Depression. About 1930, a friend of the author's dug bulbs by hand for 10 hours a day for $1.00 in Whatcom County. By 1939, the rate for general labor in Pierce County had risen to 35¢ an hour, 65¢ an hour in 1942, $1.10 in 1952 and $4.50-$5.00 an hour in 1991. The scarcity of labor and its increasing cost accelerated the change to mechanization.

Bulb growing was strictly a hands-on operation before 1900 when bulbs were planted in beds 3-15 feet wide. Horses were used sometimes for plowing the land to prepare it for cultivation, but all other operations were done by hand. The beds were opened to a depth of 4-6 inches, marked, and the bulbs were placed upright with definite spacing, then covered with soil removed from the next bed to be planted (Figure 6-1). Most weeding was done by hand and cultivating was done with a hoe. Bulbs were dug on hands and knees using a small shovel. Such procedures permitted almost anyone to grow bulbs whether it was economical of labor or not.

By the early 1900s, some growers, such as Canfield at Bellingham, had begun planting bulbs in rows, often using furrows opened with a horse and plow (Figure 6-2). Bulbs were still spaced and set upright by hand. Only about one-half to one-third as many bulbs could be planted per acre as with the bed system but planting, cultivating and digging were easier than when bulbs were grown in beds. Later, bulbs were planted by just scattering them in the furrow without spacing or setting them upright. The latter was a radical change and was only slowly adopted although the yield was almost as good as that obtained by the earlier method.

Apparently there was a lot of discussion about planting in beds versus rows in the early 1900s. Dr. Griffiths's comments are interesting in this regard. He stated in 1922 that, "To determine whether there is a method superior to the bed system will require much experiment, and the question may not be settled for years; indeed, it would not be well to try to establish at this time any degree of finality in methods"(56). But, only six years later, Griffiths remarked that, "The tendency in the United States is to discard the bed system of planting in favor of planting in rows"(59).

Meanwhile, some growers had begun experimenting with mechanizing, presumably with Narcissus, at first, since Dr. Griffiths wrote in the 1922 bulletin, "For the present the subject of planting or digging Tulips by machinery may be dismissed. No machinery for either of these operations has yet been invented"(56). He had predicted in 1916 that, "It will be remarkable if the skill of the American farm implement manufacturer will not assist us very speedily in overcoming our present high labor cost in the production of bulbs, as it has in almost every other modern farm operation"(55). This was not to be the case, however; the market for such machinery was so small that growers had to do their own improvising and developing of equipment.

During a survey of the bulb industry in 1930 for a master's thesis, Riemann (105) interviewed 16 of the largest growers in Washington and Oregon. He found, in addition to other information, that only one grower

Figure 6-1. Hand planting bulbs in beds. (From USDA Bulletin 1327, 1925)

Figure 6-2. Planting bulbs in furrows, 1936. (Courtesy Chuck Lubbe)

planted by machine and the other growers planted by hand. The row system was more frequently used than the bed method.

The first mechanical planters were essentially large hoppers mounted on a platform, allowing bulbs to fall through chutes into a holding pan and then into furrows opened by a pair of discs. Each bulb was spaced by hand by a rider seated near the ground on the digger. The entire unit was pulled by a tractor. Later, Francis Chervenka and Otto Reise made the first self-propelled planters in the Puyallup valley, with engines mounted directly on the units. Belts were added to planters to feed bulbs into the hoppers, and chutes added to place fertilizer and pesticides in the soil near the bulbs. The bulbs were no longer spaced or set upright by hand. (Figure 6-3).

The efficiency of mechanization can best be appreciated by comparing the number of man-days required for digging and planting by hand with that by machine. In 1990, one large grower estimated that 20 man days would be needed to plant one acre of Iris bulbs by hand but only 0.2 man days if done by machine (Table 6-1). The cost and maintenance of the machines are not included in the estimate. This grower runs his diggers 18 hours a day in two shifts during peak seasons and harvests Iris and Tulips in bins.

Table 6-1. Number of man days required to plant or dig one acre of bulbs in 1990.

	Iris	Narcissus	Tulips
Planting by hand	20.0	20.0	20.0
Planting by machine	0.2	1.3	0.2
Digging by hand	40.0	20.0	30.0
Digging by machine	1.0	4.0	1.0

It may be pertinent to note here that, with mechanization, the Washington Bulb Company reduced its 1990 labor requirements for harvesting bulbs by about 60% as compared with those in 1985.

The planting rate varies with the type of bulb, its size and the density of planting. The rate for planting stock (small bulbs) has been about 2½ tons per acre for Iris and Tulips and 5 tons for Narcissus. Recently, the trend has been toward more dense plantings to reduce the costs of planting, harvesting and land rental. Some growers are also leaving part

Figure 6-3. Planting by machine at Frank Chervenka's about 1935.
(Courtesy Lee Merrill)

of their Narcissus stock in the ground for two years. This produces more small bulbs which are desirable for dry sales and for greenhouse pot-plant production.

Among the early pioneers in mechanization for whom records are available are Frank and Francis Chervenka, Earle Darst, Otto Reise, Howard Mansfield (of C. W. Orton), Harold Knutson (of E. C. Orton) and John Colyn (of Van Zonneveld). According to C. W. Orton, the development of mechanization was especially stimulated during World War II because labor was so scarce. Mechanization during the 1940s is covered in more detail in articles by Chervenka (26) and Wieting (151).

Although visiting Dutch growers took a dim view of the American trend toward mechanization, claiming excessive bulb injury, it is interesting to note that they, too, for economic reasons, have had to mechanize. In fact, some of the machines now being used here were imported recently from Holland. And most of the grading equipment has come either from Holland or has been essentially patterned after their machines.

Weeding

Hand weeding (Figure 6-4) was one of the most expensive of bulb farming operations in the 1940s, especially in Iris fields. It was supplemented by cultivation with equipment drawn by horses and later by tractors (Figure 6-5). In the late 1940s, effective herbicides were found by Washington State University scientists. These were applied with the same equipment used for spraying fungicides and the cost of weeding was reduced from $200 to $20 per acre.

Applying Pesticides

Before the 1920s, fungicides and insecticides were applied in the fields with knapsack-type sprayers or dusters and this must have been quite a job when several acres were involved. The mechanization of spray application proceeded slowly, from hand sprayers to horse-drawn wooden tank sprayers, to tractor-drawn steel tanks and, then, to tractor-mounted plastic rigs. However, in recent years when the soil was too wet in the spring for the use of such equipment, airplanes and helicopters were used (Figures 6-6 and 6-7).

Digging

In pioneering days, when bulbs were planted in beds, they were dug by hand with a small shovel, as shown in Figure 6-8. This was possible because the bulbs were planted at known distances from each other. Later, when growers began planting in rows, they still spaced the bulbs at the same distances and still dug them by hand.

Still later, growers discovered that, if they were very careful and, if the rows were far enough apart, they could use a horse and plow to turn over a row of planted bulbs, exposing them so they could be picked up by hand. This procedure was gradually adopted and used for many years (Figure 6-9).

Riemann (105), in his survey of the industry in 1930, found that two growers dug only by hand; four growers plowed out the bulbs and picked them up by hand; nine dug with machines and one grower used both "plowing out" and machines.

Figure 6-4. Weeding Iris by hand at C. W. Orton's in 1949.
(Photo by author)

Figure 6-5. Machine cultivation, 1991.
(Courtesy Washington Bulb Company)

Figure 6-6. Francis Chervenka spraying Iris with a fungicide
at C. W. Orton's, 1941. (Courtesy Glenn Huber)

Figure 6-7. Spraying with a fungicide, 1991.
(Courtesy Washington Bulb Company)

Figure 6-8. Digging bulbs in beds by hand.
(From USDA Circular 372, 1936)

Figure 6-9. Picking up bulbs by hand at Segers Brothers, 1931.
(Courtesy Historical Photograph Collections, Washington State
University Libraries, Neg. 92-182). [From Riemann (105)]

The first digging machines were either potato diggers or ones patterned after them, such as a type designed by Frank Chervenka in 1927. The earliest ones were pulled by horses or tractors (Figure 6-10). Later, they were made self-propelled. Subsequent improvements on diggers included the addition of vibrating shakers on the digger to remove excess soil, bars covered with rubber tubing to reduce bruising, and endless belts to enable workers to separate bulbs from clods of soil. Now, many digging machines automatically load the bulbs into bins or hopper-type trucks which can discharge the bulbs directly onto cleaning belts (Figure 6-11).

By 1931, the majority of growers had adopted the row system and many larger growers had begun to use modified potato diggers for digging bulbs. However, a few growers continued using the "plow out and pick up" method into the 1950s. Bulbs were usually left in trays in the field for a few days to cure (Figure 6-12).

While mechanization enabled Washington growers to compete more effectively with lower-priced foreign bulbs, it resulted in most of the smaller, non-mechanized growers going out of business. This is one reason why the number of Iris, Narcissus and Tulip growers dropped from almost 200 in the early 1930s to 17, today.

Cleaning

Cleaning of bulbs was done entirely by hand until the late 1920s. Old husks were removed, daughter bulbs separated and diseased or cut bulbs were discarded (Figure 6-13). The first mechanical Narcissus cleaners were the type used for potatoes. These were later modified for use on Iris and Tulips. After cleaning, the bulbs were dropped onto a moving belt, so that workers standing beside it could pick out diseased or cut bulbs and discard them before they were graded (Figure 6-14).

Grading

Iris and Tulip bulbs were graded with a set of sieves, containing round or elongated holes of different sizes, the sieve with the largest holes being at the top of the stack and the smallest at the bottom. The stack was shaken until no more bulbs would pass through the holes. These sieves were bought in sets from Dutch dealers. This system evolved into a horizontal grader containing four or more sieve-like

Figure 6-10. Tractor-drawn digger patterned after potato digger.
At Chervenka's about 1935. (Courtesy Lee Merrill)

Figure 6-11. Digging bulbs by machine, 1991.
(Courtesy Washington Bulb Company)

Figure 6-12. Narcissus bulbs stacked in trays for curing at Chervenka's.
(Courtesy Lee Merrill)

Figure 6-13. Cleaning tulip bulbs by hand.
(USDA Bulletin 1082, 1922)

Figure 6-14. Cleaning bulbs at Harold Knutson's, 1964. (Courtesy Earl Otis)

Figure 6-15. Grading tulips at E. C. Orton's in early 1940s.
(Courtesy Lee Merrill)

plates. Bulbs were placed in a hopper at one end and were gradually moved by a shaking process across the plates until they fell through holes into a chute and thence to boxes or baskets (Figure 6-15). Such grading machines were not effective for Narcissus bulbs, which had to be graded by hand, because of their shape. The first effective Narcissus grader was a type sold in eastern Washington for grading apples, with the grading based upon bulb weight. Since bulb varieties vary in size and weight, the machine had to be reset for each variety but proved to be very efficient.

Treating

One of the most effective controls for nematodes, insects, and certain fungi on Narcissus and Iris has been the immersion of the bulbs in a HWF solution (hot water at 110-111°F plus formaldehyde) for 2-4 hours. George Lawler may have been the first grower to use this procedure when, in 1924, he imported a "Barford and Perkins" hot water sterilizer. Most other growers apparently had their tanks built locally. The sterilizer or "cooker" usually consisted of a large rectangular metal tank heated by steam from pipes coming from an adjacent boiler and was controlled manually. Bulbs were placed in bags or crates and put in or lifted out of the tank by hand or with a hoist (Figure 6-16).

In 1950, Otto Reise, with assistance from a Puget Sound Power and Light Company engineer, Glen Cushing, developed a procedure which not only speeded up the process but did a much more efficient job of it. He built a large rectangular tank, making the top flush with the shed floor. The bulbs, which were in stacks of wooden flats (5" x 15" x 27"), were trucked onto a platform at the top of the tank. A heavy wire screen was fastened over the tops of the trays and the entire load was lowered into the tank by cables controlled by an electrical hoist. Steam for heating the water came from an oil burner in an adjacent shed. A circulating pump kept the water moving and a thermostat maintained the temperature within the limits of 110-111°F. A recorder was used for reference in case claims of damage were made, since Otto custom-treated bulbs for other growers as well as his own. Ten tons of bulbs could be treated at one time. Cushing also helped Francis Chervenka develop a similar cooker in 1951. This general type of treating tank was adopted, with modifications, by most growers (Figure 6-17). Propane gas, instead of oil, is often used now as a source of fuel.

125

Figure 6-16. Treating bulbs at Seger Brother about 1931.
(Historical Photograph Collections, Washington State
University Libraries, Neg. 92-184). [From Riemann (105)]

Figure 6-17. Treating bulbs at Washington Bulb Company, 1992.
(Photo by author)

126

Sometimes, bulbs need to be treated with additional fungicides and/or insecticides. Certain materials can be added to the HWF solution while others must be used separately. Some growers devised a system of using a continuous belt, with the bulbs passing under a water spray to wash off dirt, after which they were sprayed with a pesticide. Other growers dusted bulbs in the hopper with pesticides at the time of planting.

Storing

Research by USDA and WSU scientists showed that Iris and Tulip bulbs produced better forcing results in the greenhouse if they had certain heating and/or cooling treatments before shipping. In the 1950s, Glen Cushing, of Puget Power, helped design many of the storage rooms used for such treatments. The same rooms were used for storing flowers at cool temperatures during the field flower-cutting season. At present, all large growers have storage rooms which are automatically controlled for temperature, humidity and air circulation and make it possible for Iris and other bulbs to be stored and shipped at weekly intervals to greenhouse forcers and to growers of field-cut flowers in California throughout the year.

Shipping

Bulbs were originally shipped in vented railroad cars. If temperatures were mild in the Midwest, the bulbs arrived on the East Coast in good shape, but if hot or freezing weather occurred, the results were often disastrous. The advent of air-conditioned railroad cars and trucks was a godsend, but the air conditioning sometimes failed so shippers adopted the custom of placing temperature recorders in each car or truck. This was especially useful when claims for damage were submitted. Fortunately, the temperature controls are much better now and only occasional losses occur. The latest trend is toward the use of containers which are also air-conditioned and are used for both domestic and overseas shipments. The use of containers also reduces pilferage. A single 40-foot container can hold 800,000 large (10-11 cm) Iris bulbs.

Field-cut flowers were occasionally shipped in iced railroad cars in the 1920s and 1930s, but the results were often unsatisfactory. The industry was helped by the development of refrigerated railroad cars and trucks, and after World War II, especially, by the introduction of

127

reasonably-priced air freight. At the present time, field-cut and forced flowers are usually shipped by air freight to reach their markets in the East promptly. Refrigerated trucks are used primarily in the West Coast states except at peak times when they may also carry flowers to eastern states.

Although most bulbs, if not all, are now shipped by truck, it may be of historical interest to note that in 1947 there were 114 railroad carloads of bulbs shipped from Washington. This number rose to 161 in 1948 and ranged between 154 and 164 until 1955 when it started to decline, presumably because of the increased use of refrigerated trucks for shipping. Incidentally, in the early years, a "refrigerated" railroad car was one in which ice was used to keep the bulbs or flowers from being overheated.

It cost $3.03 to ship 100 pounds of bulbs by truck in 33,000 pound minimum lots from Oak Harbor to New York City in 1959. By 1991, the cost was $10 per 100 pounds with a 40,000 pound minimum load from Seattle to New York.

Bulb Yield

Accurate yield data are available for only a very few years prior to 1956 when the Washington State Bulb Commission was organized and began collecting sales data for assessment purposes. The Commission data show definite trends but do not reflect total production because: (1) the number of INT bulbs used only for flower production is excluded from the assessment charges and does not need to be reported; (2) some sales, particularly in recent years, are reported in pounds of bulbs or dollar values and only general estimates could be made of the actual numbers of bulbs involved and (3) the increased per acre density of planting. Roger Knutson stated that Knutson Farms were planting more than twice as many bulbs per acre in 1988 as in 1973.

During the last three years for which sales data are available (1988-1990), the yield of salable bulbs per acre fluctuated between 59,400 to 65,973 Iris; 19,339 to 30,314 for Narcissus and 42,868 to 49,551 Tulips. The average yield for the three years was 63,223 bulbs of Iris, 24,428 of Narcissus and 45,476 of Tulips. All yields, and especially those of Narcissus, were reduced in 1990 because of severe freezing weather in February. These and other data on sales and acreages are listed in Table 3-3 in Chapter 3.

Bulb yield is greatly influenced by weather. Tulips are very sensitive to waterlogging, as are Iris and Narcissus, but to a lesser extent. Tulips, however, are the most resistant to freezing; Narcissus and Iris, the least resistant. The influence of freezing weather is shown dramatically in the reduction of the 1979 yield after a very severe freeze in the winter of 1978/79. This freeze reduced the yield of salable Iris bulbs by 70% per acre, Narcissus by 30% and Tulips by 11% (Table 7-1 in Chapter 7).

Soil type also affects yield. For example, the USDA Soil Conservation Service estimated the average production of salable Narcissus bulbs in Pierce County was 17,000 bulbs in the Puyallup and Sultan soil series as compared with 14,000 per acre in the Orting series (154). One large grower on the latter soil, however, had even lower yields, averaging only 10,683 Narcissus bulbs a year over the four years from 1965 to 1968.

Other factors affecting yield, which are discussed elsewhere, include the variety, quality and size of bulbs planted; type of handling and storage before planting; drought; flooding and/or waterlogging; disease and insect damage and flower cutting.

The size of bulbs harvested depends primarily on the size planted and on weather conditions, in addition to the other factors mentioned above. One grower, with a large acreage, estimated that the approximate yields of different sizes of bulbs in a normal year are distributed as shown in Table 6-2.

Table 6-2. Average yield of different salable bulb sizes by percentage.

IRIS (var. Ideal)		NARCISSUS (Large Trumpet)		TULIPS	
Size in cm	%	Size in cm	%	Size in cm	%
11 cm & larger	17%	19 cm & up	17%	12 cm & larger	40%
10-11 cm	33%	17-19 cm	33%	11-12 cm	40%
9-10 cm	33%	15-17 cm	33%	10-11 cm	20%
8.5-9 cm	17%	12-15 cm	17%	---	---

CHAPTER 7

Problems

Farmers everywhere have problems and bulb growers are no exception. Some problems are created by Mother Nature and others are man made. They include land availability, labor, freezing, flooding, wet summers, drought, pests, fires, shipping mishaps and surpluses.

Land

With all its climatic advantages, why isn't Washington, instead of Holland, the bulb center of the world? The best bulb soils in Washington State are level, well drained and consist of sandy or silt loams with a pH range of 5.8 to 6.2 (5). Unfortunately, the supply of such soil in the state is relatively limited. It is becoming scarcer every year in all major bulb-growing areas with the continued encroachment of residential and commercial development, because developers also like such level and well-drained land. Most growers own part of the land they farm but, in order to practice proper rotation or to enlarge their plantings, they usually lease additional acreage. Such additional acreage is becoming harder and harder to find and more and more expensive.

Pierce County is a good example of what is happening. For many years, it led all other counties in bulb production. In 1945, there were 15,000 acres in general agricultural production. By 1984 this acreage had shrunk to 8,000, of which only 3,000 were in specialty crops, such as bulbs and berries. Urbanization was stealing about 180 acres of land from agriculture every year (98).

Some of the best bulb soils in Pierce County are the Puyallup fine sandy and the Sultan silt loams. According to a study by S. J. Rozenbaum, the amount of such land available to farmers decreased almost 10% in 9 years, from 6,859 acres in 1976 to 6,224 in 1985. This shrinkage has speeded up during the past five years because of accelerated development. Rozenbaum stated that Pierce County is "urbanizing faster than the entire Puget Sound region," and in 1988 he estimated that 35% of the remaining prime soils in agriculture would be lost by the year 2000 (114).

The Orting area in Pierce County became an important bulb-growing area when the Van Zonnevelds began growing bulbs there in 1927. They were followed by other growers but, in 1992, there isn't even an acre left in production. The last grower, E. G. Williams, Jr. sold his 400 acre farm in 1991 for development. Wally Staatz, a neighbor, formerly had one of the largest bulb farms in the area but began converting it into a golf course and housing development in 1970. Staatz and Williams still grow a few acres of bulbs but these are raised elsewhere.

Tom Knutson, co-owner of Knutson Farms, the largest bulb farm in Pierce County, recently stated that their land near Sumner "is becoming too valuable for its current use" and that they will "probably be forced out of farming, at least in this area" (145). Neil Van Lierop, owner of the other remaining large farm in Pierce County, said that he "hasn't ruled out selling his farm someday. But he hopes to keep it going as long as possible" (82).

Richard Carkner, Washington State University economist, stated at a 1990 conference on Farming on the Urban Fringe in Pierce County that "Almost a third of the farmers interviewed are interested in selling their land, planning to sell or actually in the process of selling." He also stated that "At some point it becomes too late to preserve farmland to any great extent—I think that point has been reached for much of Pierce County" (16).

A similar problem is developing in Skagit County where 13% of all agricultural acreage and 18% of the commercial acreage (over $10,000 in sales per year) was lost to development in the five years between 1982 and 1987 (124). According to Jeanette DeGoede and Leo Roozen (43), some growers in that area are wondering if there will be even enough Tulips available for a Tulip Festival 10 years from now. Continuing development results in higher land prices, higher land leases and higher taxes, all of which make the land too costly for bulb production.

Rozenbaum (114) also pointed out that "urban growth is highly scattered . . . because there is no planning system in Pierce County." In discussing this "leap-frog development," he stated that "as farms are sold to developers, agricultural regions become dissected and particular tracts of farmland may become too isolated or too small to profitably keep in agricultural production." For example, in Skagit County, the state's

131

largest bulb grower now farms over 50 separate parcels each year. This involves moving all types of equipment and personnel more often and for longer distances, all of which increases the cost of production. In addition to that, most bulb equipment cannot operate efficiently in small fields.

When developers invade farming communities, they create other problems for farmers in addition to higher prices, leases and taxes. New homeowners close to bulb fields become agitated when pesticide sprays or dusts, fertilizers and lime dusts drift across their properties, although these practices were commonly used before they bought their homes. Another problem with developers is their blockage of natural water drainage routes by covering land with stores, houses, driveways and roads. Increased water runoff pours into inadequate ditches and often causes flooding or waterlogging of fields during periods of wet weather.

As a result of these pressures, some growers have already moved. The Lubbe family left Sumner for the Elma area in 1971; the DeGoede Bulb Farms transferred from Mount Vernon to Mossyrock in 1977; and now, the Knutsons in Sumner foresee the day when they, too, will have to move from the Puyallup Valley if they wish to continue bulb farming.

The price of good bulb land was $200-$650 per acre in 1930 and rental fees ranged from $5-$20 per acre per year (105). In 1989, land of similar quality sold for about $4,000 an acre and could be rented for $200 in Skagit Valley, while such land in Pierce County was selling for $15,000-$40,000 an acre and could be leased for $150-$300 an acre.

Freezing Weather

Freezing damage is a periodic problem with bulbs. The Whatcom County area suffered disastrous losses of bulbs because of freezes in 1916, in 1925, in 1929 and at intervals thereafter from winter storms coming down from the Fraser River Valley. This occurred in spite of mulching with straw which was generally used in Whatcom County (at 600 pounds per acre) to protect bulbs from freezing, but which the wind often blew away. The repeated heavy losses eventually caused the growers either to give up growing bulbs or to move south to Skagit County.

Bulbs grown in other counties have also been severely injured at times by freezing, particularly after mild winters which stimulated early growth. Some of the most severe freezes occurred in January of 1950,

132

November of 1955, in the winters of 1964/65 and 1978/79; in February of 1990 and again in December of 1990.

The most severe freeze in recent years, as far as bulbs are concerned, was that of the winter of 1978/79. All bulb crops were affected but Iris were especially damaged. The salable Iris crop was reduced to about 30% of that of the preceding year and some growers had no bulbs to sell. Only two major growers obtained a reasonable yield of Iris that year. One field was in a protected area and the other had been planted flat instead of with the customary ridging method. The Narcissus yield was 70% of that of the preceding year, but the Tulip crop was only slightly affected (Figure 7-1 and Table 7-1).

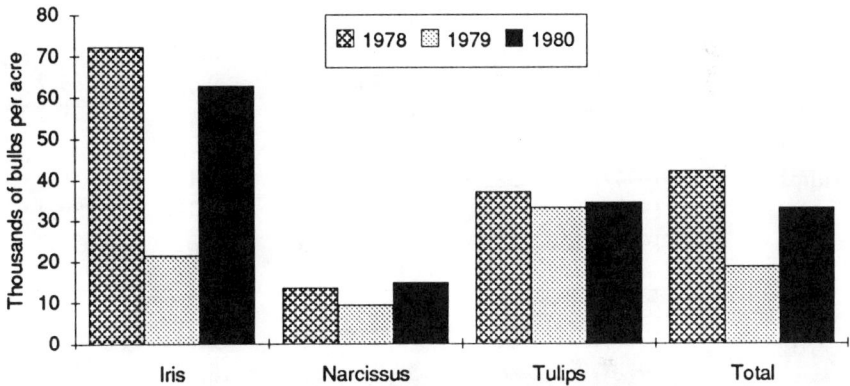

Figure 7-1. Average bulb yield in numbers per acre in years before, during and after the severe winter freeze of 1978/1979.

Another freeze occurred in February of 1989 when temperatures were below freezing for 15 consecutive days at Mount Vernon and 14 of the 15 at Puyallup. Low temperatures were 9°F at Mount Vernon and 10°F at Puyallup, but the damage was more severe in the Puyallup Valley than in Skagit County which had some snow cover. The yield of large Iris bulbs was only one half of normal that year. Narcissus flowers were also stunted and one grower lost a million dollars worth because they were too short to be sold. More bulb damage occurred in February of 1990 when the temperature was below freezing for 13 days at Mount Vernon and 12 at Puyallup. The lowest temperatures were 8°F and 18°F, respectively. The yields of salable bulbs that year were 64% of the preceding year for Narcissus, 90% for Iris and 94% for Tulips.

133

Depending upon their stage of growth, Iris are usually most susceptible to freezing injury, Narcissus are next and Tulips suffer the least. Freezing and/or prolonged cold temperatures in late winter can also damage flowers.

Table 7-1. Bulb acreage and yield of salable bulbs before, during and after the severe freeze in the winter of 1978/79.

Bulb type	Year	Number acres planted	Yield of salable bulbs	Average yield per acre	Percentage per acre of 1977/78
Iris	1977/78	727	52,491,505	72,203	-
	1978/79	742	16,025,463	21,598	29.9
	1979/80	400	25,107,119	62,768	86.9
Narcissus	1977/78	701	9,597,559	13,691	-
	1978/79	772	7,366,854	9,543	69.7
	1979/80	696	10,361,666	14,887	108.7
Tulips	1977/78	389	14,436,434	37,112	-
	1978/79	352	11,685,163	33,196	89.4
	1979/80	488	16,780,825	34,387	92.7
Total	1977/78	1,817	76,525,498	42,116	-
	1978/79	1,866	35,077,480	18,798	44.6
	1979/80	1,584	52,249,610	32,986	78.3

Floods

One of the first major losses of bulbs from flooding occurred on October 25, 1934 when the Puyallup and Carbon Rivers overflowed and ruined many bulbs in the Puyallup Valley.

In 1948, the rapidly rising Columbia River backed up into the Lewis River near Woodland and dikes were blasted to protect other areas. The resultant flooding of the farms of the United Bulb Company and of Tulips, Inc. was estimated to have destroyed between 265 and 450 acres of bulbs. A few bulbs survived but most were lost. Tulips Inc. returned to Oregon to grow bulbs, but the United Bulb Company purchased all of Ward Lawler's stock at Monroe and some other bulb stocks and planted them at Woodland in the fall. In 1975, the Washington Bulb Company lost 25 acres of bulbs when the Skagit River overflowed near Mount

Vernon. Earle Darst also lost many Iris that year from the flooding of his field near Hamilton. Some waterlogging damage has occurred at various times in all counties, following prolonged rains in sites with inadequate drainage.

The most recent and the most severe loss from water damage to bulbs occurred in November and December of 1990 when a series of heavy rains caused extensive waterlogging of bulb fields in most areas, and flooding of many fields in Skagit County. The Washington Bulb Company was reported to have had over 500 acres under water at one time, including a 43-acre field of Tulips on Fir Island which was submerged so long that the crop was a total loss. Leo Roozen estimated (108) that they lost about 25% of all their bulbs. Tulips were damaged more than any other type of bulb in all counties. In addition to the loss of bulbs, there was the extra expense of the cost of labor and equipment to remove water from fields and cleaning up afterwards (Figure 7-2).

Wet Summers

Floods are damaging and so are wet summers, but to a lesser extent. Rain toward the end of the bulb growing season and during digging not only makes harvesting more difficult but can promote the growth of certain pathogens such as Fusarium and Corticium. If the rain is prolonged, it can markedly reduce the forcing capabilities of Iris unless they are given the recommended artificial heat-curing and conditioning treatments.

Drought

If floods and wet summers are destructive, so is drought. Prolonged dry spells, especially in late spring and early summer, markedly reduce yields, particularly of Iris. This occurred frequently on Whidbey Island in the 1930s and 1940s before the growers obtained irrigation equipment. Some growers now use overhead irrigation which helps the crops and loosens the soil for digging but also encourages certain disease-producing fungi during warm weather. Severe droughts, fortunately, are rare in western Washington.

Figure 7-2. November 1990 flood of 43 acres of Washington Bulb Company Tulips on Fir Island. (Courtesy Skagit Valley Herald)

136

Diseases, Insects and Nematodes

Many horror stories are told of disastrous losses to bulb crops from diseases, insects and nematodes. Basal rot had already become a problem by 1930. Riemann (105) reported that 8 of 16 bulb growers were using cow manure as a source of fertilizer but were applying it to the soil a year before planting because they had discovered that fresh manure increased losses from the basal rot disease.

Narcissus suffer from basal rot, bulb nematodes, root lesion nematodes and bulb fly. Tulips struggle against Botrytis blight. Iris fight the bulb nematode and all of them can be infected with a multitude of serious viruses carried by aphids. Fortunately, adequate control measures are now available for these problems but, because fungi, nematodes and aphids can develop resistance to pesticides, continued research is necessary to keep ahead of these problems.

Fires

Fire is a very real danger in any farming operation. On May 8, 1954, the old Van Zonneveld bulb sheds at Orting, then owned by Harry Sather, were destroyed with a loss of cleaning and grading equipment, storage rooms, bulb trays and stored flowers. Fires in 1956 and again in 1965 destroyed records, trays, equipment and part of the warehouse at Ben Korsten's farm. An arson fire on August 14, 1971 put Francis Chervenka out of the bulb business when he lost all of his bulbs, shed and most of his equipment. The Woodland Bulb Farms owned by Ted De Groot, Jr. and Ed Maggi also lost most of its equipment, shed and bulbs in a fire on January 6, 1980. Fire also destroyed a shed, storage rooms, greenhouses, some equipment and much of their planting stock at Gardners' West Shore Acres on October 9, 1982.

Shipping

Reports in the 1930s and 1940s by R. G. Fryar and others list some of the problems the Northwest growers had with differential freight rates between East and West, North and South, truck versus rail, and even between crops. For example, it cost more to ship Iris, Tulips and Narcissus bulbs than it did to ship the same weight of Gladiolus corms. A considerable amount of time was consumed in preparing documentation about these problems and in presenting appeals to the Interstate Commerce Commission in Washington, DC, which then regulated all interstate railroad and truck rates. In this endeavor the managers of the Puget Sound Bulb Exchange were very active.

Over-heating in transit has been, and still is occasionally a problem for both Northwest and Holland bulb shipments although refrigerated railroad cars, containers and trucks are now used. At times in the past, railroad cars or trucks were sometimes sidetracked on weekends, the refrigeration system failed, or unusually hot weather occurred and the bulbs turned to mush. Most shipments now are made in refrigerated trucks and complaints are fewer, but, even now a truck may break down, or be sidetracked over a weekend or holiday. Temperature controls are so important that many shippers now include a temperature recorder with each shipment, especially when it is going to Europe, for use in substantiating claims for damage if such becomes necessary.

Bulb Surpluses

Since 1932, there have been intermittent problems with surpluses of bulbs. The first surplus years lasted from about 1932 to 1935 with Narcissus. This was probably due to a drop in demand during the depth of the Depression. As a result many growers either reduced their plantings or went out of the bulb business completely.

In 1947 and 1948, the combination of too many imports plus too much local production reoccurred. Most Washington growers lost money and dumped many of their bulbs. This situation occurred again in 1952 when both Washington and Holland growers had bumper crops, resulting in many distress sales and the discarding of about one-fourth of all bulbs. The Puget Sound Bulb Exchange alone dumped twelve railroad carloads of bulbs. The oversupply of Wedgwood Iris was estimated to have been seven million bulbs.

CHAPTER 8

Marketing the Bulbs

The markets for Washington bulbs and flowers have changed many times in the past century and some of the changes have been mentioned briefly in earlier chapters. This chapter includes a discussion of the numbers of bulbs sold, their prices and their markets including exports.

Number of Bulbs Sold

The relative importance of the different bulb types sold in any one year can be compared in three ways: by the number of bulbs sold, by the number of acres planted and by the dollar value of the crops. For example, in 1989, more Iris bulbs were sold than either Narcissus or Tulips but more acres were planted with Narcissus than with either of the others. In the same year, the total estimated dollar value of the Narcissus bulb and field-cut flower crop was twice as large as that for Tulips and Iris combined.

In 1930, an estimated 14.1 million INT bulbs were sold by Washington growers. This included 11.1 million Narcissus (37), 2.6 million Iris and only 0.4 million Tulip bulbs (105). Since Tulips were originally the major bulb crop in Whatcom County, which was the major bulb producing county in the early 1900s, the low number for Tulips is surprising.

The proportions of bulb sales continued to change in the 1940s and in the 1950s. In 1954, the total number of INT bulbs sold had increased to more than 42.4 million but more Iris bulbs were sold than Narcissus and Tulips combined (Figure 8-1 and Table 3-3 in Chapter 3).

Accurate information on the number of bulbs sold is very sketchy before 1956 when the Washington State Bulb Commission began collecting such data. Most of the available figures for the years before 1960 are reported in Table 3-3 and, for later years, in Tables 7-1 (Chapter 7) and 8-1.

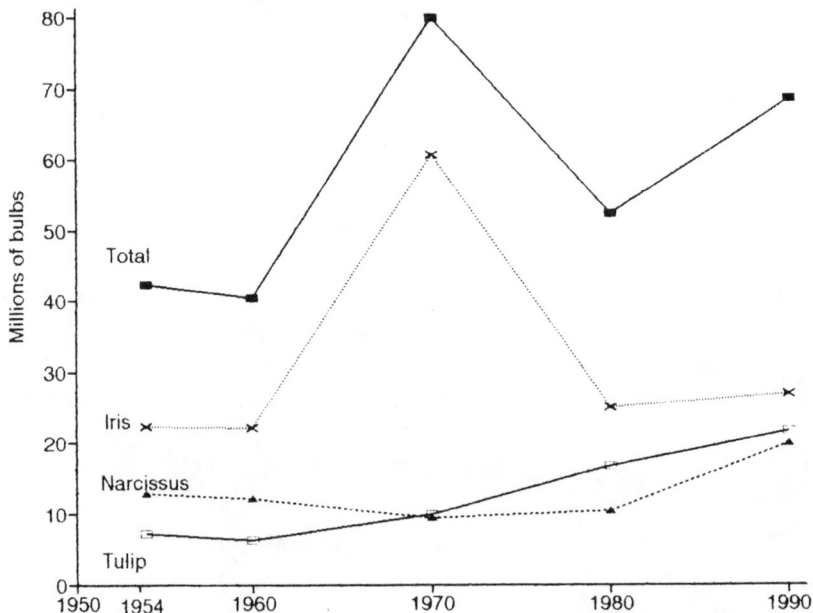

Figure 8-1. Number of Iris, Narcissus and Tulip bulbs sold, 1954 to 1990.

The number of Iris bulbs sold remained relatively stable until the early 1960s when Iris production almost exploded, in response to European demand. In 1970, growers sold a total of 79.8 million bulbs in domestic and foreign markets. Again the proportions had changed: 60.6 million Iris, 9.4 million Narcissus and 9.9 million Tulips. Three-fourths of all bulbs sold were Iris!

Freeze damage to Washington crops in the winter of 1978/79 cut production so sharply that sales of Iris bulbs dropped from 52.5 million in 1978 to 16.0 million in 1979. Narcissus sales were reduced from 9.6 to 7.4 million. Tulips were injured that winter, also, but to a lesser extent, dropping from 14.4 to 11.7 million. In percentages, there were 70% fewer Iris, 30% fewer Narcissus and 11% fewer Tulip bulbs sold in 1979 than in 1978 (Table 7-1 in Chapter 7).

The number sold of all three types of bulbs increased to a peak of 80.5 million in 1988, declined to 70.6 million in 1989 and to 68.5 million in 1990, perhaps as a result of the increased use of bulbs by growers for their own flower production.

140

Table 8-1. Sales of bulbs in millions by counties.*

Counties	1960	1970	1980	1988	1989	1990
IRIS						
Clark+Cowlitz	1,300,000	9,518,250	1,798,500	3,144,000	2,516,550	3,662,200
Lewis	—	1,538,680	8,168,650	7,850,950	6,825,675	—
Pierce	8,274,872	17,967,600	282,580	3,380,715	2,332,265	1,877,510
Skagit+Island	11,580,589	33,109,300	21,487,359	18,676,005	13,689,400	14,602,000
TOTAL	**22,155,461**	**60,595,150**	**25,107,119**	**33,369,370**	**26,389,165**	**26,967,385**
NARCISSUS						
Clark+Cowlitz	950,000	1,303,500	572,583	1,299,000	1,886,205	1,643,740
Grays Harbor	—	—	326,000	—	—	—
Pierce	8,821,580	4,273,348	2,666,490	6,091,398	4,791,716	3,765,110
Skagit+Island	2,279,256	3,793,885	6,796,593	17,103,083	17,866,427	14,437,725
Thurston	15,500	—	—	106,000	220,000	14,722
TOTAL	**12,066,336**	**9,370,733**	**10,361,666**	**24,599,481**	**24,766,348**	**19,861,297**
TULIPS						
Clark+Cowlitz	40,000	281,750	—	2,049,350	2,919,800	1,082,350
Grays Harbor	—			56,600	24,250	31,050
Lewis	—	—		4,925,250	5,035,145	—
Pierce	2,267,019	2,105,155	4,505,313	2,377,150	1,000,715	3,250,776
Skagit+Island	3,861,600	2,240,800	1,377,270	13,557,450	10,581,850	12,249,150
Thurston	40,600	7,330,355	13,298,400			
TOTAL	**6,210,969****	**9,852,885**	**16,780,825**	**22,545,863**	**19,451,865**	**21,648,471**
TOTAL BY COUNTIES						
Clark+Cowlitz	3,290,000	11,103,500	2,371,083	5,193,350	5,436,350	4,744,550
Grays Harbor	—		326,000	1,355,600	1,910,455	1,674,790
Lewis	—		3,643,835	12,673,963	12,776,200	11,860,820
Pierce	19,363,471	24,481,748	4,326,340	11,849,263	8,124,696	8,893,396
Skagit+Island	17,721,445	44,233,520	41,582,352	49,336,538	42,137,677	41,288,875
Thurston	56,100	—		106,000	222,000	14,722
GRAND TOTAL	**40,432,766****	**79,818,768**	**52,249,610**	**80,514,714**	**70,607,378**	**68,477,153**
TOTAL BY TYPE OF BULB						
IRIS	22,155,461	60,595,150	25,107,119	33,369,370	26,389,165	26,967,385
NARCISSUS	12,066,336	9,370,733	10,361,666	24,599,481	24,766,348	19,861,297
TULIPS	6,210,969	9,852,885	16,780,825	22,545,863	19,451,865	21,648,471

* Source of data: Washington State Bulb Commission. Some data were reported as bulb sales by pounds or dollars and were converted as follows: Iris-4½¢/bulb; Narcissus=6¢/bulb or 6 bulbs/lb; and Tulips=4¢/bulb or 10 bulbs/lb.

** Includes 1,750 Tulip bulbs sold in King county in 1960.

Bulb production soon reflects market demands. More Tulips were sold in Washington State in the early 1900s, more Narcissus in the 1930s. Since 1954, sales of Iris bulbs have outnumbered both of the others. Iris sales were three times those for Narcissus and Tulips combined in 1970. Proportions in the sales of all three types are more equal now.

If the 80 million INT bulbs sold in 1988 are added to an estimated 12 million bulbs used by the growers to produce field-cut and forced flowers, and these are added to an estimated 7 million bulbs of other types such as Lilies, Gladiolus and Crocus, then Washington State sold about 100 million bulbs in 1988. The bulb business indeed, has come a long way since 1930 when bulb sales totalled 14 million bulbs!

Bulb Prices

Bulb prices have fluctuated widely since the 1920s for many reasons including severe weather conditions, surpluses or shortages, fluctuations in dollar exchange values, changing demands and markets, development of better varieties and shifts in public preferences. Under normal conditions, prices obtained by Washington growers are related to Dutch prices, because their industry is so much larger. Washington bulbs do command a premium price however, because they bloom earlier, more uniformly and have more deeply colored flowers.

Narcissus prices increased rapidly in response to the Daffodil Quarantine of 1926 as would be expected (Table 8-2). Other bulb prices rose at the same time, although most were not directly affected by the Quarantine. Prices dropped as the Depression worsened after 1930 and there was a surplus of Washington Narcissus from 1932 to 1935. Prices rose moderately during the World War II years. After the war, many foreign bulbs were imported, prices dropped, and Washington bulbs were squeezed out of the late forcing market. Again, surpluses developed. In 1951, the Washington Department of Agriculture estimated that over one million Narcissus, over four million Iris and almost a million Tulips could not be sold (46). Once again prices fell. In 1952, Wedgwood Iris from Holland were selling on the East Coast for $15.80 per 1,000 bulbs wholesale while $40/1,000 was asked for Washington Iris (116), a price which later was reduced to $24. At the same time, Fryar stated that Washington production costs were twice as high as pre-war costs but that bulb prices had risen only a third (46).

Table 8-2. Average wholesale prices in dollars per 1,000 bulbs from 1920 to 1931.*

	1920	1921	1922	1923	1924	1925	1926	1927	1928	1929	1930	1931
Hyacinths	55.0	46.2	49.1	50.0	57.3	81.0	90.8	89.2	93.3	85.0	76.7	71.7
Iris	35.0	30.0	35.0	36.0	38.0	40.0	45.0	50.0	35.0	30.0	30.0	30.0
Narcissus (general)	37.6	40.3	40.9	41.5	42.8	46.1	76.6	82.3	78.9	71.5	65.3	57.9
Narcissus (King Alfred)	120.0	60.0	70.0	75.0	95.0	100.0	200.0	200.0	150.0	125.0	125.0	120.0
Tulips	37.0	31.0	31.5	32.5	33.2	38.2	40.7	36.3	35.0	32.8	31.5	29.8

*From Rieman, Table 11, p. 16; and Table B, p. 138 for King Alfred bulbs (105).

Bulb acreage slowly increased to 1,880 acres in 1949 and then gradually dropped to a low of 1,285 acres in 1959 in response to the low bulb prices. The only bright spot in this depressing period was the Iris situation. Iris acreage reached a low point of 322 acres in 1955 (Table 3-3 in Chapter 3), but rebounded faster than that of Narcissus and Tulips for reasons described later in this chapter.

The 1950s were a transition period for bulb growers and many small farmers dropped out for a number of reasons. Production costs were increasing and prices for bulbs did not keep pace. Sales of bulbs for use in greenhouses, except for Iris, were diminishing as shipments of field-cut flowers from the West Coast and other areas increased; dry sales were just beginning to pick up; and forcing by local growers was in its infancy.

Prices began to stabilize somewhat in the 1970s for both Narcissus and Tulips as growers became less dependent upon the greenhouse forcing trade. Sales to the dry sale trade and to California growers for field-cut flower production increased. More bulbs were also used by growers for production of flowers.

Prices continued to increase in the 1980s. The average prices paid by one national jobber to growers for their bulbs in 1989 are shown in Table 8-3, with the caveat that prices are variable between varieties, quantities purchased, etc. These prices are about double the prices paid in 1973.

In conclusion, the prices of both bulbs and flowers are always subject to the laws of supply and demand. If either of these crops is damaged by freezing in Holland or Washington, for example, and a shortage occurs, prices naturally rise. As one jobber said, "It's unfortunate that the good fortunes of bulb growers in one area depend upon the misfortunes of others elsewhere to a considerable extent!"

143

Table 8-3. Average prices per thousand bulbs paid to growers by one jobber in 1989. Size is circumference in centimeters.

Iris		Narcissus		Tulips	
Size in cm	Price in $	Size in cm	Price in $	Size in cm	Price in $
11 & up	60	19 & up	190	12 & up	70
10-11	55	17-19	140	11-12	55
9-10	45	15-17	100	10-11	25
8½-9	35	13-15	75		

Sales Outlets for Bulbs

The necessity for prompt response to changing markets is a way of life for bulb growers. In the early days, both bulbs and flowers were sold locally. After 1915, Mary Stewart and George Lawler began selling bulbs through catalogs. During the 1920s, the greenhouse forcing market for bulbs became increasingly important as larger quantities of Northwest bulbs were produced and it was worthwhile for eastern jobbers to handle them. By 1930, about 90% of Narcissus and, presumably, of Iris and Tulip bulbs as well, were sold for greenhouse forcing in the Midwest and East (105).

Bulb sales slowed during the Depression years of 1932 to 1935, surpluses of Narcissus developed, and many small growers quit, while others retrenched. Money was scarce. Si Van Lierop worked for Ed Orton and remembered that sometimes he was paid off in bulbs or flowers which he and his wife then sold in Puyallup and Tacoma.

As economic conditions returned to normal, the demand for Washington bulbs for forcing continued to grow until the Daffodil Quarantine was revoked in 1938 by the Reciprocal Trade Agreement Act. Large numbers of Dutch bulbs began to arrive, competing with Washington bulbs for American markets. Then, the outbreak of World War II cut off the importation of most foreign bulbs after 1939 and the demand for Washington bulbs took all that the growers had available. Gasoline rationing and labor shortages, however, kept growers from expanding much during those years. When bulbs were imported again after the war, surpluses again developed and prices dropped.

Dick Fryar described these conditions in 1952: "In the past, let us say up to 1941, we had a market of sorts; from 1942 to 1945 we had a war market that took everything we could produce; since 1945 we have had a market fraught with many vexations and not very much surety, either as to distributions or monetary returns" (46).

Fryar continued: "In the present market which roughly has continued since 1946, the one big item of change has been brought about by the effect of imports upon the obtainable price to be had for domestic stocks . . . The principal result has been to force the domestic producer out of the big late forcing market for daffodil stocks . . . In conclusion, . . . we would say that the markets of the past were passable, those of the present are palatable if not perfect and those of the future packed with peril" (46).

In 1944, Galvin stated that "About ninety percent of all Washington tulip and narcissus bulbs are used in the greenhouse forcing trade" (47). By 1950, the greenhouse-forcing market was still the major outlet for Washington bulbs but the future for it did not appear to be very bright. Fortunately, two other markets were opening up. One was the demand for Washington bulbs for field-cut flower production which is discussed elsewhere. The other actually began in the late 1930s when increasing numbers of Washington bulbs, especially Tulips, were needed for the dry sale trade in seed stores and for the catalog trade. These sales continued and, later, included many Narcissus and a few Iris bulbs as well. At the Bulb Growers Short Course in 1955, George K. Ball (George J. Ball, Inc., Chicago) commented that: "During the past decade, the market for forcing bulbs has decreased while the market for bulbs for outdoor home planting has attached itself to the coat-tails of the building boom and really has gone places . . . I firmly believe that expansion into this dry-bulb market is one of the master keys to your prosperity as individual growers and to the entire Northwest bulb growing industry" (9).

In 1956 Ted Sabelis said, in regard to the dry sale trade: "It is, relatively speaking, a brand new field for the Northwest and we are making some serious mistakes in our approach to it. This may have come about because the first efforts in this direction were made with surplus bulbs and the Northwest considered the dry sale trade at first as a sort of salvage operation for surplus bulbs . . . It will not be long now before there are more bulbs going into the dry sale trade than the entire florist trade absorbs, and since we undoubtedly will have to depend on this type of trade for the greater part of our future livelihood, it is high time we approach it with the respect it is due" and "our future in the flower industry because of new merchandising methods still has to be proven; in the dry sale trade, we know it is there. After all, the surpluses we talk about, may seem big to us, but they are very small indeed if you consider the enormous potential market that we have not even scratched yet" (117).

Fortunately, this dry sale market continued to grow and in 1990 absorbed about 40% of the Washington Narcissus, 30% of the Tulips and 5% of the Iris bulb production (Table 8-4).

Table 8-4. Estimated markets by percent for Washington-grown bulbs in 1990.*

	Bulb Type		
Sold or used for	Iris	Narcissus	Tulips
Forcing elsewhere	35%	15%	0%
Forcing and field-cut flower production by Washington growers	10	40	70
Field-cut flower production in California	50	5	0
Dry sales	5	40	30

* Estimated by Ted Sabelis.

Although sales of Narcissus and Tulip bulbs to greenhouse forcers diminished, those of Iris bulbs continued in the United States. In addition, the demand in Europe from 1954 to 1980 for Washington Iris bulbs was especially strong for reasons explained in the next section.

As George Ball pointed out in 1955 (9), the greenhouse forcing market for Washington Narcissus bulbs had been adversely affected by the shipping of field-cut flowers from North Carolina, Texas, California and the Northwest. The introduction of cargo planes and refrigerated trucks hastened the decline of the greenhouse market for bulbs because flowers could be delivered faster and in better condition to eastern markets from the West Coast. The field-cut flower market became an increasingly important source of income to growers in the spring. After all, as one large grower stated in 1990, "Why concentrate only on selling bulbs when you can sell an Iris flower for 10-20¢, which is at least twice as much as the bulb would bring?"

Development of the California field-cut flower industry along the coast from San Francisco to San Diego provided another market for Washington bulbs. Since the climate in southern California does not favor bulb production, the growers purchase large numbers of Washington Iris and some Narcissus bulbs each year to renew their plantings.

The latest development is the forcing by growers of their own bulbs in plastic or glass greenhouses. A few growers, such as Case Van Lierop at Bothell, began forcing bulbs and selling the flowers on the local market in the 1930s but the major development started in the 1950s and 1960s when growers decided to begin forcing their surplus bulbs themselves. This market has continued and expanded. At present, over 70% of the income of the Van Lierop Bulb Farms and many other large farms comes from forced and field-cut flowers. The Washington Bulb Company, the largest bulb farm in Washington, has 7½ acres in greenhouses in which they force millions of their own bulbs, as well as imported bulbs, every year. Forcing, at first, was a way to use extra large or surplus bulbs or varieties the trade didn't like. Now, varieties are grown specifically with the cut-flower market in mind.

A few other current trends should be mentioned. Bulbs, especially Narcissus and Tulips, are now sold in smaller quantities. Earlier, sales to greenhouses were often 100,000 bulbs or more at a time; now, a sale of 10,000 Narcissus constitutes a large order. On the other hand, millions of Iris may be ordered at one time by California field-cut flower producers, but are not all shipped at once. Instead they are programmed for certain conditioning treatments such as heating and cooling, held in storage by growers or jobbers and then shipped weekly to California.

To summarize the current sales outlet situation, most Washington Iris bulbs are now sold for greenhouse forcing or for field-cut flower production in California. Most Tulips are forced by bulb growers, used for field-cut flower production or sold for dry sales. Most Narcissus are used for field-cut flower production, or for grower-forcing or sold to the dry sale market. The greenhouse demand for large Narcissus bulbs has been decreasing while orders for smaller bulbs to plant in pots has been increasing. Table 8-5 gives an estimated breakdown of past and present major markets.

147

Table 8-5. Relative importance of different markets for Washington-grown bulbs from 1900 to 1989 (+ = minor to +++++ = major).*

Bulb type	Type of market	1900	1910	1920	1930	1940	1950	1960	1970	1980	1990
IRIS	Local retailing of bulbs and flowers	+++++	++++	+++	++	++	++	++	++	++	++
	Catalog sales	-	+	+	++	++	++	++	++	++	++
	For greenhouse forcing elsewhere in the United States	-	-	+	+++	+++	++++	+++++	++++++	+++++	++++
	For greenhouse forcing by local growers	-	-	.	.	.	+	++	++	++	++
	For field-cut flower production by local growers	-	-	.	.	.	+	+	+	++	+
	To California growers for field-cut flower production	-	-	.	.	.	+	++	+++	+++	+++++
	"Dry sales" to seed stores, etc.	-	-	.	.	.	+	+	+	+	+
	For greenhouse forcing in Europe and British Isles	-	-	.	.	.	.	++++	+++++	++	+
NARCISSUS	Local retailing of bulbs and flowers	+++++	++++	++++	++	++	++	++	++	++	++
	Catalog sales	-	-	+++	+++	++	++	++	+++	+++	++
	For greenhouse forcing elsewhere in the United States	-	-	+	+++++	++++++	+++++	+++	+++	+++	+++
	For greenhouse forcing by local growers	+	-	.	.	.	.	++	++	+++	++
	For field-cut flower production	+	+	+	+	++	+++	++++	++++	++++	+++++
	To California growers for field-cut flower production	-	-	.	.	.	+	++	++	+	+
	"Dry sales" to seed stores, etc.	-	+	+	+	+	++	+++	++	++	+++++
TULIPS	Local retailing of bulbs and flowers	+++++	++++	+++	++	++	++	++	++	++	++
	Catalog sales	-	+	+++	+++	++	++	++	++	++	+
	For greenhouse forcing elsewhere in the United States	-	-	.	+	+++	+++	+++	+++	+	.
	For greenhouse forcing by local growers	-	-	.	.	+	+	++	+++	++++	+++++
	For field-cut flower production by local growers	-	-	.	.	.	+	+++	+++	+++	+++
	To California growers for field-cut flower production	-	-	.	.	.	.	+	++	++	+
	"Dry sales" to seed stores, etc.	-	+	.	+	+++	+++	+++	++++	++	+++

* Based upon literature review and comments by Ted Sabelis. The same bulbs which produced field-cut flowers in the spring may be sold for dry sales in the summer.

148

Exports

Although most Washington-grown bulbs are used within the United States, some have been exported every year to Canada and, at times, to other countries as well. Since 1969, bulbs were exported in one or more years to thirteen countries: Argentina, Australia, Canada, Denmark, France, French Polynesia, Germany, Japan, Netherlands, New Zealand, Russia (USSR), South Africa and Switzerland. Exports have been of all types of bulbs. In 1963, growers shipped to Canada: 458,750 Iris bulbs, 241,835 Gladiolus corms, 157,587 Tulip bulbs, 51,300 Narcissus bulbs and 2,500 Crocus bulbs. Unfortunately, such data on the number of bulbs of specific types were seldom reported by the Washington State Department of Agriculture.

Nor does the United States Department of Commerce report on the numbers of different types of bulbs exported from Washington State. It does provide data on the total numbers of bulbs, tubers, corms, crowns, rhizomes, etc. and their total value. Other data indicate that bulbs were the major component of this group. As to the dollar value, the department reported in 1991 that $790,317 worth of bulbs were shipped to Canada, $6,791 to France and $111,836 to Japan. Exports to Japan have doubled since 1988.

The dollar values of bulbs, corms, etc. exported from the Seattle Customs District to major countries between 1969 and 1991 are shown in Table 8-6. Some Washington bulbs may have been exported also from the Columbia-Snake River (Portland) Customs District.

Although all kinds of Washington bulbs have been and still are being exported, Iris was the most important type from 1955 to 1981 but the numbers have fluctuated widely. The Iris export data, reported by the Washington Department of Agriculture for the years 1955 to 1986, are shown in Figure 8-2 and listed in Table 3-3 (Chapter 3). Unfortunately, the data specify the number of bulbs sent to Europe in the following three years only: 1957 (when 0.9 million bulbs were exported), 1963 (14.2) and 1981 (3.8). Some additional data were found in newspapers, magazines, etc.

Prior to 1953, the demand for Wedgwood Iris, the most popular forcing variety at the time, had been relatively stable, but both Dutch and American growers finally produced so many bulbs that surpluses developed and prices fell sharply. To reduce this surplus, more than 90% of Washington growers voluntarily reduced their acreage by 25% in 1953 and Dutch growers also cut their production of Wedgwood bulbs that year. Ironically, in the winter of 1953/54, Holland experienced an unusually severe freeze. Bulb yields, in general, and those of Iris, in particular, were drastically reduced and, in 1954, several Dutch bulb dealers bought Washington-grown Iris to fulfill their contracts.

Table 8-6. Exports of bulbs, corms, crowns, tubers, rhizomes, etc. from Seattle in thousands of dollars, 1969-1991.*

Year	Canada	Netherlands	France	Others	Total
1969	$ 40	$ 0	$ 0	$ 1	$ 41
1970	66	0	0	16	82
1971	36	57	0	1	94
1972	74	68	8	51	202
1973	72	0	1	7	80
1974	147	34	1	36	217
1975	198	7	6	8	219
1976	221	234	0	19	473
1977	251	0	0	6	257
1978	383	83	3	13	482
1979	481	167	0	9	657
1980	443	225	29	9	706
1981	680	217	0	30	927
1982	757	0	41	4	802
1983	677	35	0	4	716
1984	506	17	0	8	531
1985	269	8	5	15	297
1986	305	6	0	9	320
1987	553	68	0	16	637
1988	460	10	14	7	491
1989	323	5	0	57	385
1990	454	0	0	76	530
1991	790	0	7	112	909

* Data from United States Department of Commerce, Bureau of the Census. Data rounded off.

The dealers had reason to feel comfortable about purchasing Washington bulbs because Joe Berger and Cor Roozekrans (of the old Washington Bulb Company) had sold some Iris to a jobber and a forcer in Holland in 1952 and/or 1953 and the bulbs had produced excellent flowers. The 1954 importation introduced the high quality, deep color,

PICKING TULIPS, Mount Vernon, 1984
(Washington Bulb Company)

DAFFODILS, Orting, 1966, with Mt. Rainier
in the background (C. Gould)

HYACINTHS,
Hatch Ranch,
McMillan,
1969
(C. Gould)

CROFT EASTER LILIES,
Westport, 1940s (Roy McCue)

QUEEN'S FLOAT, Puyallup Valley Daffodil Festival, 1961
(Roy McCue)

IRIS FIELD, Mossyrock, 1987
(Jack DeGoede)

'FIRECRACKER' LILIES, Mossyrock, 1976
(Ed McRae)

TULIPS, Mount Vernon, Washington Bulb
Company, 1985 (C. Gould)

earliness and uniformity of bloom of Washington Iris bulbs to the entire European continent. This high quality was primarily due to Washington's climate. Another major contributing factor, according to growers, was the use of heat curing and other treatments resulting from the cooperative research of USDA and WSU scientists from 1948 to 1971.

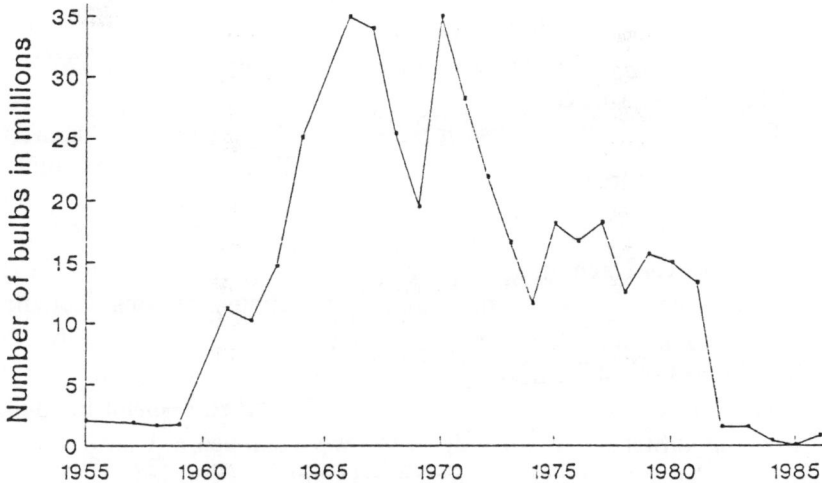

**Figure 8-2. Exports of Iris bulbs to foreign countries
from Washington State, 1955 to 1986.**

The number of Iris bulbs shipped to Europe in 1954 is unknown, but almost two million were sent in 1955. Demand, at first, was greatest in Sweden where Iris forcing during the dark winter months is difficult. In 1957, 857,750 Iris bulbs were sold to Sweden and 76,000 to Holland in addition to those exported to Canada. Other markets in Europe soon opened up including those in France, Denmark, Finland, Western Germany, England and especially those in the Channel Islands of Guernsey and Jersey, which became Washington's best customers.

By 1958, Washington growers couldn't fill the demand but Iris acreage increased only slightly from 322 acres in 1955 to 367 in 1958. The growers' reluctance to expand their acreage at first, was probably due to their vivid memory of plowing under 25% of their crop in 1953. The European market for Washington Iris, however, continued to increase dramatically and growers then began to enlarge their plantings. Iris acreage almost doubled from 367 acres in 1958 to 622 acres in 1965.

151

Washington bulbs were a desirable commodity. Ted Sabelis quoted the *Guernsey Press* for February 1, 1965 about recent experiments run at the Guernsey States Experiment Station: "Eighty-eight samples of Wedgwood Iris originating from several countries—Holland, the State of Washington and France—were grown under identical circumstances and, in every instance, the Washington-grown bulbs bloomed earlier, more vigorously and with a much higher percentage of bloom." The report concluded that "American Iris appeared much more suitable for earliest forcing" and recommended its findings to the 1,400 flower growers on the Island of Guernsey.

Twenty-five million bulbs, or 40% of Washington's Iris crop, were exported in 1964 (39). In 1966 and, again in 1970, almost 35 million Iris bulbs were exported each year (40), of which half were reportedly sent to the Channel Islands (13). In the seven years from 1966 to 1972, 199 million Iris were exported. Exports continued to increase until 1970, after which they tapered off for a number of economic reasons, including increased competition from French, Israeli and treated Dutch bulbs; the increased cost of oil for heating greenhouses; adverse fluctuations in the United States dollar exchange rate; and the increased demand for bulbs in the United States. Only 4 million Iris were shipped to Canada and to Europe in 1981—a huge drop from the 35 million exported in 1970.

After the initial success of Washington Iris in Europe, some Dutch bulb firms tried contracting for production with local vegetable farmers in the Brittany area of France and, by 1967, these farmers had bulbs available for early forcing. Brittany is located at about the same latitude and has about the same average temperature and total rainfall as does Washington State. The major difference between them is the timing of rainfall. Brittany gets most of its rain during the summer; Washington's rainfall is lightest in summer. Drier summers accelerate the maturing, digging and curing of bulbs. Washington Iris are still considered the best for color, size and number of blooms produced, although Brittany's bulbs bloom slightly earlier.

The production of Iris bulbs for early forcing was tried also in other countries including the Island of Malta and the Galilee area of Israel, where flowers naturally bloom earlier. The Dutch also began experimenting with heat curing and other treatments which improved the earliness and quality of their Iris. By 1970, the Israeli Iris were the earliest to bloom in greenhouses, followed in sequence by those from France, Washington State and Holland.

Washington bulbs still had the same high quality but they were also more expensive. Competition in world markets increased and Washington Iris bulb exports declined from 35 million in 1970 to 0.8 million in 1986, the last year for which a record is available. Limited numbers of bulbs are still exported occasionally when there is severe freezing weather in Holland, as occurred in 1987. Although bulb exports to most other countries have diminished, those to Canada have continued, as can be seen in Table 8-6.

CHAPTER 9

Flower Sales

The sale of flowers was probably the major source of income for the bulb pioneers in the early 1900s. Bulb sales gradually became more important after 1920, but now flowers are once again the most important overall source of revenue for Narcissus and Tulip growers. Only Iris producers still receive more income from bulbs than from flower sales.

Narcissus flowers were being sold in Tacoma by Edwin Wines at least as early as 1910, and this may have provided the stimulus which caused George Lawler to get into the cut-flower business the same year. Lawler sold first to Tacoma florists but, when they could no longer absorb his output, he began selling Narcissus on street corners and, still later, began shipping them to Seattle and other nearby cities. The numbers sold were small by today's standards but they represented an important step in the evolution of the bulb business in Washington State (Figure 9-1).

After the explosive increase of bulb acreage in the mid-twenties, the local flower markets were soon saturated, so growers had to develop new outlets for their flowers and began shipping to eastern markets. The March 31, 1928 issue of the *Tacoma News Tribune* shows a picture of Frank Chervenka, president of the Puget Sound Bulb Exchange, loading an iced railroad car with 400,000 Narcissus blooms destined for Chicago. Smaller lots also were being shipped daily by express. Unfortunately, these flowers had a relatively short shelf (vase) life because of the long trip and unreliable temperature controls on the trains. Greenhouse forcers in the midwest also began complaining about the importation of such flowers and argued that they competed directly with their own flowers forced from bulbs bought from Northwest bulb growers. In response to those complaints, when the Northwest Bulb Growers Association was reorganized in 1930, one of its first acts was to urge all members to stop cutting flowers and the majority of growers adhered to the request for a while.

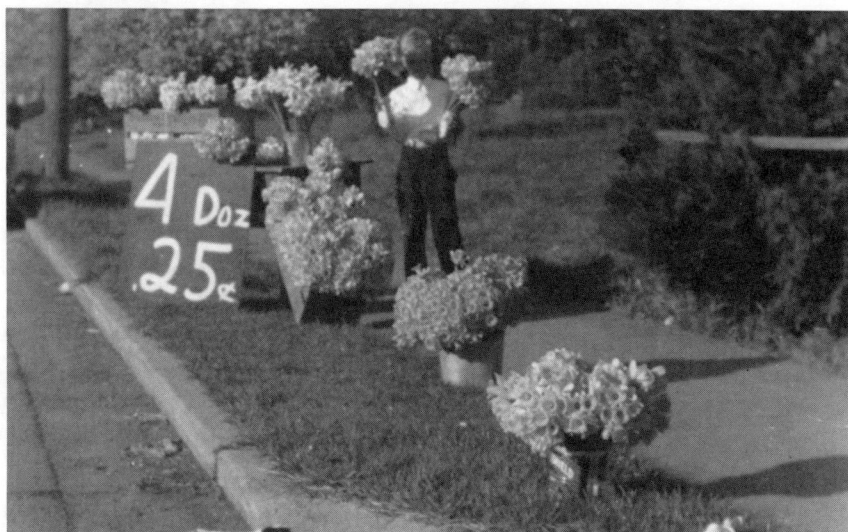

Figure 9-1. Young Chuck Lubbe selling Daffodils on a
Puyallup street corner, 1941. (Courtesy Chuck Lubbe)

Riemann (105) stated in 1931 that "to the commercial producer of bulbs, the flowers may properly be regarded as a by-product of no great value." Flower prices must have been very low at that time to justify such a statement.

In addition to the complaints from midwest greenhouse forcers, another factor contributed to the growers' decision to restrict flower sales. This was the belief that flower cutting substantially reduced subsequent bulb yield, because the flower stem functions as a leaf in food production. In later research, Kalin (77) showed that picking Narcissus flowers in the bud stage reduced bulb yield by about 2% in total weight but decreased the yield of large bulbs by 7.4%. One large grower who cuts many flowers stated that he harvests about the same size of bulbs that he plants, but he has to replace the stock every few years because of the accumulation of viruses and other problems. This applies to Narcissus on which the leaves are not cut. When he harvests Tulip flowers, he is careful to leave at least two leaves on each plant. His field-cut Iris flowers are usually obtained only from small (8 cm) heat-treated bulbs or from "mother" bulbs which had produced flowers the previous year and were, therefore, unsalable.

The anti-flower cutting effort survived reasonably well until the depth of the Depression when some growers began augmenting their income

155

with field-cut flowers. These growers argued in favor of cutting because the financial return on bulbs was inadequate; the flowers gave them a source of income in the spring without their having to borrow money from the banks to carry them through to the fall sales of bulbs; and cut flowers were already being shipped to major markets from North Carolina, California and elsewhere.

Flower sales continued to increase because, as R. G. Fryar stated in 1948: "There is growing concern among some wholesale buyers of bulbs concerning the effect of field-grown flowers being shipped into the midwest and some Eastern markets. There are instances where rather large forcers have refused to buy anything more than their "pre-cool" requirements because of these field-grown shipments. If this should really get bad, we would only have the pre-cool market to supply and that would make for a surplus of [King] Alfred bulbs right now" (45).

Growers' interest in selling flowers continued to increase for several reasons. Large imports of foreign bulbs created surpluses and depressed bulb prices; the introduction of refrigerated railroad cars and trucks enabled growers to deliver fresher flowers which commanded a better price; and flower shipments and their value increased even more when air transportation became increasingly available and cost-competitive after World War II.

The *Seattle Times* rotogravure printed a picture on April 14, 1946 of Narcissus flowers being packed in Seattle for shipment to Minneapolis on Northwest Airlines. By 1948, United Airlines was sending one or two cargoliners full of flowers daily to California and the eastern United States. The airlines advertised that the flowers picked one day went on sale the next day in New York City (122).

Field cutting of Narcissus flowers continued to increase and, between 1951 and 1955, the annual sales ranged from 18 to almost 23 million blooms. Disappointingly, prices per thousand flowers dropped steadily from $10.34 in 1951 to $6.51 in 1954 rising slightly to $6.63 in 1955 (36). In an effort to stabilize prices, reduce expenses and obtain more uniformity in grading, eight growers organized the Puyallup Valley Flower Cooperative in 1956 with Francis Chervenka as president and manager. The Cooperative handled only King Alfred flowers the first year, but later included all Narcissus varieties. It was so effective for Narcissus that, in 1959, a similar cooperative, Tulip Flowers, Inc., was organized to sell Tulip blooms, with Wallace Staatz as manager. The two flower cooperatives merged in 1964 to share the advantage of a single marketing agency for all types of bulb flowers. Refer to Chapter 17 for more details.

In 1976, the Puyallup Valley Flower Cooperative alone shipped more than 15 million Narcissus, 6 million Tulips and 1 million Iris flowers to markets all over the United States. It also sold another 3 million Narcissus blooms for use during the Daffodil Festival for floats, street sales and other purposes. This Cooperative is still active but its membership is now down to three local grower members.

The latest trend in flower production is that of growers forcing their own bulbs in glass or plastic greenhouses. The bulb types used are primarily Tulips and Narcissus with fewer Iris and Lilies. The largest forcer is the Washington Bulb Company which built its first greenhouse in 1967 and, in 1991, had 7½ acres under plastic and glass. It produces several million cut-flowers of Narcissus, Iris, Tulips and Lilies annually.

The forcing of their own bulbs, coupled with the increased field-cutting of flowers and the decreased sales of bulbs of Narcissus and Tulips, has resulted in a dramatic shift of income to bulb growers. Many growers now obtain 70% or more of their total income from sales of forced and field-cut flowers (Figures 9-2 and 9-3).

The number of flowers picked per acre varies with the type, variety and sizes of bulbs planted; the density of planting; the weather; the availability of pickers; and, naturally, with the demand, which is greatest at holiday periods. During the early 1950s, the average number of Narcissus flowers cut ranged from 10,000 to 50,000 per acre. Now, with denser plantings, it is possible to pick 77,000 flowers per acre as one grower did in 1988, when he shipped a total of 5 million Narcissus blooms from his 65-acre field. The harvest of Tulip flowers ranges from 25,000 to 50,000 or more per acre, while the yield of Iris may vary from 10,000 to 25,000 flowers per acre depending upon the size of bulbs planted. A major limiting factor in field-cut flower sales in recent years has been the lack of enough flower pickers during peak times, especially when the weather is cold and wet.

The price paid to growers for field-cut flowers in 1989 was about 10-20¢/flower for Iris, 7-10¢ for Narcissus, and 10-15¢ for Tulips. Since flower prices are often higher than bulb prices, it is not surprising that many growers now obtain a large percentage of their income from flower sales.

Figure 9-2. Picking Narcissus. (Courtesy Washington Bulb Company)

Figure 9-3. Forcing Tulips. (Courtesy Washington Bulb Company)

Questions are often asked as to the number of flowers sold by Washington State growers. Since official statistics on flower production are not available, only estimates can be made. Using conservative averages for flower production per acre and the number of acres involved in flower production in 1989, the totals may have been about 5 million Iris, 50 million Narcissus and 15 million Tulips for a grand total of 70 million flowers. Estimates of the dollar value of those 70 million flowers in 1989 approximate $6 million. If the number of greenhouse-forced INT flowers, field-cut Gladiolus and Lilies are included, the total number could be over 80 million flowers.

There is considerable competition for markets. California field-cut Narcissus flowers are usually available in January and February; those from coastal Oregon come in February and March; Washington flowers bloom in March and April. Naturally, weather can accelerate or delay blooming by one or two weeks, so, when the southern regions are late, and the northern ones early, a glut occurs and prices drop. Timing is everything. Holidays bring heavy demand and good prices. Unfortunately, the weather and the bulbs do not always cooperate!

The flower markets themselves are changing also. Most flowers originally were sold to local florists or used for street sales. When growers began shipping flowers in large quantities, they were usually sold to wholesalers in major cities who resold some to florists, and sold others for street sales and for special events such as promotions by large department stores. Many bulb flowers are now sold through supermarket chains which have established flower shops in their own stores.

In summary, a reduced number of Washington-grown Narcissus bulbs are sold now for greenhouse forcing elsewhere and these are only for the earliest market, for the quality trade or for planting in pots. Growers are using most of their bulbs for forcing and for the field cutting of flowers. Most of the growers' income from Tulips also is derived from flower sales with only a small proportion coming from the sale of bulbs to the dry sale trade. Income from the sale of Iris flowers, however, is still less than that from the sale of Iris bulbs.

Demand is increasing for unusual flowers and colors. Although the average American still prefers his Narcissus to be large and yellow and his Iris to be a dark blue, he or she is beginning to buy more pastel shades of Tulips. This reflects the popularity of the lavenders, mauves, pinks and paler colors which have been so popular recently in the fashion world. Growers, such as Marilyn Gardner, Leo Roozen and Tom De Goede, now must anticipate trends in colors years in advance (144). Reports indicate that flower sales are increasing in the United States.

CHAPTER 10

Washington State's Flower Bulb Industry
What's It Worth?

Flowering bulb fields catch everyone's eye. They not only attract tourists but they provide material for festivals, TV shows, calendars and authors. They enable Chambers of Commerce to brag about their locations and they stimulate the sale of thousands of rolls of color film. The flower bulb industry receives lots of public attention during the blooming season but its contributions to Washington State's agricultural economy are seldom noted or appreciated.

Bulbs are not even listed among the forty most important agricultural commodities in the annual reports published by the Washington Agricultural Statistics Service. Instead, they are lumped with nursery and greenhouse products. Even mushrooms, mink and sheep are included in this list although their economic values are much less than that of bulbs. Washington leads all other states in the production of Iris, Narcissus and Tulip bulbs, but this is rarely mentioned in official publications. In addition to their value, an impressive 70 million bulbs and 70 million flowers were sold in 1989 (Figure 10-1).

This industry is much more than just beauty. It's dollars, too. Total gross income for 1989, alone, is estimated to have been over $2 million for Iris, almost $3 million for Tulips and more than $6 million for Narcissus (Table 10-1 and Figure 10-2). If an estimated gross yield of $5,000 for each of the 133 acres of Lilies, Gladiolus and minor crops is added, the total value of the Washington State bulb industry exceeded $12 million in 1989. This would place it 27th in the list of the top 40 agricultural commodities in the state, just below carrots and much above strawberries, cranberries and oats! (146) And that $12 million figure does not include an estimate of the additional income to growers who force many of their own, as well as millions of imported bulbs, in their greenhouses.

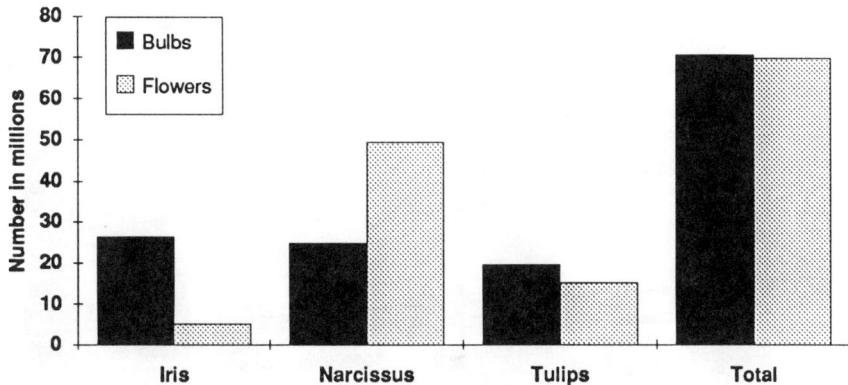

Figure 10-1. Number of bulbs and estimated
number of field cut flowers sold in 1989.

Table 10-1. Estimated total gross income from sales of Iris, Narcissus and Tulip
bulbs and field-cut bulb flowers in Washington State in 1989.

Crop	Iris	Narcissus	Tulips	Grand total
Bulbs	$1,297,200	$3,076.822	$1,069,640	$5,443,662
Flowers (field-cut)	775,500	3,455,550	1,824,000	6,055,050
Total gross income	$2,072,700	$6,532,372	$2,893,640	$11,498,712

The calculations in the paragraph above are based upon the data and estimates shown in Table 3-3 and Chapters 6, 8 and 9. This includes the Washington Department of Agriculture figures for the number of acres in bulb production and the author's data for additional acreage used only for flower production in 1989. It should be noted, however, that the figures for flower production and its value are general estimates only, obtained from several growers. They are not supported by actual data such as those for bulb sales as reported to the Washington State Bulb Commission.

Bulb and flower production and the income received from them are subject to many variables including those of weather, labor supply, markets and surpluses as discussed in Chapters 6 and 7. Annual returns for individual crops could be double that reported above in a better than average year, but half or less in a poor year. Farming is still a gamble, even with modern technology and, consequently, growers' incomes may vary considerably from year to year.

161

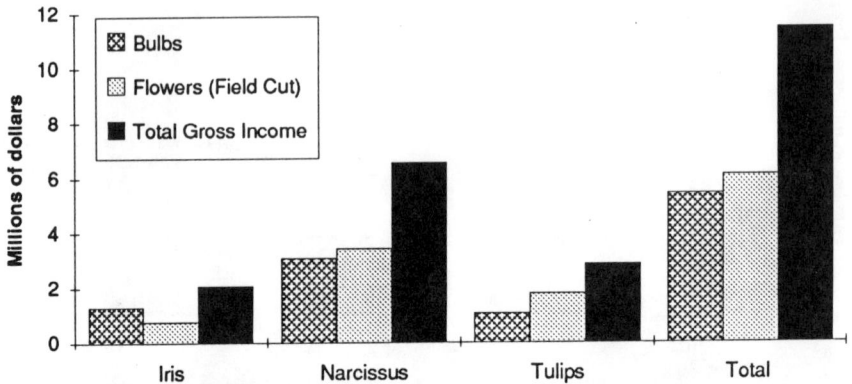

Figure 10-2. Estimated value of sales of bulbs and field-cut flowers in 1989.

The value of the bulb industry has grown rapidly in the past 21 years. The estimated 1989 income of $12 million is almost seven times larger than the $1,804,520 estimated in 1968 (149). In that year, income from flower sales was about a third of that from bulbs ($407,595 for flowers; $1,396,925 for bulbs). Since 1968, however, the number of flowers sold by growers has risen dramatically and the price of flowers has increased at least five-fold, greatly increasing growers' income. The price of bulbs however, only doubled during the same period, so the natural trend has been toward an increase in flower sales and a leveling off of bulb sales. Many growers have stated that, in 1991, more than 70% of their gross income was derived from the sales of field-cut and forced flowers.

Most of the $12 million income from the bulb industry remains in Washington State. It provides year-round employment for hundreds of people as well as part-time work for two to three thousand more during flower picking and bulb harvesting periods. The industry buys large quantities of local products including equipment, fertilizers, pesticides and many other materials. It also contributes substantially to the tax income of local, state and federal governments.

But, no matter how valuable the bulb industry is in terms of dollars and cents, the general public probably will continue to believe its greatest contribution is the beauty it brings to western Washington at a dark and gloomy time of the year.

CHAPTER 11

Quarantine and Inspection

Commercial production of bulbs in Washington State increased rather slowly from 1900 to the early 1920s. In 1922, it was greatly stimulated by a decision of the United States Department of Agriculture (USDA) to restrict entry of Narcissus and certain other bulbs after January 1, 1926. In announcing the regulation (No. 14) made under Quarantine 37, the USDA stated on December 22, 1922 that: "Information derived through inspection of import shipments of bulbs since 1919 indicates that there is a considerable element of danger in such importations in that they carry insect pests, the risk of establishment of which in this country cannot be entirely eliminated by inspection and disinfection. That risk increases directly with the volume, variety and diversity of origin of the imports. Continuance of this risk through such imports is, therefore, only justified for such reasonable time as may be required to establish the commercial production of the several important species of bulbs in the country" (143). This regulation applied not only to Narcissus, but also to Iris, Gladiolus, Montbretias and Dahlias.

A domestic quarantine (No. 62) also was placed by the USDA on Narcissus in 1926 "as an additional safeguard to prevent further distribution of these pests [nematodes and insects] in this country, all shipments of Narcissus bulbs imported under permit in limited quantities for propagation purposes were given hot water treatment under the supervision of inspectors of this [USDA] Department" (143). The state Department of Agriculture issued a similar order (No. 5) regarding the control of nematodes in Narcissus bulbs in Washington. According to the USDA restrictions, the importation of Narcissus bulbs after 1926 was limited to 100,000 bulbs per permittee until 1929 when it was reduced to 25,000. Varieties such as King Alfred and Spring Glory, of which there was ample domestic production, were not allowed to be imported. Then, in 1931, the limit was raised again to 100,000 for certain varieties which were needed for propagation in the United States.

163

Prior to the quarantine, Dr. Griffiths of the USDA had fought an uphill battle trying to get American farmers interested in raising bulbs. As Rockwell reported, "Griffiths made little progress until the Department of Agriculture, alarmed at the entry into the United States of such pests as the Japanese beetle and the Dutch elm disease, decided to apply quarantine regulation to some imported bulbs and tubers" (107).

The anticipated quarantine spurred farmers in Washington and other states, as well as representatives of Dutch bulb firms, to import Narcissus bulbs into the United States before the deadline. Imports rose from 77 million in 1922 to 142 million in 1926 (Table 12-1, Chapter 12).

The quarantine was in effect for about 10 years but efforts were started early by importers and others to weaken its provisions. In opposition, about 1934, H. F. Gronen of Puyallup organized the American Narcissus Growers Association with representatives from all the major Narcissus-producing states, to fight for continuing the quarantine. It was revoked on December 15, 1936 with the provision that imported Narcissus bulbs had to be given the latest improved treatment in hot water plus formaldehyde, which adversely affected flowering the first year. Two years later, such treatment was ruled unnecessary under the Reciprocal Trade Agreements Act of 1938 (effective August 15, 1939), provided the bulbs were inspected and found to be free of pests. The number of imported Narcissus bulbs rose from 0.6 million in 1936 to 3 million in 1938, and jumped to 11 million in 1939. Imports during the World War II years were negligible.

Still later, the USDA became concerned with the golden nematode present in certain foreign bulb fields. It was a very dangerous pest, not only to bulbs, but to other crops as well. As a result, the USDA issued an order, effective July 11, 1950, requiring all imported bulbs to be free of soil and to be accompanied by a certificate stating that the bulbs were grown on land uninfested by golden nematodes, and that inspection had been made during both the growing and the shipping seasons.

Another development was the adoption in 1951 of a pre-entry or foreign-site inspection at foreign locations from which bulbs were exported. This was done to speed up inspection, reduce delays in shipping, and to reduce costs. The USDA paid the salaries of its inspectors but foreign cooperators paid all other expenses.

USDA inspectors in Seattle previously examined bulbs grown in Washington and issued Phytosanitary Export Certificates for export to foreign countries. Now (1992), the Washington State Department of Agriculture does all the inspecting and issuing of "Phytos."

A change in inspection requirements was announced in 1991. All of the previous rules (WAC 16-484-020 through WAC 16-484-100) pertaining to Washington State's Narcissus Bulb Quarantine were repealed by the Washington State Department of Agriculture on June 15, 1991. However, there will be both field and shed inspection of Iris and Narcissus bulbs intended for export. Bulbs which will be used only for domestic flower production by the growers will not be inspected.

Washington State Department of Agriculture Inspection

Through its inspection, the State Department of Agriculture has helped growers to keep bulb diseases and insects under control and has also helped to prevent the introduction of pests on imported bulbs. The first available inspection report was one made by Ralph Marble in 1927. This inspection was primarily done to check for the nematode (*Ditylenchus dipsaci*) and bulb fly (*Merodon equestris*) in Narcissus. It was later expanded to include the nematode *(Ditylenchus destructor)* on Iris.

George Eade, Chief Nursery Inspector, reported that, in 1944, 10% of the Narcissus acreage in Washington State was still infected with the bulb and stem nematode. It was, also, not uncommon to find bulb fly larvae ranging from 1-8% and basal rot from 2-20% in salable bulbs. However, by 1963, the nematode-infestation was less than 1% and it was unusual to find bulb fly larvae. In the late 1940s the percent of nematode-infested Iris ranged from 0 to 30% of salable bulbs. By 1963, nematodes were found only occasionally and in a very low percentage (38).

Formerly, WSU and USDA scientists and extension workers cooperated frequently with the horticultural inspectors, assisting them in the diagnoses of unusual problems and in recommendation of treatments. Now, in 1992, the Washington Department of Agriculture has its own staff of professionals, including five entomologists, one plant pathologist and a technician, working with ten field inspectors of which three or four work on bulbs whenever necessary. C. Alan Pettibone is the present Director of the Department of Agriculture; Bill Brookreson is assistant Director of the Plant Services Division; Don Alexander is the Plant Protection Branch Manager; Thomas Dabalos is Nursery Field Staff Supervisor and Don Williams is Plant Pathology Program Manager. The inspectors in 1992 were: Bellingham (John Wraspir), Kent (Thomas Dabalos, Dennis Mangun, Doug Colley and Shelly Haywood), Mount Vernon (Gary Whitwer), Spokane (Richard Webley), Vancouver (Scott Rose) and Yakima (Phil Beauchene and Sherryl Stoltenow). John S. Burnett is in charge of the USDA Plant Quarantine Office in Seattle and Dr. Mitchell Nelson is their Plant Pathologist.

Biographical information, unfortunately, is available for only a few of the inspectors. Three are provided below and three others (Ted Knoblauch, Ralph Marble and Henry Reynolds), who grew bulbs at one time, are included in Chapter 5. The State Department of Agriculture does not have a complete list of their bulb inspectors, but the names and dates that we have been able to find are listed in Table 11-1.

Eade, George W.

George Eade (1905-1988, Sumner) was born in South Dakota and received his M.S. degree at South Dakota State University in 1931. He began working for the USDA in 1929 on barberry eradication in South Dakota and, in 1943, became a farm planner for the Soil Conservation Service. In 1944 George became an inspector in the Washington State Department of Agriculture. He was made Chief Nursery Inspector in 1948 and, in 1963, was placed in charge of plant certification in Washington. He retired in 1968. George was very likeable, knowledgeable and firm, but fair, in his dealings with bulb growers.

McCue, Roy

Roy McCue (Sumner) was raised in Yakima and started as a horticultural inspector for the Washington State Department of Agriculture in eastern Washington in 1939 checking on pear psylla. He was transferred to Vancouver in 1943 where he first became acquainted with the inspection of bulbs. In 1962 he was moved to Bellingham where he specialized in certified potato tuber production. Of course, like all inspectors, he was often called on to inspect many other plants including those in farms and nurseries as well as bulbs. He retired on January 1, 1970 to devote more time to his hobby of photography.

Whitinger, Clyde B.

Clyde Whitinger (Mount Vernon) was born in 1904 on a farm near Ames, IA. In 1911 his parents, with their four sons, moved to an apple

166

farm at Cashmere and later to another one near Brewster, WA. Clyde began working for the Washington Department of Agriculture as a part-time apple inspector in 1926, was transferred to western Washington as a full-time inspector in 1928 and to Mount Vernon in 1934, retiring there in 1969. From 1970 to 1980 Clyde was a part-time consultant-inspector for several bulb companies and, from 1982 to 1987, he worked full time during the bulb grading season for the Washington Bulb Company.

Table 11-1. Horticultural inspectors who were active in bulb inspection in Washington State.

Inspector	(Born-Died)	Years known to have been active in bulb inspection
Andrews, Howard		1945-1949
Bach, Jim		1988 - ?
Bjork, Mervin		1954-1957
Brown, Wm. (USDA)		1965 - ?
Bryan, Homer R. (USDA)		1965-1976
Burnett, John S. (USDA)		1965-1993
Dabalos, Thomas		1971-1993
DeGrave, Bernard		1965 - ?
Eade, George	(1905-1988)	1948-1968
Fulmer, W. L.		1943-1948
Ginnis, Tom		1959-1972
Grubb, Wayne		1946-1948
Huff, Henry (HY)		1923-1927
Hurd, Art		1971-1977
Kern, Ray		1946-1965
King, Louis	(? - 1992)	1946-1963
Knoblauch, Ted A.	(1908-1990)	1930-1965
Luce, Paul		1946-1973
Mangun, Dennis		1974-1993
Marble, Ralph S.	(1898-1983)	1927-1930
McCue, Roy		1947-1970
O'Donnell, Dan		1942 - ?
Paul, Clarence		1965 - ?
Rebhan, Robert		1978-1988
Reynolds, Henry	(1899-1972)	1925-1942
Rodenhurst, R. J.		1945-1949
Rose, Scott		1986-1993
Stillinger, Ray (USDA)		1933 - ?
Stoltenow, Sherryl		1992-1993
Truong, Thuan		1989-1991
Whitinger, Clyde		1946-1965
Whitwer, Gary		1977-1993
Williamson, Henry		1947-1948
Wraspir, John		1979-1993
Zerwekh, Vernon J.		1946-1948

CHAPTER 12

Bulb Imports and Tariff Rates

Commercial bulb growing had been slowly increasing in several areas of the United States for fifty or more years prior to 1922. On December 22 of that year it received a strong impetus when the USDA announced that imports of Narcissus and certain other bulbs would be curtailed in 1926 for the phytosanitary reasons described in Chapter 11.

As a result, imports of Narcissus bulbs jumped from 77 million in 1922 to 142 million in 1926 as shown in Table 12-1. A few Narcissus of certain desired varieties were imported subsequently for propagation purposes by growers under a special permit, but the numbers were relatively small. The quarantine was lifted in 1938 and large imports were resumed but the 142 million figure for imports of Narcissus bulbs in 1926 has never been exceeded.

Table 12-1. Narcissus bulbs. Imports into the United States, 1922-1939[*]

Year	Numbers of bulbs	Year	Numbers of bulbs	Year	Numbers of bulbs
1922	77,270,548	1928	15,869,000	1934	918,977
1923	77,193,281	1929	12,770,000	1935	247,825
1924	92,659,666	1930	6,003,563	1936	662,511
1925	106,314,049	1931	1,085,656	1937	6,056,103
1926	142,384,199	1932	1,048,474	1938	2,802,846
1927	40,506,000	1933	274,605	1939	11,381,571

* Source: Riemann (105) and United States Department of Commerce.

The Quarantine was supposed to go into effect on January 1, 1926. Therefore, either the date was extended, or a large number of special import permits were issued to growers, in order to account for the huge number of Narcissus bulbs imported in 1926.

Total imports of Iris (I), Narcissus (N) and Tulip (T) bulbs from all countries steadily increased from 106 million in 1920 to 209 million in 1929, decreased somewhat during the Depression and especially during the World War II years. They ranged between 152 to 222 million bulbs until 1979 when imports began a dramatic rise, increasing to 500 million INT bulbs in 1991. This appears to be a startling number but it actually averages out to only two bulbs per person in the United States. The import data for INT are shown for 10 year intervals from 1920 until 1990 in Figure 12-1 and are listed by years in Table 12-3.

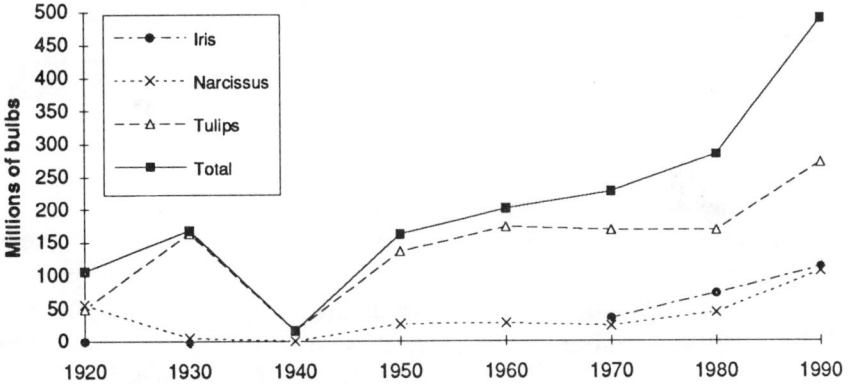

Figure 12-1. Imports in millions of Iris,Narcissus and Tulip bulbs into the United States in representative years.

Tulips have always been the most popular type of bulb imported into the United States and represented 47% of total imports of INT in 1920 and 57% in 1991, increasing in actual numbers from 50 to 286 million bulbs during that time. Iris imports increased proportionally more than Tulips did, rising from 100 thousand in 1920 to 92 million in 1991, while Narcissus doubled from 56 to 121 million. Hyacinth imports have remained relatively stable since 1947, ranging between 20 and 32 million bulbs in spite of the increase in United States population from 106,021,537 in 1920 to 248,709,873 in 1990.

Many countries have sent bulbs to the United States but Holland has been the major supplier for many years and now leads in all the main types of bulbs and corms. It shipped 760 million bulbs or 94% of the total bulb imports to the US in 1990. The other main suppliers are the United Kingdom and Israel. These three leading countries sent us 99.8% of all bulbs imported in 1990 (Table 12-2).

169

Table 12-2. Imports into the United States of major flowering bulbs and corms in millions by country of origin in 1990.*

Country	Crocus	Gladiolus	Hyacinth	Iris	Lily	Narcissus	Tulips	Total
Afghanistan							.03	.03
Australia				.02				.02
Canada		.10			.10		.06	.26
China					.57	.03		.60
Hong Kong					Tr	Tr		Tr
Israel			.02	4.40	Tr	14.66		19.08
Japan	.02		Tr	.18	.01	.04	.09	.34
Malaysia					Tr			Tr
Netherlands	60.42	162.26	29.79	107.40	59.60	70.48	270.33	760.29
New Zealand					.15			.15
United Kingdom	.26		.06		.47	25.81	.80	27.40
Total	60.70	162.36	29.87	111.98	60.93	111.02	271.31	808.17

* Source: IM 146. United States Imports for Consumption, Bureau of Census, United States Department of Commerce. Totals are rounded off. Tr = fewer than 10,000 bulbs.

Although the Narcissus acreage in England is over twice as large as that in Holland (Table 1-1), the latter country sent us almost three times more of these bulbs in 1990. Imports of Narcissus from Israel jumped from 1.9 to 14.7 million between 1978 and 1990 and imports of Iris, from 0.9 to 4.4 million bulbs. Japan's main bulb export recently, has been Tulips and, during the last ten years, the numbers usually ranged between two and three million bulbs, but in 1990 they shipped only 93,400 to the United States. Mali was a new bulb exporter to the United States in 1989, sending 60,000 Narcissus, 160,000 Tulips and 40,000 Hyacinths, but none in 1990.

Lilies have been imported from many countries. Bermuda was a major exporter of Lilies before 1900 until a virus disease wrecked its industry. Subsequently, Japan became a major Lily producer and, in 1937, exported over 40 million bulbs to all countries, including the United States. Japan, of course, lost the American market to the West Coast Croft Lily growers during World War II and never recaptured it. However, since 1984, imports of Lily bulbs have increased dramatically. Holland is now the major supplier, sending 98% of the 61 million Lily bulbs imported into the United States in 1990.

The total number of bulbs imported into the State of Washington has also increased. There were three million INT bulbs imported in 1978 and 16 million in 1988. Iris imports for the same period rose from 0.8 to 9.8 million bulbs; Tulips climbed from 1.8 to 6.1 million; while Narcissus dropped from 0.4 to 0.2 million. Many of these, especially Tulips, were probably imported for forcing by Washington growers.

170

Table 12-3. Imports of certain bulbs and corms into the United States in millions from 1920 to 1991.*

Year	Gladiolus**	Hyacinths	Iris	Lilies	Narcissus	Tulips	Total INT**
1920	3.1	16.4	.1	14.5	56.0	50.0	106.1
1921	3.3	22.6	4.0	22.5	78.0	55.1	137.1
1922	1.3	24.8	.6	8.2	77.3	64.8	142.7
1923	6.4	29.1	2.2	9.1	77.2	76.7	156.1
1924	8.1	32.2	3.0	9.7	92.7	92.5	188.2
1925	1.6	27.9	4.5	11.2	106.3	96.3	207.1
1926	1.9	23.7	2.5	16.0	142.4	106.8	251.7
1927	.8	23.7	4.2	16.2	40.5	129.7	174.4
1928	1.6	22.1	6.3	19.9	15.9	161.9	184.1
1929	.4	21.5	4.1	21.5	12.8	192.0	208.9
1930	.02	20.3	1.3	20.7	6.0***	163.6	170.9
1931		19.9	2.9	17.5	1.1	120.9	124.9
1932				14.2	1.0	91.0	92.0
1933				16.8	.3	66.6	66.9
1934				18.0	.9	71.0	71.9
1935				20.9	.2	75.2	75.4
1936				24.3	.7	88.6	89.3
1937		19.1		26.2	6.1	100.1	106.2
1938		17.5		23.4	2.8	98.4	101.2
1939		19.8		24.3	11.4	112.3	123.7
1940		.2		26.4	.2	16.1	16.3
1941		.2		1.8	.1	34.4	34.5
1942		.5		1.5	.01	27.3	27.3
1943		.2		2.2	.001	13.6	13.6
1944		.1		2.1	.003	4.0	4.0
1945		8.5		3.0	11.5	51.2	62.7
1946		17.7		3.3	32.0	100.3	132.3
1947		16.6		2.3	24.6	96.0	120.6
1948		19.6		2.2	21.4	107.3	128.7
1949		22.9		4.6	23.5	129.0	152.5
1950		24.3		4.6	26.5	136.3	162.8
1951		23.7		5.8	25.1	141.0	166.1
1952		24.9		6.3	28.3	166.0	194.3
1953		26.6		6.0	30.3	171.3	201.6
1954		27.2		5.4	27.8	167.7	195.5
1955		27.1		5.1	26.9	168.2	195.1
1956		26.8		5.7	25.8	167.1	192.9
1957		27.7		6.0	28.6	178.4	207.0
1958		28.5		5.4	28.0	178.9	206.9
1959		27.5		7.1	26.9	179.3	206.2

*   1920-1930 data from Riemann (105). Other data from IM 146, U.S. Department of Commerce. Totals are rounded off.

**   Iris and Gladiolus import data combined with data on miscellaneous bulbs by U.S. Department of Commerce for years 1931-1962. (171)

***   Estimated.

171

Table 12-3. (Continued). Imports of certain bulbs and corms into the United States in millions from 1920 to 1991.*

Year	Gladiolus**	Hyacinths	Iris	Lilies	Narcissus	Tulips	Total INT**
1960		27.5		5.4	27.6	173.2	200.8
1961		24.2		5.4	23.4	160.7	184.1
1962	3.9	23.4		5.9	21.5	150.1	171.6
1963	6.8	19.7	22.6	2.2	17.6	112.1	152.3
1964	86.2	21.4	26.2	4.1	19.5	142.4	188.1
1965	127.7	22.4	23.6	3.4	19.6	153.1	196.3
1966	115.5	21.6	21.8	3.8	21.7	155.5	199.0
1967	86.6	21.6	38.8	3.0	21.1	153.7	213.6
1968	104.1	24.5	22.3	2.9	23.1	152.0	197.4
1969	125.7	25.1	31.7	3.3	24.2	164.3	220.2
1970	119.9	24.6	27.5	3.2	25.6	168.8	221.9
1971	114.7	21.9	24.0	3.7	24.8	147.8	196.6
1972	118.6	24.5	30.4	4.7	25.7	156.4	212.5
1973	99.9	21.3	29.6	3.5	26.3	155.3	211.2
1974	88.1	20.9	32.6	3.3	30.0	158.9	221.5
1975	44.4	21.6	32.1	2.6	30.9	151.9	214.9
1976	76.2	21.4	29.3	2.3	29.0	143.6	201.9
1977	75.7	22.8	28.1	2.7	27.5	141.9	197.5
1978	100.4	23.4	34.3	2.5	30.3	140.6	205.2
1979	92.4	25.0	62.4	2.5	35.4	157.0	254.8
1980	84.8	22.5	72.5	3.9	43.5	167.8	283.8
1981	67.6	21.5	54.8	6.0	52.2	180.6	287.6
1982	73.1	22.6	59.1	5.7	51.8	186.2	297.1
1983	77.3	24.6	67.9	7.7	59.6	205.0	332.5
1984	81.0	27.0	95.5	15.5	72.9	246.7	415.1
1985	73.2	31.2	93.7	26.0	84.9	287.9	466.5
1986	118.6	29.9	99.2	35.8	89.2	287.4	475.8
1987	136.0	27.0	79.5	36.8	85.2	254.0	418.7
1988	136.5	27.4	82.5	37.2	80.7	263.2	426.4
1989	155.5	28.5	103.3	42.6	93.4	263.5	460.2
1990	162.4	29.9	112.0	61.0	111.0	271.3	494.3
1991	155.8	31.8	92.3	62.2	121.1	286.5	499.9

Tariff Rates on Imported Bulbs

Tariffs were good fund raisers for the United States Treasury in the early years. Beginning in 1936, tariff rates on bulbs were gradually reduced despite vehement objections by United States commercial bulb growers who felt that they were entitled to as much protection as other industries had. Nevertheless, rates continued to decline. Tariff rates since 1913 are shown in Table 12-4. These were the general rates which, in

172

1990, applied to most-favored nations, including the Netherlands and the United Kingdom. Bulbs from countries in a special category, such as Israel and Canada, were allowed in free of charge. A third category included such countries as the USSR and bulbs from them were charged appreciably higher rates, such as $6 per thousand for Tulips.

Table 12-4. United States import tariffs on certain bulbs and corms, 1913-1990. * (Rates in dollars per 1,000 bulbs or percent Ad Valorem)

Bulb type	1913	1922	1930	1936	1948	1950	1952	1958	1962	1963	1968	1980
											Year	
Effective date of new rate	?	9/22	6/18	6/12	6/15	7/1	7/1	7/1	7/1	7/1	1/1	1/1
Hyacinth**	$2.50	$4	$4	15%	$2	$2	$2	$2	$1.35	$0.75	$0.72	$0.60
Lily**	$5	$2	$6	$5	$6	$6	$4.5	$3	$2.37	$1.75	$1.57	$0.87
Narcissus	$1	$2	$6	$6	$6	$5	$3	$3	$2.55	$2.10	$2.10	$2.10
Tulips	$1	$2	$6	$3	$3	$3	$2	$2	$1.70	$1.40	$1.40	$1.40
Iris**	$5	30%	30%	15%	10%	10%	7.5%	7.5%	6.5%	5.5%	5.5%	5.5%
Gladiolus	$5	30%	30%	15%	10%	10%	7.5%	7.5%	6.5%	5.5%	5.5%	5.5%

* Data based upon a summary prepared by Mr. Lin Su for Mr. E. Gil Whitson, Chief, Publication Division Office of Tariff Affairs and Trade Agreements, United States International Trade Commission, Washington, D.C., and 1913 data from an accompanying report on Tariffs (November 19, 1990).

** Staged rate reductions (Kennedy Round) beginning January 1, 1968 for Hyacinths and Lilies and January 1, 1980 (Tokyo Round) for Iris.

CHAPTER 13

Bulb Varieties

This history is concerned primarily with Narcissus (Daffodils), bulbous Iris and Tulips because they have been the basis of the bulb industry in Washington State for at least the last 80 years. The acreages of Gladiolus and Lilies were appreciably smaller. Allium, Colchicum, Crocus, Dahlias, Hyacinths, rhizomatous Iris and other minor bulb types have often been grown also, but in limited quantities.

Few of the bulb types grown commercially in Washington are native to the United States. Most came originally from foreign countries, particularly those around the Mediterranean Sea, but the bulbs have been altered by extensive hybridization and by the selection of sports. Much of this work has been done in England for Narcissus and in Holland for the other types of bulbs, but many good varieties have been developed in the United States and other countries by both amateur and commercial growers. As a result, thousands of new varieties of Iris, Narcissus, Tulips and other types of bulbs and corms have been introduced during the past three hundred years. For example, during the 20-year period from 1968 to 1987, 3,466 new varieties of Narcissus were registered by the Royal Horticultural Society of London.

Fashions in flowers and popular demand have caused a shift in production from one variety or genus to another. Few of the varieties grown in volume even 50 years ago are commercially important today. Old varieties were replaced by new ones because they had some special feature such as larger and brighter flowers, more rapid propagation, better disease and insect resistance or other more favorable features. Pastel colors, for example, have recently become increasingly popular in Tulips for floral arrangements. Gladiolus were much more popular 40 years ago than they are today. Economic factors also cause production changes. At one time there was a small, but thriving, Hyacinth industry in Washington State and high quality bulbs were produced. Growers finally stopped raising them because they required too much hand labor

175

during the busy harvesting season of other bulbs. Some of these trends and the reasons for them are discussed in the following pages.

The first bulbs planted in Washington State before 1900 were of many different types. Hyacinths, Tulips, Freesias and Lilies were perhaps the most common ones at first, followed by Narcissus and still later by Iris.

In the early 1900s, growers in Whatcom County concentrated on Tulips while growers in other counties raised more Narcissus. Beginning in 1922, Narcissus became the favorite, especially as the 1926 Quarantine deadline approached. By 1930, Narcissus was planted on 90% of the total bulb acreage in Washington State and even today occupies the largest acreage although Iris and Tulip bulbs are produced in greater numbers.

Gladiolus and Easter Lilies were much more popular in the 1940s and 1950s than they are today, but, even at their peak, the total area planted probably never exceeded 200 acres each. Interest in their culture in Washington decreased when the coastal areas of California and Oregon were found to be better culturally for Easter Lilies and when Gladiolus proved too susceptible to Botrytis blight and Stromatinia corm rot to justify large-scale commercial production in western Washington.

The bulb industry of Washington State developed around three bulb varieties: the King Alfred Narcissus, the Wedgwood Iris and, to a lesser extent, the Croft Easter Lily. Narcissus, Iris and Tulips are discussed in the following pages, and Gladiolus and Lilies in separate chapters.

Narcissus

Golden Spur was the leading variety until the 1920s when King Alfred became more popular and remained in the lead until the 1970s. In 1951 King Alfred accounted for 95% of the 40 million Narcissus planted in Pierce County. It is a tetraploid variety and is hardy, propagates well, is reasonably disease resistant and produces a beautiful large yellow flower which holds up well in shipping. Unfortunately, the amateur English grower and hybridizer who developed it never lived to see his creation bloom. He was John Kendall, who may have crossed *Narcissus pseudonarcissus hispanicus* with the variety Empress (a triploid) to obtain this variety (153). His sons introduced King Alfred in 1899 at $30 per bulb. Oddly, the Royal Horticultural Society (England) did not consider it to be much good when it was first shown in 1912 and gave it a poor rating. The Society later changed its mind and the rating.

By 1923, George Lawler said that it had just passed the novelty stage in western Washington. King Alfred certainly proved its merits in the Pacific Northwest and elsewhere and was "King" for many years. But times change, and so do preferences for different types of flowers.

The most popular Narcissus varieties in 1989 in Washington included Dutch Master, Golden Harvest, Standard Value and Unsurpassable. These are all large yellow trumpets and indicate the American preference for that type of Narcissus.

The Washington Department of Agriculture and the USDA made an extremely comprehensive inspection of all Narcissus plantings in Washington in 1933. They reported that 51,809,700 bulbs had been planted of 393 different varieties and species. For historical purposes, the varieties of which more than 1 million bulbs were planted are listed in Table 13-1. King Alfred was the most popular followed by Golden Spur and Emperor. Very few of these varieties are grown today.

Table 13-1. Leading Narcissus varieties in Washington in 1933 by numbers of bulbs planted.*

Variety	Number in millions
Emperor	5.0
Glory of Sassenheim	1.7
Golden Spur	5.3
King Alfred	9.0
Laurens Koster	1.5
Minister Talma	2.2
Poeticus Recurvus	1.4
Sir Watkin	2.8
Spring Glory	1.9
Van Zion	2.2
Victoria	3.4

* Source: Stillinger, C.R. Varieties of Narcissus Reported in Washington in 1933 (Wash. Dept. Ag. Data). Mimeo.

Data on current acreages of different Narcissus varieties in production in Washington are not available. In order to demonstrate the trends in production, recent data for Holland are shown in Table 13-2 for the different classes and for individual varieties of which more than 25 acres were planted in 1991/92. Among the major classes, the acreages of Yellow Trumpets and Large Crown Narcissus have decreased the most while the Double and Cyclamineus types have increased. The following five varieties represented over 50% of the total Narcissus acreage in Holland in 1992: Carlton, Ice Follies, Dutch Master, Tete-A-Tete and Golden Harvest. Acreages of Carlton and Golden Harvest, however, have been declining since 1986, while those of Tete-A-Tete and Salome have been increasing. Only three acres were planted with King Alfred bulbs in 1991/92.

Table 13-2. Narcissus. Number of acres of major varieties and classes in Holland.*

Class	Variety	1985/86	1988/89	1991/92
YELLOW TRUMPET	TOTAL	1,045	1,005	859
	Dutch Master	335	380	307
	Exception	10	23	29
	Golden Harvest	456	360	299
	Gold Medal	29	31	31
	Standard Value	31	31	34
	Unsurpassable	63	45	29
BICOLOR TRUMPET	TOTAL	43	60	77
WHITE TRUMPET	TOTAL	37	41	44
	Mt. Hood	34	37	39
LARGE CROWN	TOTAL	1,888	1,921	1,476
	Carlton	1,100	901	621
	Flower Record	63	69	54
	Gigantic Star	47	51	56
	Ice Follies	337	444	302
	Prof. Einstein	30	30	26
	Salome	29	88	107
	Yellow Sun	92	84	60
SMALL CROWN	TOTAL	97	97	75
	Barrett Browning	70	67	43
DOUBLE	TOTAL	329	467	409
	Bridal Crown	11	23	31
	Cheerfulness	46	46	33
	Dick Wilden	56	110	84
	Flower Drift	38	49	30
	Sir Winston Churchill	10	15	25
	Tahiti	22	35	32
	Van Sion	40	45	41
TRIANDUS	TOTAL	51	55	38
CYCLAMINEUS	TOTAL	286	474	483
	February Gold	73	59	47
	Tete-A-Tete	154	347	360
JONQUILS	TOTAL	38	44	54
TAZETTA	TOTAL	107	152	143
	Geranium	40	39	58
	Minnow	27	61	47
POETICUS	TOTAL	11	10	14
SPECIES	TOTAL	7	9	15
SPLIT CROWN	TOTAL	32	86	73
OTHERS	TOTAL	39	34	26
GRAND TOTAL		4,002	4,454	3,786

* Source: Flowerbulb Inspection Service (BKD), Lisse, the Netherlands.

Iris

Blue has always been the most popular color in bulbous Iris, both here and in Holland, and the current trend is toward an ever darker blue for use in arrangements. Wedgwood, a variety of *Iris hollandica* Hoog., was one of the first varieties to be imported and grown by Washington growers and, by 1932, it was being grown in quantity. Wedgwood was probably developed in Holland but the circumstances are unknown. It became very popular, grew well and was very adaptable to early forcing in greenhouses with the proper heat curing and other temperature treatments. In 1964 about 80% of the Iris acreage in Washington State was devoted to this variety. Wedgwood remained the most popular variety until about 1970 when it was replaced by one of its own sports, a darker blue, called Ideal. Two other promising sports, Blue Sail and Blue Diamond, have been developed from Ideal. Blue Diamond is a darker blue than Ideal and eventually may replace it.

The most popular Iris variety in 1992 in Holland was Blue Magic which came from a cross of White Perfection x *I. tingitana*. Telstar is another good dark blue Iris. It is comparable to Ideal in bulb production and in foliage. Telstar blooms later than Ideal but earlier than Blue Ribbon does. Blue Ribbon (Prof. Blaauw) has been very popular both in the United States and in Holland. It is a blue Iris which is darker and larger but blooms later than does Wedgwood. Another blue, somewhat lighter in color than the others, is called Hildegarde. It has become very popular, especially for field-cut flower production. It was named for the wife of one of the pioneer bulb growers in Whatcom County, Harry Van Waveren.

One of the best white Iris is another sport of Wedgwood called White Wedgwood. It occasionally reverts to a blue tint but is still the most popular white variety grown in Holland.

Since data on Iris variety acreages in Washington are unavailable, the trends can be shown by data on major classes and varieties which were grown in Holland in recent years. See Table 13-3. Over 60% of the total Iris acreage in Holland in 1991/92 was represented by only four varieties: Blue Magic, Ideal, Blue Ribbon and Blue Diamond. Of these, only Blue Magic and Blue Diamond have increased in acreage since 1986 while Blue Ribbon, Ideal and White Wedgwood have decreased appreciably. Purple varieties have been growing in popularity while most other classes have been decreasing. Wedgwood acreage is now down to 0.8 of an acre in Holland.

Table 13-3. Iris. Number of acres of major varieties and classes in Holland.*

Color	Name	1985/86	1988/89	1991/92
BLUE	TOTAL	1,470	1,332	838
	Blue Diamond	49	116	135
	Blue Sail	6	15	17
	Blue Star	43	44	32
	Deep River	.02	1	11
	Hildegarde	69	123	70
	Ideal	674	448	241
	Prof. Blaauw			
	(Blue Ribbon)	511	468	213
	Sapphire Beauty	22	21	11
	Telstar	72	73	80
PURPLE	TOTAL	334	445	539
	Blue Magic	281	388	487
	Harry Hylkema	7	19	17
	Purple Sensation	39	21	22
YELLOW	TOTAL	79	69	61
	Royal Yellow	29	30	24
	Yellow Queen	7	9	12
YELLOW/WHITE	TOTAL	117	95	81
	Apollo	77	74	64
	Symphony	31	16	13
WHITE	TOTAL	281	199	137
	White Bridge	43	32	20
	White Cloud	28	22	16
	White Van Vliet	34	26	14
	White Wedgwood	155	108	64
AMBER, etc.	TOTAL	14	36	32
	Saturnus	8	25	18
RETICULATA + HYBRIDS	TOTAL	48	72	76
	Danfordiae	18	27	28
	Harmony	9	8	11
	Reticulata	18	31	27
ENGLISH	TOTAL	22	8	6
OTHERS	TOTAL	10	11	12
GRAND TOTAL		2,376	2,266	1,782

* Source: Flowerbulb Inspection Service (BKD), Lisse, the Netherlands.

180

Tulips

Tulips were one of the bulb types first planted by George Gibbs in 1892 and they have been grown ever since in Washington. However, there are so many different colors, sizes, etc., that it is difficult to summarize trends. The first varieties were presumably those most popular for home gardens but later the greenhouse-forcing types were raised most often commercially. Today, a combination of suitable types for forcing and for field production of cut flowers is usually grown. Since the 1950s, some of the most popular garden types in the United States have been those with huge, colorful blossoms, such as Red Emperor, developed by Dirk Lefeber in Holland.

There is an increasing demand, however, for pastel shades in Tulips for cut-flower sales. According to growers' comments in the 1990 Skagit Valley Tulip Festival Guide (144), there is more public demand for new colors than for new bulb varieties. Growers now have to anticipate flower color preferences two or three years in advance by watching trends in clothes and home decorating.

Tulips are still the most common type of bulb grown in Holland with 18,331 acres representing 66% of all spring-flowering bulb acreages in 1991/92. The largest acreage was in Triumph varieties, followed by Darwin hybrids. Acreages of the Greigii and other species, and of double-late and single early varieties increased while Darwin, single-late varieties and Fosteriana decreased the most between 1988 and 1992.

BREEDING NEW VARIETIES

Some hybridizing and selecting of sports has been done in Washington State with most bulb types. The work on Gladiolus and Lilies is described in their respective chapters. Hybridization of the others is discussed below.

Narcissus

The development of new Narcissus varieties never became as popular in Washington as it did in Holland, England and even Oregon. A few growers did some hybridizing but none of the varieties developed in Washington is in large scale production. A. N. Kanouse and his wife specialized in pink varieties and introduced several hybrids. Jac Lefeber

181

developed the popular Flower Record in Holland and continued hybridizing when he emigrated to Washington State. H. F. Gronen developed some hybrids and even Dr. Griffiths tried his hand at it, but no outstanding varieties seem to have resulted from these efforts.

Iris

C. W. Orton did considerable hybridizing of bulbous Iris, beginning about 1932. From his work came several varieties of which Pacific Gold, Yellow Prince, Moonlight, Snowdrift and Blue Princess were very promising in the USDA/WSU forcing tests at Beltsville, MD. Blue Princess is still grown on a limited scale. Earle Darst developed Moonlight Mist, Enchantress, Blue Pacific and several other varieties of which Henry De Goede had about four acres under cultivation for the dry sale trade in 1989. Other hybridizers include De Goede, Ed Orton and Burch Lemon. Lemon had several promising selections but, when he died suddenly, his stocks were lost.

Tulips

Since so many commercial growers and amateurs tried hybridizing other bulb crops, it would be surprising if they had not experimented with Tulips, but the only record we have is of three hybrids introduced by Karl Koehler sometime before he died in 1942.

* * * * * * * *

For information on distribution and classification of bulbs and related plants and descriptions of genera, species and cultivars, the reader is referred to the book on *Bulbs* by John E. Bryan, published by Timber Press, Inc., Portland, OR, 1989.

CHAPTER 14

Gladiolus

The popularity of all flowers appears to wax and wane and Gladiolus are no exception. Through the 1930s, and into the 1950s, they were much in demand but are much less popular today, at least in the Pacific Northwest.

Glads (Gladiolus) were probably brought in by the pioneers but did not become much of a commercial venture in Washington State until the 1920s. The fragmentary data available show a peak planting of 125 acres of Gladiolus in 1947. In recent years the acreage has probably ranged between 50 and 100 acres, with the majority being grown in the Yakima-Prosser area of eastern Washington where the corms grow larger, and with less disease, than they do in western Washington. The 88 acres of Glads in Washington in 1992 were grown primarily for cut-flower production.

Because of the former popularity of the flowers, there probably have been hundreds of persons who raised Gladiolus in Washington State but research has uncovered the names of only 134 commercial growers. Most of these were located in Western Washington. A list of some of the larger growers in the past includes Ralph Pommert at Pacific, Orville Roe and Ira Gregg at Auburn, Warren Dowling at Monroe, Earle Darst at George and Coupeville, and Henry DeGoede at Mount Vernon and Quincy. Both George and Quincy are in eastern Washington. After the early 1950s, the number of growers declined so that, by 1959, there were only three large commercial ones left in the Puget Sound area: Warren Dowling, Ira Gregg and Henry DeGoede. These and other known commercial Gladiolus growers in Washington State are listed in Appendix Table B.

Although Gladiolus are less popular today than they were previously, they are still used extensively by florists and are grown by many hobbyists and home gardeners. The popularity of varieties probably changes more rapidly with Gladiolus than with any other type of bulb.

Since there are no data available for the varieties currently being grown in Washington State and because of the close interaction between Washington and Holland, recent data on the 16 most popular varieties in Holland are shown in Table 14-1. These 16 made up 64% of the total (corm+cormel) acreage in that country in 1991.

Table 14-1. Gladiolus. Number of acres of major varieties and classes in Holland.*

Class	Variety	1990	1991	1992
RED	**TOTAL**	**779**	**824**	**747**
	Mascagni	222	252	208
	Traderhorn	262	265	242
LIGHT-RED	**TOTAL**	**810**	**769**	**724**
	Eurovision	159	174	166
	Hunting Song	368	338	275
	Victor Borge	213	200	214
ORANGE	**TOTAL**	**394**	**332**	**374**
	Peter Pears	303	226	296
YELLOW	**TOTAL**	**341**	**380**	**453**
	Nova Lux	143	163	232
ROSE	**TOTAL**	**1,008**	**1,018**	**1,129**
	Friendship	168	94	95
	Priscilla	223	221	273
	Rose Supreme	158	180	128
	Spic & Span	179	195	270
WHITE	**TOTAL**	**785**	**931**	**776**
	Amsterdam	79	91	86
	White Friendship	318	355	311
	White Prosperity	190	289	205
PURPLE	**TOTAL**	**260**	**316**	**362**
	Fidelio	71	88	91
SALMON/ APRICOT	**TOTAL**	**162**	**152**	**183**
	Jessica	70	60	89
NANUS	**TOTAL**	**60**	**54**	**54**
BLUE	**TOTAL**	**53**	**42**	**38**
TUBERGENII	**TOTAL**	**29**	**34**	**45**
ALL OTHERS	**TOTAL**	**100**	**106**	**83**
GRAND TOTAL		**4,781**	**4,958**	**4,968**

* Source: Flowerbulb Inspection Service (BKD), Lisse, the Netherlands. The 1992 data is preliminary.

Washington Gladiolus Society, Inc.

After some preliminary organizational meetings headed by Ralph Pommert in late 1928 and early 1929, the Washington Gladiolus Society was officially organized in 1929 and held its first annual meeting and show on August 16, 1929 at Woodland Park, Seattle. Fourteen members attended and elected Ralph Pommert as president; Fred L. Delkin, vice president and F. S. Martin, secretary/treasurer. Dues were set at $1 per year and anyone interested in Gladiolus could join. Most of the members were amateurs but many commercial growers also joined and they were the ones upon whom most of the burden of the shows fell. Some of the commercial growers served as officers at various times and, often, more than once. Growers also donated trophies such as silver cups, plaques, medals and ribbons to be awarded at the shows.

The annual show was the highlight of the year's activities, and was most often held in either Auburn or Tacoma about the middle of August. The 1952 show, for example, was held in Auburn on August 16 and 17, had 1,300 entries and was attended by 7,000-8,000 persons. There were dozens of different categories for both amateur and commercially grown flowers including 396 general categories with first, second and third prizes in each, in addition to special awards for junior growers and about 40 major awards involving permanent trophies, cups and medals for the best in each section or division. Grand prizes included the Grand Champion Spike, Reserve Champion Spike, Best Recent Introduction and Best Basket in the Show. Ribbons were bestowed generously. Almost anyone with good flowers went home with at least one or more awards.

The Society was very active from the 1940s to the 1960s, but as the popularity of Gladiolus flowers began to wane, so did the fortunes of the Society. For example, there were only 500 entries in the annual show in 1958 as compared with 1,300 in 1952. Available records show that there were 69 members in 1942, and 105 in 1947. After that the membership gradually declined. The Society held its last show in 1982 and it was decided in 1983 or early 1984 to disband. Ralph Pommert was asked to send the Society's records and remaining funds to the International Gladiolus Hall of Fame at the James A. Michener Library, Greeley, CO in the fall of 1984.

The fragmentary records available do not contain a complete list of Society presidents but they do include the names of Ralph Pommert,

Stewart Perry, Orville Roe, Warren Dowling, Erle Moran, Dan Rees and John Huff.

Hybridizers

More amateur and commercial growers probably have experimented with Gladiolus hybridizing than with all other bulb crops combined, in Washington, and hundreds of varieties were developed. F. S. Martin, at Puyallup, was one of the first hybridizers in the state and, by 1926, he had introduced several new varieties including two crosses (Tacoma and Wanita) which he made in 1917. Ralph Pommert, of Pacific, developed several excellent varieties. Two of these were All American selections: Royal Stewart and Captain Busch.

Growers

Darst, Earle

Earle Darst (Coupeville) was primarily an Iris grower and is discussed more fully in that section. However, he also grew Gladiolus commercially for corm production from 1964 until 1976, beginning first in eastern Washington. At his peak in 1967, he was probably Washington's largest Glad grower with 95 acres at George. Later, he raised Gladiolus on the Skagit Flats and on Whidbey Island until 1976. About 1980, he decided to get back into the cut-flower business and, by 1992, was growing about 10 acres of Gladiolus and 8 acres of Iris on Whidbey Island.

DeGoede, Henry

Henry (Hank) De Goede (Mossyrock) is another grower who likes all types of bulbs and is discussed more fully elsewhere. He raised Gladiolus from about 1951 until 1967, both in eastern Washington (Quincy), and in western Washington at Mount Vernon and on Whidbey Island. At his peak, he had about 40 acres of Glads at Quincy.

Huff, John and Thelma

John Huff (1908-1990, Orting) and his wife, Thelma, started raising Gladiolus about 1938 and sold cut flowers in surrounding cities from about 1946 until 1960, when they retired. They had about an acre at their peak, and also, did some hybridizing. John was president of The Washington Gladiolus Society twice and before that was secretary/treasurer for many years. Thelma started a newsletter for the Society in 1942.

The Pommerts - Ralph, Marguerite and Robert

At one time, Ralph Pommert (1895-1992, Pacific) was one of the leading Gladiolus growers and hybridizers in the Northwest. His father had grown Glads in southern Ohio where Ralph was born. Ralph was in the Army in World War I from 1918 to 1922. He met and married Marguerite in Belgium in 1921. After he was discharged and returned to the United States, they grew Glads for a few years in Illinois. About 1925, Ralph's sister persuaded him to come to Washington State where he continued growing Glads. With Marguerite's assistance, they reached a peak of about 25 acres in 1940, selling both cut flowers and corms.

Ralph had a knack for hybridizing and his Royal Stewart, named for a Puyallup friend, Stewart Perry, was introduced in 1955 as the first All American Gladiolus selection. Royal Stewart was a superb Glad with glorious color and had much promise. Unfortunately, the corms proved to be highly susceptible to Fusarium basal rot when they were grown in eastern and southern United States, so it was withdrawn from commerce. He later introduced another All American selection called Captain Busch, named for his wartime captain. This was an excellent field-cut flower type and was used primarily for commercial flower production. Other hybrids that Ralph developed included Marguerite in 1939 named for his wife; Maryln, named for his daughter; Julia Mae, named for his mother, and Anna Mae named for a Miss Washington.

Ralph was the "spark plug" for the organization of the Washington State Gladiolus Society, was very active in it, and served as president several times. He ran an All American Gladiolus trial garden in 1959, one of 26 such trials in the United States. He was also president of the North American Commercial Gladiolus Growers Association in 1950 and received, that same year, a Gold Medal Award from the New England

187

Gladiolus Society for his services to the industry. In addition, he was awarded a bronze plaque by the North American Gladiolus Council in appreciation for his contributions, and, in 1959, received a Citation for Distinguished Achievement in Horticulture from the Washington State Federation of Garden Clubs. In 1982, he was elected to the International Gladiolus Hall of Fame. Ralph also served as a mayor of Pacific at one time and was active on the Auburn School Board.

Mrs. Pommert, their daughter Maryln, and their son, Robert, also worked in the business. In 1950, Ralph and Marguerite turned it over to Bob while Ralph continued to hybridize and test new varieties as well as to judge at shows. Bob (1923-1985, Pacific) continued the corm and cut-flower business until 1954.

Roe, Orville R. and Doris

Orville Roe (1900-1952, Roe's Glad Gardens, Auburn) gave his wife, Doris, one hundred Gladiolus corms for a Christmas present in 1932. A few years later, they began selling cut flowers under Doris's supervision while Orville continued as a fieldman for the Libby Cannery. In 1945, he quit his job in order to grow Glads full time. By 1949, the Roes had 31 acres planted in Gladiolus and were shipping over 10,000 cut flowers a day to Seattle and Tacoma markets, as well as selling millions of corms to eastern markets during the winter. In 1950 or 1951, he and Doris reached their peak of 43 acres which was probably the largest planting in the Puget Sound area at that time. Their daughters, Shirley and Joy, assisted in the business in the early years. Shirley's husband, Clyde Painter, joined the Roes as a partner in 1951. Orville died in 1952 and, in 1954, Mrs. Roe and Clyde sold the business to Ira Gregg.

Sather, Harry

Harry Sather (Puyallup/Mount Vernon) was another general bulb grower who raised mostly Iris, Narcissus and Tulips but grew Gladiolus in the 1970s. At his peak he had two acres at Puyallup and ten at Mount Vernon.

CHAPTER 15

Lilies

Lilies have been grown commercially in Washington ever since George Gibbs made the first planting in 1892. They, together with Freesias, were his main source of income during the early 1900s.

Unfortunately, however, the records for Lily production in Washington State are far less complete than those available for Iris, Narcissus and Tulips. F. S. Flickinger raised Regal and Easter Lilies in 1925 at Richmond Beach. George Sheffield began growing Regals on Vashon Island in 1928. By 1931, there were about 35 others producing 3 million Regal bulbs a year. All were members of the Vashon Island Lily Growers Association. Frank and Lucie Wilson began growing the Lucie Wilson and other cultivars of *Lilium speciosum* var. *rubrum* near Everson in 1943. Then came the boom in Croft Easter Lilies from about 1944 to 1955, after which the industry gradually declined in this state. Most of the 357 known commercial Lily growers in Washington listed in Appendix Table C raised only Croft Lilies.

The total Lily acreage has always been small in comparison with that of Iris, Narcissus and Tulips. The recorded peak acreage was reached in 1951 with 112 acres (Table 3-3, Chapter 3). This figure, however, may be exceeded soon by growers raising Oriental types (such as Star Gazer) and Asiatic types (such as Connecticut King) for both bulb and flower production. The major producers of these bulbs in 1992 were Philip Bowman (Mak-Leek Lilies, Inc.) in eastern Washington and the Holland America Bulb Farms, Inc. and Van der Salm Bulbfarm, Inc., both in the Woodland area. Van der Salm began raising Asiatic Lilies at Woodland in 1980, added Orientals in 1981 and, more recently, the trumpet and Aurelian types. Most of their Lilies are now grown at Hermiston in eastern Oregon. They have an extensive program under way for the development of new varieties headed by Ed McRae.

Many of the new Lilies were developed in Gresham at the Oregon Bulb Farms, which was founded in 1928 by Jan de Graaff's father, M. B. McKay and Arthur Bowman. It is reported to have been the largest Lily bulb farm in the world at one time. Jan de Graaff became owner in 1934. He and his associates developed the famous line of Mid-Century hybrid (Asiatic) Lilies of which Enchantment has been the best known and the most widely grown and forced. They raised Enchantment, Connecticut King and many other varieties at Grandview in eastern Washington from 1975 to 1980, reaching a peak of about 80 acres.

The interest in these and other new Lilies has increased dramatically, but, while some hybridization continues in the United States, especially for garden-types, the center for development of new varieties for forcing has shifted to Holland. That country is now exporting millions of Lily bulbs, which are kept dormant at 28°F., to the United States each year.

Washington State growers have become increasingly interested in raising and/or forcing the new Lily varieties. There is no data available on the production of Lily varieties in Washington but, since Holland is the primary Lily bulb-producing country of the world, the acreage data on their major varieties may be of interest in showing recent trends. Table 15-1 lists the number of acres planted with one- and two-year-old bulbs in 1990, 1991 and 1992. In addition, Lilies were propagated from scales on 934 more acres and also grown in 60 acres of greenhouse space in 1991; similar data for 1992 were not available.

The 19 listed varieties made up 51% of all Dutch Lily acreage in 1992. As noted in Table 15-1, the leading variety, Star Gazer, was grown on 1,064 acres and comprised 19% of the crop in 1992. Planting of the formerly popular variety, Enchantment, however, dropped from 205 acres in 1990 to 72 in 1992.

Easter Lilies (*Lilium longiflorum*)

Washington State was a comparatively large producer of Croft Easter Lilies in the late 1940s and early 1950s but the Easter Lily industry is now centered in the coastal region of southwest Oregon and northwest California where the growing conditions are apparently better.

The history of the Croft Lily may have started in Washington State. About 1919, Dr. David Griffiths gave some of his hybrid seedlings to Louis S. Houghton to grow in Oregon. In 1925, Houghton gave one of the choice bulbs to his neighbor, Sydney Croft, in Bandon, OR. This plant apparently became the famous Croft Lily, although there is still some argument as to its exact origin. Croft propagated the variety, began selling bulbs about 1930 and, by 1934, was shipping thousands to greenhouse forcers. Others had similar success. About 1936 Croft sold six large bulbs and ten bulblets for $1 to Mrs. Dave Watson in Markham, WA. She prospered with them and, in 1938, sold her first crop for $748. Dee Linder at Westport, WA bought an acre of land in 1942 for $100, planted Crofts, and, by 1947, had sold $100,000 worth. By 1946 over 20 acres had been planted by 100 growers in Grays Harbor County alone and there were many other plantings scattered throughout western Washington. The Croft Lily was later replaced by the Ace and Nellie White varieties.

Table 15-1. Lilies. Number of acres of major varieties in Holland.*

Name	Type**	1990	1991	1992
Apeldoorn	A	68	59	58
Avignon	A	92	77	86
Casa Blanca	O	90	93	86
Connecticut King	A	343	261	273
Dreamland	A	67	50	53
Enchantment	A	205	92	72
Gelria	L	32	71	86
Gran Paradiso	A	78	78	83
Le Reve (Joy)	O	50	67	107
Mona	O	45	62	71
Montreux	A	84	82	77
Olympic Star	O	29	56	70
Polyanna	A	136	139	147
Roma	A	67	65	63
Sancerre	A	57	64	70
Snow Queen	L	100	159	213
Star Gazer	O	871	1,109	1,064
Sun Ray	A	165	164	123
Toscana	A	29	52	52
Other registered varieties	--	370	487	418
Non-registered varieties	--	408	451	647
Seedlings	--	205	153	90
GRAND TOTAL		**5,240**	**5,322**	**5,614**

* Source: Flowerbulb Inspection Service (BKD), Lisse, the Netherlands.
** A = Asiatic; L = Longiflorum; O = Oriental.

Hybridizing of New Lily Varieties in Washington State

Most hybridizing of Lilies was done with the garden types in Washington State. A. N. Kanouse and his wife made some crosses at Olympia but no other information is available. Other known hybridizers are discussed below.

Griffiths, Dr. David

Dr. David Griffiths (USDA) was probably the first major hybridizer of Lilies in Washington State. His main accomplishments were the Croft seedling selection and the development of the "Bellingham Hybrids." These hybrids were garden Lilies which came in a variety of colors and shades and were crosses of the closely related Pacific Coast wild Lilies, *Lilium humboldti*, *L. parryi*, and *L. pardalinum*. The varieties Shuksan and Star of Oregon were the most popular. The hybrids failed to thrive, however, in the hot summers of the southern and eastern United States and most have disappeared. Griffiths named most of his varieties after local geographical features or persons. Two of these people were Cyrus Gates and Mrs. Frances Larrabee who, together with William McKay, donated the land for the enlarged USDA Bulb Station in Bellingham in 1917 (110).

Freimann, LeVern

LeVern Freimann (Bellingham) was a county agent, first in Island County and then in Whatcom County, until he retired in 1966. His hobby was Lilies. He knew Dr. Griffiths and cooperated with him on many experiments. Although Vern sold some bulbs and flowers, his main interest was in the development of new Lily varieties which he began hybridizing in 1928. He also developed fertile lines from infertile ones by making them tetraploid, using colchicine from ground-up colchicum bulbs. In 1954, LeVern won three special awards at the American Lily Show in Seattle. His original goal was to develop golden yellow and clear pink trumpet varieties. As of 1990, however, his most popular hybrid has been a brilliant red called Scarlet Delight, registered in 1966 as a tetraploid Asiatic of the Auratum type, capable of growing in a wide range of climatic conditions.

McRae, Edward A.

Ed McRae (Van der Salm Bulbfarm, Woodland) began hybridizing Lilies in 1961 for Jan de Graaff at the Oregon Bulb Farms, producing such popular Asiatic cultivars as Polyanna, Chinook and Sterling Star; the Pixie series of pot Lilies; and various trumpet and Oriental hybrids. Some of these were included in the display by Oregon Bulb Farms at the Floriade in Holland in 1972 and helped stimulate the beginning of the "Lily-mania" in that country. In 1988, Ed moved to the Van der Salm Bulbfarm, where he has continued hybridizing and selecting new clones. The company is especially interested in producing new varieties of tetraploids, pot Lilies and new colored Oriental types. Judith McRae, his wife, (Columbia Platte Lilies, Inc., Boring, OR) has been specializing in garden varieties since 1980 and has introduced several hybrids, including Tiger Babies, Viva and Black Gold.

Wilson, Frank and Lucie

Lucie and Frank Wilson (Nookvale Farms, Deming/Everson) discovered several clumps of a new strain of *Lilium speciosum* var. *rubrum* growing in a nearby chicken yard in 1940. Mrs. Wilson purchased the entire stock in 1943 and began to propagate them. Frank named the new variety Lucie Wilson in her honor and it became quite popular. They also developed several other varieties of *L. speciosum*, including Grand Commander, Rosemede, Cinderella, Elite and Ellabee. Many of these became very popular in Holland, especially the intense red Grand Commander. At their peak, Lucie and Frank grew three major varieties of Lilies on about 20 to 25 acres. They were still selling bulbs in the early 1960s.

Lily Societies

The **Vashon Island Lily Growers Association** was a cooperative of 30-40 members growing Regal Lilies in 1931 and was, presumably, organized for the marketing of their bulbs. According to Griffiths (60) it was the first Lily growers association in the United States.

The **Seattle Lily Society** was organized November 9, 1951 by 15 growers and apparently was designed for persons primarily interested in garden-type Lilies. About 1952, the name was changed to the Puget Sound Lily Society and, perhaps still later, to the Washington State Lily Society. It published a newsletter called *Lilylore*. L. N. Freimann was president and W. L. Fulmer, secretary, of both the local society and the North American Lily Society when the latter held its annual meeting and show in Seattle in 1954. Our last report from the Puget Sound Lily Society was dated 1968.

The **Washington State Croft Lily Growers Association** was organized in July 1947 and held its first annual meeting that year in Aberdeen, WA. It was formed for "the promotion of education" about Lilies but was also used as a marketing unit, according to its newsletters. The last report available from them was for the fiscal year 1952-53.

Although there is no longer a Lily Society in this state, 43 amateur and commercial Washington growers belong to the **Pacific Northwest Lily Society** (PNLS), also known as Lilies-Northwest, Inc., incorporated in 1980. This society has a total of 343 members in several states and foreign countries but most of them are in the Pacific Northwest. Many members also belong to the North American Lily Society. The PNLS hosted the North American annual show and meeting in 1981 and in 1987, and will do so again in 1994. For more information, write to Dick Malpass, Treasurer, at 10804 NW 11th Avenue, Vancouver, WA 98685.

CHAPTER 16

Festivals and Display Gardens

It seems to be a natural development for people living in areas where flowering bulbs are grown to organize flower shows and festivals so that the entire community as well as visitors can enjoy the blossoms. The first such festival in Washington State was held at Bellingham in 1920. Many others have developed since then and are discussed in this chapter.

FESTIVALS

Bellingham Tulip Festival

This festival, an idea of Mrs. R. A. Welsh, was promoted by G. W. Nash and W. C. Weir and was first held in May 1920. The date implies that bulb growing was extensive enough at that time in Whatcom County to provide sufficient flowers for such an event. The first Tulip Flower Show was held in a tent, but the next one, in 1921, was located in the basement of the J. B. Wall Department Store in Bellingham.

Following the 1921 Festival, a Tulip Festival Association was formed and 1,200 members were enrolled at $1 each. Volunteers planted 100,000 bulbs (presumably Tulips) which helped make the Festival of 1922 "a tremendous" success. Volunteers even made 100,000 paper Tulips to add to the live ones for use in decorations. In 1922, and in subsequent years, many other communities participated including Seattle, Vancouver and Victoria as well as the Tulalip Indian tribes. During the festivities in 1922, time was taken to honor George Gibbs, who had planted the first commercial bulbs in 1892, as well as C. X. Larrabee, C. T. Canfield and Cyrus Gates who helped promote the industry in the early 1900s. Also, in 1922, the Tulip was named the official flower of the city of Bellingham.

The 1922 Festival sponsored a three-day flower show, visits to the USDA Bulb Station, ball games, band concerts and the official parade which included 75 floats, 50 decorated cars and 5,000 persons representing various organizations, cities, etc. Two airplanes even dropped Tulip flowers on the crowds.

In addition to the customary parade (Figure 16-1), the Tulip Queen Coronation was a very spectacular event. The Queen, from either Skagit or Whatcom County, was chosen by a popular vote based upon the number of votes purchased for each candidate. There was considerable competition among the various clubs and counties, and one man bought $5,000 worth of votes one year to help his Skagit candidate. In 1926, the Queen was awarded a European tour. In other years the Queen was sent to Alaska, to Hollywood or to some other glamorous place. Festival enthusiasts took their Tulips and their Queens seriously.

In 1928, they had a baseball team called the "Bellingham Tulips." There were motorboat races which were won by Tacoma and Seattle boats and one boat set a "possible world record speed of 37 miles per hour."

This delightful festival was, unfortunately, brought to an end by two calamities: the Depression and the fierce northeastern freezes which often killed many of the bulbs in the fields in Whatcom County. The last Tulip Festival was held in 1930 and the only festivities after that were the crowning of a grade school queen and a few school events at Battersby Field.

The fact that the Tulip Festival was not revived after the Depression ended implies that commercial bulb production had been drastically reduced in the county by that time. At present, the only Tulips grown there are in private gardens.

In 1936, some citizens promoted a "Spring Festival" and various groups intermittently continued to support it until 1947 when a new name, "Blossom Time," was chosen and, in 1948, a "Northwest Blossom Time, Inc." group was organized to carry it on. The last report of it was in 1953. There is a current celebration at Bellingham, called the "Sea to Ski Festival," but it has no connection with bulbs.

Grays Harbor Tulip Show

Tulip shows were held in Aberdeen in May in both 1928 and 1929. They were put on to "encourage better gardens and more beautiful homes" in the hope of stimulating more bulb growing in Grays Harbor (121).

196

Figure 16-1. Bellingham Tulip Festival float, 1924.
(Courtesy Washington State Historical Society, Curtis Collection No. 47075)

Figure 16-2. A Puyallup Valley Daffodil Show in Sumner, late 1940s.
(Courtesy Lee Merrill)

Grays Harbor South Beach Lily Festival

This two-day Festival arose as a result of the development of the Croft Lily bulb industry in the coastal area around Westport, Markham, Aberdeen and Hoquiam during the 1940s and 1950s but nothing more is known about it.

Holland Happenings at Oak Harbor

North Whidbey Island was settled in the mid-1890s by many Dutchmen and in the late 1920s, they and other community supporters organized a day-long "Holland Days" Festival which was repeated annually for many years at Oak Harbor. It was revived in the late 1930s, but was discontinued during the World War II years. In 1969, a new group began organizing a "Holland Happenings" with a parade and a Tulip Show in 1970. The original purpose of the festival was to honor North Whidbey Island's early settlers and the committee in charge sent to Holland for Dutch costumes, wooden shoes, lace caps, etc. It has now become a three-day affair and is held the last weekend in April. Although the emphasis is on Holland, other nationalities participate in the festivities. The Festival is complete with Dutch foods, traditional Dutch costumes, a flower show, musicals, dances and a parade.

In addition to the festival, a park, maintained in Oak Harbor, is called the "Holland Gardens," where thousands of Tulips are displayed. In 1990 a new park, the Hal Ramaley Memorial Park, was dedicated and it also contains a large planting of Tulips. Most of the other Tulips used for decorations and floats are imported from Skagit County because none are produced commercially on the island any more.

Puyallup Valley Daffodil Festival

The Puyallup Valley Daffodil Festival is reported to have been, at one time, the third largest flower festival in the United States. Unlike some of the others, it was not born overnight but evolved gradually between 1926 and 1934.

Narcissus flowers were used for decorations at the Rainbow Trout dinners in Sumner beginning in 1913, and also at the Steelhead Banquets put on by the Sumner Commercial Club in 1925 and 1926. With the increasing importance of the bulb business, it was only natural and

198

logical that the name of the Steelhead Banquet be changed to the Bulb Banquet in 1927. This banquet was attended by about 300 guests and several scientists from Washington, Oregon and even Washington, DC, were invited to talk on bulb growing. The Bulb Banquets continued at Sumner until the middle 1930s when they gradually evolved into the "Queen's Ball."

Meanwhile, on April 6, 1926, a Daffodil Tea was held at the home of the C. W. Ortons near Sumner. It was sponsored by the Sumner American Home and Country Club, of which Mrs. Orton was president, the Sumner Civic Club and the Sumner PTA as a gesture to support the big new Narcissus industry. Huge baskets of Narcissus flowers were provided by 18 growers from the Puyallup Valley. Between 300 and 500 growers, representatives of local cities and officers from nearby Fort Lewis attended. Records show that the tea was held again in 1928, and, presumably, in 1927 as well.

The first bulb shows in Pierce County of which records were found, included a Tulip Show in 1928 and Narcissus Shows in 1928 and 1929. Both were sponsored by the Pierce County Horticultural Society (organized in 1926) and were held in the Winthrop Hotel in Tacoma.

The first "float," a 3 x 8 foot wooden Dutch shoe filled with 11,000 Narcissus flowers, was built in 1929 by John Colyn of Van Zonneveld of Washington at Orting and displayed for a week in the lobby of Tacoma's Winthrop Hotel. The following year several other local growers also built similar floats and displayed them on Pacific Avenue near the old City Hall in Tacoma.

In 1931, R. G. Fryar organized the first show of 200-300 Narcissus varieties from commercial growers at the Sumner High School Gymnasium. Over 8,000 persons viewed it—for free. Fryar continued running and enlarging the show (Figure 16-2) until 1949 when he turned it over to Henry Reynolds and the show was moved to Tacoma. It stayed there until 1958 when it was shifted to Puyallup. It is now sponsored jointly by the Daffodil Festival Board and the Hill and Dale District Garden Clubs.

In 1932, the increasing interest in bulbs prompted the Northwest Bulb Growers Association and local Chambers of Commerce to adopt a suggestion by George Lawler to organize a "Bulb Sunday," when people could visit the fields and receive free flowers. The Northern Pacific Railroad ran a special "Daffodil Express" train from Tacoma to Orting so that visitors without cars could enjoy the acres of flowers. Another

Bulb Sunday was held in 1933, but the event proved to be too popular. The roads were jammed with so many cars that the event had to be discontinued.

The Daffodil Festival, as it is known now, really began in 1934. Lee Merrill, a commercial photographer in Tacoma, had seen a bulb parade in Holland in 1927 and he may have seen the Tulip show in Bellingham. He recommended having a similar parade in the Puyallup Valley with Daffodil- decorated bicycles and cars parading from Tacoma through Puyallup to Sumner. Merrill also suggested the use of the name "Daffodil Festival." His ideas were adopted, he was made chairman of the parade committee, and the festival was expanded to a two-day event. Merrill was the official photographer and publicist for many years. He was followed by Bill Worden and later by Bob Sconce in the same capacity. The festival has been held every year since 1934 except during World War II (1942-1945).

The parade now starts in Tacoma, passes through Puyallup and Sumner and ends in Orting. Twenty-five floats participated in 1937. In 1989 the parade included 35 floats, 34 bands, 10 marching units and 20 other groups for a total of 99 units. The estimated audience was 125,000 in addition to the thousands who watched it on television.

The total number of flowers used on the floats has ranged from 1 to 3 million. One float alone in 1956 bore 250,000 Daffodils. The average in 1989 was about 28,000 flowers per float. The parade is an all-day affair and usually takes more than two hours just to pass the reviewing stand in Tacoma.

In 1936 the Queen did not ride on a float. Instead, she reviewed the parade from a throne on a 30-foot high pylon covered with 250,000 Daffodils, at South 10th and Pacific in Tacoma.

The first Queen (Elizabeth Wotton) came from Puyallup in 1934. From then until 1956, the choice of "Queen" and "attendant" alternated between Sumner and Puyallup. The word "attendant" was changed to "Princess" in 1937. Later, queens were chosen also from Tacoma and Orting high schools, and, in 1959, the Board decided to allow other Pierce County high schools to nominate princesses to compete for the honor of being the Queen. There were 18 Princesses in 1989. There are two requirements for a high school or community that wishes to enter a princess in the competition: it must enter a float and a band in the parade the preceding year. All candidates must be high school seniors.

The Queen and Princesses participate in many community activities including parades at other festivals of which there were 15 in 1989. Two floats are kept on hand in case two festivals occur at the same time, in which case the Queen goes to one and one or more Princesses to the other. Floats are accompanied by the Daffodilians, a group of 66 men who act as hosts to visitors in Tacoma and as honor guards to the Queen and float when it is on the road. The Queens and Princesses are accompanied by a Queen Mother and her assistants who help select costumes, plan meetings and talks before various groups, arrange and chaperon trips. The first such Queen Mother was Mrs. Leola (Orville) Brown, of Sumner, selected unofficially in 1947 and appointed officially in 1948.

The Queen receives a $2,000 scholarship award. Recently a Daffodil Festival Foundation was established in an effort to raise more funds for additional scholarships.

The financing of such festivals has always been a problem and continues to be so. In an effort to provide a more sound basis for it, the non-profit Puyallup Valley Daffodil Festival, Inc. was organized in 1937 for the purpose of promoting and encouraging the bulb industry. It had a budget goal of $1,000 to be raised by selling charter memberships. It is now sustained by the sale of booster buttons and by the solicitation of five categories of sustaining memberships. Individual floats are financed by business firms, various organizations and communities.

The Festival now has a full-time secretary with an office in Tacoma. The budget in 1991 was $160,000. The Board of Directors is composed of 50 active members from local Chambers of Commerce, various clubs, the Northwest Bulb Growers Association and Past Presidents of the Board. In addition, there are local community committees to handle the details of the festival in each city. R. G. Fryar was the first president, and several local bulb growers as well as non-growers served as presidents in later years.

Local bulb growers support the Festival in many ways, especially by supplying flowers at a price much below the cost of production. In 1988, for example, bulb growers provided the Festival Board with about one million Narcissus blooms at $30/1,000 when they could have been sold for $60/1,000 in the usual floral markets. Flowers were often a surplus commodity from the 1930s to the 1950s and could easily be supplied for festivals. Today, there is a large demand for them across the country so grower assistance to the Festival should be recognized as being very generous.

The original goal of the Festival was to "promote and encourage the bulb industry." It did, indeed, focus attention on the Northwest and on the bulb industry through the widespread coverage of its colorful glamour in newspapers, magazines and on television. Promotions were arranged throughout the United States, including many at department stores, such as a mammoth display at Nieman Marcus in Dallas in 1954.

The main Festival has also grown from the two-day affair in 1934 to one which lasts eight days and now includes, besides the Main Parade: the Junior Daffodil Parade, Princess Promenade, Queen's Luncheon, Queen's Coronation and Ball, Flower Show, Tacoma Yacht Club Daffodil Marine Parade, a Good Sam Fun Run and a host of other related events. In 1992, its related activities ran from January 29 to April 26. The Festival proper lasted from April 12 to the 25th, with the Grand Parade on April 25. This is quite a contrast to the one-day "Bulb Sunday" celebration in 1932.

In addition to the Festival events described above, recognition should be given to the annual display of souvenirs from previous festivals, including gowns and Lee Merrill photographs, which are exhibited at the Ryan House Museum in Sumner during Daffodil Festival week.

For more information, write to the Daffodil Festival at 741 St. Helens, Tacoma, WA, 98402 or call 1-206-627-6176. Festival dates for 1993 are April 3-18 with the Grand Parade on April 17.

Skagit Valley (La Conner) Tulip Show

Beginning about 1946 an excellent three-day Tulip Show attracted thousands of visitors to La Conner each year. The show was usually held in late April or early May and was organized by the La Conner Civic Garden Club. Profits from the show were used for local beautification projects. Both amateurs and professionals participated. Tony Van Waveren, a bulb grower, captured permanent possession of the trophy for the most popular exhibit in 1957 after winning it for three successive years. The Tulip Show ended about 1971 and its sponsors sold many of the "props" to a group in Oak Harbor who organized the "Holland Happenings" there.

Skagit Valley Tulip Festival

The Skagit Valley Tulip Festival is a community celebration that involves every major city in Skagit County. It was officially opened in 1984 when the Mount Vernon Chamber of Commerce, under the direction of its president, Jerry Diggerness, decided to set up various events and festivities for the enjoyment of the thousands of visitors who came to the Skagit Valley every year to see the Tulips in bloom. From a small beginning, the festival has grown rapidly, attracting even more visitors and, in 1991, attendance was estimated to have been 400,000.

The best part of the festival, of course, is the opportunity to visit the colorful Tulip fields in the area which are a photographer's paradise. Every year the Eastman Kodak Company builds a stand near one of the fields for better picture-taking. Display gardens and local greenhouses are also alive with color and may be visited. Tulip Transit buses, provided by the festival committee, make it easier for people to view the fields and display gardens. They make frequent bus tours to the fields and riders may get on and off at various stops as they choose.

Two fairs held at the same time include the Downtown Mount Vernon Street Fair and the GTE directories Community Fair. Both fairs have arts and crafts shows, entertainment and festival foods. A "10K run" and a "slug run" are sponsored for would-be athletes. The "10K" is a timed race while the "slug run" is a predicted time run for slower runners or walkers.

The Skagit-Mount Vernon Kiwanis Salmon Barbecue provides a complete salmon dinner at Hillcrest Park. The Kiwanis Club also sponsors the Great Skagit Duck Race on the Skagit River. About 8,000 toy ducks are sold at $5 each for this race and the duck which crosses the finish line first wins a car or other substantial prize for its owner. "Duck money" profits are used for philanthropic purposes in the community.

The Skagit County Historical Museum in La Conner offers exhibits concerning local history as well as a spectacular view of the Skagit River Valley. The Breazeable-Padilla Bay Interpretive Center, which is headquarters for a National Estaurine Research Reserve, houses an interpretive museum with exhibits, saltwater aquaria and a special "hands-on" room for children.

Several art shows, pony rides, a gymnastic meet, a "Tulip Pedal" bicycle ride, a golf tournament, a sock-hop and fashion shows help to fill the sixteen days of the festival and, each year, the number of activities has increased.

Financial support for the festival comes from city and county governments and from more than 200 individual and business sponsors. The festival also receives royalties from sales of shirts, posters, wine and souvenir items. The festival committee is part of the Mount Vernon Chamber of Commerce but has its own budget and board of directors. "Tulipmania,"© written by Stephen Herold, was published as the Official Festival Guidebook in 1989 (66). The Skagit Valley Herald also publishes an annual souvenir edition Tulip Festival Guide.

Festival dates for 1993 are April 2-18 and for 1994, April 1-17. For more information, write to the Skagit Valley Tulip Festival, P.O. Box 1007, Mount Vernon, WA 98273, or call 1-800-4-TULIPS.

Spring Tulip Festival at Mossyrock

This Festival, held annually at the end of April, was started in the spring of 1988. It is a cooperative effort between the Mossyrock Chamber of Commerce and the DeGoede Bulb farms. It involves flower shows, craft fairs, concerts, food and other features including one that the author admired in Holland, but has never seen before in the United States: a display of "mosaics." In the Mossyrock Festival, the mosaics are pre-arranged patterns laid out on the ground, and filled with fresh Tulip blooms, seeds and other materials. A different theme is chosen for each year's mosaics. In 1990, the theme was "The Title of a Musical Composition" and 34 beautiful mosaics were laid out using that motif.

BULB GROWERS DISPLAY GARDENS

Many bulb growers maintain collections of bulb varieties near their home offices, both for their own enjoyment and also to show to visitors. A few gardens, however, are designed specifically for general display purposes and are described below.

DeGoede Gardens

Henry DeGoede and his family have developed a display bulb garden adjacent to their retail garden shop near Mossyrock. It contains many different types of bulbs but especially Tulips. Open houses are held every spring to exhibit bulb flowers and every fall to show perennials. This garden is located at 409 Mossyrock Road West, Mossyrock.

The DeGoedes had previously developed, with the help of John Conijn, the beautiful Chuckanut Gardens near Mount Vernon which resembled the famous Keukenhof Gardens in Holland on a miniature scale. The Chuckanut Gardens, unfortunately, were discontinued when the DeGoedes moved to Mossyrock.

Roozengaarde

This "Roozen Garden" was the brainchild of Bill Roozen, past president of the Washington Bulb Company. It was started in 1984 and now includes a collection of many varieties of different bulb types planted along paths among a group of fruit trees. A miniature Dutch-type windmill provides an irresistible background for photographs. A retail shop is adjacent to the garden for the sale of flowers, bulbs and associated gift items either directly or through catalogs. So many visitors come during the blooming season that two parking lots have had to be provided with attendants to direct traffic. This garden is a subsidiary of the Washington Bulb Company and is run by Bernadette Miller, a daughter of Bill and Helen Roozen. It is located at 1587 Beaver Marsh Road, Mount Vernon.

Van Lierop's Variety Garden

This display garden near Puyallup attracts thousands of sightseers during the blooming season from February 1 to May 1. There is a steady succession of blooms of more than 150 different varieties of Crocus, Hyacinths, Narcissus, Tulips and Iris. In an adjacent retail shop, the Van Lierops sell both cut and potted flowers and floral arrangements. They take orders for bulbs for gift mailing as well as for fall delivery. Neil's wife, Bonnie, and their daughters, Cynthia, Anne and April, run the shop and manage the display garden. It is located at 13409 80th Street East, Puyallup.

Westshore Acres

These gardens, near La Conner, include a two-acre planting of thousands of plants and more than 100 varieties of Daffodils and Tulips in a pleasant tree-covered setting with 40-year-old rhododendrons, hollies and other trees surrounding an 1886 Victorian home. The gardens are open, with an adjacent retail shop, from March 15 to May 1. John and Marilyn Gardner are the owners. Their location is 956 Downey Road, Mount Vernon.

CHAPTER 17

Bulb Associations, Cooperatives and the Bulb Commission

Northwest Bulb Growers Association

The Northwest Bulb Growers Association was organized to bring bulb growers together and to encourage educational activities for the promotion of bulbs. State Senator and berry farmer William H. Paulhamus called a meeting on March 27, 1924 in Puyallup for all persons interested in growing bulbs. Talks were to be given by A. G. Pruyser, Joe Smith, George Lawler and others already active in the bulb industry. About thirty interested persons attended and an unknown number formally organized the Association. George Ward Lawler of Fife was elected president, Joe Smith became secretary and Harry D. Locklin was named treasurer. The dues were set at fifty cents per year and anyone interested in bulbs could become a member. According to Smith, the same officers were re-elected at the next annual meeting which was held on April 14, 1925 in Tacoma (125).

Most, if not all, of the early bulb pioneers became members. At first, the Association was composed mainly of amateurs, according to Ed Orton, but were replaced by commercial growers in the late 1920s. On May 17, 1930 the Association was apparently reorganized and membership was restricted to commercial growers, although the original name was retained.

Present officers include an elected president, vice president and an appointed secretary/treasurer. The Board of Directors includes the three officers and four growers who represent different bulb-growing areas in Washington and Oregon. Known officers are listed in Table 17-1. Unfortunately, early records of the Association have been lost and the list is incomplete.

Table 17-1. Northwest Bulb Growers Association Officers.

Year	President	Vice President	Secretary	Treasurer
1924-1925	George Ward Lawler		Joe Smith	Harry D. Locklin
1926-1929	?			
1930	F. C. Riggs (?)	Frank Chervenka		
1931-1933	Arthur Bowman			
1934-1935	?		Secretary/Treasurer	
1936	Arthur Bowman		A. B. Flagg	
1937-1938	C. W. Orton	S. B. Hall	A. B. Flagg	
1939-1940	?			
1941-1942	John Colyn			
1943	John Colyn	Jan DeGraaff	C. W. Van Rooy	
1944-1945	?			
1946	Si Van Lierop			
1947	?			
1948	S. W. Staatz	Francis Chervenka	R. G. Fryar	
1949-1951	Francis Chervenka	Marinus Lefeber	R. G. Fryar	
1952-1953	Henry Edmondson	Joe Berger	Ben Korsten	
1954-1955	Joe Berger	Wallace Staatz	Dick Nowadnick	
1956-1958	Wallace Staatz	Earle Darst	Dick Nowadnick	
1959-1960	John Twohy	C. E. Van Lierop	Dick Nowadnick	
1961-1962	C. E. Van Lierop	Francis Chervenka	Dick Nowadnick	
1963-1964	Henry DeGoede	Tony Van Waveren	Dick Nowadnick	
1965-1966	Tony Van Waveren	Neil Van Lierop	Dick Nowadnick	
1967-1968	Ozzie Williams	Bill Roozen (W. A.)	Dick Nowadnick	
1969-1971	Bill Roozen	Ted DeGroot, Jr.	Dick Nowadnick	
1972-1974	Ted DeGroot, Jr.	Wilmer Reise	Dick Nowadnick	
1975-1976	Bill Lefeber	Roger Knutson	Dick Nowadnick	
1976-1977	Roger Knutson	Henry DeGoede	Dick Nowadnick	
1978-1979	John Roozen	Henry DeGoede	Dick Nowadnick	
1980-1981	John Roozen	Jack DeGoede	Dick Nowadnick	
1981-1982	Jack DeGoede	Dan Lefeber	Dick Nowadnick	
1983-1984	Leo Roozen	Cynthia Van Lierop	Dick Nowadnick	
1985-1989	Cynthia Van Lierop	Tom DeGoede	Dick Nowadnick	
1990-1991	William M. Roozen	Kris Lubbe-Edem	Dick Nowadnick	
1991-1992	William M. Roozen	Kris Lubbe-Edem	Dick Nowadnick	
1992-1993	Bob Hulbert	April Van Lierop	Dick Nowadnick	

After the 1930 reorganization when only commercial growers were members, the Association became primarily concerned with supporting the Daffodil Quarantine, raising tariffs, reducing transportation charges, restricting field flower-cutting, and promoting the Puyallup Valley Daffodil Festival. Still later, it placed more emphasis on advertising and on supporting research. The members who served as chairmen of the research committee are listed in Table 17-2.

Table 17-2. Chairmen of the Research Committee.

1954-1958	Ted Sabelis
1959-1971	Francis Chervenka
1972-1975	Ted DeGroot, Jr.
1976-1977	Roger Knutson
1978-1981	John Roozen
1982-1983	Jack DeGoede
1983-1984	Leo Roozen
1985-1989	Cynthia Van Lierop
1990-1991	William M. Roozen

At first, members were from Washington and Oregon only, but were joined in later years by growers from British Columbia and California. The Association now includes members from the entire West Coast (Table 17-3), although the officers are usually from Washington. Growers and jobbers in other states have also occasionally been members or associate members.

Table 17-3. Number of members of the Northwest Bulb Growers Association.

	1948	1956	1991*
Washington	81	61	30
Oregon	6	2	9
California	0	0	6
British Columbia	0	0	9
TOTAL	**87**	**63**	**54**

* Includes 20 Associate members.

According to Secretary R. L. Nowadnick, the objectives of the Association are (95):

1. To promote and safeguard the common business interests of its members.
2. To establish and maintain friendly relations among those engaged in the growing and selling of bulbs.
3. To enlist a membership among those engaged in the production of bulbs in the states of Washington and Oregon and to take united action on all matters affecting the welfare of the trade at large. This includes lobbying for the industry. [Members are now accepted from other states and from British Columbia].

The Association has prepared colored charts and streamers for advertising, has reprinted recommendations for forcing Northwest bulbs and kept its members informed with the *Northwest Bulb Growers Newsletter* published from 1948 to 1972 intermittently. This newsletter was started by R. G. Fryar in 1948. The editors were: R. G. Fryar (1948-1951), C. J. Gould (1952), R. L. Nowadnick (1953-1964), R. A. Wearne (1965-1967) and B. G. Wesenberg (1968-1972).

The Association sponsored an annual Bulb Growers Short Course/Conference, in cooperation with Washington State University, from 1948 to 1987. Since 1987 the Association has taken the initiative in organizing the conferences in consultation with WSU scientists. In 1957, it published a *Handbook on Bulb Growing and Forcing*, edited by C. J. Gould, through the fund-raising efforts of Ted Sabelis, chairman of the research committee.

To support these activities, the Association raised its annual dues in 1930 to $10 per member. This included a $5 membership in the Northwest Florists Association which did a great deal of lobbying in Washington, DC on behalf of all bulb growers in the Pacific Northwest. By 1950, dues had dropped to $5 but there was an added assessment of $2 per acre up to a limit of 100 acres. The dues for 1992 are $100 for growers and $50 for associate members (those in allied industries).

Annual meetings are usually held in conjunction with the Bulb Growers Conference in late November or early December, currently held in the Seattle area. Richard L. Nowadnick has been Secretary/Treasurer of the Association since 1954. The Association's address is: P. O. Box 303, Mount Vernon, WA 98273.

Washington State Bulb Commission

The formation of a bulb commission was authorized under the Washington Agricultural Enabling Act (Chapter 16-524 WAC), which was passed by the State Legislature and became effective June 9, 1955. The Act makes it possible for producers of agricultural commodities to organize and assess themselves for the purpose of taking certain actions relating to their agricultural commodities.

The Act provided for marketing orders and marketing agreements for the following purposes:

1. To establish plans and conduct programs for advertising and sales promotion.
2. To provide for research studies.
3. To provide for improving standards and grades by defining, establishing and providing labeling requirements.
4. To investigate and take necessary action to prevent unfair trade practices.

The Northwest Bulb Growers Association appointed an Industry Committee, which in turn took the necessary steps to form the Commission, and presented its petition the first day the Enabling Act became law. After several hearings and a final overwhelmingly favorable vote by growers, the Director of Agriculture approved formation of the Bulb Commission effective April 16, 1956 (123,128).

According to the provisions of the Act, it became mandatory for all producers of Iris, Narcissus and Tulip bulbs to belong to the Commission if the individual or firm sold 500 or more bulbs annually. Producers were required to pay assessments on those bulbs sold by them either inside or outside of Washington State. The original assessments were 20¢ per 1,000 for Narcissus bulbs, and 15¢ per 1,000 for Iris and Tulip bulbs. In July, 1986, the assessments were increased to 25¢ per 1,000 for Narcissus and 20¢ for the others, or 1.25% of value if sold by weight. At first, special stamps were issued and placed on each invoice, but this practice was discontinued in 1960.

The Director of the Washington State Department of Agriculture is authorized to assist in the formation, administration and enforcement of the marketing orders for all commodity commissions. The affairs of the Bulb Commission are administered by a board of seven, together with the Director of Agriculture or a representative as an ex-officio member. Five of the board members are elected by all the members of the Commission and must be growers; the two remaining members are chosen by the five and may be either growers or persons interested in the industry. The first five elected in 1956 were John Onderwater and Joe Berger from Mount Vernon and Miles Hatch, Francis Chervenka and Stanley Staatz from the Puyallup Valley area. The other two, selected later, were R. G. Fryar and Sam J. Stewart. The terms of Commissioners were for three years except for those of the first five who were elected for 1, 2 or 3 years in order to stagger future terms. Fryar was elected the first chairman, Staatz the vice-chairman and Chervenka the secretary-treasurer. R. L. Nowadnick has been secretary/ treasurer since 1960, but the other positions have rotated among growers as shown in Table 17-4.

Table 17-4. Washington State Bulb Commission officers.

	Chairman	Vice Chairman	Secretary/Treasurer
1956-1957	R. G. Fryar	Stanley Staatz	Francis Chervenka
1958	Miles Hatch	Bill (W. A.) Roozen	Francis Chervenka
1959-1960	Francis Chervenka	Stanley Staatz	R. G. Fryar
1961-1963	Francis Chervenka	Stanley Staatz	R. L. Nowadnick
1963-1964	Francis Chervenka	Henry DeGoede	R. L. Nowadnick
1965-1968	Ted Sabelis	Earle Darst	R. L. Nowadnick
1969-1971	Earle Darst	Harold Knutson	R. L. Nowadnick
1972-1973	Ozzie Williams	Henry DeGoede	R. L. Nowadnick
1973-1974	Ozzie Williams	C. E. Van Lierop	R. L. Nowadnick
1974-1975	Wallace Staatz	Bill (W.A.) Roozen	R. L. Nowadnick
1976-1977	Bill (W.A.) Roozen	Wallace Staatz	R. L. Nowadnick
1978-1979	Wilmer Reise	Bill Lefeber	R. L. Nowadnick
1979-1980	Wilmer Reise	Bob Hulbert	R. L. Nowadnick
1980-1981	Bob Hulbert	Roger Knutson	R. L. Nowadnick
1982-1983	Roger Knutson	Bill (W.A.) Roozen	R. L. Nowadnick
1984-1986	Bill (W.A.) Roozen	Ozzie Williams	R. L. Nowadnick
1987-1988	Ozzie Williams	Henry DeGoede	R. L. Nowadnick
1989-1990	Henry DeGoede	Roger Knutson	R. L. Nowadnick
1990-1991	Roger Knutson		R. L. Nowadnick
1991-1992	Roger Knutson	Ozzie Williams	R. L. Nowadnick
1992-1993	Roger Knutson	Jack De Goede	R. L. Nowadnick

In its early years, the Commission was very active in advertising and even had a movie made for promotional purposes in 1963 entitled *Flower Bulbs of Western Washington*. Most of the scenes were taken in the Puyallup Valley. It is still available from the Puget Sound Bulb Exchange, Sumner, Washington. Through the efforts of Ted Sabelis, the Commission joined with the Associated Bulb Growers of Holland in 1962 to "stage an intensive publicity campaign on behalf of spring flowers and provide attractive point-of-purchase material for retail florists" (91). Cooperation on this project continued until 1969.

In recent years, the major emphasis of the Commission has been its very active support of research on bulb problems. The results of some of this scientific work are reported in Chapter 19 on research.

At one time, there were 70 members in the Commission, but by 1989, the number had dropped to 17. Total acreage did not diminish, however, and this reflects the trend toward larger but fewer farms (Table 17-5). It is important to remember that growers selling only flowers are not required to join nor to report on the number of bulbs used for that purpose. In 1989 there were three firms that sold only flowers, which raises the total number of Iris, Narcissus and Tulip growers that year to 20. Also, some small growers, who dig their bulbs only every other year, make reports accordingly. Gladiolus and Lily growers do not belong to the Commission.

Current (1992) members of the Commission are: Bowen Bulb Farms, Inc., DeGoede Bulb Farm, Holland America Bulb Farms, Inc., Hulbert Farms, Inc., Knutson Farms, Inc., Lefeber Bulb Co., Inc., Charles Lubbe, Satsop Bulb Farm, Skagit Valley Bulb Farm, Wallace Staatz, Van der Salm Bulbfarm, Van Lierop Bulb Farms, Inc., Ward and Van Lierop, Washington Bulb Company, Westshore Acres, E. G. Williams, Jr. and Woodward Bulb Farm.

Table 17-5. Number of growers reporting bulb sales to the Washington State Bulb Commission.[*]

Year	No.	Year	No.	Year	No.	Year	No.	Year	No.
1956	75**	1964	36	1972	21	1980	21	1988	16
1957	70**	1965	32	1973	19	1981	20	1989	17
1958	56	1966	32	1974	19	1982	16	1990	17
1959	53	1967	25	1975	19	1983	21	1991	17
1960	51	1968	25	1976	19	1984	19	1992	17
1961	46	1969	21	1977	21	1985	16		
1962	42	1970	21	1978	20	1986	16		
1963	36	1971	21	1979	18	1987	16		

[*] Commission members include only growers who sell over 500 bulbs of Iris, Narcissus and/or Tulips annually. They do not include those selling flowers only.
[**] Estimate.

Puget Sound Bulb Exchange

Twelve bulb growers, mostly from the Puyallup Valley area, met at the Woodland Park Floral Greenhouses in Sumner on January 30, 1926 and decided to form the Puget Sound Bulb Exchange (105). These growers were: Frank Chervenka, L. R. Clarke, H. F. Gronen, L. M. Hatch, H. D. Locklin, Gregg McKinnon, C. W. Orton, E. C. Orton, W. J. Orton, Otto Reise, Sr., E. C. Royer and C. L. Van Slyke (80). By the end of 1926, thirteen more local growers had joined the Exchange and only George Lawler of Fife and Van Zonneveld of Washington at Orting remained independent in the Puyallup Valley area. The number of members has fluctuated since then, reaching a peak of 47 in 1930 and again in the late 1940s, but dropped as the total numbers of growers diminished. In 1956 there were 30 members. Although most members were from the Puyallup area, H. L. Willis from Mount Vernon was an early member and a few others from Mount Vernon also joined in the 1960s. A shake-up occurred in 1972 and several members withdrew. By 1992 only five growers were left, a figure which correlates with the general reduction of bulb acreage in the Puyallup Valley. From 1926 to 1990, however, a total of at least 83 bulb growers were members at one time or another. Known members are listed in Table 17-7.

The first president and sales manager in 1926 was Frank Chervenka. H. F. Gronen was chosen as secretary/treasurer. Chervenka resigned in 1928 and was succeeded by C. W. Orton as president and Gronen as sales manager. Subsequent officers are shown in Table 17-6.

This Exchange became one of the most successful cooperatives organized in Washington. It was planned as a non-profit cooperative, issued no capital stock, had a $10 membership fee, seven directors and an appointed secretary/treasurer. Its original constitution provided for a 50 year life. Its main purposes were the selling, packing and shipping of members' bulbs but it sometimes served in other ways. At first it hot-water treated members' Narcissus bulbs for the control of nematodes and insects. At times it also bought planting stock as in 1926 when it purchased 50 tons of Narcissus bulbs at $600 per ton from Holland for its members and again in 1959 when it purchased the entire 70-acre Narcissus collection of Jan De Graaff which contained many fine new varieties.

214

Table 17-6. Officers and managers of the Puget Sound Bulb Exchange.[*]

Year	President	Year	Vice President	Year	Sec./Treas.
1926-1928	Frank Chervenka	1926-1928	C. W. Orton	1926-1934	H. F. Gronen
1929-1960	C. W. Orton	1929-1933	E. C. Orton	1935-1943	R. G. Fryar
1961-1977	Harold Knutson	1934-1943	Otto Reise	1944-1956	Si Van Lierop
1978-1992	Roger Knutson	1944-1956	E. C. Orton	1957-1961	Miles Hatch
		1957-1962	Si Van Lierop	1962-1964	Bill Harm
		1963-1973	Francis Chervenka	1965-1974	Wilmer Reise
		1974-1975	Wallace Staatz	1975-1983	Clarence Bowen
		1976-1992	E.G. Williams, Jr.	1984-1992	Wallace Woodward

* The 1992 Board of Directors include above officers plus Wallace Staatz and Mrs. Mable (Bowen) Nearhood.

Year	Sales Manager	Year	Asst. Manager
1926-1927	Frank Chervenka	1929-1946	R. G. Fryar
1928	Otto Reise	1949-1951	Ted Sabelis
1929-1931	A. G. Pruyser	1961-1968	Joe Frantzen
1932-1946	H. F. Gronen		
1947-1951	R. G. Fryar		
1952-1968	Ted Sabelis		
1969-1972	Joe Frantzen		
1973-1992	Roger Knutson		

From 1926 to 1965, the Exchange operated out of leased Northern Pacific sheds adjacent to the railroad tracks in Sumner. Then, in 1966, the Exchange built its own $200,000 building on five acres of land purchased from Harold Knutson. An office, warehouse and special rooms for cooling and heating bulbs were included in its 62,000 square feet. The Exchange uses it during the summer and, in the spring, rents part of the facilities to the Puyallup Valley Flower Cooperative which packs, sells and ships field-cut flowers brought in by grower-members. The building is also leased, occasionally, for other purposes during slack bulb times.

Flower sales were not a major function of the Exchange originally but, in 1928, it shipped an entire iced-refrigerated carload of 400,000 Narcissus blooms to Chicago, in addition to other smaller shipments. However, the slow transportation and the lack of adequate refrigeration at that time restricted most flower sales to the West Coast. Also, in 1930, the Northwest Bulb Growers Association frowned upon flower sales to eastern markets, believing it was more profitable to sell the bulbs for forcing purposes. So, flower sales were discontinued.

Table 17-7. Known members of the Puget Sound Bulb Exchange and years of membership.

Name	Years	Name	Years
Alway, R. M.	1951 ?	McColley, Eugene E.	1942-1980
Aves, J. K. A.	1943 ?	McColley, Everett L.	1943-1965
Balch, D. A.	1965 ?	McKinnon, Gregg	1926-1943
Bowen, Clarence	1959-1965	Merritt, Leroy	1943 ?
Bowen Farms	1965-1992	Mettler, Charles	1951-1956
Breit, J. S.	1943 ?	Morrison, G. E.	1943 ?
Bryson, Harlow	1951-1960	Oliver, O. R.	1956-1965
Chervenka, Francis	1955-1971	Oliver Bros.	1951 ?
Chervenka, Frank	1926-1928	Orton, W. J.	1926 ?
Clarke, Joseph P.	1926 ?	Orton, C. W.	1926-1964
Clerget, Joseph P.	?	Orton, E. C.	1926-1956
Coffman, W. H.	1943 ?	Orton, Stanley	1951-1955
Deeds, George	1943-1964	Page, Vernal L.	1951-1956
DeGoede, Henry	1963-1968	Peters, Peter W.	1943 ?
DeVink, William	1951-1956	Peterson, Harry	1951 ?
DeVries, E. E.	1943 ?	Picha, Lloyd	1957 ?
Edmondson, Henry	1951-1964	Picha, Warren	1957 ?
Fuller, Joe R.	1951-1956	Reise, Otto, Sr.	1926-1963
Gary, M. B.	1951 ?	Reise, Otto, Jr.	1951-1959
Grainger, Robert N.	1951 ?	Reise, Wilmer	1951-1972
Gronen, H. F.	1926-1951	Reitmeier, H. J. G.	1951 ?
Harm, W. C.	1951-1966	Ritscher, Henry	1951-1962
Hatch, L. M.	1926-1956	Royer, E. C.	1926-1962
Hatch, Miles	1957-1965	Sabelis, Ted	1960-1965
Herrman, Kermit	1951 ?	Sather, Harry	1955-1957
Iverson, P. A.	1943-1951	Smit, Maynard	1951-1956
Jansen, Albert E.	1951-1960	Smith, Joe	1931-1933
Johnson, Arthur O.	1951-1975	Staatz, Stanley	1964-1968
Kern, Raymond	1943-1951	Staatz, Wallace	1964-1992
Knoblauch, Clayton	1951 ?	Stafford, James	1943 ?
Knoblauch, Melvin	1951 ?	Stookey, E. B.	1943-1951
Knutson, Harold	1951-1965	Van Slyke, C. L.	1926 ?
Knutson Farms	1965-1992	Van Lierop, Si	1943-1962
Korsten, Ben	1955-1978	Van Lierop, Neil	1958-1971
Lee, Mrs. Lucille	1951-1965	Wahlquist, J. E.	1943 ?
Leslie, Allen	1951-1958	Wait, F. P.	1951 ?
Locklin, H. D.	1926-1935	Walters, Stanley	1951-1971
Loeb, C. E.	1951-1964	Ward, Mervin	1951 ?
Lubbe, Ralph	1943 ?	Washington Bulb Co.	1963-1969
Lubbe, Charles	1951-1972	Williams Bros.	1965-1992
Mansfield, Howard	1951-1957	Willis, H. L.	1943-1956
Mattson, F. W.	1943 ?	Woodward, Wallace	1971-1992

Bulb sales started small, with only $14,000 worth sold in 1926 and about $28,000 in 1927, but they increased rapidly thereafter, until the Depression years of the 1930s when sales slumped. The Exchange, however, shipped 2,902,205 Narcissus and 306,920 Iris bulbs in 1930 for gross sales worth $200,000. The general operating expense at the Exchange that year was 17%.

In 1934, the Exchange shipped 15 carloads to Eastern markets and shipped a total of 71 carloads in 1952. In 1966, it sold 60 million bulbs, of which about half were Iris. Twenty-five million of the Iris went to Europe.

The Exchange was one of the major pioneers in opening up European markets to Washington Iris, beginning in 1954. It even shipped 100,000 Tulips to Holland for trial purposes in 1967. Because of its size, it long had a stabilizing influence on the marketing of Northwest bulbs, and independent growers generally looked to it to set prices as guidelines.

The sales managers of the Exchange have often been industry leaders and lobbyists. H. F. Gronen led the fight to retain the Narcissus quarantine, R. G. Fryar fought to protect the struggling bulb industry by lobbying to raise tariff rates and to reduce discriminatory transportation charges, Ted Sabelis helped to gain needed financing for bulb research, expand the markets for bulbs, stabilize their prices, and establish a cooperative advertising program with the Holland Bulb Exporters Association. Although it is no longer the major bulb wholesaler in Washington, the Exchange and its members still exert considerable influence in the bulb industry.

Allied Bulb Growers Association

This cooperative was organized as a closed corporation in 1929 by some of the same growers who had helped to organize the Puget Sound Bulb Exchange in 1926 and probably included others from the Kirkland area. It had similar features, and also was organized as a non-profit cooperative which issued no capital stock. It shipped bulbs from Sumner but its office was located in Seattle.

In 1930, it sold about 1,500,000 Narcissus bulbs and 1,500,000 Iris with about 90% of them going to jobbers and 10% directly to greenhouses. We have no record as to when it ceased operations but apparently it had a short life (105).

217

Puyallup Valley Flower Cooperative, Inc.

Under a marketing agreement signed by the Director of the Washington State Department of Agriculture on December 21, 1956, this cooperative was organized by eight Puyallup Valley flower growers in the winter of 1956-57 in an effort to stabilize and expand the developing cut-flower market. The eight growers represented about 75% of the Valley's cut-flower acreage. Other growers joined later and, at one time, the Cooperative included most flower producers in Washington. It had 30 members in 1959, 24 in 1963 and 3 in 1992.

The charter members were Francis Chervenka, H. D. Edmondson, Si Van Lierop, Harold Knutson, Ben Korsten, C. W. Orton, Wilmer Reise and Wallace T. Staatz. Chervenka was elected the first president; Staatz, vice president; Orton, treasurer; and Korsten, secretary (135).

Chervenka was manager from 1956 until 1961. He was followed by Joe Frantzen who served from 1961 until 1972; Harold Knutson, from 1972 to 1977; and Roger Knutson from 1977 to the present time. Roger Knutson is also the current (1992) president of the cooperative, Wally Staatz is vice president and Wallace Woodward, secretary.

The Flower Cooperative operated in space leased from the G. R. Kirk Company in Puyallup until 1966 when leased space in the Puget Sound Bulb Exchange Building became available.

The major purpose of the cooperative was to expedite the marketing of field-cut King Alfred Narcissus flowers through cooperative packing and selling. The growers at first sold the other Narcissus varieties themselves but later decided to sell all Narcissus flower varieties through the Cooperative. In 1964, this Cooperative merged with the Tulip Flowers, Inc. Cooperative in order to benefit from the advantage of having a single marketing agency for all types of bulb flowers.

Flowers are picked in bud stage and shipped by air freight or in refrigerated railroad cars and trucks. Most of those going east of Chicago travel by air, except during the peak of the season when some go by truck. In 1963, the Cooperative shipped 12 million Narcissus and 2 million Tulip flowers. By 1985, this had increased to 15 million Narcissus, 6 million Tulips and 1 million Iris plus 3 million Narcissus blooms used by the Puyallup Valley Daffodil Festival on its floats.

Because the Flower Cooperative handled so many flowers, it was a very important stabilizing factor in the early expansion days of the cut-flower industry.

218

Tulip Flowers, Inc.

This Cooperative was formed in 1959 along the same lines and with the same general purposes as the Puyallup Valley Flower Cooperative, sharing offices and facilities with it at the G. R. Kirk Company plant in Puyallup. It started with four growers from the Puyallup Valley and ten from Mount Vernon including all but two growers in Washington State who sold field-cut Tulip flowers. The first officers were Wallace T. Staatz, president; John Onderwater, vice president; Wilmer Reise, secretary and C. W. Orton, treasurer (12). In 1964 this Cooperative merged with the Puyallup Valley Flower Cooperative.

Skagit Valley Flower Cooperative

Several Mount Vernon area bulb growers organized this Cooperative about 1958. It has also been called the Skagit Valley Flower Growers and the Skagit Tulip Flowers Inc. by various growers. The goals of the Cooperative were to sell Tulip and Iris flowers and to help regulate surpluses. Coop members included Hank Bergman, Henry DeGoede, Cornelius Koning, Neal Noorlag, John Onderwater, Bill Roozen (for two years), Sam Stewart (for the first year) and Tony Van Waveren.

Bert Hart was sales manager in 1958, followed by Henry DeGoede, president and sales manager. Tony Van Waveren was secretary. Pete Walker became warehouse manager in 1959. The Cooperative used the warehouse facilities at the Tulip Grange in 1958 and, subsequently, those at DeGoede's farm and at the Holland Bulb Company where cold storage rooms were available.

Ten Skagit growers joined the Tulip Flowers, Inc. Cooperative when it was organized at Puyallup in 1959. Presumably, most of the Skagit growers continued to market their other bulb flowers through the Skagit Valley Cooperative until late in 1962 when the Holland Bulb Co. moved to Portland. The Skagit Cooperative subsequently disbanded with some of the growers joining the Puyallup Valley Flower Cooperative and the Puget Sound Bulb Exchange.

Skagit Valley Bulb Cooperative

In 1955, John Kapteyn discussed the possible formation of a Skagit Valley Bulb Cooperative with other growers in the Mount Vernon area.

It was to have been patterned after the Puget Sound Bulb Exchange. There seemed to be considerable interest, but the general reaction was that, "it was a good idea for everybody else but not for me," and, therefore, the Skagit Valley Bulb Coop never got off the ground.

Other Bulb Associations

Other bulb associations have been organized in the past, but, to this writer's knowledge, they are no longer functioning. They include the:

American Narcissus Growers Association which was organized by H. F. Gronen sometime before 1931, with a membership of commercial growers from about 11 major Narcissus-producing states. Its goals were primarily those of maintaining Quarantines 37 and 62 and promoting tariffs. Consequently, Gronen spent a great deal of time in Washington, DC arguing on behalf of the growers. He continued as president until he retired as manager of the Puget Sound Bulb Exchange in 1946. We have no further information about it.

Snohomish County Bulb Growers Association which Case Van Lierop helped to organize. H. H. Palmer was president.

Washington State Gladiolus Society. Ralph Pommert helped organize this Society in 1929 and it lasted until about 1983/84. The majority of the members were amateurs, but most commercial growers also belonged and were very active in it. Refer to Chapter 14 for more details.

The three Lily societies which were active at one time in Washington State were the **Vashon Island Lily Growers Association, Washington State Croft Lily Growers Association** and the **Seattle Lily Society**, later renamed the **Puget Sound Lily Society**. Refer to Chapter 15 for more details.

CHAPTER 18

DAVID GRIFFITHS
Scientific Father of the Washington Bulb Industry

Figure 18-1. Dr. David Griffiths
(Courtesy International Bulb Society)

David Griffiths was born at Aberystwyth, Wales on August 16, 1867, the son of David and Rachel (Lewis) Griffiths. David came to the United States with his parents to a farm in South Dakota about 1870. He received his early education at local schools which included Aberdeen (SD) High School and then attended South Dakota State Agricultural College, graduating with a B.S. degree in 1892 and an M.S. in 1893, working his way by teaching school during the winters. From 1893 to 1898, he taught science courses at the Aberdeen High School and then left for Columbia University where he received his Ph.D. in 1900. In 1905 he married Emigene Lily, who died four years later. He married Louise Hayward in 1915 (137) (Figure 18-1).

Griffiths was appointed professor of botany at the University of Arizona in 1900, where he studied grasses, other range plants and range management. In 1901, he accepted a position with the U.S. Department of Agriculture, Bureau of Plant Industry as an agriculturist in charge of range management in the Office of Grass and Forage Plant Investigations. This work involved 15 years (1901-1916) of field studies and the collection of specimens of grasses, salt bushes and cacti, primarily in the western United States. He soon became an authority on range research and range management (72). Among his projects was the investigation of the use of spineless cacti as food sources for animals and he collected about 3,500 specimens of *Opuntia* (prickly pear cactus). This collection was eventually turned over to Luther Burbank who commercialized the spineless prickly pear cactus (42,137).

Griffiths's increasing interest in the horticultural field eventually led to his being assigned to head the USDA research on flower bulbs, in which field he continued until his death in 1935. An article by Humphrey (72) stated that he spent his first fifteen years in the USDA on range research and the last twenty on bulb research. He published an article on "The Production of Dutch Bulbs on the Pacific Coast" on Dec. 16, 1916 (55). Therefore, it is assumed that his appointment to work on bulbs was made sometime in 1916. His title was changed to that of horticulturist about 1920. About 1929 he was advanced to the rank of senior horticulturist.

Much of Griffiths's research was done at the USDA Bulb Station at Bellingham, WA which was established in 1908 (Figure 18-2). Its history is described in Chapter 19. His headquarters were in Washington, DC where he had greenhouses available for forcing tests. However, he customarily spent about two months at the Bellingham Bulb Station every spring to examine plants and flowers and another two months in late summer to check the bulbs after harvest (11). Taylor reported that "Even as senior horticulturist much of his field work was of necessity done with his own hands, frequently under weather and soil conditions which involved physical hardship and hazard to health" (137).

Figure 18-2. USDA Bulb Station at Bellingham, 1913.
(Courtesy J. W. Sandison Collection, Whatcom Museum of
History and Art, Bellingham, Wash., 1982.71.30)

Under Griffiths's direction, both research activities and publications expanded rapidly at the Bulb Station. Taylor wrote that: "Though the funds available were woefully inadequate . . . Griffiths entered the field with such enthusiasm of spirit and tenacity of purpose" . . . "that he soon became recognized as the unquestioned leader in this field" (137).

Griffiths maintained experimental plots and collections of bulb varieties in plots at the USDA Arlington Experimental Farm in Rosslyn, VA, at Willard, NC and at Charleston, SC. He also ran cooperative tests with scientists as well as with both amateur and commercial growers in many other areas of the United States (61).

His known cooperators in Washington included George Gibbs, John Macrae Smith, Floyd Kaylor, L. N. Freimann and Gerrit and Maurice Van Zanten in Whatcom County; Mary and Sam Stewart, H. L. Willis and Marinus Lefeber in Skagit County; Case Van Lierop in King County; Ralph Marble, George and Ward Lawler in Pierce County and Joe Smith in Thurston County.

In addition to assisting individual growers with their problems, Griffiths also promoted bulb growing in other ways. He gave many speeches, including one in 1917 in Seattle soon after he was appointed

223

director of the Bulb Station (120). In 1923, he visited Puyallup and urged a boyhood friend, W. H. Paulhamus, to encourage farmers in the area to try bulb growing on an experimental basis. Paulhamus did so and the interest did develop, although slowly at first (99).

In this connection, a few quotations from his obituaries will best illustrate some of his problems and predictions. "Stocky, dynamic David Griffiths, a quarter of a century ago stood almost alone in his belief that the same circumstances [climate, as in Holland] favored American production of flower bulbs" . . . "Hated and derided by the Holland growers, and laughed at by his own countrymen in the flower trade, he doggedly traveled the states from Florida to Long Island, and from San Diego to Seattle, insisting that we could grow as good bulbs as could be produced anywhere in the world, and trying to get growers to experiment with the cultural methods he had proved" (107).

By 1924, he had come to the conclusion that "On the whole, the climate of the Pacific Northwest is probably superior to any other considerable area in the country" (57). Griffiths, however, made relatively little progress in promoting bulb production in the United States until the Department of Agriculture, alarmed at the entry into the United States of such pests as the Japanese beetle and the Dutch Elm disease, decided in 1922 to apply quarantine regulations to some imported flower bulbs and tubers effective in 1926. Narcissus, but not Tulips, were to be barred. In this connection, it is interesting to note a prophecy made by Dr. Griffiths: "The moment we stop importing Dutch bulbs" . . . "we'll begin importing Dutch bulb growers" and his prediction came true (107).

By 1926, Griffiths noted: "It is considered that, in spite of shortcomings in some of the varieties, the outlook for American production of bulbs is decidedly bright. The progress made is rather remarkable, considering the short time that our growers have devoted to the industry" (58).

Griffiths's first USDA bulletin (#797) on bulbs was the *Commercial Dutch-Bulb Culture in the United States* by David Griffiths and H. E. Juenemann, published in 1919. Between 1917 and 1935, he wrote over 100 articles on bulb growing for trade magazines such as *Florists' Exchange* and *Florists' Review* in addition to many technical articles. Griffiths published a steady stream of government circulars and bulletins on all phases of bulb production. Key bulletins, such as those on Narcissus, Tulips, etc., were revised and updated every few years.

Taylor reported that: "His crisp and lucid style of presentation added greatly to the practical value of these communications" (137).

Griffiths continued and expanded the bulb research which was under way at the Bulb Station when he arrived in 1917. By 1925, he and his associates there were working with over 50 genera and varieties of bulbs (69). His research was primarily of an economic or practical nature dealing with varieties, times of planting, fertilizing, harvesting, storage temperatures and forcing conditions of all types of bulbs. Later, nematodes and insects became a problem so he even got into experiments on Narcissus with the hot water (110-111°F) plus formalin treatment.

Griffiths apparently was interested in Lilies even before he was put in charge of the Bulb Station. They continued to be his main love and he eventually worked with all the major species, especially the Regal, Madonna and Easter Lilies and three California species. The *Gardeners Chronicle* reported in 1935 that by "rigorous selection and elimination he was gradually evolving a remarkable series of hybrids of the California group of Lilies like *Lilium pardalinum, L. Parryi* and *L. Humboldtii*. In his search for fine hybrids, Griffiths had the interests of horticulture at heart more than those of pure science, and his aim was the production of a series of hybrid Lilies that should take a permanent place in the gardens of the United States" (48). In the early 1930s, he released eleven hybrids. One of these, Peter Puget, was his own hybrid while the others were selected by him from seed purchased from Carl Purdy, Ukiah, CA. Griffiths may have released other hybrids but these were the only ones for which we have a record. All of these Lilies were named for prominent people or for certain geographical features in the Puget Sound region, and included two named after persons who donated land for the Bulb Station: Cyrus Gates and Frances Larrabee (60). The Lilies were down-facing and mostly orange colored with reddish or black spots. The Oregon Bulb Farms eventually acquired many of the stocks, lumped them together and sold them under the name of Bellingham Hybrids (44).

There is also reason to believe that the famous Croft Lily, which dominated the Easter Lily industry for many years, may have been one of Griffiths's selections or hybrids originally. Refer to Chapter 15 for more information on this.

After Griffiths's death, Taylor stated that: "He had much hybridization of bulbous plants under way, particularly lilies and daffodils and had named and described a considerable number of promising new varieties, some of which are in process of dissemination" (137).

A comment by Floyd Kaylor in 1954 on Griffiths's personality is interesting: "He was a queer man in some ways—very hard to know and somewhat locked up inside. It took me two or three years to really get acquainted with him, but when his closeness broke down and he accepted me as a student of bulb growing I found him most helpful and he would tell me things he was trying to do—things he had not put into any of the pamphlets he had written" (79).

Griffiths entered the Emergency Hospital in Washington, DC on March 12 and died on March 19, 1935 of "neurosis of the liver" as listed on his death certificate. He was buried in Rock Creek Cemetery. Griffiths was survived by his wife; a son, John D. Griffiths; a daughter, Mrs. Elizabeth Griffiths Lash; a sister, Mrs. F. E. Elliott of Marysville, WA and a brother (42).

Many glowing tributes appeared after his death.

"Here was a man of unquestioned stature and soundness as a botanist and one who was at the same time a horticulturist of eminence and great common sense." (72).

The *Gardeners Chronicle* said that: "Griffiths did more than any other man to interest Americans in the home production on a commercial scale of native and foreign bulbous plants" (48).

F. F. Rockwell paid tribute to Griffiths's efforts in a 1944 article on bulbs in the *Saturday Evening Post* as follows: "If you plant tulips or daffodils this fall I suggest you set each flower-filled bulb in the soil with a thought for the late David Griffiths, senior horticulturist and bulb expert for the Department of Agriculture until his death in 1935. This comparatively unknown and little appreciated scientist paved the way for the production of flower bulbs in the United States" (107).

Taylor wrote that Griffiths "developed a rare combination of scientific accuracy in his research and sound common sense in the practical application of his discoveries" and his "leadership was largely responsible for the progress thus far made in commercial bulb production in the United States" (137).

"In the course of a few years the new industry shook down. The Pacific Northwest has become, as Dr. Griffiths predicted, the leading area for the production of "Dutch" bulbs." (107).

Therefore, for his many contributions to the bulb industry, it is appropriate that he be considered, on the 77th anniversary of the beginning of his research career on bulbs in 1916, to be the Scientific Father of the Bulb Industry in Washington State.

CHAPTER 19

Bulb Research in Washington State

Bulb growers in Washington State have benefitted from the research of more than fifty full-time or part-time scientists, beginning with Dr. P. H. Dorsett and associates at the U.S. Department of Agriculture (USDA) Bulb Station at Bellingham in 1908. Why were bulb crops so popular with scientists? The beauty of the flowers was no doubt a major attraction but, in addition, these crops provided challenging opportunities for research on new and unique problems. In addition, the excellent cooperation and financial support by bulb growers and others has continued to encourage scientists to work on bulb problems.

The research from 1908 to 1935 by Drs. Dorsett, Griffiths and their associates at Bellingham provided a solid basis for the start of bulb production in Washington State. Their work was the only research done on bulbs until after the rapid expansion of bulb plantings that followed adoption of the USDA Daffodil quarantine in 1926. Insects and nematodes, by then, had become serious problems so, between 1927 and 1929, WSU scientists at Puyallup and USDA scientists at Sumner and Bellingham began to investigate the timing of the HWF (hot water plus formalin) treatment of Narcissus bulbs in an effort to obtain better pest control and to reduce injury. There were about 7 scientists who worked on Washington's bulb problems in the 1920s, 11 in the 1930s, 20 in the 1940s and 1950s, 14 in the 1970s. Now, in 1993, there are only three scientists in Washington State working part time on bulb problems. These figures include USDA and Oregon scientists who have been or are now cooperating with Washington scientists, or who were working on their own projects here. When bulb research was at its height in the Pacific Northwest in 1948, there were 67 different scientific bulb projects under way in Washington, Oregon, and British Columbia.

Washington scientists and bulb growers have benefitted from the cooperation and research of many scientists at other locations including:

F. P. McWhorter, A. N. Roberts, Harold Jensen, Tom Allen, James L. Green, Jack Stang, Larry Moore, Robert Doss and Robert Linderman at Oregon State University; William Newton, Bob Hastings, Jack Bosher, Jack Crossley and Harry Andison in British Columbia; and S. L. Emsweller, Neil W. Stuart, William McClellan, Marc Cathey, Sam Asen, Floyd Smith and Philip Brierley in the USDA at Beltsville, MD.

Table 19-2 lists available information about various scientists, both past and present. An asterisk marks the names of those who apparently spent at least one-third of their time on bulb research. Many of the others listed worked for only a short time on a special project, such as a Ph.D. thesis. The column labelled "years on bulb research" lists the names of those for whom we have definite information or for the years in which they published their research. A section is also included concerning scientists and others who ran the annual Bulb Growers Short Course (now Conference), edited the proceedings, etc.

This attempt to summarize the major research contributions has been very difficult because most of the scientists have died and many of their publications are not available in the files at WSU Puyallup. Lack of time has prevented a complete search of the literature and, therefore, the summary which follows is somewhat biased in favor of major and/or recent research with which the author is familiar. A few key references are listed, particularly of recent publications. The *Handbook on Bulb Growing and Forcing* (49) contains many of the research results of the fourteen contributing scientists up to the time of its publication in 1957. He especially regrets that he did not have the time to do the research necessary to include a biographical sketch of each scientist.

In addition to university funds, much of the bulb research at WSU has been supported by grants from the Northwest Bulb Growers Association before 1956 and by the Washington State Bulb Commission since then, by various chemical companies, and by the Fred C. Gloeckner Foundation which contributed funds for equipment through Ted Sabelis. The USDA, through Dr. S. L. Emsweller, provided a car, equipment and some operating funds from 1948 until 1977 for use by USDA collaborator, Dr. C. J. Gould.

Bulb Research Centers

The USDA Bulb Station at Bellingham

The first bulb research location in Washington State was the Bulb Station or Bulb Garden operated by the USDA and located near Bellingham. Prior to 1907, the USDA had been conducting experiments with bulbs on the East Coast and in many other areas. These included cooperative tests in the Bellingham area with George Gibbs, John Macrae Smith, and perhaps others, starting in 1903 or earlier (139). In the fall of 1905, the USDA sent 15,000 imported Dutch bulbs to Gibbs to be grown under contract for two years for experimental purposes. He finished planting them on November 9 (119). In 1906, the USDA shipped bulb stocks from Washington, DC for trial plantings at Bellingham, Tacoma and Spokane under the supervision of Henry E. Juenemann (139). Meanwhile, they also sent A. J. Pieters, L. C. Corbett and G. W. Oliver with Juenemann to survey possible bulb growing sites in the Puget Sound region and other locations throughout the United States where growing conditions were similar to those in Holland (30).

Gibbs, Smith and others had previously written letters and sent samples of their bulbs to the USDA so the survey group was aware of the bulb-growing potential in Washington State. It is not surprising, therefore, to learn that, in 1907, the federal government tentatively selected Bellingham as the site for its USDA Bulb Garden in the Pacific Northwest. In 1908, the Secretary of Agriculture, James Wilson, officially authorized the establishment of the "United States Bulb Garden at Bellingham" (30).

R. A. Oakley briefly described the purposes of the Garden in 1917 as follows: "In order to encourage the growing of Dutch bulbs in this country on a commercial scale and to provide American-grown bulbs of superior quality for congressional distribution, the Department of Agriculture established a bulb-propagating garden near Bellingham" (96).

Mr. L. N. Morrison, Assistant Director of the Bureau of Plant Industry, handled the negotiations for this site, which was leased by the Bellingham Chamber of Commerce to the United States Government for $1 a year. The Chamber also was obligated to prepare the land for planting, to supply a residence, storage buildings and various other items. The Bulb Garden was located on the site of old Fort Bellingham, about 2½ miles west of the city of Bellingham and consisted of a 9.2

acre field, 250 feet wide by 1,600 feet long, extending from the Marietta Road on the north to the Bellingham Bay on the south (30).

The first bulbs (170,466) were planted at Bellingham in the fall of 1908 by Juenemann under the supervision of Dorsett and Peter Bisset (30). Bulbs were grown in Dutch type beds, at first, but the row method was adopted in later years.

Members of Congress had been distributing free seeds to their constituents for many years and, in 1893, both congressmen and the USDA distributed almost 7 million packages of vegetable seeds, perhaps to encourage the development of gardens. Apparently, the politicians wanted to add bulbs to the list.

In 1912, about 33,000 bulbs were sent to congressmen to be distributed and over a million were planted for propagation at the Bulb Station in Whatcom County (30). In a letter to George Lawler on September 3, 1921, Griffiths stated that he had shipped Congress a carload of 340,000 bulbs which was worth $8,500 and that this amount was more money than he had received from Congress to run the Government Bulb Garden that year! The free seed and bulb distribution by Congress was discontinued in 1923 (62), but the Bulb Station had been established and was the largest bulb producer in Whatcom County, and perhaps in the state, for many years.

In 1913, Dorsett, director of the Garden reported that: "The work thus far has included the propagation and growing of hyacinths, tulips and narcissus" (30). The major emphasis seems to have been on Hyacinths at first. Varietal tests were under way on many bulb types and some forcing tests were made. These demonstrated the early blooming qualities of Washington-grown bulbs in comparison with those from Holland.

A USDA publication by Oakley lists only Tulips and Narcissus for distribution in 1917. Hyacinths, which had been very popular, were not included, probably because most of them had been lost after an extremely severe freeze in February of 1916. Oakley also reported that: "Comparative tests . . . indicate that American-grown tulip bulbs are freer from disease and blossom from five to seven days earlier than the same varieties imported from Europe; also that the flowers from Bellingham-grown bulbs are on longer stems and of better color and quality than those from foreign-grown bulbs" (96). Not many government publications emanated from this work, however, and the general impression is that most effort up to this time had gone into establishing the Bulb Station and producing bulbs for Congressional distribution.

Although Oakley was listed as the "Agronomist in Charge" in his 1917 publication, Dr. David Griffiths is believed to have been appointed director of the Bulb Garden and of the USDA bulb research program some time in 1916. Griffiths published an article on December 16, 1916 on "The Production of Dutch Bulbs on the Pacific Coast" (55). He also was reported on March 25, 1917 in the *Seattle Times* as being the "Expert in Charge" but, when asked in 1991, the USDA could not furnish a definite date for his appointment.

Dr. Griffiths was a strong director for the USDA Bulb Garden in Bellingham and, in 1917, probably influenced Cyrus Gates, William McKay and Mrs. C. X. Larrabee to donate 60 acres of logged-off land to the project. This land was located along the Guide Meridian Highway north of town. The superintendent, Juenemann, immediately began clearing 30 acres of stumps for the expansion of bulb experiments and, by 1925, the Station had 35 acres of land to use (69). Juenemann resigned in 1924 in order to grow bulbs commercially and B. L. Peters, assisted by H. A. Houser, took his place as superintendent of the Station (111).

In Washington, DC, the Garden was listed officially as "The Plant Introduction Field Station and Bulb Garden, Bellingham," but was usually called just "the Bulb Station."

Annual Visitor Field Days were held at the Station and, in 1916, about 2,000 people attended. Other visitors, both domestic and foreign, came to observe the varietal display gardens and to discuss results with those in charge, especially Dr. Griffiths.

Dr. Griffiths died rather suddenly on March 19, 1935 and, in 1936, the Station was converted into a nursery under the jurisdiction of the USDA Soil Conservation Service (11) for the testing of new trees, shrubs, and other plants for their adaptability and usefulness in the Pacific Northwest. The bulbs on hand were distributed to USDA scientists at Beltsville, MD and Corvallis, OR for continued research. In 1955, the Bellingham Station was turned over to the Washington Department of Agriculture for use as a plant nursery. It is now the site of a large shopping mall.

The USDA Ornamentals Insect Laboratory at Sumner

Charles F. Doucette was transferred by the USDA from California to the Puyallup Valley in 1927 to investigate insects on bulb crops. He was stationed at WSU Puyallup until January 1929, when he moved to the new USDA Entomological Laboratory at Sumner. The land, greenhouse and laboratory facilities were supplied by the Pierce County Commissioners at the request of local bulb growers led by Frank Chervenka. The laboratory was located on the county poor farm on Riverside Road near Sumner.

Doucette worked on the control of many insects, particularly the bulb fly and mites on Narcissus and aphids on Lilies. He was assisted, at times, by several other entomologists as shown in Table 19-1. Doucette retired in 1962 and was followed by Donald Coudriet. On June 30, 1969, the lab was closed and Coudriet was transferred to Beltsville, MD.

Some of their achievements, particularly those of Doucette, include studies of types of aphids on different genera of bulbs, the refinement in timing of the HWF treatment of Narcissus bulbs, the use of methyl bromide fumigation of Narcissus for control of bulb flies and mites, the control of Lily weevils with insecticides, the use of preplanting dips of Lily bulbs with systemic insecticides to control aphids, and especially the effectiveness of the chlorinated hydrocarbons (chlordane, aldrin, heptachlor and dieldrin) in controlling the Narcissus bulb fly. Doucette found that these materials gave outstanding control and could be used effectively in the HWF treatment, or be applied as dusts or sprays to bulbs in the furrow at planting time or used as drenches on the base of plants in the spring (35).

He also found that a hydrocyanic acid gas fumigation of Narcissus bulbs was somewhat effective for insect control, and it was used until methyl bromide fumigation was found to be more effective. An associate, Randall Latta, tested and recommended a vapor-heat treatment for Narcissus bulbs but it was rejected later by the growers as being less effective than the old HWF treatment for control of bulb flies, mites, etc.

Although he officially retired in 1962, Doucette continued to work for many years with bulb growers in Washington and with the Lily growers in Oregon and California.

232

Washington State University at Puyallup and Mount Vernon

WSU has actively assisted bulb growers for more than 65 years. On January 15, 1926, a "Bulb Day" for growers was held during the annual winter school session at the Western Washington Experiment Station at Puyallup to provide the latest information on bulb culture to growers and would-be growers.

The needs of the rapidly developing bulb industry in the late 1920s attracted the attention of many scientists, including H. D. Locklin and G. A. Newton of WSU Puyallup from 1927 to 1929. They attempted to determine the optimum dates in the Puyallup Valley for control of nematodes and insects with the HWF treatment of certain leading varieties of Narcissus.

About this time, another USDA scientist, Theodore H. Scheffer, was transferred to Puyallup to study the control of moles and mice in bulbs and other crops. He showed that trapping was the most effective technique but, even in 1992, an easier method is still desired by both growers and homeowners.

Another investigator, W. D. Courtney, was transferred by the USDA to the USDA Sumner Entomological Laboratory in 1933. He moved to the WSU Station at Puyallup to work on nematode problems until he retired in 1963. Like Doucette, he also worked on the refinement of the HWF treatment of Narcissus varieties. Later, with cooperators, he studied the control of nematodes on Iris bulbs and of leaf nematodes on Lilies.

Research on fungus diseases of bulbs began in 1927 when George Newton at WSU Puyallup (Figure 19-1) tried adding a mercury compound to the hot water bath for the control of basal rot of Narcissus. Not much more was done until 1934 when Dr. Glenn A. Huber, a plant pathologist, arrived from WSU Pullman. He discovered a sticking agent (Penetrol) which greatly improved the effectiveness of Bordeaux mixture in controlling leaf blights of Narcissus and Iris. He also began to work on basal rot control in Narcissus. Karl Baur assisted Huber in some of this research. In 1941, Huber added Dr. Charles J. (Chuck) Gould to the plant pathology department to take charge of the bulb investigations. During World War II, the bulb disease research was interrupted by the study of diseases of food crops. After the war, bulb diseases again became a major project. Dr. E. P. Breakey, entomologist, also started working on bulb insects and Croft Lily culture about 1941. Vernon L. Miller, chemist, began research on fungicides about 1945, at Puyallup.

Dr. Neil W. Stuart, a plant physiologist with the USDA at Beltsville, MD, and Gould began their cooperative bulb forcing experiments in 1948 and continued them until Stuart retired in 1971. Dr. Walter Apt, a USDA nematologist, arrived in 1956 to expand the research on nematodes. Dr. Robert Doss, a USDA plant physiologist, came in 1976 to continue Stuart's research on bulb forcing. Dr. Gary Chastagner, plant pathologist, arrived in 1978 to replace Gould who retired in 1977.

Research at WSU Mount Vernon (Figure 19-2) began in 1950 with weed control experiments by Dr. Martin Carstens, horticulturist. He was followed by Dwight Peabody, agronomist, in 1951 and, after his retirement, by Dr. Stott Howard in 1986. Dr. Wilbur Anderson, horticulturist, arrived in 1969 and began research in 1978 on a soil fertility study of bulb fields and, later, on the elimination of viruses in Iris by the use of tissue culture. Nematode research has been handled by Dr. William Haglund, plant pathologist, who began working on control problems in 1974.

Although the scientists mentioned above devoted much of their time to research on bulbs, there were many others, including cooperators here and elsewhere, who made significant contributions to Washington's bulb industry. These are also listed in Table 19-2.

WSU extension specialists at Puyallup have also contributed significantly to the bulb industry by organizing the Bulb Growers Short Course (Conference), editing the Bulb Growers Newsletter, organizing field days, etc. These include: Robert Wearne (1963-1967), Dr. Bernard Wesenberg (1968-1988) and Dr. Ralph Byther (1976-1992).

R. L. Nowadnick, former Dean at Skagit Valley College, has assisted WSU scientists in many ways. He has also been secretary-treasurer of the Northwest Bulb Growers Association since 1954 and of the Washington Bulb Commission since 1961. Nowadnick edited the Bulb Growers Newsletter from 1953 to 1964.

Four scientists worked on Washington bulb problems for their doctoral degrees: Neil Allan MacLean (on species of *Botrytis* which attack bulbs); Walter J. Apt (on species of *Fusarium* which rot bulbs); Gordon J. Van Laan (on methods of determining Iris maturity), all at WSU; and Elwood W. Kalin who earned his degree at Purdue University on the effect of flower removal on yield and forcing of Iris and Narcissus bulbs.

Figure 19-1. Washington State University Research and Extension
Center at Puyallup. (Courtesy Earl Otis)

Figure 19-2. Washington State University Research and Extension
Unit at Mount Vernon. (Courtesy Earl Otis)

235

Culture

Gladiolus variety tests. Arthur Myhre evaluated new varieties of Gladiolus during the 1960s at WSU Puyallup as part of the New England Gladiolus Society's nationwide trials. Art also experimented with liming and other techniques in an effort to increase the thickness of Tulip skins.

Fertilizers. Karl Baur, Todd Tremblay and Gould, starting in 1948, ran fertilizer tests on Iris, Narcissus and Tulips but discovered that bulbs did not respond as well as vegetables to fertilization. Baur's conclusion was that growers might have been overfertilizing rather than underfertilizing.

Dr. Wilbur C. Anderson and Dr. William Haglund from WSU Mount Vernon reported in 1978 that soils in several commercial bulb fields were low in pH, phosphorus, magnesium, zinc and boron (5). Anderson also found that the greatest nutrient absorption by Narcissus started at the time of leaf emergence and that fall applications of nitrogen were ineffective unless a controlled-release fertilizer was used (4).

Weed control. The cost of hand weeding Iris was estimated to be about $200 per acre in the 1940s. Baur and Gould discovered in 1948 and 1949 that the application of a pre-emergence spray of a dinitro herbicide plus IPC (isopropyl-N-phenyl carbamate) and diesel oil would control weeds in Iris and Narcissus at about one-tenth the cost of hand weeding. This mixture was used for several years.

Dr. Martin Carstens initiated some weed control research about 1950 at WSU Mount Vernon. This was greatly expanded by Dwight Peabody when he arrived in 1951. Peabody discovered the timing, rate and effectiveness of dinoseb plus chlorpropham (CIPC) in controlling winter annual weeds, the use of monuron and oryzalin for summer annual weed control, and the use of amitrole in preplant treatments for perennial weeds. These treatments were quickly adopted by bulb growers (101).

Peabody retired in 1985 and Dr. Stott Howard arrived in 1986 to continue the weed research at Mount Vernon. Howard found a new herbicide, cinmethylin (Cinch), to be very effective in controlling weeds in Iris, Narcissus and Tulips without causing injury. Cinch and oryzalin, when applied in the fall, were overall the most effective treatments in his tests (70). Howard resigned in 1989 and Dr. Kassim Al-Khatib joined the faculty on April 1, 1992 to continue the weed research.

Physiological Problems

Iris Topple is a physiological disorder which occurs occasionally during forcing but rarely in the fields. It shows up as a weakness of the flower stalk at the uppermost node with the resulting collapse of the flower bud. The problem occurs most often during short days with cloudy skies. Dr. Robert Doss found that the weakened area of the stem was low in calcium and that Topple could be prevented by adding calcium nitrate to the soil before planting or by repeated drenching of growing plants with calcium nitrate (31).

Tulip Topple resembles Iris Topple and is also caused by a calcium deficiency. Drs. Walter Mortensen and Aaron Baker of WSU Puyallup, in experiments at both Mount Vernon and Woodland, found that applications of lime before planting or sidedressing with calcium nitrate later could prevent this condition in the field.

Gladiolus Fluorine Injury. Dr. Folke Johnson and associates discovered in 1950 that a peculiar scorching of Gladiolus leaves near aluminum reduction plants, steel mills, pottery works, etc., was caused by fluorine gas and that certain sensitive varieties of Gladiolus could be used as "indicator plants" to determine if the gas were present. They also found that: other plants, such as prunes, could be injured; Gladiolus varieties differed considerably in resistance to injury; lime applied to Gladiolus leaves protected them from injury; and lime-impregnated filter papers would absorb fluorine which could then be analyzed at intervals to determine the accumulated amount of fluorine gas in the air (76,2).

Insects

The culture of Croft Easter Lilies in Washington was aided by the investigations carried on by Dr. E. P. Breakey and his associates in the 1940s who found that one hour of HWF treatment eliminated mites and the bud and leaf nematodes from bulbs, that methyl bromide fumigations would also control mites, and that production could be improved by dipping bulbs in Spergon and then dusting them with a hormone material before planting.

Breakey also found, starting in 1941, that methyl bromide fumigations would control insects on many other bulb crops such as the bulb fly and mites on Narcissus and aphids on Iris and Tulips. He worked out the optimum rates, temperatures and durations of treatment as well as other related factors. This methyl bromide fumigation was quickly adopted by the industry, primarily for use on salable bulbs, but also, when needed, on planting stock (15).

Virus Diseases

Drs. Gary Chastagner and John Hammond found a new virus (Turnip Mosaic Virus) causing flower discoloration or "breaking" of Tulips which is different from the common Tulip-Break Virus (TBV) in Washington State (65). Both of these viruses are transmitted by aphids. Research between 1985 and 1988 showed that most transmission of the TBV virus occurred during late April and early May in a normal year.

Dr. Tom Allen at Oregon State University and associates found eight virus diseases present in Iris plants in western Washington in 1982. The two most common were Iris Mild Mosaic and Iris Severe Mosaic; the other six were found only occasionally or rarely. The most destructive was the Iris Severe Mosaic Virus (1).

Dr. W. C. Anderson of WSU Mount Vernon and associates have developed techniques for obtaining virus-free Iris by excising and culturing small bulblets on special media under certain temperature and light-controlled conditions. The freedom of the Iris bulbs from viruses was confirmed by assays made by Allen. By means of these techniques, Anderson now has 18 virus-free clones of eight Iris varieties. After the cultured bulblets became sufficiently large, they were propagated in a vector-proof screenhouse at WSU Mount Vernon. Later, by using a new Dutch bulb-chipping machine, he was able to increase the numbers of virus-free bulbs to 24,000 by 1990 (6).

Bacterial Diseases

Bacterial diseases are not usually of major importance on bulbs and corms in western Washington. Bacterial Scab on Gladiolus is the most common one. Although the "Yellows" disease of Hyacinths is occasionally found in imported bulbs, it has never become a problem here, perhaps because of the acid soils and mild climate. However, there is a fluorescent *Pseudomonas* which sporadically causes an elongated streaking decay in Iris leaves in the field and a general stem rot at the base of cold-stored Narcissus flowers. Dr. Larry Moore from Oregon

State University worked on this problem in Washington in the mid-1970s.

Nematode Problems

W. D. Courtney and associates investigated many aspects of the HWF treatment for nematodes attacking Iris, Narcissus, Tulips and Lily bulbs including the response of different varieties to the treatments, the optimum dates for treating, the effect of temperatures before and after treatment, the benefit from presoaking bulbs, the addition of wetting agents to increase the effectiveness of HWF, etc. Their general results and recommendations were summarized in Washington Agricultural Experiment Station Circular 422 (29).

The **Root Lesion Nematode** (*Pratylenchus penetrans*) attacks Narcissus roots, most often in light, well-drained and warm soils. Dr. Walter Apt discovered it in 1956 and, in tests carried on between 1956 and 1961, he and Gould found that DD and other nematocidal soil fumigants controlled the nematode in the soil. However, high rates of methyl bromide and certain other materials slightly increased losses from basal rot and crown rot, presumably by destroying beneficial microorganisms in the soil (8).

Iris Nematode (*Ditylenchus destructor*) was effectively controlled in small Wedgwood Iris bulbs by use of the HWF treatment for 2-3 hours by Courtney and Gould, beginning in 1946. Certain other varieties could tolerate only a 1-2 hour treatment. The treatment was only partially effective on large bulbs. Courtney found that the best time for treating was 1-3 weeks after the basal cap slipped easily off the bulbs (52).

Dr. William Haglund arrived at WSU Mount Vernon in 1960 and began testing the effectiveness, timing and rates of various soil treatments for the control of nematodes in 1974. He obtained outstanding control of the nematode on Iris by using Nemacur and this treatment was soon adopted by the growers. Haglund recommended that Nemacur SEC be used at 6-12 pounds per acre in a 1:10 dilution sprayed in a 10-inch wide band over the bottom of the furrow just prior to planting bulbs. It can also be sprayed over the bulbs in the furrow before they are covered with soil. Nemacur is also effective against both the *Ditylenchus dipsaci* on Narcissus and the Root Lesion Nematodes. Nemacur does not move through the soil, so careful application is essential (63). Haglund is currently experimenting with a combination of Nemacur and SMDC (metam-sodium) in hopes of controlling migrating nematodes, insects, and parasitic fungi at the same time (64).

Leaf Blights

The cool, moist spring weather in western Washington favors several leaf-spotting fungi, particularly different species of *Botrytis* (51,52,53). The favorite fungicide used by the pioneers for controlling such fungi was Bordeaux spray, a mixture of copper sulfate and lime. Although it gave reasonable control of some fungi, it did not work against all pathogens nor did it adhere to the foliage as long as desired. Sometimes, it also injured leaves, particularly on Tulips.

Narcissus

In attempting to control the leaf-spotting fungi, Dr. Glenn Huber began experimenting with various "stickers" when he arrived at WSU Puyallup in 1934. He soon discovered that the addition of Penetrol to the Bordeaux mixture made it more effective in controlling Fire, caused by *Botrytis polyblastis,* on Narcissus. This combination was used by growers for many years. Some growers sprayed so enthusiastically that their plants looked blue instead of the normal green and occasionally plants were stunted by the Bordeaux. Bordeaux was a nuisance to mix. As other fungicides, such as the dithiocarbamates, became available and were proven to be effective, the growers gradually switched to them in the late 1940s.

Botrytis polyblastis seems to thrive under slightly warmer conditions than the other *Botrytis* species and was, therefore, only troublesome occasionally on very susceptible varieties. Recently, it has become more destructive. Chastagner discovered in tests made in 1978 and 1979 that it was controlled better with benomyl than with mancozeb (19).

He also found that benomyl and other new fungicides gave better control of Leaf Scorch (*Stagonospora curtisii*) on Narcissus than did mancozeb. Sprays applied every two weeks were definitely superior to those applied every four weeks (20).

Iris

Iris Leaf Spot (*Didymellina macrospora*) was controlled by Gould with zineb in 1958 and, later, with mancozeb in experiments at Puyallup. Chastagner reported in 1989 that Ornalin DF and certain other new fungicides gave even better control than mancozeb and benomyl (22).

Ink Spot (*Drechslera iridis*) has become a problem on Iris in recent years. Chastagner was able to control it with sprays of Chipco 26019 and Daconil 2787 (18).

Iris Leaf Rust (*Puccinia iridis*) is a world-wide disease of both rhizomatous and bulbous Iris. It can be extremely destructive to susceptible varieties in warm climates. Although the rust is rarely observed in Washington, it is a common problem in certain areas of California where bulbous Iris are grown for cut flowers in the field. In greenhouse spray tests in 1990, Chastagner found that most fungicides tested (Benlate, Dithane M-45, Daconil 2787, etc.) could successfully control this rust (21).

Tulips

Before 1942, Bordeaux mixture was used to control Tulip Fire (*Botrytis tulipae*) but it often did more damage to the leaves than did the disease. In 1942, Gould found that ferbam (a dithiocarbamate) gave excellent control without injury. Mancozeb proved to be even better when it became available and, more recently, the benzimidazoles have given excellent control. Chastagner and Dr. Tom Hsiang recently discovered numerous strains of *B. tulipae* in the Northwest that are resistant to the benzimidazoles, such as Benlate. Fortunately, they found that these strains could be controlled with dicarboximide fungicides such as Chipco 26019 (71).

Another *Botrytis* (*B. cinerea*) occasionally attacks the flowers of both Tulips and Lilies and is discussed in the next section.

Lilies

Botrytis Blight (*B. elliptica*) is a common problem on Lilies. Dr. Robert Doss, Chastagner and Kathleen L. Riley developed greenhouse techniques to test cultivars for their resistance to the fungus. They found enough variability to demonstrate that resistant germplasm is available and could be exploited in Lily-breeding programs. They also found that most infection occurs through the lower leaf surface so that fungicidal sprays should be applied accordingly (34).

Chastagner et al. discovered numerous strains of *B. elliptica* and *B. cinerea* that were resistant to the benzimidazole and/or dicarboximide fungicides. Fortunately, they were able to control these fungi with other fungicides, such as the dithiocarbamates and Daconil 2787. They found that these strains and those of *B. tulipae* varied in many characteristics. To lessen the chances for the development of fungicide-resistant strains of these fungi, they recommended using alternating sprays of two different types of fungicides (25). Spraying with a mixture of such fungicides at full strength has also been effective.

Bulb Rots

Although bulb-rotting *Fusarium* fungi thrive best under warm, moist conditions such as occur in the eastern United States, they still can cause trouble at times in western Washington, especially on highly susceptible varieties. One example of the effect of climate was demonstrated when Dr. William McClellan of the USDA at Beltsville, MD and Gould exchanged and planted fungicide-treated and untreated King Alfred bulbs, a moderately resistant variety, in 1947. They found that the warmer climate of the eastern United States definitely increased losses from basal rot as compared with those in western Washington. Twenty-seven percent became rotted in Maryland but only five percent in Washington.

The *Fusaria* attacking Narcissus and Tulips are rather specific to those crops. Apt, however, showed that the strain found on Iris could also rot Gladiolus, Crocus and other Iridaceous bulbs or corms. He recommended that such crops not be grown in rotation with each other. Apt also found that the Tulip Fusarium was a previously undescribed type and named it *F. oxysporium f. tulipae* (7).

Fusarium Basal Rot was especially severe on Narcissus bulbs which had been given a hot water treatment without a fungicide for the control of nematodes and insects. George Newton reported in 1928 that the addition of an organic mercury compound to the hot water treatment helped to control the fungus. Huber began experimenting with fungicides about 1935 and discovered that the addition of a wetting agent increased control with Ceresan. Ceresan and related mercurials, however, sometimes caused injury to the bulbs and flowers, so Gould and Miller continued the search for better fungicides. Hundreds of materials were tested in various ways between 1941 and 1977. Most were either ineffective or toxic to the bulbs. In 1946 tests, basal rot was controlled better with phenyl mercuric acetate than by any other fungicide available at that time, especially when the bulbs were dug early and treated immediately. In 1966, Mertect was shown to be even better and, in 1967, Benlate also was proven to be effective. These benzimidazoles also gave good control of Fusarium basal rots of Iris and Tulips. Busan was another promising fungicide in these tests. Recently, Chastagner has found that some new experimental compounds appear to be as effective as Benlate (24)

Penicillium (Blue mold) rots of Iris are sometimes a problem, especially on injured bulbs or those subjected to long shipments or storage under unfavorable conditions. Blue Mold was often made worse by the mercury treatments used for the control of basal rot. Beginning in 1946, Gould and Miller obtained partial control by treating bulbs with dithiocarbamates and, in 1967, with benzimidazoles. None of these was fully effective. The best results were achieved by using a combination of careful handling to avoid injury and storage of the bulbs at 80 to 85% relative humidity (52).

Chastagner recently demonstrated that many strains of *Penicillium* which attack both Iris and Tulip bulbs are now resistant to the benzimidazoles. Fortunately, he has also found two new fungicides, Banner and Imazalil, which appear to be promising for control of the fungus on these crops (21).

Bulb Treatment

Many factors can decrease the effectiveness of both the hot water plus formalin and fungicidal bulb treatments. These include the use of metal tanks, concrete tanks, wooden trays, the presence of soil on bulbs and repeated treatments in the same solution. Vern Miller found that the concentration of fungicides in commercial tanks was sometimes so low that growers were probably inoculating their bulbs with pathogens instead of protecting them (85,89). He and his associates searched for methods that growers could use to test the concentration of fungicides in their tanks and they developed the following testing kits for this purpose.

Formaldehyde kit	1948 (102)
PMA (phenylmercuric acetate) kit	1953 (102)
Mertect and Benlate kits	1973 (86,87)
Busan kit	1976 (88)

Growers who used these kits were able, after a year or more of experience, to determine the speed with which the fungicidal concentration became depleted and the rate of replenishment needed under their particular conditions.

Soil-Borne Rots

Crown Rot (*Corticium rolfsii*) was almost completely eliminated in Iris planting stock by treating bulbs in HWF for 2-3 hours in experiments by Gould in 1948. However, since this fungus can grow on many weeds and other hosts including Tulips, Hyacinths and Narcissus, a soil treatment was also needed. This was accomplished by treating soil in 1950 with PCNB (pentachloronitrobenzene). Later, tests showed that coating bulbs with PCNB before planting provided effective control and was much more economical. Subsequently, growers tried dusting the bulbs with the PCNB instead of dipping them. Results with this method were almost as good as dipping, it was easier and less expensive, and was used extensively. More recently, Chastagner et al. have discovered other new and very promising fungicides including benodanil and flutoanil for use on Iris and Lilies to control this fungus (23).

Black Rot or **Black Slime** (*Sclerotinia bulborum*) is a cool weather disease in contrast to Crown Rot which thrives under warm, moist conditions. The Black Rot fungus is especially destructive to Hyacinths, Iris and Tulips. Control methods were developed by Gould and Dr. Darrell McLean, of WSU Mount Vernon, using the same treatments that had proven effective against Crown Rot: HWF for bulbs in 1955 and PCNB treatments in 1965 to prevent soil-borne infection. Other tests showed that the Black Rot fungus survived for only two years in the soil in the absence of bulb hosts. This natural characteristic and the repeated use of the HWF and PCNB treatments has essentially eliminated this pathogen from western Washington bulb fields (52).

Rhizoctonia Stem and **Bulb Rot** of Iris and Tulips has become increasingly troublesome in recent years. Growers have tried in-furrow applications of PCNB but these have provided only marginal control. Chastagner is investigating other possibilities.

Gladiolus Corm Rots, mostly Botrytis Rot and Sclerotinia Dry Rot, were controlled more effectively by digging corms early and heat-curing them immediately than by treating them with any of the fungicides available for use in the 1950s by Gould and Miller.

Forcing

Griffiths was probably the first scientist to run experiments on the forcing of Washington-grown bulbs. Beginning in the late 1920s, he tested different varieties of bulbs, the best times of digging and planting, proper temperatures for forcing and many other factors. One of his experimental results was the discovery that Iris and Narcissus bulbs bloomed earlier when they were stored at warm temperatures soon after being dug. His bulletins list many other results.

H. D. Locklin was the first WSU scientist to force bulbs. He experimented outdoors at Puyallup in 1931/1932 by covering the flower beds with muslin and by heating the bulbs with buried electric cables. He found that this combination of heat and shade caused Narcissus and Hyacinths to flower two to three weeks earlier than usual and, of course, the blooms brought a higher price than did field-grown flowers. These treatments, however, did not accelerate the blooming of Tulips and Iris.

Washington-grown Iris bulbs usually bloomed earlier than did Dutch bulbs when forced in greenhouses and had a deeper color and produced a higher percentage of blooms. Occasionally, however, the forced bulbs gave erratic results. This occurred most often with bulbs grown under unusually cool and cloudy conditions in late spring or early summer. To study this situation, Dr. Neil Stuart and Gould began experimenting in 1948 with various treatments. The results in the first year showed that artificial heat-curing of Washington-grown Wedgwood Iris produced better and earlier flowers (130). In other tests run from 1949 to 1971, it was found that: heat curing should begin within 5 days after digging; heat curing should last for 10 to 14 days at 90°F, followed by storing (stabilizing) for 3 to 4 weeks at 65°F, and then 6 weeks of precooling at 50°F. After unusually cool growing seasons, the bulbs required a longer period of heat curing. A relative humidity of 85% appeared to be optimum for bulb storage in these tests. Other Iris varieties, such as Prof. Blaauw (Blue Ribbon), sometimes required longer heat curing and longer precooling. Many experiments were run to study the effect of other conditions on forcing such as time of digging, size of bulbs, varieties, forcing under artificial light and ventilation during forcing (52).

According to bulb growers, these discoveries were at least partially responsible for the success of Washington Iris when they were exported in large numbers to Europe after failure of the Dutch Iris crop from severe freezing in 1954. Because of their high quality the demand for Washington Iris continued until the 1970s as discussed in Chapter 8.

In subsequent experiments, Dr. Robert Doss of the USDA at WSU Puyallup found that longer heat curing of bulbs (4 weeks storage at 90°F), a shorter stabilization period (2 weeks at 68°F) followed by 6 weeks of precooling at 50°F were more effective for Ideal, a Wedgwood sport (32).

Another interesting discovery by Stuart and associates in 1963 was the stimulating effect of ethylene gas on Iris bulbs. Ethylene caused the bulbs to bloom earlier, more uniformly and in less time with the production of shorter leaves. The ethylene treatment was more effective if given before the 50°F precooling treatment than afterwards. These experimental results were later confirmed by scientists in Holland and France. In Holland, they also experimentally sprayed plants in the field with ethephon (an ethylene-releasing chemical) and it increased the percentage of bulbs producing flowers, when forced. Ethephon was tried commercially in fields, but it has not received widespread use because it induces excessive flowering of the smaller planting stock (132).

Doss and associates reported in 1989 that Iris bulbs treated with ethylene gas or ethephon dips did not need the full amount of heat-curing treatment. The plants also had shorter leaves and bloomed earlier in the greenhouse than those from untreated bulbs. They recommended that Ideal bulbs receive a 1 hour dip in ethephon, followed by 3 days storage at 90°F, 2 weeks storage (stabilizing) at 65°F, 6 weeks storage (precooling) at 50°F, followed by the planting and forcing of the bulbs as usual. The same procedure was recommended for Blue Ribbon (Prof. Blaauw) except that precooling for 9 weeks was recommended (17).

The optimum timing of digging and the application of different treatments was a rather hit or miss affair because no outward appearance of the Iris bulb indicates its degree of maturity. Stuart and associates developed degree-day formulas based upon air and soil temperatures to serve as guides to growers, but these were only general guidelines. Doss did not find any correlation between the bulbs' apical dome size and their subsequent flowering. Others have tried to correlate the presence of enzymes and other chemical compounds with flowering but the results have not been sufficiently accurate nor consistent enough to serve as a useful guide for the industry. An effective indicator for Iris bulb maturity remains to be found.

Yosh Kimura, in 1967 at WSU Puyallup, began reporting on chemical analyses of Iris bulbs. He and associates found various gibberellins, abscisic acid, decaneic acids and many other compounds in Iris. In 1977 he also discovered some naturally-occurring fungicides in the husks of Iris bulbs.

Techniques developed by Stuart and associates permit Washington-grown Iris bulbs to be stored and forced at any time of the year. The bulbs were retarded most effectively by storing them at 85°F and 85% relative humidity as soon as they were dug and cleaned, and then precooling them for 4 to 6 weeks at 50°F prior to forcing. Prolonged storage gradually reduced bulb quality, especially with yellow and white varieties. Millions of Iris are now being "programmed" with these treatments and shipped from Washington at weekly intervals to California and other locations for greenhouse forcing and field cut-flower production (52).

Stuart and Gould, starting in 1951, found that by precooling certain varieties of Tulip bulbs at 40°F, instead of the usual 50°F, they could be stored dry for 12 weeks and then planted directly in greenhouse benches, a technique which saved both labor and space. This 40°F treatment is now called the "Five Degree (C°) Tulips" in Holland and has come into widespread use on certain Tulip varieties but not all varieties react favorably to the lower temperature. Washington Narcissus bulbs also responded better to longer (12 weeks) than usual precooling, but they did better when precooled at 50°F than at 40°F in related tests (131).

The possibly detrimental effect on bulb yield and on bulb quality which might result from the picking of Narcissus flowers in the field has long been debated by bulb growers and others since the flower stem essentially functions as a leaf. E. W. (Woody) Kalin's (WSU Pullman) research showed that when Narcissus flowers were cut at bud stage, the bulb yields were reduced only about 2% as compared with those on which flowers were uncut. When the bulbs whose flowers had been cut in the field were forced later in a greenhouse, they produced about 3% fewer flowers than those from uncut plants (77).

247

Both producers and consumers are interested in extending the vase (shelf) life of cut flowers. Doss showed that the vase life could be extended by storing Iris, Tulip and Narcissus flowers in nitrogen gas and at low temperatures until they were sold. Tulip and Narcissus flowers also lasted longer when silver nitrate (at 25 ppm) and sucrose (1.5%) were added to the water in which they were placed (33).

Educational Activities

To keep bulb growers informed about the most recent research results and other developments, a Bulb Growers Short Course was organized by Gould in 1948 and has been held annually ever since (Figure 19-3), with the exception of one year (1960-?). The name was changed about 1961 to the Northwest Bulb Growers Conference. It was originally sponsored by WSU Puyallup, the Northwest Bulb Growers Association and the Washington State Department of Agriculture. Proceedings of the meetings were published from 1948 through 1956 and again from 1980 to date. Information is missing for a few of the meetings but details on the others are shown in Table 19-1.

Most of the 100 to 175 participants have come from British Columbia, Washington, Oregon and California but other states and/or countries are occasionally represented. The 1961 Short Course honored the "Old Time Bulb Growers" and many of them attended (Figure 19-4). In 1963, the retired bulb scientists in the Pacific Northwest were similarly recognized.

WSU has also put on Field Days each spring since the 1940s at either Puyallup or Mount Vernon so that growers could see the results of various experiments on fungicides, fertilizers, weed control, nematode control, etc. in field test plots.

In the mid-1950s, it was decided to assemble available information concerning bulb culture into a handbook on *Bulb Growing and Forcing* for the convenience of growers. This was edited by Gould and 14 scientists contributed articles. It was financed by advertising obtained by Ted Sabelis, Chairman of the Northwest Bulb Growers Research Committee and was published by the Northwest Bulb Growers Association in 1957. Two thousand copies were printed (49). A supplement was issued in 1961 to bring recommendations up to date.

Figure 19-3. Second Northwest Bulb Growers Short Course
Fruitland Grange, Puyallup, 1949. Dr. Neil Stuart discusses
1948/49 USDA/WSU Iris forcing tests. (Courtesy Charles H. Potter)

Left to right: Frank P. McWhorter, Marinus Lefeber, Neil W. Stuart, C. W. Orton, E. T. Evans, C. J. Gould, Mrs. Evans, Mrs. Gould, Mrs. Sabelis, Mrs. Walker, Dirk Kroon, Ted Sabelis, Mrs. E. C. Orton, Clifford Walker, E. C. Orton, Harold Kenealy, Mrs. Reise, Case Van Lierop, Otto Reise, C. R. Wilson, George Ward Lawler, George Deeds, Mrs. Lawler, Ralph and Mrs. Pommert.

Figure 19-4. Bulb pioneers and some of the
speakers and chairmen at the thirteenth Bulb Growers
Conference in Tacoma in 1961. (Courtesy Charles H. Potter)

249

Table 19-1. Northwest Bulb Growers Short Courses and Conferences.

Year	Date	City	Location	No. of Mtg.	Proceedings pub.	Organized by*	Sponsored by**	Attendance
1948	Apr 7/8	Puyallup	Fruitland Grange	1	+	Gould	WSU, NWBGA, WSDA	176
1949	Mar 1/2	"	"	2	+	"	WSU, NWBGA	150
1950	Feb 28-Mar 1	"	"	3	+	"	"	128
1951	Feb 27/28	"	"	4	+	Gould & Miller	"	125
1952	Feb 26/27	"	"	5	+	Gould	"	150
1953	Mar 3/4	Tacoma	?	6	+	"	WSDA	
1954	Mar 4/5	"	?	7	+	"	.	
1955	Feb 23/24	"	?	8	+	"	.	
1956	Mar 1/2	"	Bates Voc-Ed	9	+	"	.	110
1957	Mar 7/8	"	"	10	+	"	.	
1958	?	"	?	11		"	.	
1959	Feb 16/17	Mt. Vernon	Elks Club	12			.	
1960	None held?						.	
1961	Feb 28/Mar 1	Tacoma	The New Yorker	13			.	
1962	?		?	14			.	
1963	Feb 26/27	Tacoma	The New Yorker	15		Gould & Wearne	.	
1964	?	"	?	16		Gould	.	
1965	?	"	?	17		.	.	
1966	?	"	?	18		.	.	
1967	Feb 28/Mar 1	Tacoma	Winthrop Hotel	19		.	.	
1968	Feb 28/29	"	.	20		.	.	
1969	Feb 27/28	"	Sherwood Inn	21		Gould & Wesenberg	.	
1970	Feb 24/25	"	.	22		.	.	
1971	Feb 16/17	Fife	Johnny's Golden Door	23		.	.	
1972	Feb 8/9	Tacoma	Rodeway Inn	24		.	.	

* Byther, Ralph; Gould, Charles; Miller, Vernon; Van Lierop, Cynthia; Wearne, Robert; Wesenberg, Bernard.

** WSU=Washington State University at Puyallup; NWBGA=Northwest Bulb Growers Association; WSDA=Washington State Department of Agriculture.

250

Table 19-1. Northwest Bulb Growers Short Courses and Conferences. Continued.

Year	Date	City	Location	No. of Mtg.	Proceed-ings pub.	Organized by*	Sponsored by**	Attendance
1973	Dec 4/5	•	•	25		•	•	
1974	Dec 4/5	•	•	26		•	•	
1975	Dec 2/3	•	•	27		•	•	
1976	Nov 30/Dec 1	•	•	28	Gould & Byther		WSU, NWBGA	
1977	Nov 29/30	•	•	29		Byther	•	
1978	Nov 28/29	Tacoma	Rodeway Inn	30	?	Byther	•	97
1979	Nov 27/28	•	•	31	?	•	•	?
1980	Dec 3/4	•	•	32	+	•	•	97
1981	Dec 2/3	•	•	33	+	•	•	130
1982	Dec 8/9	•	•	34	+	•	•	152
1983	Nov 29/30	Fife	Executive Inn	35	+	•	•	?
1984	Nov 28/29	Tacoma	?	36	+	•	•	106
1985	Dec 10/11	Bellevue	Red Lion Inn	37	+	Byther & Van Lierop	•	70
1986	Dec 2/3	•	•	38	+	Van Lierop & Byther	•	143
1987	Nov 18/19	Seattle	Sea-Tac Mariott Inn	39	+	Van Lierop & Wesenberg	NWBGA, WSU	?
1988	Nov 30/Dec 1	•	•	40	+	•	•	?
1989	Nov 29/30	•	•	41	+	Van Lierop & Byther	•	?
1990	Nov 28/29	•	•	42	+	•	•	50
1991	Nov 25/26	•	•	43	+	•	•	110
1992	Dec 1/2	•	•	44	+	•	•	80

251

Results on bulb disease investigations and Iris forcing were summarized by Gould and Byther in three Extension bulletins published by WSU in 1979. They are *Diseases of Narcissus* (EB0709), *Diseases of Iris* (EB0710) and *Diseases of Tulips* (EB0711), all available from Cooperative Extension, WSU, Pullman, WA.

The first International Symposium on Flower Bulbs took place at Noordwijk, Holland in 1970. It was convened to enable scientists to exchange information on all phases of bulb culture. Subsequent symposia were held every five years in Europe until 1989 when the fifth symposium took place in the United States at Seattle, WA, July 10-14. It was organized by Drs. Byther, Chastagner and Doss. More than 70 participants representing 14 countries in both hemispheres attended and gave 89 oral or poster presentations. The most recent symposium was held in Poland, May 12-15, 1992. The next is tentatively scheduled for March, 1996 in Israel.

* * * *

Mention of vendor, trademark or proprietary product does not constitute a guarantee or warranty of the product by the author or publisher and does not imply its approval to the exclusion of other products or vendors.

Table 19-2. Scientists and Their Research on Washington-grown Bulbs.

	Born	Died	Active in bulb research*			Inst.***	Field****	Type of research on bulbs
			From	To	City**			
Al-Khatib, Kassim			1992	1993	Mt.V.	WSU	Agron.	Weed control.
Anderson, Wilbur C.		1938	1978	1992	Mt.V	WSU	Hort.	Fertilizers; soil analyses; tissue culture to eliminate viruses in Iris.
Allen, Tom			1975	1991	Corv.	OSU	Virol.	Virus problems. Coop with Anderson.
Apt, Walter J.			1956	1962	Puy.	USDA	Nema.	Root lesion nematode control; types of Fusaria attacking bulbs.
Allmendinger, D. F.	1909	1982	1947	1950	Van.	WSU	Hort.	Fluorine injury to Gladiolus, prunes, etc.
Asen, Sam			1963	1964	Belt.	USDA	Phys.	Ethylene effect, analyses of Iris bulbs.
Baker, Aaron			1959	1967	Puy.	WSU	Soils	Fertilizers. See under Mortensen.
Baker, William W.	1897	1990	1927	1945	Puy.	WSU/ USDA	Ent.	HWF treatment of bulbs (with Newton and Locklin).
Baur, Karl	1909	1986	1937	1951	Puy.	WSU	Soils	Weed control; fertilizer use on bulbs.
Breakey, E.P.	1900	1979	1945	1952	Puy.	WSU	Ent.	Insect control, especially on Lilies.
Carstens, Martin		1961	1950	1951	Mt.V.	WSU	Hort.	Chemical weed control.
Chastagner, Gary A			1978	1993	Puy.	WSU	P.P.	Fungus and virus diseases of bulbs.
Coudriet, Don			1962	1969	Sum.	USDA	Ent.	Insect control on bulbs.

* Approximate dates only.
** Bell. = Bellingham, WA; Belt. = Beltsville, MD; Corv. = Corvallis, OR; Mt.V. = Mount Vernon, WA; Pull. = Pullman, WA; Puy. = Puyallup, WA; Sum. = Sumner, WA; Wen. = Wenatchee, WA.
*** OSU = Oregon State University; PSPL = Puget Sound Power & Light; SVC = Skagit Valley College; USDA = United States Department of Agriculture; WSU = Washington State University.
**** Agron. = Agronomist; Biol. = Biologist; Chem. = Chemist; Eng. = Engineer; Ent. = Entomologist; Hort. = Horticulturist; Nema. = Nematologist; Phys. = Plant Physiologist; P.P. = Plant Pathologist; Soils = Soils Scientist; Stat. = Statistician; Virol. = Virologist.

253

Table 19-2. Scientists and Their Research on Washington-grown Bulbs. Continued.

	Born	Died	Active in bulb research*					Type of research on bulbs
			From	To	City**	Inst.***	Field****	
Courtney, Wilbur D.	1896	1965	1933	1963	Puy.	USDA	Nema.	Nematode control in bulbs.
Cushing, Glenn			1946	1950	Puy.	PSPL	Eng.	Use of electricity in heating storage rooms and for HWF treatment, etc.
Dorsett, P.H.			1908	1917	Bell.	USDA	Hort.	Culture of various bulb types; variety testing.
Doss, Robert	1945		1976	1989	Puy./Corv.	USDA	Phys.	Iris forcing (ethylene, temperature, etc.); & Botrytis on Lilies and disease resistance.
Doucette, Charles F.	1898	1983	1927	1962	Sum.	USDA	Ent.	HWF treatment of Narcissus; fumigation and dips to control insects on all types of bulbs.
Eide, Paul M.	1906	1980	1941	1945	Sum.	USDA	Ent.	Bulb insects.
Emsweller, S. L.		1966	1948	1966	Belt.	USDA	Hort.	Head of ornamentals section USDA; cooperated with WSU; Lily genetics and breeding, etc.
Gould, Charles J.	1912		1941	1977	Puy.	WSU	P.P.	Bulb diseases; fungicide tests with Miller; forcing tests with Stuart; etc.
Griffiths, David	1867	1935	1917	1935	Bell.	USDA	Hort.	Cultural studies on all types of bulbs; forcing; HWF tests on Narcissus.
Hammond, John			1985	1992	Belt.	USDA	Virol.	Virus studies. Coop. with Chastagner.
Haglund, William A.	1930		1960	1992	Mt.V.	WSU	P.P.	Nematode control, especially with Nemacur soil treatment.
Howard, Stott	1957		1986	1989	Mt.V.	WSU	Agro.	Weed control.
Hsiang, Tom			1988	1990	Puy.	WSU	P.P.	Botrytis diseases of Tulips and Lilies.
Huber, Glenn A.	1899	1986	1934	1944	Puy.	WSU	P.P.	Fungicidal sprays for leaf blights; basal rot control on Narcissus.

254

Table 19-2. Scientists and Their Research on Washington-grown Bulbs. Continued.

Name	Born	Died	From	To	City**	Inst.***	Field****	Type of research on bulbs
			Active in bulb research*					
Jensen, Harold J.			1950	?	Corv.	WSU	Nema.	Nematodes on bulbs.
Johnson, Folke			1947	1950	Puy.	WSU	P.P.	Effect and control of fluorine damage to Gladiolus.
Kalin, E. W.			1948	1954	Pull.	WSU	Hort.	Effect of flower removal on yield and forcing of Narcissus.
Kimura, Yosh	1924		1957	1973	Puy.	WSU	Chem.	Chemical analyses of Iris; estimates of amount of curing needed using heat-degree days.
Latta, Randall			1930	1942	Sum.	USDA	Ent.	Bulb insects; vapor-heat on Narcissus bulbs.
Linderman, R. G.				1992	Corv.	USDA	P.P.	Diseases of Lilies and other bulbs.
Locklin, H. D.	1891	1979	1927	1933	Puy.	WSU	Hort.	Optimum dates for HWF use on Narcissus.
Martin, C. H.			1942	1946	Sum.	USDA	Ent.	Bulb insects.
MacLean, Neal A.			1948	1949	Pull.	WSU	P.P.	Types of Botrytis attacking different genera of bulbs.
McClellan, William D.	1914	1981	1941	1956	Belt.	USDA	P.P.	Bulb rots and leaf blights; effect of nutrition, fungicides, etc.
McLean, Darrell			1950	1954	Mt.V.	WSU	P.P.	Soil treatment for black rot of bulbs.
McWhorter, Frank P.	1896	1985	1930	1967	Corv.	OSU/USDA	P.P.	Virus diseases of bulbs; diseases of Lilies.
Miller, Vernon L.	1910	1988	1945	1976	Puy.	WSU	Chem.	Fungicides for control of bulb rots; testing kits for fungicides.
Moore, Larry			1972	1976	Corv.	OSU	P.P.	Bacterial blights of Iris and Narcissus.

255

Table 19-2. Scientists and Their Research on Washington-grown Bulbs. Continued.

	Born	Died	Active in bulb research*		City**	Inst.***	Field****	Type of research on bulbs
			From	To				
Mortensen, Walter P.	1909	1966	1959	1967	Puy.	WSU	Soils	Control of Tulip Topple with calcium nitrate; effect of potassium on forcing of Lilies.
Myhre, Arthur			1960	1966	Puy.	WSU	Hort.	Tulip skin tests; national Gladiolus variety trials.
Nelson, Robert H.			1931	1932	Sum.	USDA	Ent.	Bulb insects.
Newton, George A.			1927	1929	Puy.	WSU	P.P.	Optimum dates for HWF treatment of Narcissus.
Norton, Robert A.			1973	1974	Mt.V.	WSU	Hort.	Use of artificial light for forcing bulbs.
Peabody, Dwight			1951	1985	Mt.V.	WSU	Agron.	Weed control with oryzalin, monuron, amitrol and chlorpropham.
Riemann, Alfred O.			1930	1931	Pull.	WSU	Econ.	MS thesis on bulb production in WA and OR.
Russell, Tom			1961	1965	Pull.	WSU	Stat.	Gladiolus and Iris diseases.
Scheffer, Theodore H.			1927	1936	Puy.	USDA	Biol.	Mole and mice control in bulbs by trapping.
Schomer, H. A.			1954	?	Wen.	USDA	Phys.	Prolonging flower life with polyethylene and ethylene films.
Schopp, Ralph			1941	1944	Sum.	USDA	Ent.	Bulb insects.
Segelman, H. W.			1954	?	Wen.	USDA	Phys.	Prolonging flower life with polyethylene and ethylene films.
Spruit, F. J.			1928	1929	Sum.	USDA	Ent.	Bulb insects.
Stitt, Lloyd L.			1945	1953	Puy.	WSU	Ent.	Insect control; hot water treating tanks.
Stuart, Neil W.	1908	1988	1936	1971	Belt.	USDA	Hort.	Bulb physiology; forcing of Iris, Lilies, Tulips, etc.; ethylene effect on Iris.
Tremblay, Todd			1950	1952	Puy.	WSU	Soils	Use of fertilizers on bulbs.
Van Laan, Gordon J.			1950	1953	Pull.	WSU	Hort.	Chemical changes in Iris bulbs with maturing.

Table 19-2. Scientists and Their Research on Washington-grown Bulbs. Continued.

					Active in bulb research*		
	Born	Died	From	To	City**	Inst.***	Field****	Type of research on bulbs
Others who assisted the bulb industry.								
Byther, Ralph			1976	199	Puy.	WSU	Ext. PP	Chairman Bulb Growers Conference 1977-1985; Program Chairman 1989-1992.
Dodge, John		1988	1955	1971	Puy.	WSU	Ext. Hort	Assisted with Conferences and Field Days.
Nowadnick, R. L.	1923		1953	1993	Mt.V.	SVC	Dean	Secretary/Treasurer NWBGA (1954-1993) and the Bulb Commission (1961-1993). Ed. Newsletter (1953-64).
Wearne, Robert A.			1965	1967	Puy.	WSU	Ext. Hort	Editor Bulb Growers Newsletter 1965-1967; assisted conference, 1963.
Wesenberg, Bernard	1932	1992	1968	1988	Puy.	WSU	Ext. Hort	Co-chair Bulb Growers Conference 1987-1988, Ed. Newsletter 1968-1972.

CHAPTER 20

Summary

Washington State has been for many years the major producer of Iris, Narcissus and Tulip bulbs in the United States and ranks only behind the Netherlands and Great Britain in the acreage of these bulbs in the world. Why has this state been so successful?

Several factors have contributed to this success. They include good soil, intelligent and creative farmers, scientific research assistance and especially a very favorable climate. The cool, moist winters in western Washington encourage root growth which produces larger, better quality bulbs than those grown elsewhere in the United States while the warm, dry summers facilitate digging and proper curing. The relatively cooler spring and summer weather in this area also helps to control certain diseases which cause severe losses in warmer climates.

The question is often asked as to how Washington bulbs can compete with the cheaper and more plentiful bulbs from overseas. The answer is quality. Washington bulbs produce flowers that are larger, have a deeper color and are more uniform in blooming. They also bloom about two weeks earlier than do those produced in Holland and, therefore, command a premium price in the bulb and flower markets. The successful mechanization of many operations by Washington growers has helped to keep the cost of production reasonably competitive.

Bulbs for private gardens in Washington State were brought in by some of the earliest settlers, but the oldest available record of commercial bulb production refers to a planting in 1892 by George Gibbs on Orcas Island. Gibbs later moved to Bellingham in 1899 and his success with bulbs there apparently stimulated others in the vicinity to get into the business so that Whatcom was probably the leading bulb county in the state until about 1920.

In 1906 and 1907, the United States Department of Agriculture (USDA) sent a team of scientists around the country to look for suitable areas for research on bulb growing. Gibbs and others had previously sent letters and samples of their bulbs to the Department and had cooperated with them in experiments so it was not surprising that the scientists chose Bellingham as a major test site in 1908, and established a Bulb Station there. The USDA had two major goals: to determine whether bulbs could be produced commercially in the United States and to raise bulbs for congressmen to give away to their constituents, a political custom at the time.

Experiments began at the Station in 1908 and continued until 1935. Dr. David Griffiths became supervisor of the Bulb Station at Bellingham about 1917 and deserves much of the credit for its success. He was an excellent promoter for the fledgling bulb industry and much of the information in his bulletins is still valid today. If we consider Gibbs to be the "Commercial Father" of the Washington bulb industry, then Dr. Griffiths certainly rates the title of the "Scientific Father."

Washington's bulb industry grew slowly at first. Sales of cut flowers were probably the main source of income, with bulb sales being secondary. Among the earliest growers were Mrs. Mary Stewart on Samish Island (Skagit County), and Edwin Wines on Fox Island (Pierce County), both starting about 1908. George Lawler began raising Narcissus at Fife (Pierce County) in 1910, initially for cut flower production, and, by 1920, was probably the largest bulb grower in the state. By that time, there were also several others growing bulbs in smaller plantings in several counties.

The greatest stimulus to American bulb production was the USDA announcement of a quarantine against the importation of Narcissus and certain other bulbs, imposed in an effort to protect domestic bulbs from invasion by insect and nematode pests carried on imported bulbs. It was announced in 1922, but did not go into effect until 1926. During the interval, many American farmers in several states imported bulbs for planting and several Dutch firms sent representatives and bulbs, in order to establish their own bulb farms in the United States.

The federal quarantine was modified in 1936 and revoked in 1938 but, by that time, the Washington State bulb industry was well established. Some contraction occurred during the Depression years from 1932 to 1935 when many small growers went out of business. Markets were good during World War II but manpower shortages and higher costs affected production and profits.

The wartime shortage of labor and rising costs accelerated the trend toward mechanization in digging, cleaning, planting and other operations. Mechanization proved to be very cost-effective. By hand, 40 man-days were required to dig an acre of Iris. With machines, it took just one man-day. Mechanical planting of Iris went even faster, requiring only 0.2 of a man-day by machine as compared with 20 man-days per acre when done by hand. Because the demand for such mechanical equipment was small, however, none of the commercial farm equipment manufacturers were interested in producing it. Growers had to invent, build and maintain their own machines.

After World War II, a heavy influx of Dutch bulbs at lower prices caused many Washington growers to reduce their acreages or to quit raising bulbs entirely. Iris growers, for example, plowed under 25% of their crop in the spring of 1953 because of surpluses and poor prices. Ironically, this was followed by a large increase in demand for them by Dutch bulb dealers in 1954 after an extremely severe freeze during the winter of 1953/54 damaged the Iris crop in Holland. Overseas orders for Washington Iris increased annually after that, reaching a peak of over 30 million bulbs in the late 1960s. Between 1966 and 1972, 199 million Washington Iris were exported to England, Europe and Canada. The demand tapered off, subsequently, for a number of reasons.

In general, the largest bulb acreage in Washington has usually been in Narcissus, followed by Bulbous Iris, Tulips, Lilies, Gladiolus and a few acres in Hyacinths, Crocus and other minor crops. Most of the Gladiolus are now grown in eastern Washington while the other bulb types are raised in a 180-mile strip between Woodland and Mount Vernon in western Washington. Most of the Lilies grown now are of the Oriental and Asiatic types but Washington once had a small and thriving Croft Easter Lily industry. The center for Easter Lily production is now located in the coastal areas of northwestern California and southwestern Oregon.

The total acreage of Iris, Narcissus and Tulips (INT) bulbs in Washington is estimated to have been about 5 acres in 1900 and perhaps 100 in 1920. It then climbed rapidly to 1,796 acres in 1942. Since 1942, it has fluctuated between 1,285 and 2,355 acres. In 1989, for both bulb and flower production, there were 517 acres of Iris, 1,097 of Narcissus, 608 of Tulips, 77 of Lilies, 50 of Gladiolus and 6 of miscellaneous bulbs. This 2,355 acres included the farm of the Washington Bulb Company in Skagit County which grew bulbs on 1,310 acres and is the largest producer of Iris, Tulips and Narcissus in the United States. The present bulb acreage in Washington State is one of the largest on record.

More than 900 Washington farmers have grown bulbs since 1892. The list includes 520 INT growers, 357 Lily growers and 134 Gladiolus growers. Undoubtedly, there are many more growers of whom no record has been found so far. The total number of growers has declined since the 1920s. Although there are no data on the number of Iris and Tulip growers in 1929, there were 162 Narcissus growers that year but only 15 in 1989. There were 80 INT growers in 1947, but only 17 in 1991. Three others grew bulbs in 1991 but only for cut flowers.

As the number of growers became smaller, average farm size became larger. In 1929, the average planting was 3 acres for Narcissus, the bulb type which accounted for 86% of the total bulb acreage that year. In 1947, the average for all three major bulb types was 22 acres per farm. This grew to 69 acres in 1970 and to 117 acres in 1990.

The number of INT bulbs sold rose from 14.1 million in 1930 to 80.5 million in 1988. The latter figure includes 33.4 million Iris bulbs, 24.6 million Narcissus bulbs and 22.5 million Tulip bulbs. In addition, there were probably another 10 million INT bulbs used solely for flower production. That number, plus an estimated 12 million of the Gladiolus, Lilies and miscellaneous bulbs and corms produced, would have brought the grand total of all bulbs sold in Washington to 100 million in 1988.

The largest market for Washington Narcissus originally was for greenhouse forcing in the eastern United States. Now, most Narcissus bulbs are used by local growers for field-cut flower production and for their own forcing, although a few are sold to the dry sale trade. Bulbous Iris are still in heavy demand for greenhouse forcing elsewhere in the United States and for sale to California producers for field-cut flower production. Most Washington Tulip bulbs are now used for local forcing or field-cut flower production with only a few going into dry sales.

The bulb varieties upon which the industry was founded are not often seen now in the festivals and display gardens. The excellent King Alfred Narcissus reigned for over 40 years, but has been replaced by larger new yellow trumpet varieties, such as Dutch Master and Unsurpassable. Wedgwood was the most popular blue Iris from 1930 to about 1970, but has yielded its throne to one of its sports, the variety Ideal.

The sale of field-cut flowers has become big business. Official data is not available but the total number of flowers sold in 1989 was estimated to have been about 70 million. This included 50 million Narcissus, 5 million Iris and 15 million Tulips.

Sales of forced and field-cut flowers have become so important that they now represent 70 to 90% of the total gross income of many growers, a situation almost completely the reverse of that in 1940 when income from bulb sales was far more important. Estimated gross income for INT growers was over $5 million for bulbs and over $6 million for field-cut flowers in 1989. This $11 million total does not include the income received from flowers forced in the growers' own greenhouses.

Bulb growers are no different from other farmers in having problems, some natural and some man-made. Natural problems include drought, freezing, flooding, insects and diseases while man-made problems include warehouse fires, bulb surpluses, labor shortages and the urbanization of land.

Natural problems, such as periodic severe freezes, caused bulb growing to die out in Whatcom County over 40 years ago. The most destructive freeze of all occurred during the winter of 1978/79 and affected all bulb types in all areas of western Washington.

Another natural problem, flooding, by the Columbia and Lewis Rivers, destroyed over 265 acres of bulbs at Woodland in 1948. This figure, however, has been dwarfed by the losses from a combination of flooding, waterlogging and freezing weather in the winter of 1990/91 when many Tulips, Iris and some Narcissus were destroyed in both Pierce and Skagit Counties.

Man-made problems include fires which put two growers out of the bulb business and caused serious losses at three other farms. Bulb surpluses have been an intermittent problem but were especially severe in the late 1940s and early 1950s when large imports from overseas coincided with good crops in Washington State. This surplus situation occurred at a time of changing markets and the combination was largely responsible for the decline of INT acreage from 1,800 acres in 1949 to a low of 1,285 acres in 1959, before it began to climb again. The latest man-made problem is the increasing shortage of suitable land, resulting from uncontrolled industrial and residential development. It has already crowded out most of the bulb industry in Pierce County and threatens to do the same in Skagit County where 70% of the state's bulb acreage was located in 1989.

Several bulb cooperatives have been organized in Washington and two are still active. Growers in the Puyallup Valley organized the Puget Sound Bulb Exchange in 1926 to sell, pack and ship its members' bulbs. The other organization is the Puyallup Valley Flower Cooperative which was established in 1956 to sell and ship field-cut flowers.

In order to facilitate the exchange of cultural information, bulb growers organized the Northwest Bulb Growers Association in 1924. Later, they developed the Washington State Bulb Commission in 1956 to provide additional funds for research and advertising. Both of these groups have cooperated, since 1948, with scientists from Washington State University at Puyallup and Mount Vernon in sponsoring annual Bulb Grower Conferences which keep growers up to date on new developments.

Bulb production has been aided by the research of many state and federal government scientists. The first research got under way in 1908 at the USDA Bulb Station at Bellingham where the major emphasis was on cultural techniques. Later, other USDA and WSU scientists at various locations worked on the control of diseases, insects, nematodes and weeds, as well as on improved methods for handling and forcing bulbs.

When beauty came by the acre, it was only natural for bulb festivals to spring up. The first large one was an annual Tulip Festival held at Bellingham from 1920 to 1930, followed by the beginning of the Puyallup Valley Daffodil Festival in 1926. The LaConner Civic Garden Club in Skagit County put on a Tulip Show from 1946 until about 1971. In 1970, Oak Harbor on Whidbey Island started its Holland Happenings which originally included a Tulip Show. Next to develop was the Skagit Valley Tulip Festival which was organized by the Mount Vernon Chamber of Commerce in 1984. The most recent one is a Tulip Festival held in Mossyrock during the month of April every year.

But times change. Bulbs were once the major source of income for growers; now flowers are. The center of bulb production shifted from Whatcom County south to Pierce County and now has moved back north to Skagit County. As mentioned before, the most crucial issue facing bulb growers today is not climate but land. There may not be enough bulbs left by the year 2000 to supply flowers for even the local festivals unless some method is found to preserve it. Meanwhile, the 2,000 acres of blooms which are still available in western Washington should be fully appreciated and enjoyed now.

Appendix Table A. Commercial Growers of Iris, Narcissus and/or Tulips in Washington State.*

Name (Born-Died)	Nearest city	Grew Bulbs		Number of acres in peak years**							Max.***
		From	To	G	H	I	L	N	T	M	Acres
Albertson, W. E. (1856----)	Seattle	1919	1924	+					+	+	1
Allen Lily Gardens	Sedro Wooley	1935	1942		+				+		
Alquist, Emil	Mount Vernon	1949	1950		+				+		
Alquist, Leonard	Mount Vernon	1947	1949		+				+		1
Alway, Ralph M.	Sumner	1942	1952				1	+			
Anderson, Edgar (Sammamish Bulb Company)	Tacoma	1933					1				1
Anderson, Leroy	Tacoma	1947	1949		+		+		+		1
Andrews, Mrs. George	La Conner	1933					4	4			4
Applequist, Frank	Seattle	1933					+				
Averill, F. A.	Snohomish	1935	1942			+					
Aves, J. A.	Puyallup	1933	1948				1			+	1
Baarslag, H. S. (Baarslag Bulbs)	Tacoma	1942	1943		+		+				
Bailey, H. F.	Sumner	1925	1942		+		1				1
Baker, Fred A.	Seattle	1933			+		+				
Ballinger, R. L.	Puyallup	1933				+	1			+	1
Barrie, Donald	Kirkland	1947	1958		+		+		3	3	3
Bates, William E.	Burton	1933	1942		+		+				
Barder, Henry	Puyallup	1947	1956				6	6			6
Beaver, R. S.	Sumner	1933					1				1
Beaver, R. T. & R. L.	Sumner	1942	1943				1	1			1
Beckenhauer, L. F.	Montesano	1933					1				1
Bellingham Bulb Company	Bellingham	1923	1926	+					+		5
Bennedict, Lucy W.	Puyallup	1933						+			
Berger, Joe (1913-1985) (Washington Bulb Company)	Mount Vernon	1947	1956	14	9		2	7	+		32
Bergman, Henry A. (1909-1962)	Mount Vernon	1947	1961	6	8		8	6	+		25

* Based upon available records or comments by other growers; + indicates the name was found on a list but the number of acres was not reported or was less than one; ? indicates the location and/or year is unknown.

** G=Gladiolus, H=Hyacinths, I=Iris, L=Lilies, N=Narcissus, T=Tulips, and M=Miscellaneous.

*** Maximum number of acres.

265

Table A. Commercial Growers of Iris, Narcissus and/or Tulips in Washington State. Continued.

Name (Born-Died)	Nearest city	Grew Bulbs From	To	G	H	I	L	N	T	M	Max*** Acres
Bernhard, Henry	Sumner	1942	1944					3			3
Bernhoft, George (Berhoft & Buurman)	Mount Vernon	1947	1950		+						
Boden, C. W.	Everett	1933				2		2			2
Boldue, Leo	Kirkland	1942	1948			5		5			5
Boulevard Park Nursery	Seattle	1950				+		+			
Bowen Bulb Farms	Puyallup	1983	1992			10		10			10
Bowen, Clarence (1926-1983)	Puyallup	1959	1983		+			+	+		35
Bowen, George	Sumner	1942	1943			2		2			2
Brainard, A. W.	Seattle	1933	1942		+			1			1
Brainard, S. A.	Seattle	1942	1944			+		+			1
Breckenridge, J. C.	Centralia	1947				+		+			
Bredall, Peter C.	La Center	1933	1948					6	+		6
Breit, J. S.	Sumner	1943	1948					1			1
Bruene,	Mount Vernon	1949									5
Bryce, J. J.	Bellevue	1933	1942		+			12			12
Bryden, Florence	?	1942								+	+
Bryson, Harlow	Puyallup	1951	1959					4			4
Buurman, G.	Mount Vernon	1948	1950		+						6
Cabes Floral Patch	Elma	1950			+						
Cacatian, Fermin	Orting	1933						1			1
Calbom, Sam	Mount Vernon	1950			+		+				
Canfield, C. T. (1851----)	Bellingham	1899	1904							+	
Carvasso, A. H.	Bellingham	1933	1942				10	10			10
Chambers, Seward	Olympia	1933	1942		2			2			2
Chambers, Tom E.	Olympia	1942			+			1			1
Chervenka, Frank A. (1880-1966) (Chervenka Bulb Farms)	Sumner	1923	1944		15		+	40			55
Chervenka, Francis (Chervenka Bulb Farms)	Sumner	1944	1971		10		+	45	2		52
Christensen, Ron	Oak Harbor	1977	1983		2			2			2
Christianson, Mrs. L. P.	Stanwood	1950			+				+		
Clapp, I. C.	Kirkland	1950		+	+						

Table A. Commercial Growers of Iris, Narcissus and/or Tulips in Washington State. Continued.

Name (Born-Died)	Nearest city	Grew Bulbs		Number of acres in peak years**							Max*** Acres
		From	To	G	H	I	L	N	T	M	
Clark, L. R.	Sumner	1925	1950	+				+	+		
Clark Bulb Farm	Sequim	1950							+		
Clerget, Joseph P.	Sumner	1942	1961			1	1			1	
Clizbe, Alan	Mount Vernon	1939	1966	+		1	+		2		10
Cochran, Emmett	Seattle	1933			3			3			3
Cochrane, John	Seattle	1933	1935		+		+	+			
Coffman, W. H.	Sumner/McKenna	1935	1948		+		+				
Colhours Bulb Farm	Keyport	1950				+					
Connely, Edward	Puyallup	1950		+							
Connena, Vito (Connena Bulb Farm)	Snohomish	1933	1950		+		5	5	+		5
Conner, E. L.	Yakima	1950			+			1			
Conrad, Fred	Puyallup	1942					1	+			1
Cook & Dow	Puyallup	1958				+					
Cooke, George	Coupeville	1933	1935			+					
Coons, N. D.	Aberdeen	1933					+	+			
Cowell, Ray	Mount Vernon	1949	1961		5			1	3		8
Crowder, J. H.	Bellevue	1933					+	+			1
Curtis, Mrs. Frank	Seattle	1933				+					
Darst, Earle (Darst Bulb Farms)	Coupeville	1932	1992	95	137		+		+		182
Darst, Glenn (1893-1971)(Darst Bulb Farms)	Coupeville	1932	1969	137	137	+	+	+	+		137
Davis, M. R. (M. R. Davis Bulb Company)	Marysville	1933						+			
Deeds, George H. (1874-1969)	Puyallup	1933	1965		3		5	5	+		10
De Goede, Henry with Hildegarde (wife), Jack, Dennis & Robert (De Goede Bulb Farms)	Mount Vernon/Mossyrock	1951	1992	40	80	80	50	80	+		250
De Goede, John P. with Anna (wife), Ben, Phil & Paul (Windmill Greenhouses)	Mount Vernon/Sumner	1955	1966	+	+	+	+	+	+		
De Goede, Tom with Jeanette (wife) (Skagit Valley Bulb Farms)	Mount Vernon	1955	1992	25	50	18	150	50	+	3	52
De Groot, Ted, Sr. (1893-1982) (United Bulb Company)	Woodland	1929	1979	50	18	150	50	+			250
De Groot, Ted, Jr. (1926-1984) (Woodland Bulb Farm)	Woodland	1978	1980	+	40	40	+				80
Delkin, Fred (Delkin Bulb Farm)	Bellevue	1933	1950	+	+	20	20	+			20
Deselem, Fred	Olympia	1950						+			
Devink, William J. (1927-1985)	Sumner	1951	1956	7	7						7

Table A. Commercial Growers of Iris, Narcissus and/or Tulips in Washington State. Continued.

Name (Born-Died)	Nearest city	Grew Bulbs From	To	G	H	I	L	N	T	M	Max*** Acres
DeVries, E. E.	Sumner	1942	1948								2
Dobbe, Benno (Holland America Bulb Farms, Inc.)	Woodland	1980	1992	20	10			2	25		55
Doty, L. W.	Sumner	1947						+			
Doverspike, S. E.	Raymond	1933									1
Downie, George	Kirkland	1942			+						
Duris, Steve	Puyallup	1956						1			1
East View Nursery	Stanwood	1950						+			
Edem, Mrs. Kristen (Lubbe) (Satsop Bulb Farm)	Elma	1976	1992					10	2		12
Edmondson, Henry D. (1901-1979) (Edmondson & Mansfield)	Sumner	1946	1964					12	8		20
Edwards, Gordon (The Lily Gardens)	Bellevue	1935	1946		+			+			
Edwards, Ira J. (W. E. Bulb Farm)	Woodinville	1947	1956	3	3						6
Eerkes, Erwin	Mount Vernon	1940	1952		5			1	6		20
Egbert, Arthur	Woodinville	1950			+			+			
Elske, William	Marysville	1947	1950		1				3		4
Engle, Carl T.	Coupeville	1935	1937		2			2			2
Engle, Ralph	Coupeville	?			2						2
Engle, Robert P.	Coupeville	1935	1964		25			2	2	+	29
Engle, Will	Coupeville	1935	1937		2						2
Essex, J. W.	Seattle	1933						+			
Evetts, R. S.	Bellevue	1935	1942		+						
Eylar Gardens	Renton	1950			+						
Failor, Paul L.	Bellevue	1932	1942		+			2			2
Fender, C. F.	Seaview	1933						+			
Fixter Bulb Gardens	Longview	1944								+	
Flagg, Alvin B. (A. B. Flagg Company)	Seattle	1933	1950					1	1		1
Forbes, R. R.	Kirkland	1933	1942		+			1			1
Forehand, J. A.	Sumner	1933			3			3			3
Franco, Gary & Alberta (Madrona Farms)	Lopez Island	1985	1992	+	+		+	+	+		4
Fredson, Mrs. Frank	Shelton	1933			+			+			
Fredson, Mrs. Jean T.	Shelton	1933						+			

Table A. Commercial Growers of Iris, Narcissus and/or Tulips in Washington State. Continued.

Name (Born-Died)	Nearest city	Grew Bulbs		Number of acres in peak years**							Peak Acres
		From	To	G	H	I	L	N	T	M	
Fuller, F. B.	Puyallup	1942				+					
Fuller, Joe R.	Sumner	1942	1956			2					2
Furbush Gardens	Kirkland	1950	1951			+					
Furnar, E.	Mercer Island	1933				+					
Gardener, R. L.	Yakima	1947				+					
Gardner, John with Marilyn (wife) (Westshore Acres)	Mount Vernon	1964	1992			120			6		120
Gary, Mark B.	Sumner	1947	1952		+	+	+	+	+		1
Gibbs, George (1832-1919)	Orcas/Bellingham	1892	1917	+			+	+	+	+	5
Giese, O. L.	Bellingham	1922	1948			+					
Goelzer, Lester (1901-1975)(Kirk & Goelzer)	Puyallup	1942	1958			60			+		60
Gonnason, Victor	Fall City	1950			+	+					
Gordon, Edward P. & Eddie G. (North Coast Bulb Farm)	Mount Vernon	1947	1958		+	16		10			26
Government Bulb Farm	Bellingham	1933				1					1
Grainger, Robert N.	Sumner	1947	1952			1					1
Grant, Fred	Mount Vernon	1947				+			+		
Gronen, Hamilton F. (1874-1968)(Gronen's Daffodil Garden)	Puyallup	1923	1952		+	13					13
Gronen, Roger H. (Gronen's Daffodil Garden)	Puyallup	1947	1951			10					10
Guldemond, Arie (Est. by A. G.)(United Bulb Company)	Woodland	1944	1979	125	2	200	75		+		402
Guthrie, Harry	Chehalis	1947				+			+		
Hagler, Curtis E.	Kirkland/Monroe	1950	1952			+					
Hale, Peter	Puyallup	1933	1951		+	8					8
Ham and Son	Everson	1933	1942			2					2
Hammerly, Harry	Marysville	1947	1950						+		
Hansen, A. W.	Seattle	1933				1					1
Hansen, Emil	Mount Vernon	1947				+			+		
Hansen, Harry	Mount Vernon	1947	1950			+			+		
Hanstad, Robert	Conway	1950			+						
Hardy Flower Gardens	Spokane	1935	1942							+	
Harm, J.	Sumner	1942	1948			+			+		
Harm, William C.	Puyallup	1939	1968			13			+		13

269

Table A. Commercial Growers of Iris, Narcissus and/or Tulips in Washington State. Continued.

Name (Born-Died)	Nearest city	Grew Bulbs		Number of acres in peak years**							Max***
		From	To	G	H	I	L	N	T	M	Acres
Hartkopf, Mrs. Maude	Kirkland	1950				+					
Hatch, L. M. (1880-1964) (Hatch Ranch)	Puyallup	1925	1948	+	+		5	+			17
Hatch, Miles B. (Hatch Ranch)	Puyallup	1948	1972	+	+	6	17	+			20
Hathaway, George	Kirkland	1950				+					
Hayes, John P.	Kirkland	1933	1942			+	1				1
Hayley, Roy	Lynden	1933					+				
Heather Hills Farm	Oakville	1950								+	
Hebechuch, Catherine	Puyallup	1950					+				
Hensley,	Mount Vernon	1949									3
Herr, Edith	Puyallup	1942					+			+	
Hermann, Kermit	Sumner	1951	1952				+			+	
Herzog, Cora	Port Townsend	1950						+			
Hickcox, F. T.	Puyallup	1942						2			2
Hickcox, Kermit	Puyallup									+	
Higgens,	La Center	1942						1			1
Highland Nursery	Kirkland	1950								+	
Hill, Albion S.	Seattle	1950							+		
Hobby Iris Gardens	Camas	1950									
Holland Bulb Grower	Mount Vernon	1948	1952					+	+		
Hollguts, Luke	Whidbey Island	1934			4			+	+		4
Holt and Sons	Auburn	1933		+				+			
Homan, Dr. Clyde (1903-1984) (Tulips, Inc.)	Woodland	1947	1948		5		20	40			65
Hornbeck, E. N.	Centralia	1942						+			
Houslin, Jim	Coupeville	?			2						2
Houston, J. P.	Coupeville	?								+	
Howell, Tom	Whidbey Island	1947		4			4				4
Hoyt, Mrs. Fred	Puyallup	1933	1943	+			2				2
Hubbard, George	Burlington	1949	1956	10			2				10
Huber, Walter F.	Elma	1950		+	+			+			
Hulbert Farms, Bob, Jim (& Sons Jack & Tom)	Mount Vernon	1974	1992	+	+		65				65

Table A. Commercial Growers of Iris, Narcissus and/or Tulips in Washington State. Continued.

Name (Born-Died)	Nearest city	Grew Bulbs		Number of acres in peak years**								Max***
		From	To	G	H	I	L	L	N	T	M	Acres
Hull, Albert F.	Seattle	1950										
Hutcheson, Leo	Puyallup	1942							+			
Ilton, R. H.	Montesano	1933	1942		2				2			2
Ingals, Roy	Sumner	1942							+			
Iotte, Leland E.	Pacific	1950	1961							2		4
Iris City Gardens	Walla Walla	1950							+		+	
Iverson, Peter A.	Puyallup	1942	1952						3	+		3
Jacobs, Grover	Enumclaw	1946	1948							+		
Janig, Alfred	Puyallup/Orting	1933	1948						+			
Jansen, Albert E.	Sumner	1947	1959						4	+		4
Jeul, Oscar	Puyallup	1933							+			
Johnson, Adolph	Mount Vernon	1944	1956			+	+		+	+		3
Johnson, Arthur O.	Puyallup	1950	1975			2			2	+		15
Johnson, E. W.	Sumner	1933							1			1
Johnson, Fred	Anacortes	1933							+			
Johnson, Richard	Kirkland	1950				+						
Jones, S.	Orting	1933					+		+			
Jonkheer, Tony (Mt. Vernon Bulb Company)	Mount Vernon	1955	1963							+	+	
Jueneman, Henry E. (Jueneman Bulb Company)	Bellingham	1924	1926							+	+	
Kanada, S. (South Park Greenhouse)	Seattle	1933	1942			+	+		+			
Kano, S.	Sumner	1933										
Kanouse, Aaron N. (1902-1980) (Floravista)	Olympia	1922	1973	+		+			3	+		3
Kapteyn, John (Holland Bulb Growers)	Mount Vernon	1946	1947						1	1		1
Kaylor, Floyd C. (1876-1960) (Kaylor Nurseries)	Blaine	1910	1954						1	+		1
Keel, J. H.	Puyallup	1933							5			5
Keen, Mrs. W. H.	Walla Walla	1950									+	
Keeney, Esther S.	Seattle	1950							+			
Kenealy, Harold R. (1900-1975)	Mount Vernon	1929	1965	2		17			15	20		54
Kenley, Dave (Northwest Rose Growers)	Woodland	1978	1992			20			33			53
Kennedy Floral Gardens	Everett	1933	1946						+			

Table A. Commercial Growers of Iris, Narcissus and/or Tulips in Washington State. Continued.

Name (Born-Died)	Nearest city	Grew Bulbs		Number of acres in peak years**							Max***
		From	To	G	H	I	L	N	T	M	Acres
Kern, Raymond F.	Sumner	1942	1952		+			5	+		5
King, Mrs. Ritah	Ferndale	1933						1			1
Kirk, George R. & Paul, Sr. (Kirk & Goelzer)	Tacoma	1942	1958					60	+		60
Kirsch, Ted (Sun Valley Bulb Farm)	Mount Vernon	1981	1984		+			+			
Knoblauch, Clayton	Sumner	1951	1952							+	
Knoblauch, Henry	Sumner	1933	1942					1			1
Knoblauch, Melvin A.	Sumner	1950	1952					+			
Knoblauch, Ted	Sumner	1928						+			
Knutson, Harold (1913-1977) (Knutson Farms)	Sumner	1957	1977		+			105	+		250
Knutson Farms, Mrs. Harold, Tom & Roger	Sumner	1977	1992		60			135	74		269
Koehler, Karl (1874-1942) (Koehler Farms)	Orting	1930	1942	+	+			+	+	+	15
Koehler, Mrs. Karl (Elsie) (1895-1980) (Koehler Bulb Farm)	Orting	1942	1960						+	+	1
Koehler, Louise (Anderson) (Koehler Bulb Farm)	Orting	1958	1966					+	+		1
Koetji, Tom & Sons	Oak Harbor	1950				+		+			
Koning, Cornelius	Mount Vernon	1948	1990		2			4	+		20
Koren, J. D.	Olympia	1933						+			
Korsten, Ben, Jr.	Sumner	1942	1968		10			45	16		61
Krains Bulb Gardens	Enumclaw	1950			+			+			
Kuss, J. N.	Seattle	1950							+		
Ladd & Holden	La Center	1933					22				22
Ladd & Marble	La Center	1942						70			70
Lafky, A. F. J.	Longview	1950			+			+			
Lakedell Nursery	Bothell	1950						1			
Lane, R. G.	Sumner	1942						+			1
Langdon, A. W.	Sumner	1944	1951					+	+		
Langlois Floral Gardens	Vancouver	1933						+			
Larrabee, C. X. (1843-1914)	Bellingham	1899								+	
Lavaughns Dahlia Gardens	Buckley	1950			+						
Lawler, George (1861-1948) (Lawler Bulb Company)	Fife/Roy	1910	1948		+			120	+	+	200
Lawler, George Ward (1886-1974) (Lawler Bulb Company)	Roy/Monroe	1941	1962		+			+	+	+	200

272

Table A. Commercial Growers of Iris, Narcissus and/or Tulips in Washington State. Continued.

Name (Born-Died)	Nearest city	Grew Bulbs		Number of acres in peak years**							Max***
		From	To	G	H	I	L	N	T	M	Acres
Leckenby, Jim (Leckenby Seed Company)	Mount Vernon	1949	1952			5					5
Lee, C. E.	Olympia	1933	1947					1			1
Lee, Mrs. Lucille (Lubbe) (1904-1989)	Puyallup/Sumner	1931	1977		+			11	+		15
Lefeber, Bill (Lefeber Bulb Company)	Mount Vernon	1949	1989		34			76			110
Lefeber, Dan (Lefeber Bulb Company)	Mount Vernon	1989	1992		19			80	+		99
Lefeber, Jac	Olympia/Mount Vernon	1948	1967	+	+			5	1		9
Lefeber, Marinus (1893-1982) (Lefeber Bulb Company)	Lynden/Mount Vernon	1928	1970		24			26	8		58
Legros Brothers (Broadway Floral)	Everett	1933						+	+		
Lemon, Burch	Coupeville	1944	1950		+			+	+		3
Leslie, Allen	Sumner	1951	1957					2			4
Lindbloom, Fred	Mount Vernon	?	1943							+	
Linder, Carl	Mount Vernon	1942	1943					1			1
Lingham, Alfred (Linghams Lily Gardens)	Tacoma	1935	1946			+	+			+	
Linn, Pierce	?	1951									
Linn, W. C. & W. A.	Kirkland	1948	1956		+			+		+	3
Lively, E. E.	Seattle	?								+	
Lloyd, A. H.	Port Townsend	1942	1956		+						
Lloyd's Gardens	Seattle	1950		+				+	+		
Locklin, Harrison D. (1891-1979)	Puyallup	1924	1935					1			1
Loeb, C. E.	Sumner/Puyallup	1951	1965					14			14
Longley, William E.	Bellingham	1922	1942		+					+	
Loomis, R. P.	Bellingham	1950						+		+	
Love, J. J.	Olympia	1942						+			
Lovelace, Glenn E.	Kirkland	1950			+			+		+	
Lubbe, Charles M.	Sumner/Elma	1949	1992					27	+		27
Lubbe, Kurt	Elma	1971	1992					9			9
Lubbe, Ralph W.	Puyallup	1942	1948					5			5
Ludington, Roy	Anacortes	1933						+			
Lynden Bulb Company	Lynden	1930									
McCandless, Mrs. Frank	Olympia	1933						2			2

273

Table A. Commercial Growers of Iris, Narcissus and/or Tulips in Washington State. Continued.

Name (Born-Died)	Nearest city	Grew Bulbs From	To	G	H	I	L	N	T	M	Max*** Acres
McClane, William	Sumner	1933					+				
McColley, Eugene E.	Sumner/Buckley	1942	1981		4		15		1		15
McColley, Everett L. (1897-1975)	Sumner	1943	1965				12				12
McCreedy, W. R.	Bellevue	1933	1942				1				1
McGuire, Monte (Northwest Rose Growers)	Woodland	1980				+	+				
McKay, R. J.	Mount Vernon	1947	1950				10				10
McKinnon, Gregg	Sumner	1925	1948				1				1
McLean, J. R. (1897-1977) (McLean Bulb Company)	Elma/Puyallup	1933	1965			+	40		6	+	46
McNaughton Bulb Farm	Bellingham	1933	1948				1				1
McSpaden, Ted	Mount Vernon	1949	1951								1
Magee, Jack	Sumner	1942	1956			+	+		1		1
Maggi, Ed (Woodland Bulb Farms)	Woodland	1978	1980			+	40	40			80
Mahaffey, Charles C.	Kirkland	1950					+	+			
Maire, E. L.	Bellingham	1933	1942				2				2
Mansfield, Howard (Edmondson & Mansfield)	Sumner	1946	1964			+	12		8		20
Marble, Ralph S. (Marble Bulb Company)	Sumner/La Center	1934	1948	+	+		+				
Mason, F. E.	Kirkland	1950			+		+			+	
Mattson, Fred W. & Son	Sumner	1933	1943				3				3
Maupin, Margaret (1896-1980) (Walker & Maupin)	Mount Vernon	1949	1979			+	10	+			10
Meadow Mountain Bulb Farm	Granite Falls	1933	1942			+	2				2
Merritt, Leroy M. (1880-1963)	Sumner	1933	1949				4				4
Mettler, Charles	Tacoma	1951	1956				9				9
Middlecoff, George	Vashon Island	1935	1942		+						
Missall, Fernie	Kirkland	1950			+						
Moldenhouer, W. A.	Chehalis	1935	1942		+						
Monrad, Olaf (Monrad Bulb Company)	Tacoma/Seattle	1929	1950		+		+				
Montgomery Gardens	Colville	1935	1942		+						
Moody, Forrest C.	Puyallup	?								+	
Morey, E. R.	Seattle	1933	1942		+		+				
Morgan	Puyallup	1942			+		+				

Table A. Commercial Growers of Iris, Narcissus and/or Tulips in Washington State. Continued.

Name (Born-Died)	Nearest city	Grew Bulbs From	Grew Bulbs To	G	H	I	L	N	T	M	Max*** Acres
Morisse, Carl F.	Puyallup	1942	1956							+	
Morrison, George E.	Puyallup	1926	1948					2			2
Mt. Baker Bulb Company	Mount Vernon	1950				+	+			+	
Mt. Rainier Bulb Company	Mount Vernon	1950				+	+	+			
Mullens, Jesse	Kirkland	1942				+				+	
Nakatsuka, J. A.	Kent	1933						3			3
Nasuca, J.	Renton	1933						1			1
Nearhood, Sam (Bowen Bulb Farm)	Puyallup	1985	1992				10	10			10
Nelson, Nels	Mount Vernon	1947	1950				+	+			1
Nelson & Dundle	Nahcotta	1933					10	10			10
Ness, Peter	Edgecomb	1933						9			9
Newell, Mrs. A. B. (Cedarmere Gardens)	Kirkland	1933				+		+			
Noorlag, Neal (1906-1989)	Oak Harbor/ Mount Vernon	1930	1983	6	20	+	20	15			46
Norblad, Frank	Bay Center	1942						1			1
Nordrum, H. P.	Kirkland	1950				+					
Norton, W. Leroy	Kent	1950			+	+					
Oliver Brothers	Sumner	1951	1956			4		4			4
Oliver, C. Fred	Puyallup	1942	1950		+			2			2
Oliver, Orno R. (1901-1990)	Puyallup	1934	1975			20		20	5		25
Oliver, R. H.	Sumner	1951								+	
Olympia Perennial Gardens	Mud Bay	1933						+			
Onderwater, John (1896-1962)	Mount Vernon	1941	1961	+	3	8	+	+	16	+	30
Orton, Charles W. (1879-1963)	Sumner	1924	1963		70	100	+	100	30		200
Orton, Edward C. (1881-1975)	Sumner	1923	1956		40	+	40	100	30		200
Orton, Stanley P.	Sumner	1946	1952		4	4	8	+			12
Orton, W. J.	Renton	1925	1926								
Ottesen, Andrew	Oak Harbor	1944	1954		3				+		3
Overholt, D. W.	Sumner	1925							+		
Page, Vernal L.	Sumner	1947	1956		2			3			5
Page, W. W.	Sumner	1948	1956						+		

275

Table A. Commercial Growers of Iris, Narcissus and/or Tulips in Washington State, Continued.

Name (Born-Died)	Nearest city	Grew Bulbs		Number of acres in peak years**							Max***
		From	To	G	H	I	L	N	T	M	Acres
Palmer, G. A.	Whidbey Island	1935				4					
Palmer, H. H.	Arlington	1933	1948				1	+			1
Parks, Ray	Kirkland	1950				+					
Paulhamus, W. H. (1864-1925)	Puyallup	1924						+			
Payzant & Gallup	Chehalis	1942						+			
Perron, Frank J.	Bellevue	1950								+	1
Peters, Peter W.	Puyallup	1942	1943				1				1
Peterson, Dan (Novelty Bulb Gardens)	Everett	1947	1950				+		2		2
Peterson, Harry J.	Sumner/Yelm	1947	1956		+		2		4		7
Peterson, O. S.	Sumner	1925	1927						1		1
Peterson, Walfred	Grayland	1925						+			
Picha, Lloyd D. (----1988)	Puyallup	1950	1961		1		11				30
Picha, Warren	Puyallup	1942	1961		3		16		1		30
Ping, J. R.	Sumner	1942	1946				1				1
Pohl, F. G.	Tacoma	1933						+			
Polinder, Kryn	Lynden	1933	1948		+						
Portman, A. M.	Brewster	1956								+	
Pruyser, August G.	Puyallup	1923	1933				19				19
Pudor, O. M. (Pudors, Inc.)	Puyallup	1923	1942		+						
Rae, Donald M.	Kirkland	1950			+					+	
Rawlings, J. W.	Tacoma	1933					2				2
Ray's Garden	Vancouver	1935	1942		+						
Reininger Floral Farm	Lynden	1942	1948	1			10				10
Reise, Otto, Sr. (1896-1981)	Puyallup	1925	1959		1		40		1		40
Reise, Mrs. Otto, Sr.	Puyallup	1940							1		1
Reise, Otto, Jr.	Puyallup	1947	1956				10		+		10
Reise, Wilmer	Puyallup	1936	1984		5		30		2		35
Reitmeier, H. G.	Puyallup	1951	1952							+	
Reynolds, Henry (Reynolds & Vaughan Co.)	Sumner	1941							+		
Rhitto, Henry	Bellevue	1942		+							

Table A. Commercial Growers of Iris, Narcissus and/or Tulips in Washington State. Continued.

Name (Born-Died)	Nearest city	Grew Bulbs		Number of acres in peak years**							Max.***
		From	To	G	H	I	L	N	T	M	Acres
Rhitto & Peterson	Bellevue	1933						1			1
Richardson, Ralph	Seattle	?								+	
Rickers, Mrs. W. H.	Kirkland	1950				+					
Rideout, G. H.	Puyallup	1924	1957					8		+	8
Rise, Herman	Seattle	?								+	
Ritscher, Henry B.	Sumner	1942	1959			+		8		+	8
Roberson, Leonard (1904-1967)(L. N. Roberson Co.)	Seattle	1927	1950				+			+	
Roberts, Burton	Olympia	1942	1943				+				
Robertson, Lillian (L. Robertson Nursery)	Elbe	1950								+	
Roods Bulb Farm	Shelton	?								+	
Rodzant, Hank & John	Oak Harbor	1940	1945			+		+	+		
Roodzant, Herbert (1897-1989) & Pete	Oak Harbor	1940	1956		20		10	4			34
Roozen, William A. with Helen (wife), John, Leo, Richard, William M., Michael & Bernadette (Washington Bulb Co., Inc.)	Mount Vernon	1950	1992	2	330	50	530	400			1310
Rosaia Brothers (Thomas Floral)	Seattle	1925	1942			+		1			1
Royer, E. C.	Sumner	1925	1959			+		5			5
Sabelis, Ted	Buckley	1961	1962					1			1
Sanders, H. M.	Monroe	1933	1942					1			1
Sather, Harry M. (1912-1991)	Sumner	1953	1975	12	7		14		3		20
Saul, Joseph T.	Auburn	1933					+				
Schaeffer, L. D.	Vashon Island	1932					+				
Schemper, Charles	Mount Vernon	1949	1950		+			+			5
Schindele, H. J.	Mount Vernon	1947	1950		+		+				
Schindele, Ted	Mount Vernon	1947	1950		+						
Schleicher, F. E.	Seattle	1935	1942		+						
Schluh, Eugene	Mount Vernon	1947	1949	2	+	+					3
Scholz, Alfred	Puyallup	1934	1950					4	2		6
Schroeder, Kenneth W.	Mount Vernon	1950			+						
Schwan, Fred	Sumner	1956							+		
Scramlin, Marchall	Kirkland	1950	1956		+						
Segers Brothers	Lynden	1925	1942		+		22				60

Table A. Commercial Growers of Iris, Narcissus and/or Tulips in Washington State. Continued.

Name (Born-Died)	Nearest city	Grew Bulbs		Number of acres in peak years**							Max***
		From	To	G	H	I	L	N	T	M	Acres
Selset, Reidar K.	Kirkland	1950			+						
Setter, Al M.	Galvin/Centralia	1947	1956		+		+	1			2
Shane, Dan	Mount Vernon	1950			+		+				
Shannon, E. C.	Puyallup	1950					+				
Sharp, Harry	Seattle	1951	1952			+					
Sheffield, George (Sheffield Bulb Farm)	Burton	1928	1942		+	+	+				
Shorey, Samuel	Orcas Island	1904								+	
Simoni, Andrew	Seatle	1948									
Simpson & Hubbard	Everett	1933					+				
Slagle Gardens	Puyallup	1950			+						
Slettengren, A.	Redmond	1950			+						
Smiley,	Mount Vernon	1949									5
Smit, L. Maynard	Puyallup	1933	1956		+		+				10
Smith Brothers	Bellevue	1950			+		+	+			
Smith, George & Knight	Coupeville	1935	1948		10	10			+		10
Smith, Gilbert	Burton	1935	1946		+	+					
Smith, Joe (Olympia Bulb Farm)	Olympia	1919	1933	2	+	+	2	20	2		40
Smith, John W. Macrae (1866----)	Bellingham	1901	1942		+	+	+	+	+		1
Smith, Karel (Lubbe) (Satsop Bulb Farm)	Satsop	1971	1992		10		10	2			12
Smith, Karl	?	?								+	
Smith, Robert L.	Bellevue	1933	1942		+		3	3			3
Smith, Robert	Sunnydale	1933	1935		+		+	+			
Snow, L. M.	Sumner	1933			+		2	2			2
South Park Iris Garden	Seattle	1950			+		+				
Staatz, Stanley W. (1894-1968) (Staatz Bulb Farm)	Sumner	1937	1968	20	+	+	40	16			140
Staatz, Wallace T. (Staatz Bulb Farm)	Sumner	1952	1992	20	+	+	50	15			140
Stafford, James	Sumner	1933	1944		+		+	+			
Staiff Bulb Farms	Sumner/Snohomish	1947					+				
Stelling, Jacob	Puyallup	1924									
Stephenson, M. E. (Billmyrt Gardens)	Kent	1935	1942		+		+				

Table A. Commercial Growers of Iris, Narcissus and/or Tulips in Washington State. Continued.

Name (Born-Died)	Nearest city	Grew Bulbs From	To	G	H	I	L	N	T	M	Max*** Acres
Steuber & Richardson	Seattle/Falls City	1933	1942			+	36				36
Stewart, Fred	Anacortes	1933				+					
Stewart, Mrs. Mary Brown (1870-1958)(Tulip Grange)	Bow	1908	1947			+	+		+	+	
Stewart, Sam J. (1902-1972)(Tulip Grange)	Mount Vernon	1925	1972		30	108		50			153
Stiembi, Fred	Lynden	1933					+				
Stinson, Harry L.	Seattle	1950			+						
Stoley, Olaf	Kirkland									+	
Stone, Mrs. Cora B.	Puyallup	1933					1				1
Stookey, E. B. (---1961)	Olympia	1933	1951					4	1		5
Stremler, Fred & Sons	Lynden	1942	1948				2				2
Stubbs, G. S.	Vancouver	1947					+				
Stroud, W. L.	Seattle	1950							+		
Sumner Floral Company	Sumner	1933					1				1
Sunnen, Joe	Puyallup	1956					3				3
Sutter, S. S.	Puyallup	1940	1946				2				2
Svoboda, John	Puyallup	1944	1948		3						3
Svoboda, Leo	Puyallup	1949	1964						+		
Swanson, August S.	Seattle	1935	1942		+						
Swenson, Alfred	Bow	1950			+	+					
Symbiosis Gardens	Kent	1950			+						
Taylor, A. J.	Marysville	1924	1946				+				
Taylor, Walter R.	Olympia	1924	1943				3				3
Thole, F. A.	Seattle	1942			+						
Thomas Floral Company	Kent	1933					+				
Thompson, Hugh	Marysville	1933	1942		+		1				1
Thuesen, N. H.	Seattle	1933	1942		+		+				
Tillinghast Seed Company	La Conner	1950			+						
Tober, Leo	Sumner	1950			+						
Torgerson, Mary V. (Lakeside Iris Gardens)	Seattle	1950			+						
Trafton, George M.	Seattle	1933	1942				1				1

279

Table A. Commercial Growers of Iris, Narcissus and/or Tulips in Washington State. Continued.

Name (Born-Died)	Nearest city	Grew Bulbs		Number of acres in peak years**							Max*** Acres
		From	To	G	H	I	L	N	T	M	
Trusdale, I. N.	Seattle	?								+	1
Tubbs, Harry E.	Puyallup	1948	1956				1				1
Tulip Town Bulb Garden	Bellingham	1922						+			
University Flower & Bulb	Seattle	1942			+						
Urahama,	Sumner	1933				+					1
Vallentgoed, Rutgert (Vallentgoed & Murray)	Bellingham	1922	1926			+			+		5
Van Aalst, Frank	Lynden	1926					+	+			
Van Aalst, John (----1950) (Van Aalst Bulb Farms)	Kirkland	1920	1946			+	5		+		5
Van Aalst, Rudolph	Stanwood	1961							+		
Van Amam, Philip E.	Vancouver	1947				+					
Van der Griend, Gewet	Lynden	1933	1943			2		2			2
Van der Mey, C. M.	Puyallup	1948	1952			+		+			2
Van der Pol, Nicholas (Van der Pol & Ronning)	Seattle	1947	1950			+		+			1
Van der Salm, Jerry (Van der Salm Bulbfarm, Inc.)	Woodland	1980	1992			+	100	10	10	10	100
Van Lierop, Case E. (1886-1961)(Vans Bulb Farm)	Bothell/Conway	1924	1961			12	+	10	18		80
Van Lierop, Cornelius (1918-1973)(Vans Bulb Farm)	Bothell/Conway	1940	1973			12	+	10	18		80
Van Lierop, C. Pete with sons Jeff & Peter (Ward & Van Lierop)	Olympia	1981	1992					25		+	25
Van Lierop, Mrs. E. H.	Bothell	1935							+		
Van Lierop, Neil with Bonnie (wife), Cynthia, Anne & April (Van Lierop Bulb Farm, Inc.)	Puyallup	1950	1992			40		60	25		120
Van Lierop, Simon (1900-1962)(Van Lierop Bulb Farm, Inc.)	Puyallup	1931	1962			8		21	4		35
Van Rooy	Orting	1942						30			30
Van Slyke, Clifford (1905----)	Puyallup	1921	1926	+	+						2
Van Waveren, Antonio (1914-1979)(Tony's Bulb Gardens)	Mount Vernon	1946	1968			8		6	10		24
Van Waveren, Harry	Lynden	1930	1949					+			5
Van Zanten, Gerrit (1902-1959)(Van Zanten Bulb Company)	Lynden	1926	1959			5	+	115	+		120
Van Zanten, Maurice (Van Zanten Bulb Company)	Lynden	1928	1949			5	+	115	+		120
Van Zonneveld, Arie (1899-1948)(Van Zonneveld of Washington)	Orting	1925	1948			+	138	+			165
Van Zonneveld, Robert	Mount Vernon	1947	1951						+		
Vaughn Bulb Farm (Vaughn & Reynolds)	Sumner	1941						+			
Wahlquist, J. E.	Puyallup	1942	1948					4			4

Table A. Commercial Growers of Iris, Narcissus and/or Tulips in Washington State. Continued.

Name (Born-Died)	Nearest city	Grew Bulbs From	To	G	H	I	L	N	T	M	Max*** Acres
Wait, Fred P.	Sumner	1951								+	
Walker, Pete (Walker & Maupin)	Mount Vernon	1949	1979					10	+		10
Walters, Stanley W.	Puyallup	1946	1978		3			5			8
Wanamaker, Herman L. (---1963)	Coupeville	1935	1950		5						5
Ward, George	?	?							+		
Ward, Mervin (1906-1989)	Puyallup	1950	1956					8		+	8
Ward, Mervin Lee (Ward & VanLierop)	Olympia	1981	1992					25			25
Warwick, Tom	Bellingham	1922								+	
Watson, Frank	Centralia	1947	1951							+	
Watson, Halsey R.	Olympia	1924	1943					2			2
Watsons Bulb Acres	Olympia	1942	1946					+			
Waugh, A. C.	Auburn	1933						+			
Webster, H.	Kent	1933						1			1
Webster, L. T.	Olympia	1950								+	
Weeks, J. A.	Bremerton	1935								+	
Weyers, H. L.	Mount Vernon	1961	1965							+	
Wheadon, Percy	Kirkland	1933	1944					6			6
Wheeler, Alta M.	Seatle	1933						+			
Whidden, Sam	Puyallup	1933						2			2
Wight, Arthur E.	Fox Island	1927	1942	+				4	+		4
Wight, C. Leland	Woodinville	1942	1947					8			8
Wight, William C.	Fox Island	1927	1934	+				3	+		3
Wight, Steve	Fox Island	1930						1			1
Williams, Earl	Sumner	1942						+			
Williams, Elmer G., Sr. (1895-1976)(Williams Bros.)	Orting	1941	1958		+			40	+		40
Williams, (Ozzie) Elmer G., Jr. (Williams Bros.)	Orting	1956	1992		15			50	15		80
Williams, Hyacinth G.	Kent	1950								+	
Willingham Bulb Specialists	Puyallup	1950						+			
Willis, H. L. (1869-1956)(Hollyhurst)	Mount Vernon	1910	1956		5		+	3			10
Wilson, Charles N. (Wilshire Gardens)	Hoquiam	1942	1947					3			3

Table A. Commercial Growers of Iris, Narcissus and/or Tulips in Washington State. Continued.

Name (Born–Died)	Nearest city	Grew Bulbs From	Grew Bulbs To	G	H	I	L	N	T	M	Max*** Acres
Wilson, D. M.	Sumner	1933					1				1
Wimer, W. C.	Bellingham	1942	1943		+		+				
Wimer, W. D.	Bellingham	1942					1				1
Wincer, W. C.	Bellingham	1933					+				
Wines, Edwin (1862-1934)	Fox Island	1905	1924				5				5
Winters, Fred W. (1882-1968)	Bellevue	1924	1943		+		7				7
Woodland Park Floral	Sumner	1942	1947				2				2
Woods, H.	Seattle	1933					+				
Woodward, Wallace (Woodward Bulb Farm)	Puyallup	1963	1992				4	1			5
Wymer, J. B.	Kirkland	1950		+							
Yaba, George	Kent	1956	1958	+			+	+	+		1
Yahami, G.	Vashon Island	1933					+	+			
Youngman, Adrian	Whidbey Island	1933	1934		+						
Zeilstra, Henry	Oak Harbor	1947	1950	+							

Appendix Table B. Commercial Gladiolus Growers in Washington State.*

| Name (Born-Died) (Company)** | Nearest City | Grew Gladiolus | |
		From	To
Albertson, W. E.	Seattle	1924	
Applequist, Frank	Seattle	1946	1947
Berke, Nels (Viking Gardens)	Tacoma	1942	1946
Bloomquist, Mrs. Lenora	Sequim	1950	
Bonney Boone Gardens	Yakima	1946	1947
Brown, Harry L.	Tacoma	1950	
Cassidy, H. N.	Yakima	1946	1947
Christiansen, Mrs. L. P.	Stanwood	1950	
Clark, Elliot K. (Clark Bulb Farm)	Sequim	1950	
Clark, L. R.	Sumner	+	
Cobb, Virgil A.	Lynden	1950	
Cohoons Glad Gardens	Arlington	1950	
Colburn Gardens	Spokane	1946	1947
Connel's Glads	Tacoma	1989	
Conner, E. L.	Yakima	1950	
Darst, Earle**	Coupeville	1964	1992
DeGoede, Henry**	Mount Vernon	1951	1967
Desellem, Fred	Olympia	1950	
Dissen, Mrs. W. C.	Ellensburg	1950	
Dowling, Warren	Monroe	1941	1959
East View Nursery	Stanwood	1950	
Ericksen, E. F.	Marysville	1950	
Fernbriar Gardens	Issaquah	1950	
Ferry, R. H. (Mountainview Glad Gardens)	Tacoma	1947	1950
Figgins, Burl T.	Yelm	1950	
Ford, F. E.	Seattle	+	
Foulk, E. K.	Tacoma	1946	
Frederick, R. E.	Renton	1947	1950
Friend, Clarence	Zillah	1957	1992
Friend, John P.**	Outlook	1957	1992
Friend, Klaas	Soap Lake	1955	
Friend, Nick	+	+	
Fry, Homer L.	Granger	1950	1991
Gebaroff, A.	Seattle	1946	1947
Gilbert Gardens	Sunnyside	1950	
Gillilans Flowers	Eatonville	1950	
Glad-Croft Gardens	Bellingham	1950	
Gordon, A. D.	Spokane	1946	1947
Gregg, Ira (Sunnyside-1942)**	Auburn	1954	1959
Hammerly, Harry**	Marysville	1950	
Hardy, Maynard N.	Sunnyside	1950	
Hedstrom's Flowers	Olalla	1950	
Herzog, Cora	Port Townsend	1950	
Hobby Iris Gardens	Camas	1950	
Huber, Walter F.	Elma	1950	

* Based upon available records or estimates by other growers. A + indicates the name was found on a list but no date was reported.

** Grew 10 acres or more of Gladiolus according to available records or comments.

283

Table B. Continued. Commercial Gladiolus Growers in Washington State.*

Name (Born-Died) (Company)**	Nearest City	Grew Gladiolus From	To
Huff, John (1908-1990)	Orting	1938	1960
(Huffs Glad Patch)			
Hughes, William F.	Redmond	1950	
Iris City Gardens	Walla Walla	1950	
Kanouse, Aaron N. (1902-1980)	Olympia	1922	1941
Kaylor, Floyd (1876-1960)	Blaine/Tacoma	1941	1954
(Peace Arch Nursery)			
Kennedy Flower & Bulb Garden	Pinehurst	1946	1947
Kirk, Arthur R.	Yakima	1946	
Kirk, Arthur W.	Fort Lewis	1950	
Knopf (or Knapp), Robert	Walla Walla	1950	
Krains Bulb Gardens	Enumclaw	1950	
Kress, G. M.	Vashon	1950	
Kuss, J. N.	Seattle	1950	
Langdon, A. W.	Sumner	1947	1950
Leinbach, Jack	Yakima	1950	
Libby	Yakima	+	
Lively, E. E.	Seattle	1950	
L & L Bulb Farm	Chehalis	1950	
Loomis, R. P.	Bellingham	1950	
Lost Lake Bulb Farm	Elma	1950	
Love, Don (Don Love Gardens)	Elma	1950	
McHaffey, Charles C.	Kirkland	1950	
McKay, R. J.	Mount Vernon	1950	
McLeof, J. W.	Pacific	1946	1947
Mann, A. B.	Puyallup	1923	
Marine View Gardens	Edmonds	1941	
Martin, F. S.	Puyallup	1926	1929
Mayvalor Gardens	Vancouver	1950	
Moeller, A. J.	Tacoma	1942	1947
Montgomery Gardens	Colville	1946	1947
Moran, Erle E. (1906-1982)	Chehalis	1932	1982
Moyers, E.	Spokane	1950	
Mt. Baker Bulb Company	Seattle	1950	
Mt. Rainier Bulb Company	Seattle	1950	
Norris, R. L.	Wapato	1950	
Norton, W. Leroy	Kent	1950	
Olson, Jacob	Milton	1946	1947
Onderwater, John (1896-1962)	Mount Vernon	1950	
Orton, E. C. (1881-1975)	Sumner	1946	
Oyster Bay Dahlia Gardens	Bremerton	1950	
Painter, Clyde & Mrs. Roe	Auburn	1952	1954
Peckenpaugh, D. G.	Opportunity	1946	1947
(Rockland Bulb Farm)			
Pommert, Ralph J. (1895-1992)**	Pacific	1925	1950
Pommert, Robert (1923-1985)**	Pacific	1950	1954
Purdin, Walter	Yakima	1946	1947
Purple, Dan	Seattle	1946	1947

Name (Born-Died) (Company)**	Nearest City	Grew Gladiolus	
		From	To
Randwood Bulb Gardens	Montesano	1950	
Rees, Dan	Puyallup	1942	1957
Reetz, Marvin H.	Ridgefield	1950	
Rich Avenue Gardens	Spokane	1946	1947
Rise, Herman	Seattle	1950	
Robertson, J. T.	Sunnyside	1941	1947
Roe, Orville R. (1900-1952)**	Auburn	1932	1952
Roe, Mrs. Doris & C. Painter**	Auburn	1952	1954
Rood's Bulb Farm	Shelton	1950	
Sather	Chehalis	+	
Sather, Harry**	Sumner	1970	1980
Schinkelshock, Garrit**	Prosser	1989	1991
Schuler, A. J.	Puyallup	1950	
Searls, Edgar	South Prairie	1946	1952
Setters Bulb Farm	Galvin	1947	1950
Sheehy, Harold D.	Sumner	1950	
Short, B. M.	Bremerton	1950	
Silers Cut Flowers & Bulbs	Elma	1942	1950
Smith, George W. & Knight	Seattle	1946	1947
Smith, Joe	Olympia	1922	1930
Smith, Leslie J.	Kennewick	1946	1947
Stillings, J. R.	Yakima	1946	1947
Stroud, W. L.	Seattle	1950	
Summer's Gardens	Tacoma	1950	
Sunnyside Bulb Farm	Grandview	1950	
Suquamish Flower Gardens	Suquamish	1950	
Sutter, S. S.	Puyallup	1946	1947
Swayne, Violet (Swaynes Gardens)	Puyallup	1952	1958
Swenson, Mrs. Merle	Bremerton	1950	
Tacoma Glad Farms	Tacoma	1950	
Terryhill Gardens	Suquamish	1950	
Tyner's Gardens	Seattle	1950	
Updike Bulb Gardens	Vancouver	1950	
Webster, M. E. (Websters Glads)	Tacoma	1946	1950
Weilers Greenhouses	Spokane	1946	1947
Whitaker, Ron	Olympia	1989	
White, D. H.	Tacoma	1947	1950
White House Glad Company	Longview	1950	
Wight, W. C., A. E. & C. E.	Fox Island	1927	1942
Wilkins, J. D.	Otis Orchards	1946	1947
Williamson, David & Ben	Elma	1950	
Wilson, Charles N. (Wilshire Gardens)	Hoquiam	1950	
Womack, Homer E.	Seattle	1950	
Wood, J. P. & Sons (Floralwood Gardens)	Yakima	1950	

Appendix Table C. Commercial Lily Growers in Washington State.*

Name (Company)**	Nearest City	Grew Lilies From	To
Anderson, N. P.	Mount Vernon	1950	
Armstrong, E. K.	Olympia	1950	
Arnold, Claude	Kirkland	1950	
Arnold, Eugene O.	Edmonds	1950	
Baisden, P. C.	Monroe	1950	
Baker, Floyd	Grayland	1947	
Baldwin, James	Elma	1947	
Bell, Herbert S.	Grayland	1947	
Berger, Joe**	Mount Vernon	1947	1956
Bergman, Henry A.	Mount Vernon	+	
Berry, A. W.	Silverdale	1950	
Betterley, Griffin & Spellacy	Grayland	1947	
Bigelow, E. C.	Sequim	1949	1950
Birkinshaw, Faye	Westport	1947	
Blair, Wilson	Seaview	1947	
Blake, Ernie	North Cove	1947	
Bloomquist, John	Hoquiam/	1946	1950
(B. Bros. Lily Bulbs)	Grayland		
Bothwell, F. B.	Port Orchard	1950	
Bottemiller, Fred	Vancouver	1949	
Bowker, Clarence	Port Orchard	1950	
Bowman, Philip (Mak-Leek Lilies Inc)	Pasco	?	1992
Boydston, R. D.	Westport	1947	
Brain, Mrs. James	Thorp	1950	
Brandner, Lloyd	Westport	1947	
Brandner, Fred	Westport	1947	
Brautlacht, L. J.	Bremerton	1956	
Brown, Elmer	Grayland	1947	
Brown, P. P. (Brown's Gardens)	Ridgefield	1949	
Breakey, E. P.	Puyallup	1947	
Bunch, John L.	Kirkland	1950	
Bush, Henry	Elma	1949	
Butz, F. R.	Ethel	1949	
Byrum, W. O.	Everson	1946	
Calbom, Sam	Mount Veron	1950	
Caldwell, Byron	Westport	1947	
Carey, Dortha	Grayland	1950	
Carey, W. E.	Grayland	1949	
Carlson, J. E.	Grayland	1950	
Carossino, Frank (Oceanside Nursery)	Westport	1947	
Carstenson, John	Westport	1947	1950
Casanova, William	Aberdeen	1947	1949
Cefalu, Antonio	Westport	1946	1949
Cefalu, H.	Westport	1947	
Chambers, V. P.	Kirkland	1950	
Chervenka, Frank	Sumner	1927	

* Based upon available records or estimates by other growers. A + indicates the name was found on a list but no date was reported.

** Grew 10 acres or more of Lilies according to available records or comments.

286

Table C. Continued. Commercial Lily Growers in Washington State.*

Name (Company)**	Nearest City	Grew Lilies From	To
Chichester, Ed H.	Port Orchard	1950	1956
Chichester, F.	Bremerton	1950	
Christianson, H. P.	Grayland	1947	1956
Clark, J. M.	Hoquiam	1949	
Cranguyma Farms	Long Beach	1949	
Dalrymple, Harry	Grayland	1947	
Darrow, Lynn	Grayland	1947	
Darst, Glenn	Coupeville	+	
Davies, Miles A.	Westport	1947	
Davis, A. H.	Grayland	1947	
Davis, Brisbon	Edmonds	1950	
Davis, Mart	Port Orchard	1950	
De Graaff, Jan (Oregon Bulb Farms)	Grandview	1975	1980
DeGroot, Ted (United Bulb Company)**	Woodland	1947	1956
Delkin, Fred L.	Bellevue	1947	
Desellem, Fred	Olympia	1950	
Dexters by the Sea	Tokeland	1947	
Diedrick, Gustof	Westport	1947	
Dobbe, Benno**	Woodland	1980	1992
(Holland America Bulb Farms, Inc.)			
Dodge, C. H.	Bremerton	1950	1956 ..
Dorman, J. E.	South Bend	1949	
Douglas, George F.	Vancouver	1949	
Dragg, Frank	Montesano	1947	
Duncombe, Will (D & O Croft L.B.C.)	Redmond	1950	
East View Nursery	Stanwood	1950	
Edlund, A.	Montesano	1949	1950
Edwards, G. G.	Aberdeen	1947	1949
Edwards, Gordon T.	Bellevue	1946	
Edwards, Mrs. Glenn T. (Glenacres)	Westport	1947	
Edwards, Ira J.	Woodinville	1947	1956
Ellerbeck, A. D.	Mount Vernon	1950	1956
Eramo, Edward	Satsop	1947	
Espedal, E.	Hoquiam	1947	
Espedal, Osmund A.	Hoquiam	1947	1950
Evans, L. R.	Everett	1946	
Everett, K. B.	Westport	1947	
Everson, Albert S.	Oakville	1950	
Everson, Laurence O.	Oakville	1947	
Fabritz, Leo E.	Port Orchard	1950	
Falls Creek Lily Gardens	Elma	1947	1949
Fields, George H.	Quinault	1946	1947
Flatt, Floyd	Grayland	1947	1949
Flickinger, F. S.	Seattle	1925	1927
Ford, F. E.	Seattle	1950	
Freimann, LeVerne L.	Bellingham	1928	1989
Frost, Rosetta	Aberdeen	1947	1950
Fulmer, W. L.	Seattle	1950	
Gary, Mark	Sumner	1947	
Genoe, H.	Port Orchard	1950	
Gerwig, Louis	South Bend	1947	1949

287

Table C. Continued. Commercial Lily Growers in Washington State.*

Name (Company)**	Nearest City	Grew Lilies From	To
Getchell, C. D.	South Bend	1947	
Gibbs, George	Orcas/Lynden	1892	1907
Giese & Novolich	Aberdeen	1947	
Glad-Croft Gardens	Bellingham	1950	
Goheen, Guy C.	Ridgefield	1949	1950
Gonnason, Victor	Fall City	1950	
Gotchy, S. L.	Westport	1947	
Gronen, Robert H.	Puyallup	1947	1951
Gross, John	Aberdeen	1947	
Grossman, Herbert	Markham	1946	1947
Guldemond, Arie (United Bulb Co)**	Woodland	1947	1956
Gustafson, Dayton N.	Sumner	1956	
Haley, E. R.	Grayland	1947	
Hall, C. R. D.	Montesano	1946	
Hall, Joe	Montesano	1947	
Hall, Price	South Bend	1947	1949
Hamblem, D. D.	Markham	1946	1947
Hamblem, Howard	Aberdeen	1949	
Hamblem, T. B.	Aberdeen	1947	
Hamblem Lily Farm	Aberdeen	1950	
Hammer, David J.	Marysville	1950	
Hammerly, Harry	Marysville	1947	1950
Harms, Leonard C.	Westport	1947	
Hanson, Harry	Mount Vernon	1947	
Harnden,Henry	Aberdeen	1947	
Hattebaugh, W. & Strubel	Elma	1947	1949
Hattebaugh, Mrs. Walt	Elma	1950	
Hebert, Leo	Tokeland	1947	
Henry, George P.	North Cove	1947	
Henry, R. H.	Grayland	1947	
Herzog, Cora	Port Townsend	1950	
Hickerson, D.	Aberdeen	1947	
Hickerson, Herbert	Grayland	1947	
Hickman, James H.	Aberdeen	1947	1949
Hill, J. C. & Son	Grayland	1947	1950
Hill, Charles	Westport	1947	1949
Hogan, Katherine	Westport	1947	
Homanberg, E. A.	Port Orchard	1956	
Houghtaling, C.	Everett	1946	
Hubers Bulb Gardens	Elma	1947	1949
Huber, Walter F.	Elma	1950	
Hueneka, Fred E., Sr.	Orting	1950	1956
Hunt, J. T.	Ocosta	1947	1949
Hunt & Sylvia	Markham	1947	
Iris City Gardens	Walla Walla	1950	
Irish, W. E.	Riffe	1949	
Irvin, A. M.	Grayland	1947	
Island View Gardens	Bremerton	1950	
Jackson, R. A.	Westport	1947	
Jacobson, R.	North Cove	1947	1949

288

Table C. Continued. Commercial Lily Growers in Washington State.*

Name (Company)**	Nearest City	Grew Lilies From	To
Johnson, Arthur F.	Grayland	1949	1950
Johnson, Charles R.	Westport	1947	1950
Johnson, Curtis G.	Aberdeen	1947	
Johnson, Clarence	Mount Vernon	1950	
Johnson, Helen	Grayland	1949	
Johnson, James G.	Olalla	1950	1956
Johnson, K. A.	Sumner	1956	
Johnson, L. F.	Edmonds	1950	
Johnson, Lloyd O.	Grayland	1947	1949
Johnson, Matt	Port Orchard	1956	
Johnson, Werner	Grayland	1947	
Joubert, Foy H.	Poulsbo	1950	
Joyce, Erwin	Montesano	1949	
Kajfas, Mrs. Frank	Aberdeen	1947	
Kanouse, Aaron N.	Olympia	1929	1973
Kaufman, Gretchen	Bellingham	1950	
Kechter, Carl	Aberdeen	1947	
Keehnel, S. J.	Centralia	1947	
Kemp, W. O.	Grayland	1947	
Kepner, K. M.	Elma/Poulsbo	1947	1950
Keppert, H.J.	Olympia	1950	
Kilgore, Mike	Montesano	1947	
Kivi, Matt	Aberdeen	1947	
Knight Bulb Farm	North Cove	1947	
Knight, George	Tokeland	1947	
Knutsen, Louis	Montesano	1947	
Krause, Frank	Westport	1947	
Krueger, Otto F.	Port Orchard	1950	
Kviz, Fred (Vista Nursery)	Seattle	1950	
Labreck, E. W.	Poulsbo	1950	
Laier, Carl	Aberdeen	1947	
Lake, James	Aberdeen	1947	
Larson, Siebert	Montesano	1947	
Larson, William M.	Bremerton	1950	
Laughlin Lily Gardens	Vashon	1946	1950
Lawson, C. J.	Orting	1956	
Leckenby, Jim	Mount Vernon	1949	1952
Lennox, S. A.	Seattle	1950	
Levering, Frank E. (Izora Gardens)	Westport	1946	1949
Linder, Dee	Westport	1946	1950
Linder, T. E.	Westport	1946	1950
Lindstrom, Fred	Raymond	1947	
Lindstrom, Joe	Westport	1947	
Linghams Lily Gardens	Tacoma	1946	
Linkleter, F. W.	Aberdeen	1947	
Linzell & Huber	Elma	1947	
Lively, E. E.	Seattle	1950	
Livingston, L. C.	Satsop	1947	
Lockhart, Robert A.	White Salmon	1949	
Lowe, M. L.	Aberdeen	1947	

289

Table C. Continued. Commercial Lily Growers in Washington State.*

Name (Company)**	Nearest City	Grew Lilies From	To
Lund, Ernest	Port Orchard	1956	
Lund, Herbert E.	Port Orchard	1956	
Lundgren, C. W.	Aberdeen	1947	
Lyford, N. C.	Seattle	1950	
McAninch, Arthur M.	Montesano	1947	
McCallum, A. C.	Montesano	1947	1949
McCormick (Shorty Rick)	Grayland	1947	
McDonald, Kenneth	Grayland	1947	
McGill, G. W.	North Cove	1949	
McKay, D. W.	Oakville	1947	
McKay, R. J.	Mount Vernon	1950	
McLean, J. R. (J.R.McLean Bulb Farms)	Elma/Puyallup	1947	1950
McLean, Homer	Grayland	1947	
McMahill, H. E.	Poulsbo	1950	1956
McTaggert, W. A.	Aberdeen	1947	
Manchewsky, Geoge	Westport	1947	
Marble, Ralph	La Center	1947	
Mason, Claude	Montesano	1947	
Matthews, C. H.	Aberdeen	1947	1950
Matthews, Esther	Aberdeen	1949	
Matthews, E. S.	Grayland	1949	1950
Matthews, Shirley	Aberdeen	1950	
Mauer, Dr. A. J.	Rochester	1947	
Miller, A. C.	Oakville	1947	
Miller, John L.	Elma	1947	
Miller, Lewis J.	Westport	1947	
Mooers, King	Renton	1956	
Moore, A. J.	Puyallup	1950	
Moore, J. Frank	Longview	1950	
Morgan, Victor	Westport/ Humptulips	1946	1947
Morris, Oliver S.	Hoquiam	1947	1949
Morriss Croft Lily Farm	Port Orchard	1950	
Mt. Baker Bulb Company	Seattle	1950	
Mt. Rainier Bulb Company	Seattle	1950	
Mountain Meadow Bulb Farm	White Salmon	1950	
Mowes Croft Lily Research Farm	Elma	1947	
Mumaw, R. H.	Westport	1947	
Nelson, Chris	Tokeland	1947	1950
Nelson, Nels	Mount Vernon	1947	
Nelson Ranch	Tokeland	1947	
Niemi (Nimi-?), John	Grayland	1946	1947
Noorlag, Neal	Oak Harbor	1947	1950
Northern Cross Lily Farms	Bow	1950	
Onderwater, John	Mount Vernon	1947	
Orton, E. C.	Sumner	1947	1948
Osborne, E. S.	Hoquiam	1947	
Ostergaard, Alvin	Elma	1947	1949
Paris, William Carl	Port Orchard	1950	
Peck, James	Grayland	1947	
Pederson, Caroline	La Center	1950	

Table C. Continued. Commercial Lily Growers in Washington State.*

| Name (Company)** | Nearest City | Grew Lilies | |
		From	To
Pederson, Mrs. E.	La Center	1949	
Pelmulder, Jay	Rochester	1950	
Perry and Johnson	Hoquiam	1950	
Peterson, Walfred	Grayland	1949	1950
Peuhkurinen, J.	Aberdeen	1947	
Pezella, Paul	Auburn	1950	
Phelps, Leonard (South Arbor Bulb Farm)	Markham	1946	1949
Picharts Bulb Farm	Sumner	1950	
Potter, Ernest	Westport	1947	
Prettyman, Robert	Westport	1947	
Prosch, Edwin L.	Ridgefield	1949	1950
Purdy, George W.	Port Orchard	1950	
Rader & Painter	Seattle	1950	
Randwood Bulb Farm	Montesano	1947	
Rendig, John	Ethel	1950	
Renier, Earl S.	Nordland	1947	
Richards, Ray L.	Grayland	1947	
Richardson, V. D.	Hoquiam	1947	
Riverside Gardens	Renton	1950	
Roberson, L. N.	Seattle	1927	1935
Rodenberger, Glen H.	Olga	1947	1950
Rodgers, John	Westport	1947	
Rogers, Edward	Westport	1947	1949
Roozen, Wm. A. (Washington Bulb Co.)**	Mount Vernon	1955	1992
Rosenbach, Victor (Rosenbach Nursery)	Markham	1946	1950
Rosselli, Emil	Chehalis	1947	1956
Sartor, Herman E.	Port Orchard	1950	
Schluh, Eugene	Mount Vernon	1947	1949
Schwab, F. W.	Tacoma	1950	
Sederberg, Roy & Oscar	Port Orchard	1950	
Sharp, Harry	Sumner	1951	1952
Sharpf, Everett	Puyallup	1950	
Shay, S. G.	Olympia	1947	1950
Sheffield, George	Vashon Island	1928	1931
Shipman, Harry	Tokeland	1947	
Shorey, Samuel	Orcas Island	1904	
Short, B. M.	Bremerton	1950	
Shride, Claude L.	Vashon	1946	
Sigurdson, G.	Grayland	1947	
Siler, C. L.	Elma	1949	
Skur, Mrs. Ilme	Grayland	1947	
Smith, Gilbert	Burton	1946	1947
Smith, Joe	Olympia	1919	1925
Smith, Paul E.	Alderwood Manor	1950	
Smrz, Frank	Edmonds	1950	
Soehl, Fred	Aberdeen	1947	1950
Spangberg, W.	North Cove	1947	
Spaar, A.	Grayland	1947	
Spaulding, Isobel	Montesano	1949	
Spence, A. I.	Everett	1950	

291

Table C. Continued. Commercial Lily Growers in Washington State.*

| Name (Company)** | Nearest City | Grew Lilies | |
		From	To
Stalding & Son	Grayland	1947	1950
Stalding, Victor	Grayland	1949	
Stalding, Ward	Grayland	1947	1950
Stark, Harry	Aberdeen	1947	
Stauffer, Fred	Tokeland	1947	
Stolberg, Henry	Oakville	1950	
Stone, A. G.	Puyallup	1950	
Stolts, Barney	Westport	1947	
Strubell, Clarence	Elma	1950	
Sundstrom, Dr. J. H.	Montesano	1947	1950
Tackitt, Mrs. Paul	Westport	1947	
Tagliar, Angelo	Satsop	1947	
Tanata, Joe	North Cove	1949	
Taylor, A. J.	Marysville	1946	
Taylor, Walter R.	Olympia	1946	1947
Tessman, William	Westport	1947	
Teveldahl, John	Grayland	1947	
Thornberg, Oscar R.	Hoquiam	1947	1949
Thurston, W.	Grayland	1947	
Tobey, L. W.	Elma	1947	1950
Traverso, Enrico	Grayland	1949	1956
Trigg, L.	Westport	1947	1949
Van der Salm,Jerry (V.d.Salm Bulbfarm)**	Woodland	1980	1992
Van Lierop, Case	Bothell	1947	
Van Zanten Brothers	Lynden	1950	
Vining, Minnie	Westport	1947	
Vinson, J. L.	Westport	1947	1949
Vista Nursery	Seattle	1950	
Wagner, Mitchell	Stanwood	1956	
Wahl, O. H.	Aberdeen	1947	
Waite, E. E.	Stanwood	1956	
Waite, M. R.	Kent	1950	1956
Walden, L. M.	Aberdeen	1947	
Walker, Margaret	Elma	1949	
Waldron, Roy	Grayland	1947	
Ward,James L.	Kelso	1947	
Warren, Earl	Grayland	1947	1950
Watson, Chester C.	Aberdeen	1946	1949
Watson, D. A.	Markham	1946	
Watson, E. E.	Montesano	1946	1947
Watson, Frank	Centralia/ Grayland	1947	1950
Watson, Mabel	Olympia	1947	
Watson, Maude E.	Markham	1947	1950
Watson's Nursery	Montesano	1949	
Watson & Wherry	Olympia	1950	
Welk, E. A.	Onalaska	1949	
West Shore Gardens	Aberdeen	1950	
Whalen, J. W.	Westport	1947	
White, Mrs. Anna G.	Seattle	1950	
Willingham Bulb Specialties	Puyallup	1950	

Table C. Continued. Commercial Lily Growers in Washington State.*

| Name (Company)** | Nearest City | Grew Lilies | |
		From	To
Willis, H. L.	Mount Vernon	1950	1956
Wilson, C. L.	Westport	1947	
Wilson, Charles N. (Wilshire Gardens)	Hoquiam	1950	
Wilson, Frank & Lucie**	Everson	1943	1960
Wiitamaki, William	Montesano	1947	1949
Wood, J. P. & Sons (Floralwood Gardens)	Yakima	1950	
Wood, R. W.	Montesano	1947	
Wroth, Ben R.	Montesano	1947	
Young, Blanche	Aberdeen	1947	1949
Younger, Robert	Bay City	1949	1950
Youngs, Croft Lily Ranch	Poulsbo	1950	
Zerwekh, Vernon J.	Chehalis	1947	1949

293

BIBLIOGRAPHY

1. Allen, Tom, Wilbur C. Anderson, Gary Chastagner and Robert Doss. 1983. Virus disease survey of Northwest iris stocks. Proceedings 35th Annual Northwest Bulb Growers Conference. p.8.

2. Allmendinger, D.F., V.L.Miller and Folke Johnson. 1950. Control of fluorine scorch of gladiolus with foliar dusts and sprays. Proceedings Amer. Soc. Hort. Sci. 56:427.

3. *American Standard*, Sumner, WA. 1925. Takes up bulb growing. Sept. 18, front page.

4. Anderson, W.C. 1985. How important is nitrogen fertilizer for bulb production? Proceedings 37th Northwest Bulb Growers Conference.

5. Anderson, Wilbur C. and William A. Haglund. 1978. Summary of soil fertility survey on bulb crops grown in western Washington during the spring of 1978. Washington State University, N.W. Washington Research and Extension Unit. Mimeo.

6. Anderson, Wilbur C., Kathryn A. Mielke, Patricia N. Miller and Tom Allen. 1990. In vitro bulblet propagation of virus-free Dutch iris. Acta Horticulturae 266. p. 77-81.

7. Apt, Walter J. 1958. Studies on the Fusarium diseases of bulbous ornamental crops. Doctoral thesis. State College of Washington.

8. Apt, Walter J and Charles J. Gould. 1961. Control of root-lesion nematode, *Pratylenchus penetrans*, on Narcissus. Plant Disease Reporter Vol 45 No. 4, p. 290.

9. Ball, George K. 1955. Trends in merchandising of Northwest bulbs. Proceedings of 7th Northwest Bulb Growers Short Course. p. 20.

10. Bell, Mrs. Marilyn. 1989-1992. Personal correspondence regarding Gibbs. Woodinville, WA.

11. *Bellingham Herald*, Bellingham, WA. 1953. Experimental nursery farm helps conserve west's soils. April 26.

12. Bence, Erna. 1959. Tulip co-op ships first flowers here. *Tacoma News Tribune*, Farm News, April 5. p. B-6.

13. Bence, Erna. 1972. Bulb growers worry if common market in England will cut demand for U.S. flower bulbs. *Tacoma News Tribune*, Country Life Section, Feb. 9.

14. *The Blade*, New Whatcom, WA. 1898. Puget Sound's Bulbs. Aug. 9.

15. Breakey, E.P. 1952. Uses and Misuses of Methyl Bromide. Proceedings 1952 Northwest Bulb Growers Short Course. p. 32.

16. Carkner, Richard. 1990. Farming on the urban fringe in Pierce County, Washington. Speech presented at Farmland Preservation Conference. Nov. 30, Mt. Vernon. Mimeo.

17. Cascante, X.M., Robert P. Doss, and Y. Ozeri. 1989. Development of methods for the use of ethylene or ethephon to improve early forcing performance of Dutch iris grown in the Pacific Northwest of the United States. Special Report 836 Oregon State Univ. Ag. Exper. Station in cooperation with the USDA Ag. Res. Service.

18. Chastagner, Gary. 1981. Iris foliar diseases and their control. Proceedings of 1981 Northwest Bulb Growers Conference. p. 42-46.

19. Chastagner, G.A. 1983. Narcissus fire: prevalence, epidemiology and control in western Washington. *Plant Disease* 67:1384-1386.

20. Chastagner, Gary. 1985. Efficacy of fungicides in controlling leaf scorch on field grown daffodils. 1985 test results. Proceedings 1985 Northwest Bulb Growers Conference. p. 36.

21. Chastagner, Gary A 1990. 1989-90 bulb disease research Washington State University. Mimeo.

22. Chastagner, Gary and John M. Staley. 1989. Fungicidal control of foliage diseases on tulips, daffodils and bulbous iris. Proceedings 41st Northwest Bulb Growers Conference. p. 4-8.

23. Chastagner, Gary A, John M. Staley and Kathy Riley. 1990. Control of *Sclerotium rolfsii* on bulbous iris and lilies with in-furrow fungicide applications. Acta Horticulturae 266. p. 457-467.

24. Chastagner, Gary A, John M. Staley and Valerie McQuarrie-Baker. 1991. Effectiveness of preplant fungicide dips in controlling basal rot on 'Golden Harvest' daffodils. Proceedings 1991 Northwest Bulb Growers Conference. p. 19-21.

25. Chastagner, Gary A and Kathy Riley. 1990. Occurrence and control of benzimidazole and dicarboximide resistant Botrytis spp. on bulb crops in western Washington and Oregon. Acta Horticulturae 266. pp. 437-445.

26. Chervenka, Francis. 1948. Mechanical aids to bulb culture. Proceedings of the first Northwest Bulb Growers Short Course. p. 27.

27. Chervenka, Francis. 1989. Interview by C. J. Gould. May 9.

28. Chervenka, Frank. 1954. Personal communication. Mar. 14.

29. Courtney, Wilbur D. 1963. Control of nematodes affecting bulbs by hot water treatment. Washington Ag. Exp. Sta. Circular. #422.

30. Dorsett, P.H. 1913. Experiments in bulb growing at the United States bulb garden at Bellingham. USDA Bull. #28.

31. Doss, R.P., J.K. Christian, J.M. Langager. 1979. Calcium deficiency and occurrence of topple disorder in bulbous iris. Canadian J. Plant Sci. 59:185-190.

32. Doss, R.P. 1981. Effects of durations of 32°C and 20°C postharvest bulb treatments on early forcing of Ideal iris. Can. Jour. Plant Sci. 61:647-652.

33. Doss, Robert P. 1984. Preliminary examination of some factors that influence the vase life of cut bulb flowers. Proceedings 1984 Northwest Bulb Growers Conference. pp. 20-30.

34. Doss, Robert P., Gary A Chastagner and Kathleen L. Riley. 1986. Screening ornamental lilies for resistance to *Botrytis elliptica*. Scientia Horticulturae 30:237-246.

35. Doucette, Charles F. 1959. Soil drenches for control of the Narcissus bulb fly. Jour. Econ. Entomology 52:348.

36. Eade, George. 1956. The bulb and flower industry of the State of Washington. Proceedings of the 8th Northwest Bulb Growers Short Course, p. 9 & 10.

37. Eade, George W. 1959. A look at the bulb industry in Washington. Northwest Bulb Grower, Northwest Bulb Growers Association. Newsletter No. 73. Mimeo.

38. Eade, George. 1963. How healthy are our bulbs? Northwest Bulb Growers Assn. Newsletter #92, Apr.

39. Eade, George W. 1964. Annual report of State Department of Agriculture-Division of Horticulture. Plant certification and nursery inspection. Mimeo.

40. Eade, George. 1971. Washington State bulb acreage and exports (1966-1971). Washington State Dept. of Agriculture Nursery Inspection Report. Mimeo.

41. Fletcher, S.W. 1904. Transplanting a million-dollar industry. From *Country Life in America*. Reprinted in *Seattle Post-Intelligencer* Feb. 7, p. 46.

42. *Florists' Review*. 1935. Obituary of Dr. David Griffiths. Mar. 28, p. 28.

43. Flynn, Tony. 1990. Tulip festival 2000 may never happen. *The Argus*, Vol 99, No. 18, front page.

44. Freiman, L.N. 1989. Personal communication.

45. Fryar, Richard. 1948. Northwest Bulb Growers Association Newsletter, Jan. 15.

46. Fryar, R.G. 1952. Our bulb markets—past, present and future. Mimeo copy of talk given at 4th Northwest Bulb Growers Short Course. Feb. 20, 1952.

47. Galvin, J.P. 1944. The bulb industry of western Washington. *Economic Geography.* Jan. pp. 20-24.

48. *Gardeners' Chronicle.* 1935. Obituary for Dr. David Griffiths. Apr. 13, pp. 5-6.

49. Gould, Charles J., ed. 1957. Handbook on bulb growing and forcing. Northwest Bulb Growers Association, Mount Vernon, WA. 196 p.

50. Gould, Charles J. 1957. The Flower Bulb Industry. Washington Agricultural Experiment Stations Circular 318.

51. Gould, Charles J. and Ralph S. Byther. 1979. Diseases of Narcissus. Washington State Univ. Ext. Bull. #709.

52. Gould, Charles J. and Ralph S. Byther. 1979. Diseases of bulbous Iris. Includes a section on Iris forcing. Washington State Univ. Ext. Bull. #710.

53. Gould, Charles J. and Ralph S. Byther. 1979. Diseases of Tulips. Washington State Univ. Ext. Bull. #711.

54. Gould, Charles J. 1990. History of Bulb Growing in Washington State. Fifth International Symposium on Flower Bulbs (1989). Acta Horticulturae 266. pp. 15-23.

55. Griffiths, David. 1916. The production of Dutch bulbs on the Pacific coast. *Florist's Exchange.* Vol. 43, #25, Dec. 16.

56. Griffiths, David. 1922. The Production of Tulip Bulbs. USDA Bull. No. 1082, p. 8.

57. Griffiths, David. 1924. The production of narcissus bulbs. USDA Bull. No. 1270. Oct. 11, p. 24.

58. Griffiths, David. 1926. American bulbs under glass. USDA Bull. No. 1462.

59. Griffiths, David. 1928. A score of easily propagated lilies. USDA Circular No. 23.

60. Griffiths, David. 1933. Some hybrid Martagon lilies. USDA Circular No. 299, p. 8.

61. Griffiths, David. 1936. Speeding up flowering in the daffodil and the bulbous iris. USDA Circular No. 367.

62. Griffiths, David. 1936. Tulip Culture in the United States. USDA Circular No. 372, p. 3.

63. Haglund, William A. 1982. Efficacy of selected nonvolatile nematicides on control of *Ditylenchus destructor* in Iris. Jour. of Nematology. Vol. 14, No. 4, pp. 92-96.

64. Haglund, William A. 1991. Soil fumigation with Metam on ornamental bulbs in northwest Washington. Proceedings 1991 Northwest Bulb Growers Conference., p. 22-24.

65. Hammond, J. and G. A Chastagner. 1988. Natural infection of tulips with turnip mosaic virus and another potyvirus isolate distinct from tulip breaking virus in the USA. Proceedings 7th Int'l Symposium on Virus Diseases, San Remo, Italy.

66. Herold, Stephen. 1989. Tulipmania: the Skagit Valley tulip festival. Celestial Arts, Berkeley, CA. Official Festival Guidebook in 1989.

67. Hill, R. G. 1931. A survey of the United States bulb industry. A preliminary report. U.S. Dept. of Agriculture, Bureau of Agricultural Economics.

68. Horstman, T. 1983. Bulb and flower cultivation in Skagit Valley, Washington. Term paper for a history class at Western Washington University, Bellingham.

69. Houser, H. A. 1925. What the government bulb farm at Bellingham is doing for the bulb industry. Proceedings of the 21st annual meeting of the Washington State Horticultural Assn.

70. Howard, Stott W., Carl R. Libbey and Eric R. Hall. 1988. Weed control research in ornamental bulbs. Proceedings 40th Northwest Bulb Growers Conference. pp. 24 & 25.

71. Hsiang, T. and G.A. Chastagner. 1991. Ecological and parasitic fitness of dicarboximide and benzimidazole resistant *Botrytis* species. Can. J. Plant Pathology 13:226-231.

72. Humphrey, H. B. 1961. Obituary of David Griffiths 1867-1935, in Makers of North American Botany. Ronald Press, NY, pp. 101-103.

296

73. *The Islander*, Friday Harbor, WA. 1898. Gibbs elected president of Orcas entertainers. Mar. 10.

74. *The Islander*, Friday Harbor, WA. 1898. Gibbs shipping wild currants to eastern markets. Apr. 14.

75. *The Islander*, Friday Harbor, WA. 1898. Gibbs planting 50,000 Holland bulbs. Oct. 27.

76. Johnson, Folke, D.F. Allmendinger, V.L. Miller and C.J. Gould. 1950. Leaf scorch of gladiolus caused by atmospheric fluoric effluents. Phytopathology. Vol. XL. 239-246.

77. Kalin, Elwood W. 1954. Flower removal in the field and its effects on bulb production and forcing quality of *Narcissus pseudonarcissus* var. King Alfred. Proceedings of Amer. Society for Hort. Sci. 63:473-487.

78. Kansas City Historical Society. 1881. History of Johnson County, Missouri.

79. Kaylor, Floyd C. 1954. Personal communication. Apr. 12.

80. Knutson, Roger. 1989. Personal communication. Dec. 19.

81. Lefeber, Marinus. 1972. Personal communication.May 27.

82. Leovy, Jill. 1992. Bloom is off daffodil farming. *Seattle Times*, Apr. 3, Sect. A-2.

83. Lingham, A. 1907. An article on bulb growing. *Puyallup Valley Tribune*, May 25. p. 5.

84. Merrill, William, Eastsound, WA. 1989-1992. Personal correspondence.

85. Miller, V.L., W.D. Courtney and B.L. Anderson. 1950. Stability of formaldehyde solutions used in bulb treatments. Phytopathology. Vol. 40:627.

86. Miller, V.L., C.J. Gould and E. Csonka. 1974. Estimation of thiabendazole in the milligram and submilligram ranges. Jour. Agr. Food Chem. Vol 22:90-92.

87. Miller, V.L., C.J. Gould and E. Csonka. 1974. Estimation of benomyl in the milligram range. Jour. Agr. Food Chem. Vol 22:93-95.

88. Miller, V.L., E. Csonka and C.J. Gould. 1976. Estimation of milligram and submilligram amounts of Busan fungicide. Jour. of the AOAC. Vol 59:737-739.

89. Miller, V.L., C.J. Gould and R. Byther. 1978. Quick tests for formalin, Mertect, Benlate and Busan fungicides used in the bulb industry. Washington State Univ. Mimeo.

90. Montgomery, Tom. 1926. Diversified Farming on Gronen Ranch. *Puyallup Valley Tribune*, Aug. 14, p. 5.

91. *Northwest Bulb Growers Association Newsletter*. 1962. International effort to promote spring flowers. #88. August.

92. *Northwest Horticulturist*. 1906. The flower bulb industry. June No. 6. p. 2.

93. *Northwest Horticulturist*. 1906. Report of the 4th annual meeting of the Pacific Coast Assn. of Nurserymen, Tacoma, WA. July No. 7. p. 1.

94. *Northwest Horticulturist*. 1906. Photograph of hyacinth bulbs grown by Gibbs. Oct. No. 10. p.234.

95. Nowadnick, R. L. 1983. What is the Northwest Bulb Growers Association? Proceedings 35th Northwest Bulb Growers Conference. pp. 17-73.

96. Oakley, R.A. 1917. Distribution of Tulip and Narcissus Bulbs in 1917. USDA, Bur. of Plant Industry. S.D.-37.

97. Orton, C.W. 1954. Personal interview by C. J. Gould.

98. Otis, Earl. 1985. Pierce county agriculture. News release. March. Mimeo

99. Paulhamus, W.H. 1923. Suggests bulb production as possible local industry. *Puyallup Valley Tribune*. Apr. 21.

100. Paulhamus, W.H. 1924. Narcissus growing. *American Standard*, Sumner. Apr. 4, front page.

101. Peabody, D.V. 1981.Use of registered (and nonregistered) herbicides in ornamental bulbs. Proceedings 33rd Northwest Bulb Growers Conference.

297

102. Polley, D., V.L. Miller, C.J. Gould and W.D. Courtney. 1953. Tests for fungicidal solutions of formaldehyde and of several mercurials. Phytopathology. Vol. 43:598.

103. *Puyallup Valley Tribune*. 1924. Senator Paulhamus's suggestion for planting bulbs in the Puyallup Valley. Mar. 28.

104. *Puyallup Valley Tribune*. 1925. Bulb culturists plan meet here. Mar. 21. p. 7.

105. Reimann, A.O. 1931. Bulb production and marketing in the United States, particularly in Washington and Oregon, considered as to its economic aspects. MS thesis in Agric. Economics. Washington State College. p. 119.

106. Ripp, Bart. 1992. King of the Tideflats. [Tacoma] *Morning News Tribune*. Soundlife. Sect. D. p. 3.

107. Rockwell, F.F. 1944. Holland was never like this. *Saturday Evening Post*, Sep. 30. Quoted by permission of the *Saturday Evening Post* (Dec. 18, 1992).

108. Roozen, Leo. 1992. Personal communication. Oct. 2.

109. Roth, Lottie R. 1926. History of Whatcom County. Vol. I:482-483.

110. Roth, Lottie R. 1926. History of Whatcom County. Vol. I:781-782.

111. Roth, Lottie R. 1926. History of Whatcom County. Vol. II:152-153.

112. Roth, Lottie R. 1926. History of Whatcom County. Vol. II: p. 158.

113. Roth, Lottie R. 1926. History of Whatcom County. Vol. II: p. 757.

114. Rozenbaum, Scott J. 1988. Monitoring losses of important farmlands through the Landsat-based geographic information system. MS thesis. Washington State Univ., Dept. of Agronomy and Soils. May.

115. Ryan, Jack. 1969. Flower festival failing; daffodil costs up. *Seattle Post-Intelligencer*. May 30. p. 10.

116. Sabelis, Ted. 1952. The Wedgwood price-war. Northwest Bulb Growers Newsletter. Jun. 25.

117. Sabelis, Ted. 1956. New trends in merchandising bulbs. Proceedings of 8th Pacific Northwest Bulb Growers Short Course. p. 21.

118. San Juan County Commissioners. 1890. Lease of 121.45 acres to George Gibbs. Records of Island Title Co., Friday Harbor, WA. Vol II, Deeds. p. 382. (Courtesy of Mrs. Art Grove).

119. *The San Juan Islander*. 1905. Who stole Gibbs' trees? Dec 2, front page.

120. *Seattle Times*. 1917. Bulbs affected by great war in Europe. March 25. p. 22.

121. *Seattle Times*. 1929. Grays Harbor plans second tulip show. May 12. p. 5.

122. *Seattle Times*. 1948. Planeloads of daffodils sent. Apr. 7. p. 4.

123. Sincock, Robert L. 1956. Bulb Commission out to regain markets. *Washington Farmer*. Aug. 2. p. 5.

124. Skagitonians to Preserve Farmland. 1992. Farmland preservation in Skagit County: Program options and recommendations. Prepared for the Skagit County Board of County Commissioners. p. 183.

125. Smith, Joe. 1925. Bulb Association. The Joemma Bulletin. Vol. 7, No. 3, Jun. 1. p. 4.

126. Smith, Sally S. 1990. An obituary of George Gibbs summarized from an article in the *American-Reveille*, Bellingham, WA, Mar. 18, 1919. Bellingham Public Library. Personal communication. Oct 14.

127. Splitstone, Fred John. 1954. Orcas, Gem of the San Juans. Pub. by Fred T. Darvill, Eastsound, WA. p. 78.

128. Staatz, Stanley. 1956. The Bulb Commission. Proceedings of the 1956 Northwest Bulb Growers Short Course. p. 13.

129. Stewart, Mary. 1933. Bulbs of quality and distinction. Tulip Grange, Inc. catalog.

130. Stuart, Neil W. and C. J. Gould. 1950.Iris curing and storage temperatures discussed in report. *Florists' Review*. Jul. 20.

131. Stuart, Neil W. and Charles J. Gould. 1953. Tulip forcing as affected by curing and storage temperatures. *Florists' Review*. Vol. 113:31-32.

132. Stuart, Neil W., Sam Asen and Charles J. Gould. 1966. Accelerated flowering of bulbous iris after exposure to ethylene. *Hort. Sci.* Vol 1:19-20.

133. *Sumner News Index*, Sumner, WA. 1940. History of the Puyallup Daffodil Festival. Mar. 8.

134. *Tacoma Ledger*, Tacoma, WA. 1910. A general article about George Lawler. Jan. 30.

135. *Tacoma News Tribune*. 1957. Flower Co-op sets out to firm prices. Jan. 6.

136. Taylor, Mrs. Walter R. 1961. Personal communication.

137. Taylor, William A. 1935. David Griffiths obituary. *Science* n.s. 81:426-427. May 3. Permission to use quote from ®AAAS (Sept. 2, 1992).

138. Taylor, William A. 1935. Dr. David Griffiths. *American Amaryllis Society 1935 Year Book*, p. 23. Permission to use photograph from the International Bulb Society. Photo from Dr. Marc Cathey.

139. Teck, Frank C. 1907. Government to establish flower bulb station on Puget Sound. *Seattle Post-Intelligencer*. 13 Oct. Sec. 2, p. 11.

140. Thornton, A.W. 1921. Article on George Gibbs, A Friend. *Bellingham Herald*. Apr. 30.

141. U.S. Census Bureau. 1900. Washington State printed census for Whatcom County. Marietta township. (Courtesy of Mrs. Marilyn Bell).

142. U.S. Census Bureau. 1910. Washington State, Whatcom County printed census, Clearbrook township. Vol. 3, W 79. (Courtesy of Mrs. Marilyn Bell).

143. United States Senate. 1940. Hearings before a subcommittee of the committee on agriculture and forestry, 76th Congress, third session of Senate Resolution 143. p. 2

144. Valdez, Christine. 1990. Tulip colors closely linked to decorating, fashion trends. *Skagit Valley Herald*. Tulip Festival. p. 10.

145. Washburn, Kim. 1990. Families sink roots in business community. *Pierce County Herald*, Oct. 20. Business Sect. p. 1.

146. Washington Agricultural Statistics Service. 1990. Agriculture! Washington State's #1 Industry. Washington Dept. of Ag.

147. Washington Board of Health. Bureau of Vital Statistics. 1919. Certificate of death of George Gibbs. Whatcom County Record #60. (Courtesy of Mrs. Marilyn Bell).

148. Washington Territory Census. 1889. Island County, Washington Territory. (Courtesy of Mrs. Marilyn Bell).

149. Washington State University Cooperative Extension. 1972. Value of ornamental horticultural crops grown in Washington in 1968. EM3707.

150. Wiederspohn, Helen. 1990. Biographical information on George Gibbs supplied by Mrs. William Perry, Lynden Chamber of Commerce. Personal letter of Jun. 4.

151. Wieting, Carol. 1949. Northwest bulb growers expedite jobs with special machinery. *Florists' Review*. Feb. 17.

152. Winters, Frederick W. 1989. Historic Structure Report of Winter's House. City of Bellevue, WA. WJE No. 890981.

153. Wylie, Ann P. 1952. The history of garden Narcissi. *Heredity*. Vol 6, part 2. pp. 137-156.

154. Wyman, Rachael. 1988. Skagit Valley bulbs: a continuing frontier. Entry in national competition for National History Day. Mount Vernon, WA. Mimeo.

155. Zulauf, Allen S. 1979. Soil survey of Pierce County area, Washington. USDA Soil Conservation Service in cooperation with Washington Agric. Exp. Sta.

SUBJECT INDEX

Washington Bulb Company, 22, 23, 43, 52, 89-91, 115, 134, 135, 150, 167, 205, 213

West Shore Acres, 23, 44, 51, 61, 137, 213

Williams Brothers, 51, 69, 88, 108-109

Windmill Greenhouse and Nursery, 57

Woodland Bulb Farms, 33, 59, 68, 137, 213

Woodward Bulb Farm, 213

Counties: 27-49; Asotin, 28; Clallam, 27; Clark, 27, 33-34; Cowlitz, 27, 33-34; Grays Harbor, 28, 34; Island, 28, 34-35; Jefferson, 27; King, 27, 36-37; Kitsap, 27; Lewis, 37-38; Mason, 27; Pacific, 27; Pierce, 27, 38-41; San Juan, 42; Skagit, 27, 42-45; Snohomish, 27, 45-46; Spokane, 27; Thurston, 27, 46-47; Whatcom, 27, 47-49; Yakima, 28.

Crocus, 17, 175

—D—

Data, sources of, 17, 20, 27-28, 139

Diseases, 237-245

Display Gardens, 204-206
  Chuckanut Gardens, 205
  De Goede Gardens, 38, 204
  Roozengaarde, 205
  Van Lierop's Variety Garden, 205
  Westshore Acres, 206

—E—

Exports, 24-26, 149-153

—F—

Farms: 24-26; locations in 1990, 15; number, 19; size, 21-23.

Festivals and flower shows, 195-204
  Bellingham Tulip Festival, 48, 195-197
  Grays Harbor South Beach Lily Festival, 34, 198
  Grays Harbor Tulip Show, 34, 196
  Holland Happenings, 198
  Puyallup Valley Daffodil Festival, 41, 197-202
  Skagit Valley Tulip Festival, 45, 203-204
  Skagit Valley Tulip Show (La Conner), 45, 202
  Spring Tulip Festival at Mossyrock, 38, 204

Flowers, 154-159

Forcing, 245-248

—G—

Gladiolus: 183-188; number of acres in Holland, 3, 184; in USA, 3; in Washington State, 24-26; growers, 183-188, 283-285; hybridizing, 186-188; diseases, 245; research, 227-258; varieties, 175, 184; Washington Gladiolus Society, 185-186.

Growers: individual acreages in 1989, 32; biographies of, 50-111; lists of: Gladiolus, 283-285; Iris, 265-282; Lilies, 286-293; Narcissus, 265-282; Tulips, 265-282; name index, 303; number of, 19-21, 24-28, 50.

—H—

History: George Gibbs, 4-14; David Griffiths, 221-226.

Holland: number of acres: total, 1, 3; in Gladiolus, 184; in Iris, 180; in Lilies, 191; in Narcissus, 178; in Tulips, 181.

Hyacinths, 3, 175-176

—I—

Imports: 168-174; by countries, 170-173; data for 1920-1990, 171-172; tariff rates, 172-174.

Insects, 237-238

Inspection: 163-167; inspectors, 165-167; pests, 163-165; purpose, 163; USDA, 163-167; Washington State, 165-167.

International Bulb Symposium, 252

Iris number of acres: in Holland, 3, 180; in USA, 3; in Washington State, 24-26, 179-180; exports to Europe, 18, 24-26, 149-153; growers, 50-111, 265-282; hybridizing, 182; research, 227-258; sales of bulbs, 139-153; sales of flowers, 154-159; varieties, 179-180.

—L—

Labor supply, 112-116

Land scarcity, 130-132

Lilies number of acres: in Holland, 3, 191; in USA, 3; in Washington, 24-26; general, 187-188; growers, 189-194, 286-293; hybridizing, 49, 189, 190, 192-193; research, 227-258; societies, 193-194; varieties, 189-193.

—M—

Mechanizating, 112-128

—N—

Narcissus (Daffodils) number of acres: in Holland, 3, 178; in USA, 3; in Washington State, 24-26, 177; general, 18-19; growers, 50-111, 265-282; hybridizing, 181-182; number of bulbs planted in 1933, 177; research, 227-258; sales of bulbs, 139-153; sales of flowers, 154-159; value, 160-160; varieties, 176-178.

Nematodes, 239

Netherlands, The, see Holland

301

Northwest Bulb Growers Association, 20, 207-210, 228, 248

—O—
Organizations
Allied Bulb Growers Association, 217
American Narcissus Growers Association, 220
North American Lily Society, 194
Northwest Bulb Growers Association, 20, 207-210, 228, 248
Pacific Northwest Lily Society, 194
Pierce County Horticultural Society, 199
Puget Sound Bulb Exchange, 214-217
Puget Sound Lily Society 220
Puyallup Valley Flower Cooperative, Inc., 218
Royal Horticultural Society, 175, 176
Seattle Lily Society, 220
Skagit Valley Bulb Cooperative, 219-220
Skagit Valley Flower Cooperative, 219
Snohomish County Bulb Growers Association, 220
Society of American Florists (SAF), 7, 92
Tulip Flowers, Inc., 219
Vashon Island Lily Growers Association, 220
Washington Croft Lily Growers Association, 220
Washington Gladiolus Society, Inc., 185-186
Washington State Bulb Commission, 17, 28, 139, 211-213, 228
Washington State Lily Society, 194

—P—
Problems: 130-138; bulb surpluses, 138; drought, 135; fires, 137; floods, 134-135; freezing weather, 132-134; land scarcity, 130-132; land prices, 131-132; pests, 137; shipping 137-138; wet summers, 135.
Production: 112-129; bulb sizes 129; cleaning, 121; digging, 117, 121; grading, 121; land price, 132; land scarcity, 130-132; labor supply, 112; mechanizing, 113-129; pioneers, 116; planting, 112-116; problems, 130-138; shipping, 127-128, 137-138; spraying, 117; storing, 127; treating, 125-127; weather effect, 1, 2, 15; weeding, 117; yield, 128-130.

—Q—
Quarantine: 163-165; foreign sites, 164; HWF treatment, 164; insects, 163; nematodes, 163-165; phytosanitary certificates (Phytos), 164; purpose, 163, 164; USDA, 163, 164; Washington State, 163, 165.

—R—
Research: bacteria, 238-239; bulb treatment, 243-244; culture, 236; educational activities, 248-252; financial support, 228; insects, 232, 237-238; forcing: Iris, 245-248; Narcissus, 247; Tulips, 247; leaf blights, 240-242; locations, 229-235; nematodes, 239-240; physiological, 237; rots, soil borne, 244-245; rots, storage, 242-243; scientists, 221-257; vase life of flowers, 248; virus, 238.

—S—
Sales of bulbs: competition, 142-145; counties, 141; data, sources, 17, 27-28, 139; exports from WA, 24-26, 149-153; markets, 19, 144-153, 175; numbers sold, 24-26, 139-142; prices, 142-144; shipping, 137; surpluses, 138, 142, 149; value, 160-162; yield per acre, 128-129.
Sales of flowers: 154-159; competition, 159; effect of fashion, 159; field-cut, 154-159; forced, 157, 159; markets, 154-159; numbers per acre, 157; numbers sold, 159; price, 156-157; value, 159-162.
Summary, 258-264

—T—
Tariff rates, 172-174
Tulips number of acres: in Holland, 3; in USA, 3; in Washington, 19, 24-26; general, 19; growers, 50-111, 265-282; hybridizing, 182; research, 227-258; sales of bulbs, 139-153; sales of flowers, 154-159; value, 160-162; varieties, 181.

—U—
United States Department of Agriculture at Bellingham, 48, 221-226, 229-231; at Sumner, 232.

—V—
Value of the industry, 160-162
Varieties, 175-182
Virus, 238

—W—
Washington State Bulb Commission, 17, 28, 139, 211-213, 228
Washington State University at Mount Vernon and Puyallup, 39, 233-258

302

NAME INDEX

303

305

—R—
Rebhan, Robert, 167
Rees, Dan, 186
Reise
   Ludvig, 87
   Mrs. Otto (Florence), 88, 108
   Otto Carl, Sr., 14, 40, 41, 62, 69, 86,
      93, 115, 116, 125, 214, 215, 216
   Otto, Jr., 88, 216
   Wilmer, 82, 87, 88, 102, 208, 212,
      215, 216, 218, 219
Reitmeier, H. J. G., 216
Reynolds, Henry J., 80, 88, 166, 167,
   199
Riemann, Alfred O., 256
Riggs, F. C., 208
Riley, Kathleen L., 241
Ritscher, Henry, 216
Roberson
   Frances, 89
   Leonard N., 89
Roberts, A. N., 228
Rodenhurst, R. J., 167
Roe
   Joy, 188
   Mrs. Orville (Doris), 37, 188
   Orville R., 37, 183, 186, 188
   Shirley, 188
Roodzant
   Bert, 35, 89
   Hank, 35, 89
   John, 35, 89
   Pete, 35, 89
Roozekrans
   Cornelius, 43, 52, 90, 91, 150
   Nic, 91
Roozen
   Bernadette Roozen Miller, 43, 91, 205
   Helen, 43, 90, 205
   John, 43, 45, 91, 208, 209
   Leo, 43, 91, 131, 135, 159, 208, 209
   Michael, 43, 91
   Richard 43, 91
   William (Bill) A., 43, 52, 68, 82, 89, 91,
     205, 208, 212, 219
   William M., 43, 91, 208, 209
Rose, Scott, 166, 167
Rotteveel, 52
Royer, E. C., 214, 216
Russell, Tom, 256

—S—
Sabelis, Theodore (Ted), 61, 92, 106, 110,
   145, 152, 209, 210, 212, 215-217, 228,
   248
Sather, Harry M., 92, 106, 137, 188, 216
Scheffer, Theodore H., 233, 256
Scholz
   Alfred, 69, 80, 93
   Frank, 93

Schomer, H. A., 256
Schopp, Ralph, 256
Sconce, Bob, 200
Segelman, H. W., 256
Segers Brothers, 35-37, 48, 51, 76, 93, 100,
   105
Sharp
   Donn, 94
   Harry, 94
Sheffield, George, 37, 189
Shorey, Samuel, 42, 94
Smit, L. Maynard, 84, 94, 216
Smith
   Floyd, 228
   George, 35
   Harry, 108
   Joe, 36, 38-40, 46, 66, 85, 94, 207, 208,
     216, 223
   John W. Macrae, 9, 10, 47, 51, 95,
     223, 229
   Knight, 35
   Mrs. Karel (Lubbe), 34, 60, 75, 78,
     96
Spruit, F. J., 256
Staatz
   Stanley W., 51, 54, 96, 208, 212, 216
   Wallace (Wally) T., 41, 79, 96, 97,
     131, 156, 208, 212, 215, 216, 212,
     215, 216, 218, 219
Stafford, James, 216
Stang, Jack, 228
Stewart
   Frances, 98
   Mrs. Mary Brown, 10, 27, 42, 51, 98,
     107, 109, 144, 223, 259
   Sam J., 42, 45, 51, 61, 67, 77, 80,
     98, 99, 107, 212, 219, 223
Stillinger, Ray, 167
Stitt, Lloyd L., 256
Stoltenow, Sherryl, 166, 167
Stookey, E. B., 47, 216
Stuart, Neil W., 228, 234, 245-247, 256

—T—
Taylor, Walter R., 46, 95, 100
Thomas, Ray, 65
Thornton, A. W., 6, 10
Tremblay, Todd, 236, 256
Truong, Thuan, 167
Twohy, John, 84, 208

—V—
Vallentgoed, Rutgert, 48, 100
Van Aalst
   Frank, 48, 93
   John, 36, 50, 93, 100
Van der Salm, Jerry, 100
Van Der Sys, Bos, 106
Van Laan, Gordon J., 234, 256

TERMS AND ABBREVIATIONS

Cm: Abbreviation of centimeter (0.39 inch). When used in this book it refers to the circumference of bulbs.

Dry Sales: Sales of bulbs to garden centers, chain stores, catalog companies, etc., for resale to the general public. Does not include sales to growers for commercial cut-flower production in greenhouses or in fields.

Heat-curing: Artificial heat treatment of bulbs, usually applied soon after digging to hasten maturation.

HWF: A 1 to 4 hour hot water at 110-111°F. + formalin treatment of dormant bulbs to kill certain parasitic fungi, nematodes and insect pests.

INT: Iris, Narcissus and Tulips, the major bulb crops grown in Washington.

Mother bulbs: Usually large bulbs which produce daughter bulbs used for planting stock.

NWBGA: Northwest Bulb Growers Association.

Planting stock: The small bulbs, bulblets or cormels planted to produce salable-size bulbs the next year.

Precooling: Exposure of bulbs to cool temperatures (usually 40-50°F.) prior to planting to promote development of roots and flowers.

Salable: Bulbs large enough to produce flowers the first year.

Sport: A spontaneous mutation which gives rise to a new variety.

USDA: The United States Department of Agriculture.

WSU: Washington State University, formerly Washington State College.

WSU Mt. Vernon: The Research and Extension unit of WSU at Mount Vernon, WA.

WSU Puyallup: The Research and Extension Center of WSU at Puyallup, WA. Originally named the Ross Station when founded in 1894, the Western Washington Experiment Station from 1907 until 1965, the Western Washington Research and Extension Center from 1965 to 1988, and the Washington State University Puyallup Research and Extension Center from 1988 to present.

ABOUT THE AUTHOR

Charles J. (Chuck) Gould is Plant Pathologist, Emeritus, Washington State University. He specialized in diseases of bulbs, turfgrasses and other important ornamental crops at the WSU Puyallup Research and Extension Center from 1941 to 1977. He holds a bachelor's degree from Marshall University and a doctorate from Iowa State University. A Fulbright Grant enabled him to study bulb diseases at the Flower Bulb Laboratory in Lisse, Holland in 1951. He is a Fellow of the American Phytopathological Society and a Distinguished Alumnus of Marshall University.